Best of the Journals in Rhetoric and Composition

Best of the Journals in Rhetoric and Composition
SERIES EDITORS: STEVE PARKS, JESSICA PAUSZEK, KRISTI GIRDHARRY, AND CHARLES LESH

The Best of the Journals in Rhetoric and Composition series represents an attempt to foster a nationwide conversation—beginning with journal editors, but expanding to teachers, scholars and workers across the discipline of Rhetoric and Composition—to select essays that showcase the innovative and transformative work now being published in the field's independent journals. Representing both print and digital journals in the field, the essays in each addition represent a snapshot of the traditional and emergent conversations occurring in our field—from classroom practice to writing in global and digital contexts, from writing workshops to community activism. Together, the essays provide readers with a rich understanding of the present and future direction of the field.

Essays included in the "Best" series undergo a rigorous review process. First, all essays must have already crossed the threshold to be published in an academic journal in the field. Then, out of all the essays published by a journal, the editor can only select two essays. Next, the "Best" series editors create reading groups across the country. These groups feature full time faculty, adjunct faculty, and graduate students who teach in a range of institutions. In this way, all the nominated essays are assessed and ranked for how they speak to the interests of all those who work in our field – a review process which is unique to the series. The Series editors, plus one guest editor, then make a final selection of essays that have the strongest support from the reading groups for inclusion in a particular volume.

In this way, the Best of Rhetoric and Composition Journals represents the only publication in the field that can truly claim to represent the students, teachers, as well as scholars' collective insight into the pressing issues and important of the current moment. It is for this reason that authors selected for inclusion are celebrated at their home institutions and why journals actively seek to recognition for their work through the series. And it is for its ability of the series to provide the broadest conception of scholarship in our field, that the "Best" publications have found a home in introductory graduate courses and advanced undergraduate courses.

BEST OF THE JOURNALS IN RHETORIC AND COMPOSITION 2018

Edited by Jordan Canzonetta, André Habet, Laura Gonzales, David Blakesley, Jessica Pauszek, and Steve Parks

Parlor Press
Anderson, South Carolina
www.parlorpress.com

Parlor Press LLC, Anderson, South Carolina, USA

© 2019 by Parlor Press. Individual essays in this book have been reprinted with permission of the respective copyright owners.
All rights reserved.
Printed in the United States of America

S A N: 2 5 4 - 8 8 7 9

ISSN 2327-4778 (print)
ISSN 2327-4786 (online)

978-1-64317-061-9 (paperback)
978-1-64317-062-6 (Adobe eBook)
978-1-64317-063-3 (ePub)

1 2 3 4 5

Cover design by David Blakesley.
Printed on acid-free paper.

Parlor Press, LLC is an independent publisher of scholarly and trade titles in print and multimedia formats. This book is available in paper and digital formats from Parlor Press on the World Wide Web at http://www.parlorpress.com or through online and brick-and-mortar bookstores. For submission information or to find out about Parlor Press publications, write to Parlor Press, 3015 Brackenberry Drive, Anderson, South Carolina, 29621, or email editor@parlorpress.com.

Contents

Introduction   *vii*
    Jordan Canzonetta, Laura Gonzales, and André Habet

Reflective Pedagogical Practices

THE WAC JOURNAL
Inviting Students to Determine for Themselves What It Means to Write Across the Disciplines   *3*
    Brian Hendrickson and Genevieve Garcia de Mueller

JOURNAL OF TEACHING WRITING
Authentic Questioning as a Form of Inquiry: Writing in the Dialogic Classroom   *27*
    Eamon Cunningham

JOURNAL OF SECOND LANGUAGE WRITING
The Relationship Between Lexical Sophistication and Independent and Source-Based Writing   *57*
    Kristopher Kyle and Scott Crossley

TEACHING ENGLISH IN THE TWO-YEAR COLLEGE
A Partnership Teaching Externship Program: A Model That Makes Do   *89*
    Darin Jensen and Susan Ely

RHETORIC REVIEW
Making, not Curating, the Rhetorical Tradition: Ways through and beyond the Canon   *111*
    Erika Claire Strandjord

WPA: WRITING PROGRAM ADMINISTRATION
On Learning to Teach: Letter to a New TA   *133*
    E. Shelley Reid

Bodies in Composition

PRESENT TENSE
Composing Artificial Intelligence: Performing Whiteness and Masculinity   *153*
    Patricia Fancher

COMPOSITION STUDIES
Sensing the Sentence: An Embodied Simulation
Approach to Rhetorical Grammar   *163*
   Hannah J. Rule

WLN: A JOURNAL OF WRITING CENTER SCHOLARSHIP
Feminist Mothering: A Theory/Practice for
Writing Center Administration   *187*
   Michelle Miley

ENCULTURATION
From Spectacular to Vernacular: Epideixis in
Tactical Urban Design   *197*
   Blake Watson

Community-Based Writing Practices

COMMUNITY LITERACY JOURNAL
Brokering Literacies: Child Language Brokering in
Mexican Immigrant Families   *225*
   Steven Alvarez

LITERACY IN COMPOSITION STUDIES
Daughters Learning from Fathers:
Migrant Family Literacies that Mediate Borders   *243*
   Kaia Simon

REFLECTIONS
Subalternity in Juvenile Justice:
Gendered Oppression and the Rhetoric of Reform   *271*
   Tasha Golden

COLLEGE COMPOSITION AND COMMUNICATION
Veterans in the Writing Classroom: Three Programmatic
Approaches to Facilitate the Transition from the
Military to Higher Education   *303*
   D. Alexis Hart and Roger Thompson

RHETORIC SOCIETY QUARTERLY
Children Speaking: Agency and Public Memory in
the Children's Peace Statue Project   *331*
   Risa Applegarth

Introduction

Jordan Canzonetta, Laura Gonzales, and André Habet

The Best of the Journals in Rhetoric and Composition series is a curation of exceptional articles from the field of rhetoric and composition. These articles are selected by editors along with colleagues across the country who review and vote on each year's selections. *The Best of the Journals in Rhetoric and Composition 2018* offers editors the opportunity to learn how academic journals view their published work and elucidates how rhetoric and composition scholars evaluate what makes academic articles significant. In this way, *Best of* serves less as a definitive ranking of scholarship published in a single year, and more so as a finite space wherein the curation of scholarship momentarily clarifies how a specific group of rhetoric and composition graduate students and faculty are reading their field. Engaging this anthology through that lens, we hope, can help readers of this collection to consider the intersections and slippages that exist between readers' interests and those of the extended volunteer team who helped us craft and select pieces for this collection. Built through a collaborative and reflexive practice, the collection encompasses an asynchronous celebration of the many possibilities our field currently has to offer in terms of research interests, lines of inquiry, and methodological practices.

Before you get into the rhythm of these pieces, we feel it is necessary to briefly reflect on why this compilation exists in the first place. This anthology, in large part, was founded by Steve Parks, Brian Bailie, and Collette Caton in order to subsidize the cost for academic journals who want to hold promotional table space at the annual *Conference on College Composition and Communication's* (CCCC's) book exhibit but who may lack the financial resources to do so on their own. If you purchased this collection, we thank you for making it a bit easier for some academic journals to maintain their space and visibility at *CCCC*. We see this collection as another means for the labor of these journals' editors, as well as the articles' authors to receive much deserved-recognition.

Admitting the material exigence of this publication does not remove the urgent energy with which we feel these pieces ought to be circulated beyond a single journal's readership--in fact, a key reason the series was created was to expand access and visibility of them. By building this collection and continuing to expand the readership of the articles included within, we hope to continue facilitating a discipline-wide conversation about the issues concerning rhetoric and composition at this present moment. In putting together these works with the help of academic journals in the field of rhetoric and composition, we worked along with a team of readers across institutions to curate an anthology that responds to the needs of instructors and researchers in a variety of institutional contexts. Such attention to the kairotic conditions of pedagogical and theoretical inquiry pervades many of these pieces as they work to situate us in the circumstances that generated their work. Thus, before moving on to introduce the specific selections within each section of the collection, we want to give some insight into how the pieces for this collection were selected and curated based on the rigor and thoughtfulness of our team of assistant editors who repeatedly showed how to hold ourselves and our colleagues accountable for the work we select to represents our field.

Selection and Curation Process

This year, *The Best of* collection shifted its focus from exclusively reviewing independent journals to a broader, more comprehensive scope. A principal concern of the publication is to represent as wide a range of research interests, models, and publication formats as possible.

Within that framework, we as editors enlisted the help of associate editors who represent a wide range of interests and institutional locations. Associate editors were invited to participate in reviewing selections through social media efforts on Twitter and Facebook, through contacting standings groups and Special Interest Groups (SIGS) at *CCCC*, through previous contributors, and through associations all editors have maintained at various institutions. Each colleague who was contacted or responded to recruitment was responsible for inviting other participants and led their respective groups. This year's associate editing team is comprised of instructors who are teaching at research universities, comprehensive and regional institutions, and community and liberal arts colleges. We have reviewers who are tenured and part-time adjunct faculty, along with MA and PhD students. Editors of the series prioritized institutional diversity among readers. We recommend that future publications the *Best Of* series also continue developing a protocol to ensure and forefront inclusion of editors across areas of race, gender, sexual orientation, nationality, and dis/ability.

As we recruited associate editors to review selections from a variety of journals in the field, we also reached out to editors of independent journals and non-independent publications. We asked each editor (or in some cases, editors) to selected approximately two nominations they thought were fitting as contributions to the *Best Of* collection. After we received their nominations and finalized associate editor reviewing groups, we randomly assigned each group four selections, ensuring that each nomination was read by at least two groups. To determine the final works for the collection, we tallied the rankings we asked reviewer groups to create or selected their top scored pieces. We assigned a point to a work every time it was in a group's top four ranks and determined a threshold number for inclusion in the series. Every selection that received at least three to four votes was automatically considered, noting that each journal could only have one nomination in the final collection. In cases of tied pieces, the editors met and deliberated until they agreed upon a final decision about which piece to include. To ensure fairness and equal representation across journals, some works with scores of 1 or 2 were also considered and discussed between the editors. We consulted the associate editing group's comments on each piece and adjudicated discrepancies about whether certain pieces met the criteria we established as guidelines for reading groups. These criteria for *Best of* were established for the editors and associate editors when the series began and are still used today:

- Only one article from each journal can be included in the anthology.
- No author can be included more than once in the anthology.
- No article should be excluded due to production concerns (length, inclusion of photos, blend of digital/print formats, etc.).

In addition to general criteria for selection, each reading group was provided with the following initial criteria and guidelines for ranking each article:

- Article demonstrates a broad sense of the discipline, demonstrating the ability to explain how its specific focus in a subdisciplinary area addresses broader concerns in the field.

- Article makes original contributions to the field, expanding or rearticulating central premises.
- Article is written in a style which, while based in the discipline, attempts to engage with a wider audience or concerns a wider audience.
- When ranking, please use the following numeric scale:

    3 – Article does an outstanding job with this criterion
    2 – Article does a strong job with this criterion
    1 – Article does an adequate job with this criterion
    0 – Article does not address this criterion

Groups were encouraged to include their own criteria that emerged from the readings. Themes among the criteria generated by the reviewer groups were as follows:

- Importance and exigence of the topic in the field of composition and rhetoric studies
- Timeliness, kairos, relevance, and longevity of the topic
- Clarity, accessibility, and persuasiveness of the writing
- Strong theoretical grounding
- Practicality in the classroom and engaging students
- Diversity of voices
- Modeling effective use of academic language
- Praxis—i.e, how do the authors develop their theories/ideas/data?
- Engagement with existing scholarship; how does this fit with current conversations in the field?
- Article respects the agency of its subjects, negotiating issues of race, gender, class, and identity in an equitable and empowering way.
- Criteria connected to disability (relevance, accessibility of content, decenters normative experience, does not pathologize, contributes to equity and access)

After receiving each group's listing and determining the selections to be included in the collection, we as editors grouped the selected pieces into three main sections that comprise this collection. We believe that these three sections represent overall themes and interests that emerged from the scholarship published in our field this year and from the selections made by our collaborators across the country.

The pieces in *Section 1: Reflective Pedagogical Practices* illustrate the many ways in which rhetoric and composition scholars are consistently re-inventing what may be perceived as "tried and true" pedagogical practices in the composition classroom. These pieces showcase the ongoing value that readers of composition scholarship place on research that provides both theoretical and practice-based recommendations to improve our work with students in and beyond the University. In *Section 2: Bodies in Composition*, we present pieces that showcase our field's growing acknowledgement of the critical role that the body plays in the learning and teaching of writing. Several pieces in this section bring attention to embodied knowledge and its influence on learning. Finally, *Section 3: Community-Based Writing Practices* illustrates the many ways in which rhetoric and composition scholarship and pedagogies can be grounded in reciprocal models that situate writing expertise both in and outside of the University.

Section 1: Reflective Pedagogical Practices

This section begins with "Inviting Students to Determine for Themselves What it Means to Write Across the Disciplines" by Brian Hendrickson and Genevieve Garcia de Mueller in *WAC Journal*. Hendrickson and Garcia de Mueller's article is timely and built on prominent conversations about transfer, metacognition and threshold concepts, focusing specifically on Guerra's concept of "writing across difference." This piece attends to students' cultural backgrounds and socioeconomic status, which addresses a large gap in scholarship from WAC/WID. Hendrickson and Garcia de Mueller account for the varied "socioeconomically and ethno-linguistically underrepresented communities" present and underserved in composition classrooms. This piece honors students' experiences by grounding theories of transfer and meta-awareness in the "literacy values and practices" students already possess before they enter writing classrooms. In drawing attention to their own literacy practices, Hendrickson and Garcia de Mueller argue, "students' self-assessment memos reveals that students apply certain threshold concepts to acquire critical agency as academic writers, and in a manner consistent with Guerra's concept of transcultural repositioning." This piece exemplifies the criterion established by associate editor groups, who valued work from the field that "respects the agency of its subjects, negotiating issues of race, gender, class, and identity in an equitable and empowering way."

Also situating learning in students' interests and backgrounds, Eamon Cunningham's "Authentic Questioning as a Form of Inquiry: Writing in the Dialogic Classroom" (published in the *Journal of Teaching Writing*) offers an application of reading analysis pedagogies in class that scaffolds tiers of readings and invention activities to facilitate students' development of critical thinking and reading abilities. Building on his application of the "dialogic classroom" model, Cunningham "privileges critical writing models as the focal point of student work, where students construct, or co-construct, the lines of inquiry for a text." Through this work, Cunningham extends longstanding connections in reading and writing by "teaching readers and teaching writers simultaneously" through a pedagogy that is grounded in student-developed inquiries.

Our selection from the *Journal of Second Language Writing* also provides a useful framework for reconceptualizing writing pedagogy. Kristopher Kyle and Scott Crossley's "The Relationship between Lexical Sophistication and Independent and Source-Based Writing" "explores the relationship" between "newly developed indices of lexical sophistication and holistic scores of writing proficiency in both independent and source-based writing tasks." Explaining that there are "gaps in our understanding regarding (a) the relationship between lexical sophistication and independent and source-based writing task proficiency scores, and (b) whether independent and source-based tasks require different linguistic resources with regard to lexical sophistication," Kyle and Crossley present an intricate study that holds implications for how notions of writing proficiency are applied in second language writing assessment and pedagogy.

Another selection for this year's collection was touted for its necessity in filling a gap related to professional development and teaching "basic writing" (a highly contested term) in two-year colleges. Darin Jensen and Susan Ely's "A Partnership Teaching Externship Program: A Model that Makes Do" from *TETYC: Teaching English in the Two-Year College* highlights a pragmatic and essential partnership program that helps community college teachers engage with the scholarship, theory, and pedagogical practices related to basic writing. The authors suggest that graduate students who graduate and begin working in two-year institutions are largely underprepared for teaching courses some departments label "remedial," and these courses comprise a significant portion of first-year writing at these institutions. Jensen and Ely outline the partnership program between graduate students and teachers as one that "encompasses theory and practice of basic writing in a co-teaching model. We offer this model as one that demonstrates a way to build a program that meets the need of community colleges in hiring qualified instructors, that prepares graduate students for careers beyond graduate school, and that helps universities make important reforms in graduate programs to move beyond merely replicating scholars for research institutions." One assistant editing group described Jensen and Ely's partnership program as a "highly relevant and practical model, given that so many teaching candidates go into teaching at two-year institutions but lack the necessary training. The article does not fall into a trap of believing this model to be a panacea, but freely admits to many of the inter-institutional barriers in the field of "remedial" style teaching."

Continuing to expand applications of writing pedagogy beyond perceivably traditional models, Erika Claire Strandjord, in "Marking, not Curating, the Rhetorical Tradition: Ways through and beyond the Canon" (*Rhetoric Review*), introduces nonWestern understandings of classical rhetoric terminology such as 'tradition' to illustrate how such reorientations can reopen conversations regarding what and who gets read in the classroom. Strandjord argues that the rhetorical tradition has not provided a "resistance to change" on its own. Rather, the field's "misunderstanding of the rhetorical tradition as equaling the Western rhetorical canon" has rendered pedagogical limitations in the teaching of rhetoric. Strandjord describes how, by expanding the canons beyond Western frameworks, rhetoric courses can orient students toward a folklorick understanding of tradition, wherein readers are accountable for the meaning-making generated from taking up and circulating particular narratives. Through this work, Strandjord adds to broader conversations regarding how we can disrupt certain practices in the composition classroom towards a non-colonial gaze that treats canonicity as a continuously-generated and communally-deliberated practice.

This section concludes with this year's selection from *WPA: Writing Program Administration*: E. Shelley Reid's "On Learning to Teach: Letter to a New TA." Reid's work is a unique, inviting piece that welcomes new teaching assistants to the "personal, dynamic, and multifaceted" world of teaching composition to college students (p.1). Reid strikes an impressive balance in her prose: her writing is highly accessible, yet it also explicates complex theoretical concepts to new teachers who possess little pedagogical training. This accessibility is crucial for new teachers, who may feel intimidated or unprepared for teaching students within days of their teacher training. Reid offers six "strategies" for composition teaching assistants, each of which is relentlessly pragmatic and empathetic: accessing prior writing knowledge, understanding and adapting to conscious incompetence, integrating multiple learning approaches exploring "managed uncertainty" and "failing forward," and "extending your new teacher timeline." Reid's generous and forgiving strategies for new teachers are deeply empathetic, relatable, and acutely mirror the challenges many of us have faced in our first semesters of teaching.

SECTION 2: BODIES IN COMPOSITION

Section two opens with Patricia Fancher's "Composing Artificial Intelligence Performing Whiteness and Masculinity" (*Present Tense: A Journal of Rhetoric in Society*). In this groundbreaking piece, Fancher "analyzes the discourses of Eugene Goostman," a chatterbot that was deemed successful at convincing humans it was not a bot. Fancher combines feminist theory on embodiment with a technological critique of the white maleness the chatterbot performed. One group of assistant editors described Fancher's piece as an "approach to embodiment (an important and growing area of rhetorical studies) that is necessary and relevant." Describing whiteness and maleness as implicit and invisible, Fancher argues that the chatterbox "explicitly" invokes these tropes to "perform persuasive intelligence" to pass the bot off as a human. Fancher's most poignant critique is sharply articulated in her conclusion: "Eugene's performance of intelligence functions as a social mirror, reflecting cultural tropes of whiteness and masculinity that are intertwined with identifiable performances of intelligence. By reading Eugene Goostman's text for its embodied rhetoric, this discourse makes visible the continued centrality of whiteness and masculinity as the most convincing performance of intelligence. Ironically, this gendered and raced intelligence is made visible because the intelligent subject being tested has no body at all but relies upon a rhetoric of embodiment to perform convincing intelligence."

Extending the attention to embodied practice as central to rhetoric and composition scholarship and practice, section 2 continues with Hannah J. Rule's "Sensing the Sentence: An Embodied Simulation Approach to Rhetorical Grammar" (*Composition Studies*). In this piece, Rule "applies the neuroscientific concept of embodied simulation—the process of understanding language through visual, motor, and spatial modalities of the body—to rhetorical grammar and sentence-style pedagogies." By inviting students to engage in a multi-sensory envisioning the scene of a sentence, Rule was able to facilitate students' learning of how to develop the elusive 'flow' often touted as the holy grail of syntactic compliment. This piece evinces the benefits of engaging in the methods of Western scientific fields, such as neurology, while being mindful that these methods must be intersected with work from disability studies in order to engage in a broader understanding of embodied experience. In this way, Rule's approach reflects the ongoing interdisciplinary connections that push rhetoric and composition to continue developing writing pedagogies that center diverse perspectives, histories, and lived experiences.

Next, in "Feminist Mothering: A Theory/Practice for Writing Center Administration" (*WLN: A Journal of Writing Center Scholarship*), Michelle Miley describes "the devaluation of writing center work that for years scholars have connected to the feminization of writing centers." Drawing on the work of scholars like Melissa Nicolas, Miley provides an overview of scholarship that "warns against the feminization of the [writing] center," explaining how "this domesticated narrative can lead to the devaluation of writing center directors." While Miley acknowledges the importance of countering dominant "mothering" narratives about writing center work, she also "resist[s] the silencing of [her] mothering identity both at home and at the center," explaining that the notion of the writing center as a "'homey' space, a space shaped by our own insistence on listening, encouraging, nurturing, is indeed an important space to many" across the University. By (re)claiming the "mothering role" in writing center work through a feminist perspective, Miley illustrates how "feminist mothering provides a theory/practice" by which writing center directors "can embrace the nurturing/motherwork of the writing center while resisting the patriarchal trappings in the domestication of motherhood."

Moving from acknowledging the role of the Writing Center as a site for embodied learning and repositioning, Blake Watson's "From

Spectacular to Vernacular: Epideixis in Tactical Urban Design" (*Enculturation*) closes Section 2 by helping us consider the role that space plays in crafting rhetorical action. Watson demonstrates how tactical urbanism, the changing of public space as a means of activism, is both an instance of epiectic rhetoric and a means by which people have learned to demonstrate in public spaces have changed since the 1960's at the height of the Civil Act era when public demonstrations such as the March on Selma were more feasible prior to the introduction of convoluted highway protest laws. Watson studies the work published in *Tactical Urbanism*, a text that "examines the rhetorical work of vernacular epideictic design—the material construction of (often temporary) structures, affordances, and coordinative signs designed to inspire observation and reflection, to shore up and reassert shared values, and to teach a way of "seeing with" those values." Through this piece, Watson is able to use a study of *Tactical Urbanism* to demonstrate how interventions in the built environment disrupt learned understandings of the possible uses of public space through vernacular responses to the changing urban landscape.

SECTION 3: COMMUNITY-BASED WRITING PRACTICES

Our attention to community-based writing practices in section 3 is foregrounded by "Brokering Literacies: Child Language Brokering in Mexican Immigrant Families" by Steven Alvarez (*Community Literacy Journal*). In his five-year ethnographic study of how youth negotiate meaning with their families in an after school literacy program, Alvarez illustrates the intricate ways in which youth use "varying levels of bilingual practices to effectively translate, interpret, and advice between adults and family members of different ages." Through this work, Alvarez argues that "Language brokering is an everyday literacy practice, but one that in the United States gets relegated to outside classrooms." In order to continue valuing youth literacies, educators can continue "encouraging language brokering inside classrooms" specifically by "recognizing it as a tool for student involvement and multicultural interest."

In our selection from *Literacy in Composition Studies*, "Daughters Learning from Fathers: Migrant Family Literacies that Mediate Borders," Kaia Simon extends further attention to family and community literacies by explaining that "issues surrounding family literacies and relationships are particularly acute for migrant groups who arrive to the US as refugees with varying histories of literacy experiences." By presenting "an ethnographic study of twenty-three Hmong women's literacy" practices, Simon "explore[s] the multiple intersections among literacy, family, gender, and culture" commonly present in Hmong refugee communities. Through this work, Simon resists common "narratives of refugee disempowerment," instead highlighting how family and community literacies within refugee communities render powerful interactions among "education, professional careers, leadership, and advocacy." Simon's work presents important takeaways for community literacy scholars, arguing that the notion of literacy in family contexts is "complicated: at times the source of conflict and strife, at times a source of relationship building and strengthening. Family literacy practices, regardless of whether or not they directly support or related to the literacy practices of schools, workplaces, or governments, can have lifelong effects." By engaging with family and community literacy work, rhetoric and composition scholars can thus continue to honor the rich and multilayered relationships that our students and communities experience with literacies in and beyond classroom spaces.

Continuing to bring attention to issues of positionality in writing and literacy practices, Tasha Golden's "Subalternity in Juvenile Justice: Gendered Oppression and the Rhetoric of Reform" (*Reflections*) illustrates how women continue to be placed in a "subaltern status" within the justice system, positioned through "pervasive rhetorical constructions of them as others." Through her analysis of the rhetorical positioning that women in the justice system are frequently subjected to, Golden argues that the community-based projects engaging with prison populations should move away from imposing deficit-based frameworks on women's experiences. Instead, "by acknowledging the subalternity of young detained women, further studies and community collaborations can be taken up to close the distance between the actual experiences and knowledges of young women and the oppressive rhetorical constructions of them that have long informed policy, programming, and daily interaction." In this way, researchers developing community-based projects, particularly projects involving marginalized and vulnerable populations such as imprisoned women, should continue to foreground power relationships and positionalities as critical components of ethical and sustainable collaboration.

Further illustrating issues of ethical collaboration in community-based writing projects, our selection from *College Composition and Communication* is D. Alexis Hart and Roger Thompson's "Veterans in the Writing Classroom: Three Programmatic Approaches to Facilitate the Transition from the Military to Higher Education." As veteran enrollment in higher education burgeons, Hart and Thompson offer an exigent and pragmatic article that examines three different approaches for modeling veterans' courses. The authors highlight the complicated transitional struggles veterans encounter when leaving military life for a civilian role in higher education. Veterans in an "induction" phase—the liminal space in between leaving the military and "acclimate[ing] to a new environment"—can be fraught with drastic identity shifts and feelings of alienation. According to the authors, teachers in composition courses are often exposed to the challenges associated with these transitions first-hand because writing courses typically involve some form of narrative. For veterans, narrative features of pedagogy can pressure students into disclosing their military past and can contribute to their feelings of isolation and otherness (p.350). As one group of assistant editors suggested, the authors of this piece "examine the need to balance the needs of 'integrating' the veteran, while avoiding stigmatizing at the same time." Ultimately, the authors advocate for asset-based pedagogy as they deftly move between theory about veteran composition courses and practical guidelines for following these models in classrooms. This piece's strength lies in its honesty about the challenges associated with teaching an underserved population and its concrete strategies for approaching veteran courses.

Section 3 concludes with Risa Applegarth's "Children Speaking: Agency and Public Memory in the Children's Peace Statue Project" (*Rhetoric Society Quarterly*). Applegarth "examines the argumentative and organizational strategies of a group of children from New Mexico who worked in the early 1990s to publicize, design, and fund the Children's Peace Statue," a national memorial for peace developed on the 50th anniversary of the bombing of Hiroshima and Nagasaki by the United States. Through their collective efforts, the youth described in Applegarth's article funded and "reportedly petitioned the Los Alamos County Council to accept the statue as a gift to the city of Los Alamos." By analyzing "children's (unsuccessful) efforts to place the statue in Los Alamos," Applegarth illustrates the often-ignored rhetorical agency of youth, showing how "children speaking—collectively, publicly, insistently about past and future—undermine more comfortable practices that figure children as symbols of hope and goodness. Instead, children who speak designate themselves as agents who will bring about the world they desire." At a time when youth are leading activist movements resisting violence across and beyond the United States, Applegarth's argument for the value of youth agency resonates deeply, providing a model for how rhetoric and composition scholars and teachers can engage with youth in contemporary activist movements.

LOOKING FORWARD

By showcasing the selections for the 2018 *Best of* in three-themed sections, we propose a collaboratively-developed framework to help readers engage with important publications highlighted and selected by rhetoric and composition scholars and students across the country this year. While we acknowledge the value of these selections, we also recognize that the wide breadth of a constantly expanding discipline cannot be encompassed in a single collection. As the *Best of* series continues growing, we hope to continue developing new models for increasing the access and opportunities that scholars and students in rhetoric and composition have to engage with the emerging work of our field. As these efforts continue, we hope to see new initiatives for providing open-access options for reading this work, as well as new frameworks for collaborating with scholars, students, and communities that reflect multiple institutional and embodied positionalities and epistemologies. Further, we hope to expand our definition for the types of journals solicited for nominations to encapsulate non-U.S. centered approaches to literacy, composition and communication. It is our wish that future editors will be able to continue working toward enhancing dialogue with non-U.S. based publications to expand the range of methods, places, and ways of knowing represented as this journal's pieces. As this year's selections illustrate, the disciplinary, embodied, and material orientations of researchers, teachers, and students in rhetoric and composition continue to shift each year, and as such, what we deem to be the "best" in our field each year should continue to reflect this dynamic fluidity.

Acknowledgments

The editors would like to acknowledge and thank the associate editors for their labor and expert contributions to this year's collection of *Best of the Journals in Rhetoric and Composition*.

Erika Sparby, Illinois State University,
Alison Lukowski, Christian Brothers University ,TN,
Kelle Sills, University of Tennessee, Martin
Jason Tham, University of Minnesota

Iris Ruiz, UC-Mercedes
Anne Zanzucchi, UC-Mercedes
Thomas Hothem, UC-Mercedes
Heather Devrick, UC-Mercedes
Helen Sandoval, UC-Mercedes
Diana Hines, Texas A&M University - Commerce

Billy Lancaster, Texas A&M University - Commerce
Megan Opperman, Texas A&M University - Commerce
Ian Radzinski, Texas A&M University - Commerce
Judy Serrano, Texas A&M University - Commerce
Mike Smith, Texas A&M University - Commerce
Tawnya Smith, Texas A&M University - Commerce
Michelle Tvete, Texas A&M University - Commerce
Christopher Wydler, Texas A&M University - Commerce

Jessica Rose Corey, Duke University
Rajendra K Panthee, Syracuse University
Ben Erwin, Syracuse University
Marc Bousquet, Syracuse University

Jorge Gomez, El Paso Community College
Donna Munoz, El Paso Community College
Yasmin Ramirez, El Paso Community College
Joe Crisafulli, El Paso Community College
Jennifer Cedillos, El Paso Community College
Reyna Munoz, El Paso Community College

Bruce Kovanen, University of Illinois, Urbana-Champaign
Andrew Bowman, University of Illinois, Urbana-Champaign

Logan Middleton, University of Illinois, Urbana-Champaign
Nicole Turnipseed, University of Illinois, Urbana-Champaign

Patti Poblete, Henderson State University
Breanna Kreimeyer, Grand View University and Des Moines Area Community College
Jennifer Lin LeMesurier, Colgate University
Amy Wan, Queens College and CUNY Graduate Center
Chakrika Veeramoothoo, University of Minnesota
Robyn Tasaka, University of Hawai'i-West O'ahu
Natalie Perez, University of Hawai'i-West O'ahu
Aimee Takaki, University of Hawai'i-West O'ahu
Yasmin Romero, University of Hawai'i-West O'ahu
Natalie Szymanski, University of Hawai'i-West O'ahu
Andrew Burgess, Florida State University

Craig A. Meyer, Texas A&M University-Kingsville
Mary Frances Rice, University of Kansas
Anne-Marie Womack, Tulane University
Hilary Selznick, Western Michigan University
Lauren Obermark, University of Missouri, St. Louis
Dev Bose, University of Arizona
Ellen Birdwell, Alvin Community College

Kelly Blewett, Indiana University-East
Rich Schivener, University of Cincinnati
Kathleen Spada, University of Cincinnati
Katelyn Lusher, University of Cincinnati

Jacob Richter, Clemson University
Charissa Che, University of Utah
Geoff Clegg, Midwestern State University

BEST OF THE JOURNALS
RHETORIC AND COMPOSITION

THE WAC JOURNAL

WAC Journal is on the Web at http://wac.colostate.edu/journal/ and parlorpress.com/wacjournal

The WAC Journal is an open-access, blind, peer-viewed journal published annually by Clemson University, Parlor Press and the WAC Clearinghouse. It is published annually in print by Parlor Press and Clemson University. Digital copies of the journal are simultaneously published at The WAC Clearinghouse in PDF format for free download, http://wac.colostate.edu/journal/. Print subscriptions support the ongoing publication of the journal and make it possible to offer digital copies as open access. *The WAC Journal* publishes WAC-related articles on WAC techniques and applications; WAC program strategies; WAC and WID; WAC and writing centers; interviews and reviews; and emergent technologies and digital literacies across the curriculm.

Inviting Students to Determine for Themselves What It Means to Write Across the Disciplines

Brian Hendrickson and Genevieve Garcia de Mueller show how their adoption of what Juan C. Guerra refers to as "writing across difference" played out at their university, which is largely comprised of students from socioeconomically and ethnolinguistically underrepresented communities. Their pilot course needed to be responsive to individual students' racial and linguistic identities. One of the key goal of the course was thus to gain a greater understanding of the complexity of issues related to language, power, and identity within their own communities. Through a collaborative process of rubric development, their WAC program directly involved students in formulation of a rubric for writing achievement that reflected the nature and voices of a diverse student population.

Inviting Students to Determine for Themselves What It Means to Write Across the Disciplines

Brian Hendrickson and Genevieve Garcia de Mueller

INTRODUCTION

Situated in the literature on threshold concepts and transfer of prior knowledge in WAC/WID and composition studies, with particular emphasis on the scholarship of writing across difference, our article explores the possibility of re-envisioning the role of the composition classroom within the broader literacy ecology of colleges and universities largely comprised of students from socioeconomically and ethnolinguistically underrepresented communities. We recount the pilot of a composition course prompting students to examine their own prior and other literacy values and practices, then transfer that growing meta-awareness to the critical acquisition of academic discourse. Our analysis of students' self-assessment memos reveals that students apply certain threshold concepts to acquire critical agency as academic writers, and in a manner consistent with Guerra's concept of transcultural repositioning. We further consider the role collective rubric development plays as a critical incident facilitating transcultural repositioning.

COURSE RATIONALE

Although it could be said that composition courses are designed to prepare students "to meet the demands of academic writing across the disciplines"—the description for our writing program's second-year, intermediate composition course—scholars in composition studies, and writing across the curriculum and in the disciplines (WAC/WID) more particularly, have questioned the capacity of composition courses to do just that.1 Whereas J. Paul Johnson and Ethan Krase find that the first-year composition (FYC) classroom can help students transfer general argumentative skills to upper-division writing tasks, Natasha Artemeva and David R. Russell separately argue that the traditional FYC classroom cannot adequately simulate writing and learning contexts within particular academic disciplines. To better prepare students, scholars such as Linda S. Bergmann and Janet Zepernick, Amy Devitt, and Elizabeth Wardle ("Understanding") recommend a shift in composition pedagogy from teaching generalizable skill sets or particular genre conventions to sets of metacognitive strategies.

How specific those strategies are to particular disciplinary contexts is a matter of debate. Anne Beaufort argues that students develop general types of writing knowledge, but only over time and in particular disciplinary contexts. Likewise, Chris Thaiss and Terry Myers Zawacki suggest that students develop as writers in accordance with the idiosyncrasies of particular disciplines, but in generalizable developmental phases leading to metadisciplinary awareness. Linda Adler-Kassner and Elizabeth Wardle also contend that learning to write involves the acquisition and application of a cross-disciplinary set of threshold concepts, and Kathleen Blake Yancey, Lianne Robertson, and Kara Taczak observe that FYC courses foregrounding reflection and explicit instruction in threshold concepts from composition studies support students' transfer of writing knowledge and practices more effectively than those grounded in expressivism or cultural studies. Although they don't set out to study the role prior knowledge plays in transfer, Yancey, Robertson, and Taczak find that the role it does play is equally if not more important, as Mary Jo Reiff and Anis Bawarshi have previously demonstrated.

This recognition of the value of students' prior literacies aligns well with scholarship in WAC/WID that Juan C. Guerra refers to as "writing across difference," or work that urges WAC/WID scholars and practitioners to "acknowledge the value inherent in the full repertoire of linguistic, cultural, and semiotic resources students use in all their communities of belonging"; "encourage them to call on these as they best see fit"; and institute campus-wide initiatives like the "Writing Across Communities initiative that attempts to integrate the individual college classroom, the campus and our students' other communities of belonging" (x–xii). "Writing Across Communities" is the term Michelle Hall Kells coined for her grassroots approach to creating a WAC/WID initiative that operates as "a mechanism for transdisciplinary dialogue to demystify the ways we make and use knowledge across communities of practice" (94). Kells elaborates, "It is a process that must directly involve students themselves. Moreover, it is a process that should include consideration of the range of rhetorical resources influencing students' lives in and beyond the academy" (90).

Writing across difference seemed to us a particularly relevant and necessary concept for re-envisioning the function of our writing program's second-year, intermediate composition course within the larger literacy ecology of our flagship, land-grant, Hispanic-serving institution. We were concerned that our writing program had not adequately addressed how this course would help our particular student population, largely comprised of students from socioeconomically and ethnolinguistically underrepresented communities, "improve their writing skills to meet the demands of academic writing across the disciplines." The lack of any explicit attention in the course description to where our students were coming from, where they were going, and what literacies they were bringing with them, raised concerns for us similar to those expressed in Donna LeCourt's critique that WAC/WID has "forgotten the concern for alternative literacies and voices Other to the academy" (390). Drawing upon LeCourt's vision for a critical "third stage" in WAC/WID, Victor Villanueva suggests addressing the field's assimilationist tendencies through an antiracist critical pedagogy developed in partnership with scholars in other disciplines.

Twelve years after Villanueva, and seventeen after LeCourt, Mya Poe continues to call attention to "WAC's limited engagement with race," which Chris M. Anson contends is partly due to its focus on faculty development, and partly to a habit in composition studies writ large of treating "students as a generalized construct, not as individuals who bring specific histories, experiences, and 'vernacular literacies' to their learning" (23). For these reasons, and out of recognition of the local demographic context of our institution, we wanted our own course pilot to be more responsive to individual students' racial and linguistic identities. Our state consistently ranks at or near bottom in terms of overall youth well-being and chances at success (2014 Kids Count 21; "State Report Cards"). According to the US Census Bureau, 19.5% of the state's population lives below the poverty level. A minority-majority state, 47.3% of the population are Hispanic or Latino, 10.4% are American Indian or Alaska Native (39.4% are white alone), and 36% speak a language other than English at home. During the semester in which we piloted our course, our university's official enrollment report stated that 84% of the student body claimed original residence in state, so it is no surprise that the demographics of the undergraduate student body of 21,008 closely reflected those of the state as a whole: 43% Hispanic and 6.4% American Indian (38.3% white).2 That the average undergraduate student age was 23.7 years old further suggests a large nontraditional undergraduate student population.

If one reason for designing our course pilot was to better attend to where our students came from and what they brought with them, the other was to better attend to where they were going. It's difficult, though, to define what it means "to meet the demands of academic writing across the disciplines" without the assistance of a WAC/WID program capable of more systematically documenting the ways that faculty assign writing across the disciplines. At the time of our study, the university benefited from a strong grassroots network of students, faculty, and administrators advocating for a WAC/WID program with an emphasis on writing across difference, but it operated largely outside official channels, including reporting lines and budgets. The university's college for undergraduate student success did partner with the English department's core writing program to offer linked courses, or learning communities (see Nowaceck; Wardle, "Can"; Zawacki and Williams), but those offerings didn't extend beyond the first year. And though several academic units required writing-intensive courses in their majors in response to the requirements of their own disciplinary accrediting bodies, the university offered no formal oversight or support in the form of a mandate for writing-intensive upper-division courses (see Townsend). The writing program therefore offered no upper-division courses in writing in the disciplines beyond those particular to its professional writing degree concentration.

It did, however, offer two second-year writing courses as part of the university's core curriculum. Our course pilot took place in a section of one of them, English 202: Expository Writing, with the following full description: "an intermediate writing course designed for students who have passed 101 and 102, and who wish to improve their writing skills to meet the demands of academic writing across the disciplines." 202 was one of four options students could choose from to fulfill the second-year, university-wide core writing and speaking requirement, the others being professional and technical writing (201), public speaking, and reasoning and critical thinking. Though several colleges within the university, including business and engineering, required 201, only the college of fine arts required 202.

202 was billed to prospective instructors, mostly graduate students in the English department, as focusing "on one content subject, selected by the instructor, for the length of the semester." Despite the breadth of possible themes implied here, the course titles rarely reflected disciplinary interests beyond literary or cultural studies, even though at the time of our study, more than two-thirds of our university's undergraduate students had declared majors outside the college of arts and sciences, in which humanities-related disciplines were housed. As Carol Severino and Mary Traschel point out, generalist versus discipline-specific notions of academic writing are often shaped by the disciplinary or institutional context in which a course or initiative takes shape, and within the context of our English department, 202 seemed to operate under the assumption that humanities-related notions of academic writing were generalizable across the disciplines. What's more, a student planning to pursue a major complementary to the focus of a particular section would not likely know to look for the section-specific description on the writing program's website; only the general course description was included on the registration site, further suggesting that the course should be beneficial to the student regardless of its focus or their choice of major.

But was that what we were saying, and if so, were we really offering a course that could fulfill that promise? Beneath the surface of this question were other questions central to WAC/WID: "What does it mean to learn to write and teach writing within and across particular disciplines?"; "What role should core writing courses play in preparing students for the writing challenges they will face in their upper-division coursework?"; and "How can writing programs and WAC/WID initiatives best account for a particular student body's learning goals and learning incomes?"

Course Design

Our pilot course section, "Reading and Writing Our Communities," sought to productively engage with questions of disciplinarity, transfer, and identity—and in ways that honored the WAC/WID language in the course description—by prompting students to examine how their own prior and other literacy values and practices shape and are shaped by the communities to which they already belonged, then encouraging them to transfer their growing meta-awareness of that dynamic to the critical acquisition of academic discourse, i.e., the task of answering for themselves what it means "to meet the demands of academic writing across the disciplines."

In distinguishing between the kinds of literacy outcomes programs/courses privilege, Thomas Deans identifies "writing about the community" courses as emphasizing "personal reflection, social analysis, and/or cultural critique . . . [and] tend[ing] to advance academic and critical literacy goals" (18). With a writing-about-the-community pedagogy in mind, our course description read as follows: "In this course, students will develop their own academic writing identities by considering how language, power, and identity influence how we read (are shaped by) and write (shape) our communities." Similarly, our outcomes emphasize academic and critical literacy goals met through personal reflection and cultural critique:

> By actively, collaboratively, and critically engaging with course readings, community-based research, and the writing process itself, students in this course will:
> - Gain a greater understanding of the complexity of issues related to language, power, and identity within their own communities;
> - Explore the strategies of community writing centers and other community literacy initiatives for acting as responsible agents of change;
> - Reflect on their own academic literacy practices by:
>   - Analyzing and evaluating the moves made by academic writers in relevant selected readings and further scholarly research;
>   - Collectively developing assessment criteria derived from that analysis and evaluation;

> o Applying criteria in peer and self assessment and in composing drafts of major writing assignments;
> o Assembling a portfolio including revised drafts of major writing assignments and an outcomes-based self-assessment memo.

Our sequence of assignments moved from a focus on the cultural, ethnic, linguistic, professional, religious, and/or other communities to which students already belonged to the academic community to which they wished to gain entry. In each assignment, we asked students to analyze how various aspects of literacy shape and are shaped by specific communities, then apply that same analytical framework to consider how they were working in the course to acquire academic literacies. For each assignment prompt, we provided students with a rhetorical situation. Their audience was always their peers, and their context an undergraduate academic journal; as an example, we provided our own institution's publication featuring the best essays written by students in courses across the curriculum.

For the first assignment, students were asked to choose as their subject "an artifact—textual, audio, image-based, or a combination thereof—that exemplifies a particular valuable, idiosyncratic, or even undesirable literacy practice in [their] own community." In this assignment, as with the latter two, students were required to collect analyzable data from the community in question in the form of field notes, interviews, recorded images, and other texts. The purpose of the first assignment was "to demonstrate that [the] artifact is an interestingly representative example of a particular literacy practice in [their] own community." This assignment aimed to give students the opportunity to develop an understanding of literacy as shaping and shaped by a community's attempts at self-representation and to prepare students for the next two assignments, which asked them to analyze "a literacy education practice in [their] own community" and the "values and beliefs about what 'good' academic writing is (and isn't)," respectively.

Our assignment prompts allowed students a wide berth to explore what literacy means to them and their own communities. Whereas for the first assignment some students looked at textual and digital literacy practices, such as Facebook and Twitter usage among their friends, others described local street art and billboard advertisements as literacy practices reflecting the values, discursive conventions, and power dynamics within the local community. One student even analyzed how her brother's Grateful Dead shirt functioned as a literacy practice signaling his status within the touring community.

Whereas the first assignment emphasized text collection as the primary research method, the second assignment asked students to conduct actual observations and interviews. We and our students were surprised to discover that most of them were often already involved in some kind of literacy education practice beyond the university, prompting assignments about crisis center training, online home brewing forums, tour guide services, youth ministries, and even rugby practice, where a student analyzed how the rules of the game shaped how he coached and the values players were expected to learn.

If the first two assignments were intended to be more analytical than critical, the third assignment invited students to apply what they had learned throughout the semester in a more evaluative fashion. One student made an argument for greater awareness of the instructional needs of second-language writers, and another for those of students with disabilities, with a special focus on mental illness. Yet another evaluated digital literacy practices like Twitter as tools for teaching and learning that challenge traditional notions of "good" academic writing.

For each assignment, students relied on readings in composition studies and related disciplines to formulate research questions and protocols that analyzed how language and literacy practices determined membership in particular communities and how community members determined their language and literacy practices. Keeping in mind the work of Thaiss and Zawacki on differences and overlaps between academic and alternative discourses, we chose readings that modeled a range of moves that academic and nonacademic writers make, including breaks with writing conventions, whereas readings often interrogated the relationship between language, power, identity, and status in a particular community. In that respect, our course design borrowed from Douglas Downs and Elizabeth Wardle's "Writing about Writing" (WAW) pedagogy, which urges compositionists to act "as if writing studies is a discipline with content knowledge to which students should be introduced, thereby changing their understandings about writing and thus changing the ways they write" (553). As Nancy Benson et al. note regarding their WAC/WID-influenced "Guide to Writing in the Majors" course revision, WAW doesn't just teach students to write like writing studies majors; it provides them with tools for learning about writing in other disciplines. In our own course pilot,

WAW also provided tools for students to study nonacademic literacies, comparing them with the conventions found in course readings, and with the writing they were doing in their other coursework. In many respects, we used WAW in the same way that Joanna Wolfe, Barrie Olson, and Laura Wilder use what they term "Comparative Genre Analysis": with the hope that what transfers is not so much proficiency in conforming to particular writing conventions but awareness of how those conventions shape communities, and vice versa (45).

To encourage students to exercise agency in the acquisition of academic discourse, we integrated collective rubric development into our pilot course via Asao B. Inoue's community-based assessment pedagogy. Inoue provides a systematic account of collective rubric development as shifting the culminating emphasis from instructor evaluation to peer and self-assessment. The basic concept behind community-based assessment pedagogy is that students collectively develop rubrics that describe holistically what a proficient/adequate (not excellent) paragraph—and eventually position paper—should look like. The rubric evolves over time from a list of traits to categories of traits, and the language of the rubric evolves in complexity and explicitness as students apply it in peer assessment and collectively revise it during class discussion. Inoue stresses the difference between critique and assessment, coaching students to focus on potential, and focusing class time on discussing strategies for assessing peers and interpreting peer assessment, and he makes reflection on assessment an integral component of the process as well. To maintain the emphasis on peer assessment and not instructor evaluation, Inoue does not grade students on their assignments. Instead, he negotiates their grades with them during one-on-one end-of-semester portfolio conferences.

In our application of community-based assessment pedagogy, we asked students to summarize and reflect on course readings in which the authors examine literacy artifacts, then draw inferences regarding how the community "reads" and "writes" the artifact, i.e., shapes and is shaped by the literacy practices associated with the artifact, and class discussion consisted of comparing and contrasting a range of popular and academic readings and analyzing how and why different readings with similar purposes were written in different ways for different audiences. These exercises paved the way for students to work in teams on what Barbara Walvoord and Virginia Anderson call primary trait analysis, in which lists of traits evolve into categories of traits that eventually form the dimensions of a rubric (67). In our version of primary trait analysis, students identified key traits from the readings that they considered relevant to the assignment's genre and rhetorical situation, then grouped those traits into rubric categories. In performing this exercise, students were instructed not to employ superlatives but to use qualitative language to describe traits that perform the function expected of a document given its genre and rhetorical situation. Each team then posted their rubric drafts to a discussion forum on our online course site, then assessed other teams' rubrics, noting what traits and categories they would like to see included in the final rubric to be used collectively by the class. Based on commonalities across rubrics as well as students' assessment of rubrics, the teams' rubric drafts were compiled into a single course rubric to be refined during class discussion before and after the peer assessment process, in which students used the rubric to describe in memo format what they saw in at least two of their peers' first drafts. We then evaluated as a class the effectiveness of the rubric as a resource and guide for peer assessment, and we revised it accordingly before students used it again to write self-assessment memos addressed to the instructor as accompaniments to their revised second drafts. We repeated this process through the following two sequences, during which we adapted the previous rubric based on new and increasingly longer and more complex readings and writing assignments.

Some of the benefits of giving students greater agency over rubric creation and revision are apparent in the evolution of the rubric itself. The first combined rubric draft evidenced the complicated nature of accounting for seven different teams' interpretations of the genre and rhetorical situation, and the students objected to it as too wordy, impersonal, abstract, and stuffy. Take for example this trait from the rubric's "Introduction" section: "Establishes the document's rhetorical situation as described in the assignment guidelines, introducing the document's topic and purpose and the relevance between them and the document's audience." After being led through a class activity in which teams revised the rubric, then advocated for their revisions to the rest of the class, students decided on the following language: "Introduces your paper's subject, a literacy artifact, as well as your paper's purpose, and the relevance between your paper's literacy artifact, purpose, and audience."

Although the style in which the rubric was written grew simpler over time, its descriptions of genre conventions and the requisite rhetorical awareness grew in complexity. The first assignment's rubric ended up with four categories of traits: introduction, body, conclusion, and style. In the final version of its "Introduction" section, another trait read: "Explains terms and methods of analysis by referring to sources so that a general audience of your academic peers could understand." By the final draft of the third assignment's rubric, the students had decided to give that trait its own category labeled "Terms, Methods, and Literature Review" and revised it as follows: "Explains terms, methods, and scholarly context of research by referring to sources so that a general audience of your academic peers can identify what/whose conversation you're entering and what you plan to contribute to it." The changes in the second example evidence students' growing awareness of the rhetorically situated purpose of genre conventions specific to academic writing. By negotiating the terms of the rubrics that served to concretize these conventions, students gain a sense of academic discourse as evolving, malleable, and questionable.

This approach aligns with one of our underlying assumptions in designing "Reading and Writing Our Communities": that instructors cannot coach students in the critical acquisition of academic discourse while presenting them with unquestionable guidelines and rubrics, then grading them on how well or poorly their writing conforms. Our students did not therefore receive evaluations of their writing. Borrowing one of Kathleen Blake Yancey's reflective writing practices, instructor feedback took the form of a response memo that reinforced students' insights in their self-assessment memos and directed their attention to other aspects of their writing that they might not have considered in their self-assessments. Though students did receive occasional prescriptive feedback when struggling with more foundational problems, most feedback took the form of a request that the student explore in her next memo how she was attending to a particular problem. Often that request was more prescriptive of the memo itself than of the assignment to which it referred, pressing students to further develop their reflections, explaining in greater detail how and why they made particular choices. So although students did not receive evaluations of their writing, they did receive feedback that directed them in revising their drafts for inclusion in their final portfolios. The goal in withholding evaluation and directing prescriptive feedback only at the students' self-assessments and not at the primary writing assignments was to highlight the course's emphasis on developing students' awareness of how they made their choices and not necessarily the choices themselves, thereby carving out a space for students to critically reflect on their acquisition of academic discourse. This emphasis on assessing students' reflective writing also aligns with the first of what Susan H. McLeod and Eric Miraglia identify as WAC/WID's "two different but complementary pedagogical approaches . . . 'writing to learn' and 'writing to communicate,'" which they claim is a key feature of WAC/WID's success as a pedagogical change agent (5).

Because our writing program required a more thorough record than afforded by Inoue's approach to deferring grades until the end of the semester, we adapted Jane Danielewicz and Peter Elbow's contract model to fit programmatic constraints. We assigned full credit for all assignments submitted on time and meeting minimum requirements. If students met these two conditions on all assignments leading up to the final portfolio, they earned an 85% in the course, or a solid B. The remaining 15% was determined by the extent to which students demonstrated in their portfolio self-assessment memos critical engagement with their own writing in terms of the course outcomes, and we collectively developed as a class the final portfolio rubric that distinguished qualitatively between an excellent (15%), proficient (10%), sufficient (5%), and unacceptable (0%) portfolio memo.

Coding Portfolio Self-Assessment Memos

In coding students' portfolio self-assessment memos, we hoped to identify if, when, and how students articulated any threshold concepts that may have aided them in their learning. In their portfolio self-assessment memos, students were asked to first provide a brief, general assessment of their experience in the course, explaining how if at all the course influenced their own writing; their understanding of writing and/or literacy in general; and their understanding of academic writing and/or literacy in particular. For the remaining majority of each memo, students were asked to describe decisions they made while writing and/or revising each assignment, citing as evidence specific pages in drafts whenever possible, and explaining how and why they made those decisions in terms of whatever aspects of the course they deemed relevant.

Data analysis took place over eighteen hours and ten meetings, during which the two of us coded fourteen students' end-of-semester self-assessment memos. We approached our data analysis inductively, a process described by Catherine Marshall and Gretchen B. Rossman as one in which the researcher "identifies the salient, grounded categories of meaning" that "then become buckets or baskets into which segments of text are placed" (159). Throughout the process, we refined all categories and subcategories with an eye for internal convergence and external divergence, ensuring that in adding, revising, and dividing categories all remained "internally consistent but distinct from one another" (Marshall and Rossman 159).

At the first level of coding, we identified any passages in students' self-assessment memos where they explicitly discussed any element of the course that played a role in their learning. At the second level, we placed those passages into three major categories that emerged during rereading. The first major category was comprised of potential threshold concepts. Then we had to create a second major category just for references to rubrics, and a third for references to both concepts and rubrics. Although we were initially looking only for threshold concepts, the prevalence of rubric references led us to also pay attention in our analysis to the role that rubrics played in student learning.

At the third level of coding, we further divided the major categories, creating five concepts categories of academic research, academic writing, literacy, rhetorical situation, and reflection. These category labels were fairly superficial in that they didn't describe how students used each respective concept. But the level-three rubrics categories did go into greater detail regarding how students found rubrics useful: for defining terms, developing ideas, focusing inquiry, integrating sources, structuring an assignment, reflecting in general, and revising in general. We also came up with a level-three rubric utility category of collective development that we had to refine further in our level-four coding to identify how students described the utility of collective rubric development: as clarifying concepts, cultivating individual agency, and/or establishing collective investment and accountability.

Level-four coding likewise consisted of identifying five further subcategories through which we differentiated students' references to concepts categories. The subcategories noted instances wherein students discuss the utility of a particular major concept as self-empowerment as an end in and of itself; hermeneutic, or a process of inquiry and/or interpretation; sociocultural, or a way of understanding the socially constituted nature of language, identity, and agency, but without a demonstrated recognition of how that understanding gains the student access and/or agency; access, or a means of gaining access via greater agency, but without a demonstrated recognition of how that access and/or agency operates within a sociocultural understanding of the concept; and transcultural, or the need and/or ability to apply a sociocultural understanding to transition between discourse communities, i.e. the access and sociocultural subcategories combined.

In all cases, we strived to construct what Michael Quinn Patton calls "indigenous typologies," or categories and subcategories that evidence an explicit relationship between a concept or rubric reference and a claim about how it contributed to a student's learning (457). At times, however, we did have to discern implicit references to the rubric from the way a student might describe a class conversation that influenced her writing, which we knew was a conversation that emerged during and necessarily in relation to the collective development of a rubric. In other, murkier cases, a student might demonstrate an understanding of literacy as sociocultural in the way she explains decisions she made while writing, but without explicitly describing the concept, in which case we would discuss at length whether the student makes any reference elsewhere in the memo that demonstrates the influence of a course concept on that decision, or if the student's language and reasoning adequately reflects the way a concept was discussed and applied in the course.

Once we had refined all of our coding, we tabulated the number of students who referenced a concept/subcategory pairing as well as the number of instances of references within each concept/subcategory pairing, making sure to document the student's identifying number in each case so that we could maintain correspondence between our tabulations and other tables containing students' passages. We also tabulated the number of instances a concept/subcategory pairing was mentioned in conjunction with the rubric; the number of students who referenced each category of rubric utility, and the number of instances of those references; and the number of students who referenced a rubric utility category in conjunction with a concept/subcategory pairing. These tabulations provided us a clearer picture of which concept/subcategory pairings and rubric utility categories were referenced most frequently and by the most students, separately and together.

Of all the concept/subcategory pairings, students in "Reading and Writing Our Communities" most often demonstrated an understanding and application of the category of literacy, and within it the subcategories of literacy as hermeneutic, sociocultural, and transcultural, in that order. These pairings align with Beaufort's writing process and discourse community knowledge categories, as well as Adler-Kassner and Wardle's threshold concepts of writing as a continuous learning process, as a social and rhetorical activity, and as enactment and creation of identities and ideologies. In terms of categories and subcategories of rubric utility, students most often referred to the category of collective rubric development, and within it the subcategories of collective rubric development as clarifying concepts, establishing a sense of collective investment and accountability, and cultivating individual agency, in that order. Furthermore, of all the concept category/subcategory pairings, students most frequently referenced the rubric in relation to their understanding and application of literacy as sociocultural.

Students' Theories of Writing Knowledge

Identifying these concept category/subcategory pairings allowed us to further analyze the relationships students articulated between them, so that the pairings existed no longer as isolated coding categories but as what Yancey, Robertson, and Tacsak describe as the theories of writing knowledge students develop through reflective practice. One major trend we noticed in students' theories was an appreciation for the dialectical nature of literacy and learning. Take for instance Student Nine's explanation of collective rubric development as hermeneutic; in her case, this development involved an interpretation of and inquiry into not only an area of scholarship with which she was previously unfamiliar but also her own extant understanding of literacy as sociocultural, and in that respect the process of collective rubric development serves for Student Nine as one of "self-discovery":

> For major writing assignment one, I chose the petroglyphs as my literacy artifact, and I explained the conflict of the local Native Americans and suburban population fighting for the petroglyph land to illustrate the power struggle that may arise when different groups understand varying forms of literacy. At first, the prompt for this writing assignment was confusing because I

didn't understand the connection between literacy, a community, and language. However... the discussions held in class were very open-ended, and this allowed my peers and I to ask questions to sort out our thoughts.... By listening to the in-class discussions, I became aware of other concerns that had arisen and thought more critically about the major writing assignment. Before the class discussions, I received the prompt and was confused because the wording of the rubric was lengthy. However, during class we discussed how to change the rubric in groups, and thinking about how I wanted to change the rubric was a form of self-discovery. For instance, when thinking about standards for the assignment, I discovered more about my own understanding of the topic, and what I needed to learn more about, and this helped me focus my attention on certain aspects to better my understanding.

Student Nine explores the ways in which collective rubric development helped her further develop the knowledge she already possessed about her topic, and in a way that helped her rethink how she was writing about it, which in turn helped her learn that much more about her topic.

The dialectical relationship Student Nine describes between collective rubric development, conceptual knowledge acquisition, and the writing process involves a movement from confusion to greater clarity, and in a manner increasing individual agency while simultaneously emphasizing the sociocultural nature of literacy. That movement appears to play an important role in students' accounts of how a sociocultural understanding of literacy enables them to transculturally reposition as academic writers. Although the theory of transcultural repositioning had informed our course design from the start, we didn't explicitly recognize it as an outcome or look for evidence of it in students' self-assessment memos, but in coding students' self-assessment memos, we recognized that the more striking examples conformed to Guerra's definition of the term. Guerra derives the term from Min-Zhan Lu's description of learning in basic writing as repositioning, or boundary crossing catalyzed by an encounter with conflict. For Guerra, transcultural repositioning describes how all students, but especially the socioeconomically and ethnolinguistically underrepresented, overcome cultural and linguistic obstacles by transferring their prior and other literacies to the critical acquisition of new literacies.

Lu's original emphasis on the function of conflict in repositioning aligns with our own findings, as we discovered that students described their own critical acquisition of academic discourse less in terms of an explicit transfer of prior and other rhetorical knowledge and practices and more as a gradual movement from an encounter with conflict through collective rubric development to an insight into the dialectical nature of literacy understood as sociocultural; and in that respect, the notion of transcultural repositioning provided us a framework through which to examine students' individual accounts of this more longitudinal, collective process. For example, Student Seven connects her emergent understanding of literacy as sociocultural with her ability to transculturally reposition:

> Overall this class was personally challenging and rewarding. I learned about what it means to be literate, as well as the power that being extensively literate holds, and pushed [sic] me to improve my own writing.
>
> Regarding literacy and academic writing, my understanding has changed in a profound way. I now understand that literacy is based on community discourse and that the discourse of a community affects the community discourse, somewhat like evolution. This realization has changed my views on my own writing as well; my writing affects those who read it, and my writing is affected by what I read. As time goes on, I see that my writing has the power to change the discourse of its subject, and that this power comes from credibility.

Again, Student Seven acknowledges that the class was "personally challenging," and without first developing an appreciation for discourse communities as sites of contention and flux, she admits that she wouldn't see her own writing as carrying any consequence. Her understanding and application of literacy as sociocultural allows her to claim ethos and agency in the discourse communities to which she wishes to belong.

Although Student Seven doesn't mention collective rubric development in the above passage, she does mention elsewhere that the "group assignments"—i.e., collective rubric development—helped her and her group members better understand course concepts in general, suggesting that the activity likely did play an important role in her development of an understanding of literacy as sociocultural. The following passage from Student Five more explicitly connects collective rubric development with transcultural repositioning:

> I chose to analyze written communication in the workplace as a means of exploring what is defined within this certain community as "good" writing. Focusing on this form of writing allowed me to consider how determinations of "good" or "bad" writing are made and how there is a more complex dynamic that prohibits a universal definition of "good" writing.
>
> The overall activities of constructing and revising rubrics for this class seemed to be most applicable to thinking about this assignment because it made me realize that determining what qualifies as "good" writing can differ depending on the class and teacher. Working together to compose rubrics seemed to counteract this disparity and allowed us to be able to more critically engage in the writing process.

Student Five describes how collective rubric development enabled her to better appreciate academic writing as sociocultural and to exercise agency within the academic discourse community of the classroom, and she suggests that this academic literacy knowledge and practice contributed to her evolving understanding of workplace literacy knowledge and practice. Again, her description of this relationship is more dialectical than linear, offering a glimpse into how prior and other literacies, academic literacy, threshold concepts such as the sociocultural nature of literacy, and collective rubric development are synthesized for her into an understanding and performance of academic writing as neither immutable nor inaccessible. Interestingly, this knowledge and practice again appears to arise out of an encounter with conflict, in the case of Student Five, due to the ability to "counteract [the] disparity" she observes between what different teachers value as "good" writing across the disciplines.

Discussion

At the time of our study, both the writing program and university in question were undergoing significant changes, but as we write this, those changes have yet to lead to a new course description or set of outcomes for the second-year "Expository Writing" course, or an administratively supported campus-wide WAC/WID initiative. We originally set out to develop an approach that our writing program might use to better align the composition classroom with the demands of writing across the disciplines, and in a manner that empowered our students to take agency in determining what that means. However, our research offers implications of relevance beyond the successful revision of a single course at one particular institution, and beyond the composition classroom in general, for scholars and practitioners interested in exploring the possibilities of a writing across difference approach to WAC/WID.

Our analysis of students' self-assessment memos adds dimension to the definition of transcultural repositioning that we inherited from WAC/WID scholars Guerra and Kells in that we were able to observe students applying their understanding of literacy as sociocultural to the task of accessing critical agency as academic writers, suggesting that for our students, a sociocultural concept of literacy operated as a threshold concept in transcultural repositioning. This finding led us to reflect on how explicitly foregrounding the concept of literacy as sociocultural in the composition classroom might help us reframe that work as the facilitation of transcultural repositioning. It's possible that doing so might be more beneficial to certain student populations, and further research might observe the effects of explicitly foregrounding the concept of literacy as sociocultural across multiple course sections and with a larger sample population of students who self-identify as belonging to a socioeconomically and ethnolinguistically underrepresented community. Alternatively, researchers might provide a more longitudinal description of how the concept of literacy as sociocultural operates as a threshold concept facilitating transcultural repositioning throughout students' upper-division coursework.

Our research suggests that transcultural repositioning may be a valuable guiding principle for curriculum design at the course and programmatic level, and we hope that our efforts will encourage others to afford this concept the extensive scholarly attention it deserves. At the same time, not all students' self-assessment memos evidenced transcultural repositioning. More often, they evidenced students' emergent and preliminary recognition of literacy as sociocultural, or the related recognition of literacy as hermeneutic, i.e., an ongoing process of inquiry and interpretation. That an understanding of literacy as sociocultural was a necessary but not sufficient attribute of transcultural repositioning suggests that the latter may be a difficult though nevertheless rewarding outcome to aim for, if not an objective that every student should be expected to achieve.

As indicated by Lu's definition of repositioning, transcultural repositioning did not occur for our students without conflict, but the occurrence of conflict appears to indicate an intersection at which students' prior and other literacies, academic literacies, and the conceptual knowledge students gained from the course all collided, interacted, and were synthesized in a manner consistent with Yancey, Robertson, and Tacsak's description of the critical incident model of prior knowledge use, in which "students encounter an obstacle that helps them retheorize writing in general and their own agency as writers in particular" (5). The indeterminacy and deliberation involved in collective rubric development presented obstacles that ultimately appeared to help our students retheorize academic literacy and claim agency in the process of determining for themselves what it means "to meet the demands of academic writing across the disciplines." In other words, what we imagined would function as a simple form of empowerment also seemed to play an important role in students' acquisition of conceptual knowledge of writing and literacy.

Further research might look more explicitly at how collective rubric development functions as a critical incident in students' attempts at transcultural repositioning. But we might also consider the utility of collective rubric development in curriculum design at the course and programmatic level. What if, for instance, we had more explicitly invited our students into the collective activity of revising our course description and outcomes in accordance with students' actual learning outcomes (and incomes)? To do so would be to place Inoue's community based assessment pedagogy into conversation with Bob Broad's organic assessment protocol, so that actual courses take the place of focus groups in the collective process of curriculum design. Resituated within the context of WAC/WID, such an approach harkens back to Kells's insistence on "a reconceptualization of WAC through a deliberative process that engages diversity and the discursive possibilities of representation" (90). In that respect, our pilot course design also adds dimension to what such a reconceptualization of WAC/WID might look like.

Acknowledgments

We'd like to thank Jill Jeffery and Todd Ruecker for mentoring us through the course design and IRB application process; Kyle Fiore and Chuck Paine for encouraging us to experiment with our course pilot; and The WAC Journal editor, Roy Andrews, and our anonymous reviewers for their generous and encouraging feedback.

NOTES

1. We have withheld identifying information in accordance with our research protocol, using pseudonyms where appropriate.
2. We use these racial/ethnic labels to remain consistent with the sources of our demographic data.

REFERENCES

The 2014 Kids Count Data Book. Annie E. Casey Foundation, 22 July 2014, http://www.aecf.org/m/resourcedoc/aecf-2014kidscountdatabook-2014.pdf.

Adler-Kassner, Linda, and Elizabeth Wardle, editors. *Naming What We Know: Threshold Concepts of Writing Studies.* Utah State UP, 2015.

Anson, Chris M. "Black Holes: Writing Across the Curriculum, Assessment, and the Gravitational Invisibility of Race." *Race and Writing Assessment,* edited by Asao B. Inoue and Mya Poe. Peter Lang, 2012, pp. 15–28.

Artemeva, Natasha. "A Time to Speak, a Time to Act: A Rhetorical Genre Analysis of a Novice Engineer's Calculated Risk Taking." *Journal of Business and Technical Communication,* vol. 19, no. 4, 2005, pp. 389–421. *SAGE,* doi: 10.1177/1050651905278309.

Beaufort, Anne. *College Writing and Beyond: A New Framework for University Writing Instruction.* Utah State UP, 2007.

Benson, Nancy, et al. "Rethinking First Year English as First Year Writing Across the Curriculum." *Double Helix: A Journal of Critical Thinking and Writing,* vol. 1, 2013, pp. 1–16. *Double Helix,* http://www.qudoublehelixjournal.org/index.php/dh/article/view/3/78.

Bergmann, Linda S., and Janet Zepernick. "Disciplinarity and Transfer: Students' Perceptions of Learning to Write." *WPA: Journal of the Council of Writing Program Administrators,* vol. 31, no. 1–2, 2007, pp. 124–49. *CWPA,* http://wpacouncil.org/archives/31n1-2/31n1-2bergmann-zepernick.pdf.

Broad, Bob. "Organic Matters: In Praise of Locally Grown Writing Assessment." *Organic Writing Assessment: Dynamic Criteria Mapping in Action.* Bob Broad, et al. Utah State UP, 2009, pp. 1–13.

Danielewicz, Jane, and Peter Elbow. "A Unilateral Grading Contract to Improve Learning and Teaching." *College Composition and Communication,* vol. 61, no. 2, 2009, pp. 244–68. *JSTOR,* http://www.jstor.org/stable/40593442.

Deans, Thomas. *Writing Partnerships: Service-Learning in Composition.* National Council of Teachers of English, 2000.

Devitt, Amy J. *Writing Genres.* Southern Illinois UP, 2004.

Downs, Douglas, and Elizabeth Wardle. "Teaching about Writing, Righting Misconceptions: (Re)envisioning 'First-Year Composition' as 'Introduction to Writing Studies.'" *College Composition and Communication,* vol. 58, no. 4, 2007, pp. 552–84. *JSTOR,* http://www.jstor.org/stable/20456966.

Guerra, Juan C. *Language, Culture, Identity, and Citizenship in College Classrooms and Communities*. Routledge / NCTE, 2016.

Inoue, Asao B. "Community-Based Assessment Pedagogy." *Assessing Writing*, vol. 9, 2005, pp. 208–38. *ScienceDirect*, doi:10.1016/j.asw.2004.12.001.

Johnson, J. Paul, and Ethan Krase. "Articulating Claims and Presenting Evidence: A Study of Twelve Student Writers, From First-Year Composition to Writing Across the Curriculum." *The WAC Journal*, vol. 23, 2012, pp. 31–48. *The WAC Journal*, http://wac.colostate.edu/journal/vol23/johnson.pdf.

Kells, Michelle Hall. "Writing Across Communities: Deliberation and the Discursive Possibilities of WAC." *Reflections: A Journal of Writing, Service-Learning, and Community Literacy*, vol. 6, no. 1, 2007, pp. 87–109.

LeCourt, Donna. "WAC as Critical Pedagogy: The Third Stage?" *JAC*, vol. 16, no. 3, 1996, pp. 389–405. *JSTOR*, https://www.jstor.org/stable/20866089.

Lu, Min-Zhan. "Writing as Repositioning." *Journal of Education*, vol. 172, no. 1, 1990, pp. 18–21.

---. "Conflict and Struggle: The Enemies or Preconditions of Basic Writing?" *College English*, vol. 54, no. 8, 1992, pp. 887–913. *JSTOR*, https://www.jstor.org/stable/378444.

Marshall, Catherine, and Gretchen B. Rossman. *Designing Qualitative Research*. 4th ed., Sage, 2006.

McLeod, Susan H., and Eric Miraglia. "Writing Across the Curriculum in a Time of Change." *WAC for the New Millennium: Strategies for Continuing Writing-Across-the-Curriculum Programs*, edited by Susan H. McLeod, Eric Miraglia, Margot Soven, and Christopher Thaiss. National Council of Teachers of English, 2001, pp. 1–27. *WAC Clearinghouse*, http://wac.colostate.edu/books/millennium/chapter1.pdf.

Nowacek, Rebecca S. *Agents of Integration: Understanding Transfer As a Rhetorical Act*. Southern Illinois UP/Conference on College Composition and Communication of the National Council of Teachers of English, 2011.

Patton, Michael Quinn. *Qualitative Research and Evaluation Methods*. 2nd ed., Sage, 1990.

Poe, Mya. "Re-framing Race in Teaching Writing Across the Curriculum." *Across the Disciplines*, vol. 10, no. 3, 2013. *WAC Clearinghouse*, http://wac.colostate.edu/atd/race/poe.cfm.

Reiff, Mary Jo, and Anis Bawarshi. "Tracing Discursive Resources: How Students Use Prior Genre Knowledge to Negotiate New Writing Contexts in First-Year Composition." *Written Communication*, vol. 28, no. 3, 2011, pp. 312–37. *SAGE*, doi: 10.1177/0741088311410183.

Russell, David R. "Activity Theory and Its Implications for Writing Instruction." *Reconceiving Writing, Rethinking Writing Instruction*. Edited by Joseph Petraglia. Erlbaum, 1995, pp. 51–77.

Severino, Carol, and Mary Trachsel. "Theories of Specialized Discourses and Writing Fellows Programs." *Across the Disciplines*, vol. 5, 2008. *WAC Clearinghouse*, http://wac.colostate.edu/atd/fellows/severino.cfm.

"State Report Cards." *Quality Counts 2014*. Education Research Center, 3 January 2014, http://www.edweek.org/ew/qc/2014/state_report_cards.html.

Thaiss, Chris, and Terry Myers Zawacki. *Engaged Writers: Dynamic Disciplines*. Boynton-Cook, 2006.

Townsend, Martha, A. "Writing Intensive Courses and WAC." *WAC for the New Millennium: Strategies for Continuing Writing-Across-the-Curriculum Programs*. Edited by Susan H. McLeod, Eric Miraglia, Margot Soven, and Christopher Thaiss. Urbana, IL: National Council of Teachers of English, 2001, pp. 233–58. *WAC Clearinghouse*, http://wac.colostate.edu/books/millennium/chapter10.pdf.

United States, Department of Commerce, Census Bureau. *State and County QuickFacts*. 8 July 2014, https://www.census.gov/quickfacts/.

Villanueva, Victor. "The Politics of Literacy Across the Curriculum." *WAC for the New Millennium: Strategies for Continuing Writing-Across-the-Curriculum Programs*, edited by Susan H. McLeod, Eric Miraglia, Margot Soven, and Christopher Thaiss. National Council of Teachers of English, 2001, pp. 165–78. *WAC Clearinghouse*, http://wac.colostate.edu/books/millennium/chapter7.pdf.

Walvoord, Barbara E., and Virginia Johnson Anderson. *Effective Grading: A Tool for Learning and Assessment*. Jossey-Bass / Wiley, 1998.

Wardle, Elizabeth A. "Can Cross-Disciplinary Links Help Us Teach 'Academic Discourse' in FYC?" *Across the Disciplines*, vol. 1, 2004. *WAC Clearinghouse*, http://wac.colostate.edu/atd/articles/wardle2004/Index.cfm.

—. "Understanding 'Transfer' from FYC: Preliminary Results of a Longitudinal Study." *WPA: Journal of the Council of Writing Program Administrators*, vol. 31, no. 1–2, 2007, pp. 65–85. *CWPA*, http://wpacouncil.org/archives/31n1-2/31n1-2wardle.pdf.

Wolfe, Joanna, Barrie Olson, and Laura Wilder. "Knowing What We Know about Writing in the Disciplines: A New Approach to Teaching for Transfer in FYC." *The WAC Journal*, vol. 25, 2014, pp. 42–77. *The WAC Journal*, http://wac.colostate.edu/journal/vol25/wolfeetal.pdf.

Yancey, Kathleen Blake. *Reflection in the Writing Classroom*. Utah State UP, 1998.

—, Liane Robertson, Liane, and Kara Tacsak. *Writing across Contexts: Transfer, Composition, and Cultures of Writing*. UP of Colorado, 2014.

Zawacki, Terry Myers, and Ashley Taliaferro Williams. "Is It Still WAC? Writing within Interdisciplinary Learning Communities." *WAC for the New Millennium: Strategies for Continuing Writing-Across-the-Curriculum Programs*, edited by Susan H. McLeod, Eric Miraglia, Margot Soven, and Christopher Thaiss. National Council of Teachers of English, 2001, pp. 109–40. *WAC Clearinghouse*, http://wac.colostate.edu/books/millennium/chapter5.pdf.

JOURNAL OF TEACHING WRITING

Journal of Teaching Writing is on the Web at http://journals.iupui.edu/index.php/teachingwriting

Now in its thirty-seventh year of publication, the Journal of Teaching Writing (JTW) is the only national, refereed journal devoted to the teaching of writing at all academic levels, from preschool to the university, and in all subject areas of the curriculum. It publishes articles, reviews of books and pedagogical websites, and professional announcements. JTW's Editorial Board, which is composed of distinguished teachers and writers from all educational levels and geographic regions of the U.S., functions as a review team, reading and responding to submissions. With its editors and Editorial Board, the Journal aims to demystify the editorial review process and model the teaching of writing as a process of reflection and revision. Back issues can be downloaded free at http://journals.iupui.edu/index.php/teachingwriting.

"Authentic Questioning as a Form of Inquiry: Writing in the Dialogic Classroom"

Eamon Cunningham argues for a composition course featuring deep reading—including deliberate work by students to form their own questions around a cluster of readings. That's one way that students can begin to discover how inquiry leads to the construction of knowledge. The composition classroom becomes a place where *learning how to know* assumes greater importance than *conveying what is known*. The essay is notable for its inclusion of detailed student responses to the challenges and opportunities of deep reading in a dialogic classroom.

Authentic Questioning as a Form of Inquiry: Writing in the Dialogic Classroom

Eamon Cunningham

As a student, I loved the readings in my English classes—from Plato to Postmodernism—even before I had much of a clue about what these writers really meant. It's taken ten years on the other side of the desk to understand something a teacher of mine once told me a long time ago: "If you think you have everything figured out on the first reading, something must be wrong. Either you are not reading good writing, or you are not reading carefully enough." As a student, I was too often taken by the hand to the "right" answer, thinking in ways that had been mapped out for me, and writing in ways that did little for my own curiosity and sense of investigation. It was only when I began teaching and designing my own assignments that I began to read, write, and think differently. For the first time, I felt that I had the authority to question, challenge, and expand on not only the texts from class, but also my own writing and thinking: where my responses came from, the process by which I constructed knowledge, and how these processes might be expanded, intensified, or challenged. Reading and writing turned from a matter of coming up with answers to questions about a text to learning what type of questions needed to be asked in the first place. "Is it possible to replicate this essential experience I had as a teacher/reader for my students by letting them construct the lines of inquiry *they* wish to pursue for a text?" I wondered. Over the last few years, I have put this question to the test in my classroom.

Composition theory, while grounded in empirical research and sound practice, is a double-edged sword for teachers of writing. On one hand, theory provides the paradigms and methods to understand *how* one reads, *how* one builds knowledge, and *how* one makes sense of the mélange of ideas right before pen is put to paper. On the other hand, there is often a gap between the teaching of writing as conjectured by theorists and its actual practice. This gap is often filled by eager teachers' expostulations that seldom work to change students' ideas about themselves as writers. The further that practice drifts away from sound theory, the less likely it is that students will ever realize themselves as having a writerly identity. And while there is no single solution to the range of difficulties that students face in composition classrooms, deep reading—including deliberate work by students to form their own questions around a cluster of readings—is one way that students can begin to discover how inquiry leads to the construction of knowledge. In doing so, the composition classroom becomes a place where *learning how to know* assumes greater importance than *conveying what is known* (Farmer 16). What I propose is an approach to reading and writing that shifts away from class routines "where boundaries seem pre-set and whose work as a result too often consists almost entirely of teacher talk, discrete assignments, and individual assessments" (Roskelly 24). Instead, this approach privileges critical writing models as the focal point of student work where students construct, or co-construct, the lines of inquiry for a text. A scene from Shakespeare's *Macbeth* will be used as the running example in this article, but this process can be just as easily applied to historical documents, informational texts, essays, speeches, and various other forms of print and digital media found in high school and college classrooms. For a complete narrative of this process in action, please consult this article's appendix. Teachers may prefer to implement these strategies gradually—say, using Step One as an auxiliary activity to add focus and dimension to a class discussion— or go at it wholesale and utilize these steps as the superstructure of a course's entire writing program. Whatever the choice, if classroom teachers decide to challenge themselves and give it a go, these methods can be a useful tool in getting students to read with a writer's eye and write with a reader's sensibility about the complex texts found in high school, college, and work environments.

This approach draws from the body of research around Writing-to-Learn (WTL) and dialogism (Peter Elbow, Joseph Harris, Julie Christoph, Martin Nystrand, and Paul Hielker, among others) as well as "the interactive pedagogy of Paulo Freire, the learning theory taught by Leo Vygostky, and the dynamic nature of interpretation outlined by Louise Rosenblatt into the framework of a classroom" (Roskelly 23-24). Teachers need not be familiar with these theorists to enact the approach's main drive: to introduce students to the inquiry process by having them take on the imagined role of question writer where they will construct a set of questions in response to a text, provide answers to those questions, and vet these inquiries through their peers in order to have a deeper understanding of how the source text works, its internal logic and governing ideas. What's also at stake here is how WTL—a mode of discourse that is traditionally underemphasized in many English classrooms—lets students meaningfully interact with a text while not assuming a falsely authoritative voice that plagues far too many Writing-to-Show-Learning (WTSL) or summative assignment compositions. Some teachers adhere to the notion that the more formal writing students are doing, the better. But the approach of writing described in this article addresses a slightly different issue: "Do students need more writing, or do they need better assignments?" (Zemelman and Daniels 73). Of course, formal writing has a defined space in composition classrooms, but undergirding these formative assessments with regularly occurring "self-sponsored" (WTL) compositions is one way to purposefully harness the power of informal writing as a scaffold to more formal writing projects (Zemelman and Daniels 71-73). To get here, three things need to happen. First, students need to learn the characteristics of an "authentic question;" second, students need to apply these authentic questions in the persona of assignment designer, the producer (rather than the recipient) of the inquiry; third, students need to transfer the learning from these WTL exercises to WTSL compositions, thus closing the loop in the WTL-WTSL continuum.By using the processes described herein, "we end up teaching texts, teaching readers, and teaching writers simultaneously" (Goldschmidt 64).

For teachers, especially those with struggling readers, the question now becomes, "How can I get students to engage with a text in complex and sophisticated ways without force-feeding the important points?" Mary Goldschmidt's "Marginalia: Teaching Texts, Teaching Readers, Teaching Writers"—from which the term "authentic question" is drawn—is the foundational methodology upon which the approach to reading detailed in this article rests. Goldschmidt makes the case that "rhetorical" (Haas and Flower), "introspective" (Salvatori), or "practice-based" (Adler-Kassner and Estrem) reading strategies "[have] been an important undercurrent in the past three decades of composition scholarship" (Goldschmidt 51). Though most composition scholars agree about the fluid relationship between reading and writing, "it is precisely our own already-automatized expertise in reading that can often be the cause of our frustration with students, since we expect students to read *the way we read*" (Goldschmidt 57). She advocates teaching students to become "meta-readers," self-conscious, rhetorical readers who demonstrate the "very kinds of critical reading habits that [instructors] routinely use but too infrequently verbalize or model except through the kinds of questions we ask in class" (Goldschmidt 58). To launch this transformation, she suggests that as students read, they should keep marginal notes—"marginalia"— with four categories in mind: comprehension notes, interactive/ evaluative notes, rhetorical notes, and extending notes (Goldschmidt 66-67). As the titles of the notations indicate, Goldschmidt's system compartmentalizes these notes into "types" which are both multi-dimensional (reading with different purposes in mind) and scaffolded (where comprehension leads to evaluation, which leads to extension, which leads to rhetorical analysis). The virtue of these categories is just how straightforward and practical they are for helping student readers make clear distinctions between explicit, inferential, and synthetic observations of a text, while keeping things low-stakes, informal, and in the WTL realm. Figure 1 lays out an adaptation of Goldschmidt's theory, which can be scaled up or down depending on student ability.

Students will likely need a few dry-runs before this process takes, but once some degree of confidence is attained, the imagined role of question writer can begin. Here, students will be the makers (and answerers) of their own close reading assignments and develop their early observations from the marginalia activity. Students will work within an easy-to-follow, four-step process to develop their questions from the ground up. Each stage is detailed under the subheadings below, along with an explanation of how these stages can be accomplished, and why we should do them at all.

Step One: Identify the Key Ideas of the Text to Give Direction

As in any good reverse engineering or "backwards design" process, students should start by explicitly identifying their key insights into a text by writing a "significant statement," an idea that follows designs from David Bartholomae and Anthony Petrosky's *Facts, Artifacts, and Counterfacts*. Significant statements are not merely a one-line precis or summary. Rather, this is an exercise that gets students thinking in rhetorical terms by asking them to consider how the main elements of written discourse—the author, the audience, the text itself—affect the way a reader makes meaning from a text (see Figure 2). Advanced students may not need much intervention here, but for struggling readers, some focused scaffolding may be in order, such as pre-teaching some paratextual information to help students to read with more focus and purpose. There's any number of places the teacher could nudge a student towards as a starting point. Notice that Shakespeare's troubled marriage to Anne Hathaway somehow underwrites the dynamics between the Macbeths? Start there. Wonder how Shakespeare's primary audience would understand this scene in live performance differently than a twenty-first century, mediated presentation? Start there. See that Lady Macbeth buries her intentions under thick layers of metaphor and analogy? Start there.

Read the assigned text, and as you read, rather than highlighting or underlining, write notes in the margins. Since the text is sufficiently ambiguous enough to invite many interpretations, make sure that you do at least two types of "marginalia" for each category. You'll want to revisit the text at least once for each note "type;" that is, read once for comprehension, a second for interactive/evaluative concerns, a third for extending observation, and a fourth for rhetorical analysis.			
On a *first* read, make	On a *second* read, using your comprehension notes make	On a third read, using your comprehension and interactive/evaluative notes make	On a *fourth* read, using your comprehension and interactive/evaluative, and extending notes make
Comprehension Notes are marginal comments that *summarize or paraphrase*:	**Interactive/ Evaluative Notes** are marginal comments that *question, analyze, criticize, praise, agree or disagree* with:	**Extending Notes** are marginal comments that *go beyond the text* and:	**Rhetorical Notes** are marginal comments that *examine*:

The main argument /thesis A new point An example Evidence used as a sub-point Why the passage is important A contradiction	The author's idea(s) The author's logic, examples, or evidence The author's analysis The author's assumptions The author's methodology	Offer an alternative explanation Offer additional or contradictory evidence Pose new questions React emotionally to the author's style, tone, or substance Make a connection with your extra-textual knowledge (experience)	How the author attends to, or fails to attend to, the reader's needs The effectiveness of how the author responds to other scholars in the field or perspectives on the issue The scope of the author's knowledge on the issue How the author establishes or undermines his/her own (or a character's) credibility The author's implied political stance or ideological grounding

Figure 1: Marginalia Exercise for Student Readers

No reader can find everything in a text, but every reader can find one thing, and sometimes that's all it takes to get things going in the right direction. Significant statements provide focus to analysis, but more importantly, give space for students to ground their analysis in what they have found intriguing in a text. Teachers may need to nudge a bit, but once students connect with the text via their interests, the insights will unravel right along (Carter and Gradin 7). Since most good writing can address several of these concerns at once, students need not feel that they have to find the "right" direction. By having students respond in this way, passages that were silent now suddenly speak and each line of questioning allows a reader's wavering attention to be renamed and given priority as an act of attention (Bartholomae and Petrosky 21-22).

DIFFICULTIES TO ANTICIPATE IN STEP ONE

In Act III, scene iii of *Hamlet*, Claudius—overrun by his conflicting feelings of guilt and ambition—says, "I stand in pause where I shall first begin and both neglect," and students may feel similarly overwhelmed as they put pen to paper in this first step. Like any journey into an undiscovered country, my students who have shied away from Step One do so because they are intimidated by its new terminology and unfamiliar stances towards a text. If this is the case, it may be worthwhile to reframe what Step One is trying to do in terms of "prewriting," a familiar schema for most students who've been through other English courses. Because this step is interested in getting initial impressions down on paper, remind students that "not paying attention to your personal reactions may lead you to feel disconnected from the communication going on—as though some other people were arguing about something that you had no interest in" (Bazerman 119). To make explicit what you think about things *is* to involve yourself with the ongoing dialogue surrounding the issue. After reading, consider nudging students by asking, "How did you react?", "Why do feel that way?", "Did you react that way because of some experience in your life?", "Did you react that way from something you've learned in school?" Find out where students are coming from and pose a similar line of questioning to the one above to encourage students that they will eventually find a way into the text.

STEP TWO: CHOOSE PASSAGES TO FOCUS ON

Once students have clarified a text's "significant statement," they should hone in on specific lines and passages to expand upon these initial reactions. Having the student—not the teacher—select the important passages is the objective of this stage. By linking quotes to the insight generated from the significant statement (see Figure 3), students are doing what I would call "Quoting-to-Learn" since the quotes students choose should tell the teacher something about the way students have oriented themselves towards what can be extrapolated from the "significant statement." Most students tend to associate quotes with arcane rules of punctuation, citation, and integration, but quotations can't, and shouldn't, always be reduced to a simple matter of rules (Harris 28).

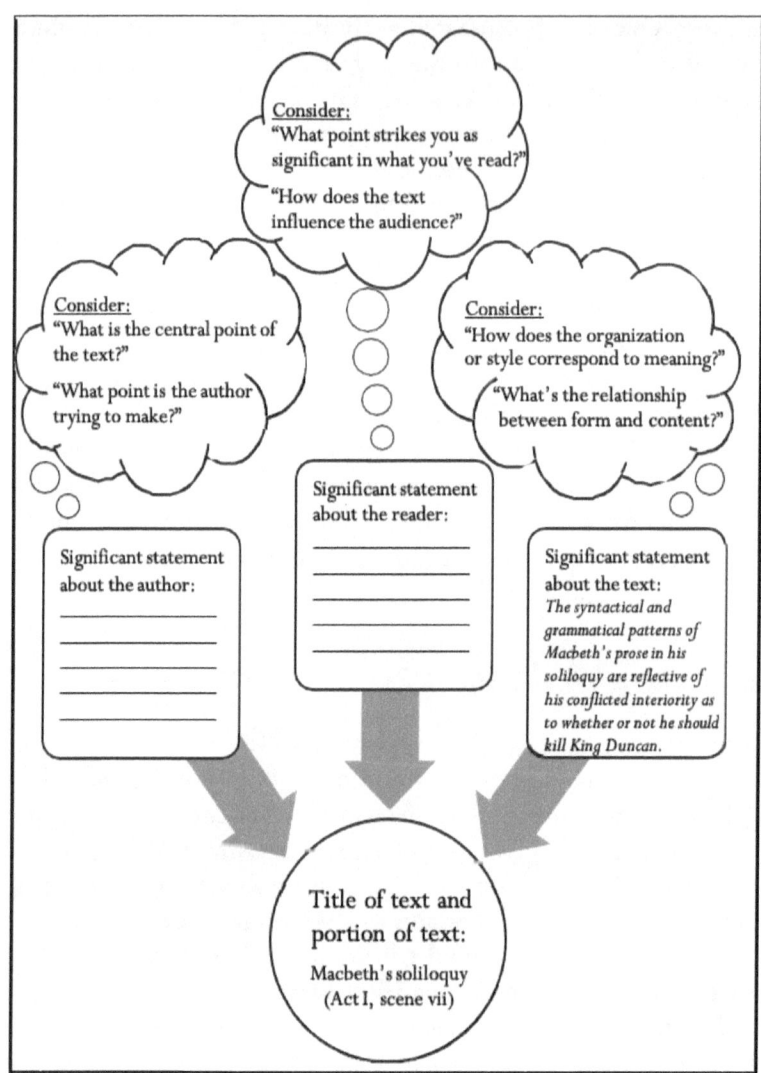

Figure 2: Significant Statement Exercise for *Macbeth* (Act I, scene vii)

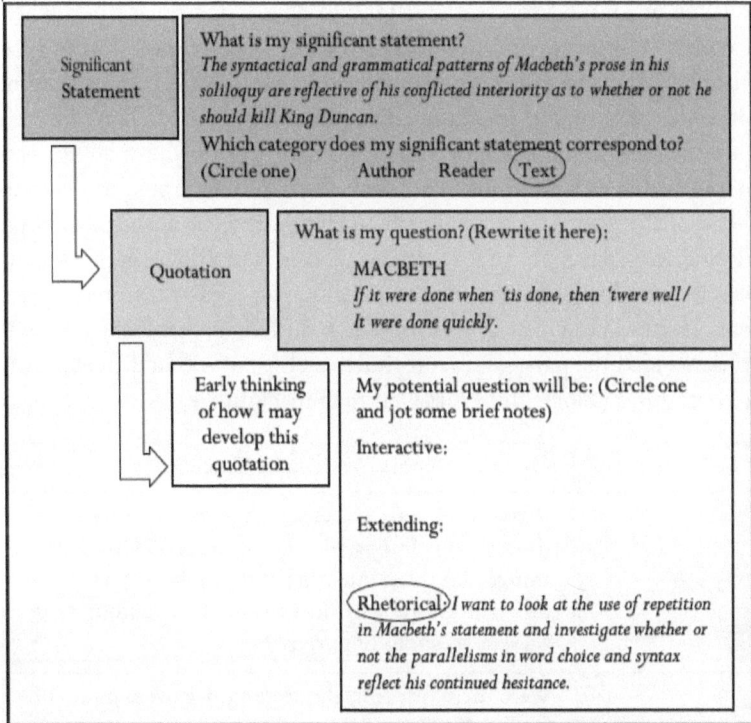

Figure 3: Quote Selection Exercise for *Macbeth* (Act I, scene vii)

The quotes students choose, then, are essential to their developing inquiry since "quotation is the very act in which one voice creatively absorbs another and defines it in relation to that second voice. When we interrupt the quoted text, interrogate it, clarify its point, or expose its ambiguities, we make an opening for our own utterances and give it shape to our own roles in the conversation" (Bialostosky 18). Students likely discover meanings or allusions that other readers have missed—it happens all the time—and such a perception of oneself as a reader is empowering and contributes to how students may make up their mind about the text they hold in their hands.[1]

DIFFICULTIES TO ANTICIPATE IN STEP TWO

Quoting is the salt and pepper of composition, and it's possible that teachers may become easily frustrated when students are reticent to work with quotes in the varied ways that Step Two calls for. I've found that many composition students tend to have a one-track mind when it comes to quotes, thinking of them as little more than backup for what's said in the paper and unable to work outside this paradigm. Since the handling of quotes in this process has only partly to do with quotes-as-proof models, not knowing other ways of how quotes can be put to use is a common roadblock. Perhaps encourage students to think of the quotes as a process of "recirculating the author's writing, highlighting parts of the texts for the consideration of others" (Harris 36) as a way to put a personal stamp on the ideas presented in the text. If more concrete intervention is required, perhaps suggest that students read the passage several times, each time with a different purpose in mind (Block and Duffy), as seen in Figure 4.

Strategy:	Question to pose to struggling student:
Predict	Were there any places in the reading where you thought the author was trying to foreshadow something? Did this come true? If it did, what tipped you off? If it didn't, why do you think the author made these suggestions of purpose?
Monitor	Were there places in the reading that were more difficult to understand than others? Why may the author have written that portion in a dense or tough-to-understand style?
Image	Were there any passages that were rich in imagery? What were the images that came to your mind? Can you connect these images to other places in the text?
Infer	Were there places in the reading that you understood because of your prior knowledge on the topic? Was it an allusion? A reference to a fact or anecdote? Do you think the author assumes the reader will know it?
Evaluate	Were there places in the reading that you made a judgement about? Do you think the author wants the reader to take a moral stance? Are they suggesting something here about the larger takeaways for the reader?
Synthesize	Were there places in the reading that you connected to things outside of the reading? How did this connection add depth and dimension to your understanding of the passage?

Figure 4: Suggestions for Struggling Readers on How to Choose Purposeful Questions

Step Three: Compose the Questions

Once students have selected a pool of quotes that link up to their significant statement, the real explication of the text can begin. Students, here, will formalize their inquiry of the text in the persona of an assessment designer tasked with developing a close-reading assignment that focuses on their selected passage. This imagined persona is certainly a bit odd, but its purpose is to help students break with the surface-level, and often predictable, handling of quotes reinforced by most standard WTSL compositions. Such a style of inquiry asks that students self-consciously identify and internalize the moves they have made while reading that will, in turn, help them to become more intentional, rhetorical readers (Goldschmidt 59). While students will certainly be encouraged to throw their thoughts and experiences into the mix as they write their questions, they should adhere to some general guidelines as they put pen to paper. Each question they write should have two parts: a "where-in-the-text-do-I-see-this" part that ties the question to the text and a "why-does-this-observation-matter" part that extends the textual observation to an interpretive or evaluative inquiry. An example of this two-pronged approach to questioning is illustrated in the "Question" box of Figure 5. As questions begin to take shape, Goldschmidt's marginalia categories can be a useful storehouse for records of a student's early thinking as well.

Example Question		Modeled Thinking of Example Question
Context statement (if needed)	In Act I, scene vii of Shakespeare's *Macbeth*, the title character considers the prospect and consequences of killing King Duncan, an action, if completed, that would result in him becoming King of Scotland. In his soliloquy, he weighs the extensive consequences of regicide (killing a king) and ultimately decides that his action is not for him.	I felt that it was important to provide a brief context setting statement here since to take any Shakespearean line out of context may misrepresent its function in the larger play. Also, in a play that is constructed around the public/private face dichotomy, it's important to note that this line is drawn from a soliloquy which, by dramatic convention, usually means that we are getting a character's true thoughts and feelings (his private face, so to speak).
Quote	MACBETH: *If it were done when 'tis done, then 'twere well/It were done quickly.*	I chose the opening line of the soliloquy because it's Macbeth's lead-off idea and all that follows in the speech flows from this line. He may counter or affirm what he says here, but he can't escape it.
Question	In the first two lines, what word does Macbeth repeat several times? How does this foreshadow his reluctance to commit the deed?	The first question is the "where" part which asks readers to simply find repetition in a small amount of text. The second question is the "why" part which asks for inference out of the textual observation.

What's my question doing? Circle one and explain how your question is:	Comprehending	For clarity, I'll include the explanation in this box of how the question is rhetorically analyzing.
	Interacting/evaluating	Rhetoric is not solely the tool of the speech giver, the essay writer, or the filmmaker. Rhetorical moves are sometimes best illustrated through the mouths of invented characters in imaginative literature. The question that I have asked keys into the rhetoric of the fictional speaker Macbeth. The opening line establishes his implied stance of hesitance ("implied stance or ideological grounding" in marginalia terms) that is initially his source of strength for *not* killing the king. He announces the results of his deliberations to Lady Macbeth, and she responds to his remarks by pressing him to follow through with the murder of King Duncan. In doing so, this initial statement, which was once a source of strength, now becomes the very thing that undermines Macbeth's virtue (or how "the author establishes or undermines his/her own [or a character's] credibility" in marginalia terms) and shows him to be a hypocritical figure.
	Extending	
	Rhetorically Analyzing	

Figure 5: Question Writing Exercise for *Macbeth* (Act I, scene vii)

DIFFICULTIES TO ANTICIPATE IN STEP THREE

Most students are adept at answering questions about a text, but few are expert at asking them. This tends to be the most difficult step for students because to ask probing questions "means making public what is private—a process dependent on explication, illustration, and critical examination of perception and ideas" (Petrosky 20). Asking good questions begs the student to engage and explore both their own knowledge and the purposes of the text. This "participative pedagogy" brings to the forefront the generative effects of having students play with subject and form as a means of exploring the text they hold in their hands (Halasek 107). Consider Figure 6 as a resource for students who may think, "I don't know what to ask."

Generative Questions for the "Where" Question	*Connecting "Why" Question*
Where does the main point of the passage show up?	Why do you think it shows up at the beginning? Why does it delay until the middle? What's gained by waiting until the end?
Where does the author/character show us that he's worth listening to? Where does he connect with you emotionally? Where does he provide hard proof?	Why are these important to your understanding of what the author/character has to say? How do these either draw you in or push you away from what's said?
Where does the author/character's proof or examples appear in the passage?	Why do you think they're in the order they are? Why may it start with a shock and work back? Why may it begin with broad claims and follow with specifics?
Where do you see the author/character making an assumption?	Why does this assumption matter to what they are saying? Why is it bias? Why does it seem honest?
Where do you see any unusually long sentences? Short sentences? Fragments?	Why would the author place these sentences where she does? How do they emphasize, or de-emphasize, the point it's making?

Where do you think the author/character may not be telling us everything they know? Where do they seem genuinely confused?	Why would the author/character not be forthright? What is gained or lost by this move?
Where do you see patterns in the writing? Where does the author/character repeat things?	Why do you think these patterns are meaningful? What is the point of using the same verbs over and over again? Adjectives?

Figure 6: Suggestions for Struggling Readers on How to Write Purposeful Questions

STEP FOUR: EXTEND THE INFERENCES— ANSWER THE QUESTIONS

The natural companion exercise to asking questions is to answer them, and here students will bring closure to their developing insight on the text. By asking students to fully write out their responses to the questions they pose, they must think even more deeply about the inquiries from Step Three and flesh out what they know, establish the limits of what they don't know, or open up new pathways for further inquiry. In other words, by answering their questions they are "making visible the thinking that is often invisible... as they grapple with the writer's writing, the reader's reading, and the mediating contexts that shape both. [By doing so], students are trained to be more intentional and rhetorically sophisticated writers themselves" (Goldschmidt 59). When answering their own lines of inquiry, students will step out of their persona from Steps One, Two, and Three and back into that of a student who is WTSL (see Figure 7). Though there will be varying levels of success and finesse with this switch, the hope is that students grasp the important ideas of the text more readily because they are translating these findings into a language they understand—their own (Davies 34).

Context Statement (if needed)	In Act I, scene vii of Shakespeare's *Macbeth*, the title character considers the prospect and consequence of killing King Duncan, an action, if completed, that would result in him becoming King of Scotland. In his soliloquy, he weighs the extensive consequences of regicide (killing a king) and ultimately decides that his action is not for him.
Quote	MACBETH *If it were done when 'tis done, then 'twere well / It were done quickly.*
Question	In the first two lines, what word does Macbeth repeat several times? How does this foreshadow his reluctance to commit the deed?
Answer	The neat thing about this line is that, depending on the way that the reader emphasizes the words in the mind's ear as they read, there are actually three plausible answers to the "where" component of the question. On first read, the repetition of "it" (and its related "'tis" and "'twere") was the first to catch my eye. On a second read, I noticed that the verb of each clause, "were," is also notably repeated. And yet, on a third read, the repetition of "done" is undeniably present, and its monosyllabic beat gives us the backing rhythm to the iambic line. So I guess now that we've noticed these repetitions we have to consider how each work in concert to foreshadow Macbeth's eventual reluctance.

Figure 7: Question Answering Exercise for *Macbeth* (Act I, scene vii)

Grammatically speaking, "it" is a pronoun, but in this syntax of this line, it is a pronoun that lacks its antecedent companion. Since this is the opening sentence of the soliloquy, we're given an ungrammatical line to start things off, and it's hard to believe that Shakespeare—so sensitive to the use of the English language—would unwittingly commit such a grammatical misstep. By obscuring the reference to the murder by proxy of the pronoun, the reader can see Macbeth's distant consideration of the deed, but he's so hesitant to consider it in "real terms" that he can't even bring himself to say the word. Likewise, the verb "were" contributes to his tone of hesitation. Every instance of this verb's appearance works to couch each of Macbeth's clauses into the conditional mode. He is flirting with the concept, but giving himself an out: if it *were* to happen, there's still an equal and opposite possibility that it *were not* to happen. The "done" repetition is an outgrowth of this effect. Never do we see a rundown of the grisly details, or even a mention of "murder." He wants the payoff of the action, but doesn't want to get his hand dirty to go through with it. He wants it to be "done," "done," "done."

DIFFICULTIES TO ANTICIPATE IN STEP FOUR

The most common misstep for students in this stage is to think that all the hard work has been done: the thinking through of significant statements, the selecting of quotations, the writing of the questions. All of those processes are what Anne Berthoff would call, "'forming activities' in which students should discard the faulty notice that when you compose you 'figure out what you want to say before you write,' and accept instead this more helpful slogan: 'You can't know what you mean until you hear what you say'" (46). Once student have formed their thoughts, it's time to communicate their final insights. For students attuned to the distinctions between WTL and WTSL—and it may be useful to make this distinction to them at this point if they are not—tell them to think of Step Four in terms of a traditional WTSL exercise. This stance towards classwork is one that is undoubtedly familiar to all students, and by explaining this step as a re-entering to familiar territory (or, writing in ways they are normally accustomed to), students should be more easily able to communicate their ideas and not just let the question "speak for itself."

The approach to inquiry writing detailed in this article will no doubt come more naturally to "experienced readers [who understand] that both reading and writing are context-rich, situational, and constructive acts" (Haas and Flower 182). Though these more sophisticated readers already have in their mind's ear the "sounds" of thought, such a process can be both generative and constructive for inexperienced readers as well. In some ways, the very absence of precision, or "error," in the question writing and answering process can be just as productive for students. In David Bartholomae's "The Study of Error" he notes that, "basic writers...are not performing mechanically or randomly but making choices and forming strategies as they struggle to deal with the varied demands of a task, a language, and a rhetoric. Errors, then, are stylistic features, information about *this* writer and *this* language; they are not necessarily 'noise' in the system, accidents in composing, or malfunctions in the language process" (Bartholomae 257). Though Bartholomae's discussion of error focuses on student missteps at the sentence level, the spirit of his comments translate to the larger interpretive issues that are at stake in this article. In other words, though the final product produced in these WTL exercise may not be "teacher-quality," its words and thoughts are still performing a vital function for the developing reader while giving feedback to the teacher about the student's present understanding and/or growth.

Whether students are "right" about a text is another thing; this process, if approached with an open mind and heart, will help students facilitate a dialogue between a text and their ideas. It can help students learn *how* to find a productive focus, craft an engaged response to class texts, develop a coherent and organized line of thought, work carefully with source materials, and support interpretations using apt examples and quotations. But more than this, it shows that complex texts are problems with which to engage; they're meant to be complex—not just a thing to demonstrate one's mastery or to declare ready-made opinions. What's produced is what the students see, and they see it because it is really there for them, and when a teacher reads what they've written, they should nod and say, "Yes, there is truth in that. It may not be the only truth, but these students have seen, and have told us honestly what they have seen."

Conclusion

It's worth acknowledging a number of questions that arise with an approach to inquiry like this: What kinds of instruction accompany this type of writing? How can this project extend into work with peer review? How does a teacher deal with the reality of giving feedback and grades for this type of writing? How much needs to be sacrificed in the existing curriculum to make space for such an involved approach to inquiry? What if students' writing "makes sense" to them but is incomprehensible to anyone else? What recourse is there if students intentionally write easy questions to reverse engineer easy answers? Each of these are important and relevant questions for teachers to consider should they choose to adopt some of this article's methodology to the teaching of reading and writing. There's not space in this article to address each one, though I will say that this process bears benefits whether it's done in full or scattered piecemeal among existing class exercises. John Locke once said, "Reading furnishes the mind only with *materials* of knowledge; it is thinking that makes what we read ours" (Locke quoted in Mann 371). The approach to reading and writing detailed in this article tries to make good on both parts of what Locke says. As students expand, intensify, or challenge their own thinking, they are doing something quite special in an English classroom: they are self-generating the insight into a text through a process in which *they* must come up with the main insights and *they* must develop these insights in light of the evidence that they've gathered. But more than this: it's a way for students to take their first steps in the direction of a dialogic stance toward writing—a stance that acknowledges that everything is prompted by and preparing for some other utterance—in a nonthreatening way. Once my students leave the borders of my classroom, they're on their own as readers, writers, and thinkers. The mountain stands in front of them, so to speak, and all I have given them here is a pickaxe and a small wheelbarrow, but moving any mountain begins by carrying away a few small stones.

Note

1. Readers especially attuned to concerns of dialogism may recognize this "making up of one's mind" as a key idea that runs through the work of Mikhail Bahktin ("ideological becoming") and Kay Halasek. Such an experience is crucial for burgeoning independent readers who, as they struggle to find and claim an orientation towards their text, will experience a liberation (however small) "from the authority of other's discourses" (Baktin quoted in Halasek 109).

Works Cited

Adler-Kassner, Linda, and Heidi Escrem. "Reading Practices in the Writing Classroom." *WPA: Writing Program Administration*, vol. 31, no. 1/2, Fall/Winter 2007, pp. 35-47.

Bartholomae, David. "The Study of Error." *The Writing Teacher's Sourcebook,* edited by Gary Tate and Edward P. J. Corbett, Oxford UP, 1999, pp. 303-17.

Bartholomae, David, and Anthony Petrosky. *Facts, Artifacts, and Counterfacts.* Heinemann, 1986.

Bazerman, Charles. *The Informed Writer.* Houghton-Mifflin, 1994.

Berthoff, Ann. *Forming, Thinking, Writing.* Boynton/Cook Publishers, 1989.

Bialostosky, Donald. "Liberal Education, Writing, and the Dialogic Self." *Contending with Words,* edited by Patricia Harkin and John Schilb. Modern Language Association of America, 1991, pp. 11-22.

Block, Cathy, and Gerald Duffy. "Research on Teaching Comprehension: Where We've Been and Where We're Going." *Comprehension Instruction,* edited by Cathy Collins Block and Sheri R. Parris. Guilford Press, 2011, pp. 19-37.

Carter, Duncan, and Sherrie Gradin, editors. *Writing as Reflective Action.* Pearson/ Longman, 2001.

Davies, Anne. "Involving Students in Classroom Assessment Process." *Ahead of the Curve,* edited by Douglas Reeves. Solution Tree Publishing, 2007, pp. 31-58.

Elbow, Peter. "Reflections on Academic Discourse: How It Relates to Freshmen and Colleagues." *College English,* vol. 53, no. 2, Feb 1991, pp. 135-55.

Farmer, Frank. "A Language of One's Own: A Stylistic Pedagogy for the Dialogic Classroom." *Freshman English News,* vol. 19, no.1, 1990, pp. 16-22. Goldschmidt, Mary. "Marginalia: Teaching Texts, Teaching Readers, Teaching Writers." *Essays in Reader-Oriented Theory, Criticism, and Pedagogy,* Fall 2010, pp. 51-69.

Haas, Christina, and Linda Flower. "Rhetorical Reading Strategies and the Construction of Meaning." *College Composition and Communication,* vol. 39, no. 2, May 1988, pp. 167-83.

Halasek, Kay. *A Pedagogy of Possibility: Bakhtinian Perspectives on Composition Studies.* Southern Illinois UP, 1999.

Harris, Joseph. *Rewriting: How to do Things with Texts.* Utah State UP, 2006.

Heilker, Paul. *The Essay: Theory and Pedagogy for an Active Form.* National Council of Teachers, 1996.

Mann, Horace. "Hand Book: Caution and Counsels." *The Common School Journal,* vol. 5, no. 24, Dec. 1843, p. 371.

Petrosky, Anthony. "From Story to Essay: Reading and Writing." *College Composition and Communication,* vol. 33, no 1, 1982, pp. 19-36.

Roskelly, Hephzibah. *Breaking (into) the Circle: Group Work for Change in the English Classroom.* Boynton/Cook Heinemann, 2003.

Salvatori, Mariolina. "Conversations with Texts: Reading in the Teaching of Composition." *College English,* vol. 58, no. 4, Apr. 1996, pp. 440-54.

Zemelman, Steven, and Harvey Daniels. *A Community of Writers: Teaching Writing in the Junior and Senior High School.* Heinemann, 1989.

APPENDIX

Example of Student Writing Output for Narrative of the Life of Frederick Douglass

What follows is a recreated example of student writing based on Chapter 2 of *Narrative of the Life of Frederick Douglass.* Each of the four steps are accompanied by the student's writing output as well as my own semi-narrative reflections that detail points to difficulty, success, and intervention. The student, "Nick," whose interests gravitated towards music and performing arts, was enrolled in my upper-level composition class, a course that focused primarily on rhetoric and composition, in the fall of 2014. The examples/reflections contained in this appendix are intended to concretize some of the article's broad goals, namely to show:

- How students may build their own scaffolding for inquiry to construct a full set of authentic questions in response to a text—and provide answers to those questions
- —in order to have a deeper understanding of how the source text works, as well as understanding its internal logic and governing ideas.
- How students can develop a thoughtful and patient approach to critical reading that allows them to appreciate the multiple forms, viewpoints, and tactics present in complex texts, and to gather perspective prior to arriving at their own writing, writing that is now more situated in the discourse of the subject.
- How teachers can emphasize the formative role of WTL as a meaningful stage in the construction of knowledge that lets students interact with a text while not assuming a falsely authoritative voice that plagues far too many WTSL compositions. WTL is not just about the act of writing; this type of writing here is really about inquiring, and it's this type of inquiring that facilitates the learning.

Students were first asked to read and annotate the opening paragraphs of Chapter 2 of *Narrative of the Life of Frederick Douglass* along the lines of the marginalia exercise (Figure 1). After recording their initial impressions, I gave students about 20 minutes to re-read and re-consider their annotations to see if any patterns emerged and organized their lines of thinking. Nick immediately honed in on Douglass's discussion of music that appears in the passage, particularly the use of technical language in the sentence, "They would *compose* and sing as they went along, consulting neither *time* nor *tune*." I wasn't surprised that Nick was drawn to this concept, and I encouraged him to see if there were other discussions of music (or suggestions of musicality) elsewhere in the chapter. He was able to locate a few but became a bit frustrated with how to stitch all of these observations together into a "significant statement." I intervened, as I did with several other students in the class, by saying, "Given that this chapter is largely an exposition on the hardships of slave life, why may Douglass have deliberately included a running discussion of music? What is *that* doing *there*?" I let the question bubble and stew with Nick as I checked in with other students. I returned a bit later to see that he had begun to make some early breakthroughs with his initial observation about music and its rhetorical function in the text. He wrote down his "significant statement" and though his word choice of "better understand" and "day-to-day experience" I felt were a bit vague, I allowed the ambiguity to remain. I told Nick that leaving things thoughtfully unresolved is sometimes a mark of maturity and sophistication as a reader and leaving some degree of fruitful ambiguity will allow for flexibility in the coming steps.

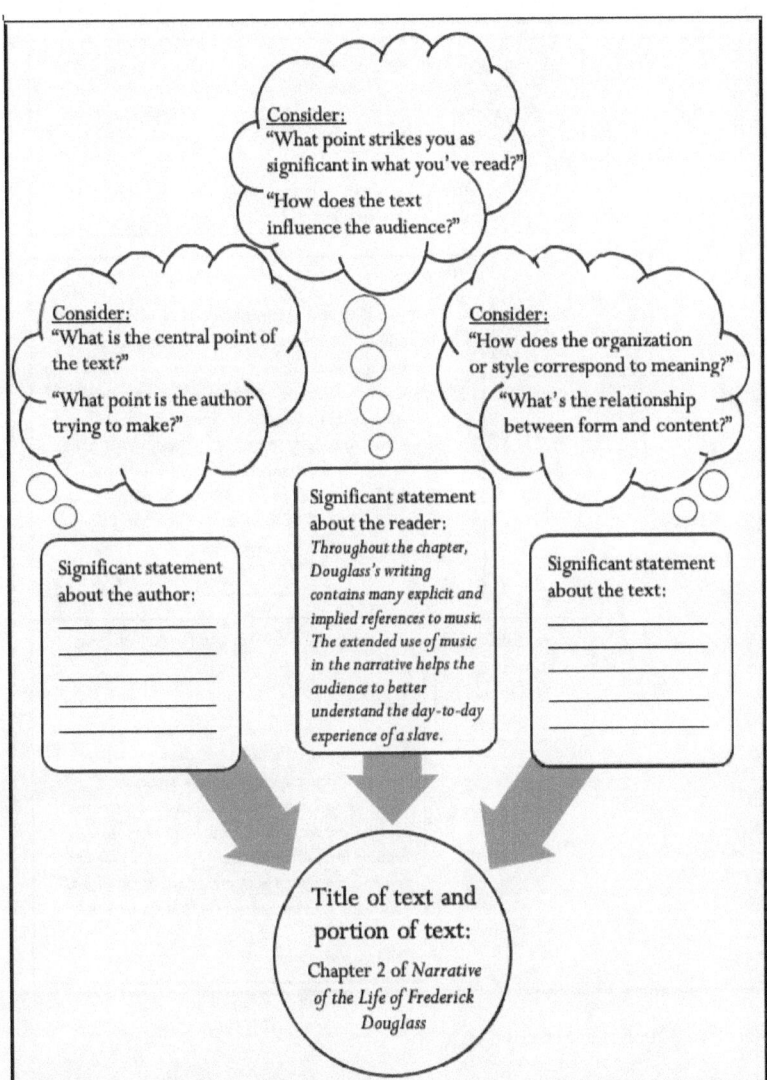

Step One: Significant Statement

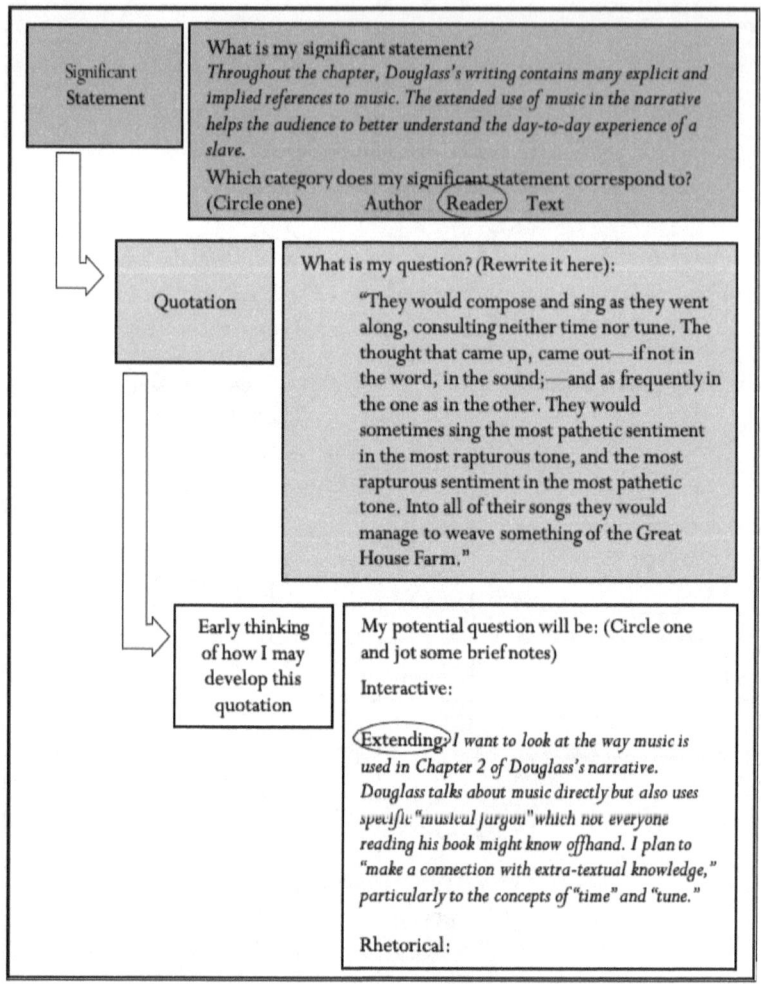

Step Two: Quotation Selection

Since Nick was drawn to Douglass's use of musical jargon in his initial reading, the quotation selection stage seemed like a no-brainer to him. He initially decided to quote, "They would compose and sing as they went along, consulting neither time nor tune." I agreed with him that this was an apt choice, but as students were given some time to make their final decisions, I circled back to Nick to discuss how he planned to develop this brief quotation with a close reading question that he must provide a detailed answer for. He seemed a bit fixated on his prior knowledge about "time" and "tune," and I worried that his extra-textual knowledge may end up causing him to digress. So, we looked again at the text. We discussed the "So What?" question of the musical terms, and I suggested possibly expanding the range of the quotation so as to give himself a little more to work with. "He talks about the lack of 'time' and 'tune,'" I said, "Do you see the prose equivalents of these concepts elsewhere in his writing?" I wasn't really sure myself what this question would yield as I asked it. When I introduced *Narrative* to the class a few days prior, I spent some time discussing how Douglass, despite being wholly self-educated, was one of the consummate prose stylists of 19th century American Literature. His style, Nick noted, is one of order and precision (or "time" and "tune," I clarified). Nick read some of the surrounding sentences in Chapter 2, looking for moments of eloquence and refinement in the style. Nick was surprised, but not entirely surprised, to find that the very next sentence which followed his initial quotation was quite difficult to read. Knowing Nick was a strong rhetorical reader, I suggested that he parse the sentence to see if he could generate some question based on the interplay of Douglass's description of the slave songs and the prose style found here in *Narrative of the Life of Frederick Douglass*. He thought for a while, and then put pen to paper.

Both Nick and I were encouraged by the insight that began to emerge. He had a substantial quote upon which to base his question and his early inquiry about the relationship of "time" and "tune" to Douglass's prose style had great potential for development. As Nick began to write his question, I reminded him (and the class) of some key considerations. I said, "The writing of the question is another stage in the clarification of *your* insights on the text. The question must urge a would-be responder to make some inference based on the quotation that you've made to be the focal point. Don't be too leading, but don't be too vague. Picture a friend in your mind's eye and write the question for him or her: someone with intelligent interests but who hasn't thought about this topic as you have." He drafted a few proto-type questions which I felt were a bit heavy on the "where-in-the-text-do-I see-this" concern. I redirected Nick to the questions from Figure 6 to help. After some trial-and-error, he felt he had found his way as he planned to ask how the lack of "time" and "tune" in the slave songs is replicated in the style of the subsequent sentence. I loved the connection, but I had to push him a bit further since this insight, on its own, felt like an unsatisfactory conclusion. "Is this merely a showing off of his rhetorical skill or is there some reason Douglass's narrative temporarily adopts the cadence of the slave songs?" I asked. I felt this was a big question that had to be accounted for, but I approached this discussion with care in order to leave Nick in control of the ultimate direction of the inquiry. After some back and forth, Nick drew the conclusion that by adopting the speech patterns of the slave songs, Douglass demonstrates an unquestionable ethos for his criticisms of the Great House Farm, and the institution of slavery, in Chapter 2. All the insights had fallen into place. Now it was up to Nick to provide some final clarification as he explained the answer to the question he successfully posed.

"By asking you to fully write out the responses to the questions you have posed," I said to the class, "you not only are asked to think critically about the inquiries you have initially presented in the questions from Step Three, but to also self-consciously identify, label, and give voice to these concerns." Nick, like most students in the class by Step Four, was excited to put the finishing touches on the self-generated insights that had been built over the last few class periods. I could see a very justified sense of satisfaction as the students began to write, despite the intellectual challenges and creative demands of what I was asking them to do. They felt like active participants in the writing who were able to put whatever thoughts and experiences they had into dialogue with the world of the text. I was thrilled to see this experience draw to a close as I observed a very justifiable sense of accomplishment and an increased "sense of writerly agency in the academy" (Goldschmidt 64). For Nick, in particular, he learned that he didn't have to check his personal passion for music at the door. He was able to see these interests as a space of possibility and potential to let knowledge flow in new directions and link into a text as never before. As a teacher, I can't think of anything more powerful than that.

Context statement (if needed)	Chapter 2 of *Narrative of the Life of Frederick Douglass* details the experiences of slaves surrounding promotion to the Great House Farm. Douglass specifically focuses on the use of music in the slave community in this chapter.
Quote	"They would compose and sing as they went along, consulting neither time nor tune. The thought that came up, came out—if not in the word, in the sound;—and as frequently in the one as in the other. They would sometimes sing the most pathetic sentiment in the most rapturous tone, and the most rapturous sentiment in the most pathetic tone. Into all of their songs they would manage to weave something of the Great House Farm."
Question	How does Douglass describe the songs of the slaves? Where else in Chapter 2 are there sentences composed with "neither time nor tune" and how do these sentences influence the reader's perception of the narrator?
What's my question doing? Circle one and explain how your question is:	Comprehending: Interacting/evaluating: Extending: My question will first ask readers to identify what Douglass literally says about music in the passage. I then plan on having responders to my question take this idea and apply it to the way Douglass himself writes. The ideas of "time" and "tune" will be a big factor of my question since I want to show how Douglass raises his ethos as a credible narrator by speaking in the same manner as the slave songs he describes. Rhetorically Analyzing:

Step Three: Question Writing Activity

Context statement (if needed)	Chapter 2 of *The Narrative of the Life of Frederick Douglass* details the experiences of slaves surrounding promotion to the Great House Farm. Douglass specifically focuses on the use of music in the slave community in this chapter.
Quote	"They would compose and sing as they went along, consulting neither time nor tune. The thought that came up, came out—if not in the word, in the sound;—and as frequently in the one as in the other. They would sometimes sing the most pathetic sentiment in the most rapturous tone, and the most rapturous sentiment in the most pathetic tone. Into all of their songs they would manage to weave something of the Great House Farm."
Question	How does Douglass describe the songs of the slaves? Where else in Chapter 2 are there sentences composed with "neither time nor tune" and how does this influence the reader's perception of the narrator?
Answer	Douglass says, "They would compose and sing as they went along, consulting neither time nor tune." To fully get what Douglass is saying, a reader needs to know the definitions of two words: "time" and "tune." "Time," or time signature, represents a uniform number of beats in each measure and "tune" refers to the correct musical pitch or key. Songs lacking these things will not be pleasing to the ear and are generally considered to be poor songwriting. Douglass is obviously not a composer, so his writing doesn't literally have time or tune. However, the question asks readers to closely analyze Douglass's syntax choices to find where the writing sounds like the slave songs he's describing.

The lines "The thought...House Farm" is written like a song with "neither time not tune." Instead of having a clear flow, the sentence has several stops and pauses which make it hard to read smoothly. The phrase "came up, came out" is the first example of this. It sounds like Douglass is missing a word but the fact that it sounds like he made an error is a perfect illustration of writing that lacks "tune." Right after this first phrase is another example when he says "—if not in the word, in the sound;—". The way Douglass uses punctuation is unusual. He puts a semicolon just before the second dash. Since both dashes and semicolons make a reader stop when they are reading, having two of them makes an extra-long pause in the middle of the sentence. This is an example of Douglass writing without "time." In addition, despite its length of 25 words, this quotation is actually a sentence fragment. The main subject, "thought," is just followed by a bunch of things that describe it which can be seen as another example of the sentence lacking both "time" and "tune."

Step Four: Question Answering Activity

JOURNAL OF SECOND LANGUAGE WRITING

The Journal of Second Language Writing is on the Web at https://www.journals.elsevier.com/journal-of-second-language-writing

The *Journal of Second Language Writing* is devoted to publishing theoretically grounded reports of research and discussions that represent a contribution to current understandings of central issues in second and foreign language writing and writing instruction. Some areas of interest are personal characteristics and attitudes of L2 writers, L2 writers' composing processes, features of L2 writers' texts, readers' responses to L2 writing, assessment/evaluation of L2 writing, contexts (cultural, social, political, institutional) for L2 writing, and any other topic clearly relevant to L2 writing theory, research, or instruction.

The Relationship Between Lexical Sophistication and Independent and Source-Based Writing

In this article, Kyle and Crossley explore the relationship between lexical sophistication and holistic scores of writing proficiency in independent and source-based writing. Included in the study are some newly developed indices of lexical sophistication such as word frequency, range, and n-gram. The results suggest that lexical sophistication indices are not strong predictors of essay quality in source-based tasks, while range and bigrams are important predictors of essay quality in independent tasks that. Also, responses to source-based tasks tend to include more sophisticated lexical items than those to independent tasks. The article concludes with important implications for second language writing assessment and pedagogy.

* Reprinted from the *Journal of Second Language Writing* 34 (2016): 12–24. © 2016, with permission from Elsevier.

The Relationship Between Lexical Sophistication and Independent and Source-Based Writing

Kristopher Kyle and Scott Crossley

Abstract

Lexical sophistication is an important component of writing proficiency. New lexical indices related to range, n-gram frequency, psycholinguistic word information, academic language, polysemy, and hypernymy have yielded new insights into the construct of lexical sophistication and its relationship with second language (L2) acquisition and writing. For example, recent studies have suggested that range and bigram indices are stronger indicators of lexical sophistication than frequency in the context of L2 acquisition and L2 writing and speaking proficiency. This study explores the relationship between these newly developed indices of lexical sophistication and holistic scores of writing proficiency in both independent and source-based writing tasks. The results suggest that range and bigrams are important predictors of essay quality in independent tasks, but that lexical sophistication indices are not strong predictors of essay quality in source-based tasks. The results also indicate that responses to source-based tasks tend to include more sophisticated lexical items than responses to independent tasks. Implications for second language writing assessment and pedagogy are discussed.

INTRODUCTION

A key measure of academic success is writing proficiency (Kellogg & Raulerson, 2007). Becoming a proficient academic writer is a challenging and multifaceted endeavor, both for first language (L1) and second language (L2) writers (Crossley & McNamara, 2009; National Commission on Writing, 2003). Academic writers must learn to navigate a number of different task types (e.g., Römer & O'Donnell, 2011) that may differ in rhetorical (Cumming et al., 2005; Hyland, 2007) and linguistic (Cumming et al., 2005; Hardy & Römer, 2013) features. Differences in task types may also require writers to employ varied skills (Plakans & Gebril, 2013; Plakans, 2008) and linguistic resources (Guo, Crossley, & McNamara, 2013). These differences make it difficult to assess writing proficiency using a single task (Schoonen, van Gelderen, Stoel, Hulstjin, & de Glopper, 2011), and suggest that the construct of writing proficiency may better be described as a set of writing proficiencies. Accordingly, some high-stakes assessment tools assess writing proficiency using multiple writing tasks. The Test of English as a Foreign Language (TOEFL), for example, includes both independent tasks (i.e., tasks that ask test takers to draw on their personal experience when responding to a prompt) and source-based tasks (i.e., tasks that ask test takers to integrate information from source texts when responding to a prompt) in an effort to better reflect the types of writing tasks encountered in academic settings (e.g., Chapelle, Enright, & Jamieson, 2008; Cumming et al., 2005). One important question that arises with the inclusion of multiple writing assessment tasks is whether the tasks elicit responses with distinct features (i.e., are assessing different aspects of writing proficiency) (Cumming et al., 2005).

Among the many features of writing proficiency that have been investigated, the role lexical knowledge plays in successful writing is well attested. Lexical knowledge can be considered both a receptive (Baba, 2009; Schoonen et al., 2011) and a productive (Kyle & Crossley, 2015; Laufer & Nation, 1995; Laufer, 1994) trait. Receptive lexical knowledge refers to an individual's ability to understand the meaning of a lexical item that is read or heard, and is often assessed using standardized tests such as the Vocabulary Levels Test (Schmitt, Schmitt, & Clapham, 2001) or the Word Associates Test (Read, 1998). Productive lexical knowledge refers to the words available to an individual when writing or speaking. Productive lexical knowledge is often assessed by examining the lexical sophistication of a speaking or writing sample. Lexical sophistication is generally related to the diversity (e.g., Engber, 1995) and/or the relative difficulty (often based on corpus frequency counts; e.g., Laufer & Nation, 1995) of the lexical items in a text.

Research has demonstrated that L2 writers pay particular attention to lexical concerns as they construct texts (e.g., Cumming, 1990; Leki & Carson, 1994; Manchón, Murphy, & Roca de Larios, 2007), and links have been reported between both receptive and productive lexical knowledge and writing proficiency scores in relation to both independent (Guo et al., 2013; Schoonen et al., 2011) and source-based writing tasks (e.g., Baba, 2009; Guo et al., 2013). One important question that has not been thoroughly addressed, however, is whether productive lexical knowledge (i.e., lexical sophistication) is uniformly important across writing task types. Previous research (Guo et al., 2013) indicates that independent and source-based writing tasks differ in the lexical features that are predictive of writing proficiency scores. Specifically, they found that word familiarity and frequency were predictive of source-based writing quality, while word length and hypernymy were predictive of independent writing. However, Guo et al. did not investigate a number of lexical features theorized to be important components of essay quality, nor did the study consider if source-based and independent tasks led to production differences in lexical output. Such differences may provide a greater understanding of how the two task types differ and provide stronger rationale for the use of the two tasks when assessing writing skills. In addition, differences in the two task types may inform automated essay scoring systems that rely on linguistic features. The current study builds on previous research such as Guo et al. (2013) by exploring a wide range of lexical features across independent and integrated tasks.

Receptive lexical knowledge and writing proficiency

A number of studies have found links between receptive lexical knowledge and writing proficiency scores in independent (Koda, 1993; Schoonen et al., 2011) and source-based tasks (e.g., Baba, 2009). Koda (1993), for example, found a strong positive relationship ($r = .70$) between receptive language knowledge and holistic scores of writing proficiency for English L1 writers of L2 Japanese. In addition, Schoonen et al. (2011) used scores on a receptive vocabulary task as a predictor of L2 writing proficiency scores, finding moderate, positive correlations ranging from $r = .53$ to $r = .57$. Baba (2009) also found moderate, positive relationships between holistic scores of quality on a summary writing task and vocabulary size ($r = .40$) and vocabulary depth ($r = .34$). Together, these findings suggest that receptive lexical knowledge may be an important indicator of writing proficiency, but do not indicate how receptive lexical knowledge translates into linguistic production.

Productive lexical knowledge and writing proficiency

Links have also been made between productive vocabulary knowledge (i.e., lexical sophistication) and writing proficiency scores. Lexical sophistication has traditionally been operationalized as the diversity of the words used in a text (e.g., the number of unique words in a text divided by the total number of a text; Engber, 1995) or by the average reference-corpus frequency of words in a text (e.g., Laufer & Nation, 1995).

Lexical diversity

One way that productive vocabulary knowledge has been measured is by using lexical diversity measures, such as the type-token ratio (e.g., Engber, 1995) or more sophisticated measures such as D (Jarvis, 2002; Malvern & Richards, 1997). Indices of lexical diversity measure the variety of words used in a text. Generally, positive relationships have been found between lexical diversity and writing proficiency scores. Engber (1995), for example, found a moderate, positive correlation between lexical diversity and holistic scores of L2 writing proficiency with regard to an independent writing task. Essays that included more diverse lexical items tended to earn higher holistic scores. A number of other studies have found similar trends with regard to holistic scores of L2 writing proficiency with independent writing tasks (e.g., Cumming et al., 2005; Grant & Ginther, 2000; Jarvis, 2002). Cumming et al. (2005) also extended these findings to source-based writing tasks, finding a positive relationship between type-token ratios and holistic scores in read-write and listen-write tasks. However, recent research has indicated that lexical diversity is more strongly related to text cohesion than lexical sophistication. Specifically, lexical diversity captures the repetition of words across a text (i.e., lexical overlap) and is thus a measure of lexical cohesion (Crossley, Kyle, & McNamara, 2015).

This contrasts with lexical sophistication indices which capture text-external features of words (such as reference corpus frequency).

Word frequency

Lexical sophistication is perhaps most often operationalized using the reference-corpus frequency of the words in a text (e.g., Attali & Burstein, 2006; Crossley, Cobb, & McNamara, 2013; Crossley & McNamara, 2012; Enright & Quinlan, 2010; Laufer & Nation, 1995). Words that occur less frequently are considered sophisticated (e.g., *solidification, octogenarians, modularized*) while frequent words (e.g., *people, place, number*) are considered less so (Kyle & Crossley, 2015). Research suggests that more proficient writers will, on average, use less frequent words when writing in response to independent tasks. Laufer and Nation (1995), for example, found that more proficient L2 writers used fewer high frequency words (i.e., words that comprise the most frequent 1000 words in English). Others have found similar results with regard to average reference corpus frequency of words in independent L2 compositions, finding that on average, more proficient L2 writers use less frequent words than less proficient ones (Attali & Burstein, 2006; Crossley & McNamara, 2012; Crossley et al., 2013; Enright & Quinlan, 2010; Guo et al., 2013). Average reference frequency has also been investigated with regard to source-based tasks. Guo et al. (2013), for example, found that frequency was negatively correlated with TOEFL source-based task scores, which is in line with studies that have explored frequency in independent tasks.

Expanding the construct of lexical sophistication

Recent studies have used newer automated indices to measure lexical sophistication in both L1 and L2 contexts. Researchers have, for example, used the average reference corpus word range (i.e., the percentage of texts in a reference corpus that a word occurs in; Kyle & Crossley, 2015), the average reference corpus bigram and trigram (i.e., two and three word sequences), frequency (Crossley, Cai, & McNamara, 2012), the use of academic words and phrases (Kyle & Crossley, 2015), the psycholinguistic properties of words (Crossley & McNamara, 2013; Guo et al., 2013), and the semantic relationships words have (i.e., hypernymy and polysemy; Guo et al., 2013) to measure the relationship between lexical sophistication and holistic scores of both L1 and L2 writing proficiency. These studies have demonstrated that indices beyond word frequency can add to models of lexical sophistication and contribute to our understanding of the relationship between lexical sophistication and L2 writing proficiency. We discuss these newer indices below.

Word range

Range, which is also referred to as *dispersion*, *entropy*, and *contextual diversity*, is a measurement of the number of texts in a reference corpus in which a word occurs (Gries, 2008). Words with high range values (e.g., *people*, *book*, *building*) occur widely throughout a number of different texts and contexts, while words with low range values (e.g., *antifungal*, *lithosphere*, *deictic*) tend to be restricted in use to a smaller number of texts and contexts. The average reference-corpus range has been shown to be negatively correlated with analytic scores of lexical proficiency (Kyle & Crossley, 2015), suggesting that words with a narrower range are more sophisticated than those with a wider range. While links between range and analytic scores of lexical sophistication have been investigated, the link relationship between range and holistic scores of writing proficiency in independent and source-based writing has not.

N-gram frequency

N-grams, or multi-word expressions of *n* words in length, have been of increasing interest in lexical sophistication over the past ten years (e.g., Biber, Conrad, & Cortes, 2004). N-gram frequency has been shown to be correlated with analytic scores of lexical proficiency (Kyle & Crossley, 2015). L2 texts that include more frequent n-grams (e.g., *one of the*, *as well as*, *as a result*) tend to earn higher analytic scores of lexical sophistication than those with infrequent n-grams (e.g., *the former east*, *their hands and*, *of the no*). The relationship between n-gram frequency and independent L1 writing has also been explored with contradictory results (i.e., n-gram frequency was negatively correlated with holistic scores of writing proficiency; Crossley et al., 2012) but has not, to our knowledge, been investigated with relation to independent or source-based L2 writing.

Academic language

Academic language has been defined as words and/or multi-word units (n-grams) that occur frequently in academic texts such as research journal articles, textbooks and academic lectures, but relatively infrequently in general corpora (Coxhead, 2000; Simpson-Vlach & Ellis, 2010; Xue & Nation, 1984). The academic word list (AWL; Coxhead, 2000), for example, includes 570 word families that represent academic language at the word level (e.g., *analyze, transmit, statistic*). The academic formulas list (AFL; Simpson-Vlach & Ellis, 2010) includes multi-word units that are frequent in academic texts, but less frequent in general corpora (e.g., *in relation to, the development of, the fact that*). Theoretically, higher proficiency writers are expected to use more academic words and n-grams when responding to academic writing tasks (Morris & Cobb, 2004; Simpson-Vlach & Ellis, 2010). Morris and Cobb (2004), for example, found that independent L2 essays written by higher proficiency learners tended to include more AWL words. Other recent research, however, has suggested academic language (i.e., words from the AWL and AFL) may occur infrequently in some collections of learner writing (Kyle & Crossley, 2015), regardless of proficiency level.

Psycholinguistic properties of words

The psycholinguistic properties of words have been of interest to cognitive scientists for some time (e.g., Coltheart, 1981; Toglia & Battig, 1978), but within the last five years have been connected to the construct of lexical sophistication. Word properties such as concreteness, familiarity, imageability, meaningfulness, and age of acquisition have been linked to analytic scores of lexical proficiency (Kyle & Crossley, 2015) and holistic scores of L2 writing proficiency (Guo et al., 2013). Kyle and Crossley (2015) found that informal L1 and L2 written texts that included less concrete, familiar, imageable, and meaningful words tended to earn higher lexical proficiency scores. Additionally, essays that included words that on average are learned later also tended to earn higher analytic lexical proficiency scores. Guo et al. (2013) found similar relationships between concreteness, familiarity, imageability, and meaningfulness and holistic writing proficiency scores for TOEFL independent and source-based writing tasks. The relationship between word age of acquisition has not, to our knowledge, been used to model holistic scores of L2 writing proficiency with regard to either independent or source-based writing tasks.

Semantic relationships

Polysemy and hypernymy are types of semantic relationships related to lexical development (Crossley, Salsbury, & McNamara, 2009; Crossley, Salsbury, & McNamara, 2010) and L2 writing proficiency scores(Guo et al., 2013; Reynolds, 1995). Polysemy refers to the number of different (but related) senses (i.e., meanings) a word form has. A word such as *table*, for example, has more senses (i.e., a piece of furniture, geographic feature, etc.) than a word such as *encephalon* (which has only a single sense). Hypernymy refers to the hierarchical relationships between words. Words with high hypernymy values have a large number of superordinate terms, while words with low hypernymy values have few (or no) superordinate terms. For example, *animal* has six hypernymic terms (e.g., organism, animate thing, etc.), while *dog* has thirteen hypernymic terms (e.g., canine, carnivore, mammal, etc.). Recently, Guo et al. (2013) found that L2 independent essays that include words with fewer senses (i.e., lower polysemy scores) tend to earn higher scores, but no links were found between polysemy and source-based writing. Guo et al. (2013) also found a positive relationship between hypernymy (for nouns) and writing proficiency scores for both independent and source-based writing tasks.

Lexical sophistication and automatic essay scoring models

Over the past decade, automatic essay scoring (AES) systems have become increasingly prevalent in standardized writing assessments (Attali & Burstein, 2006; Shermis & Burstein, 2013). Such systems can decrease the time and costs related to essay scoring while also increasing test reliability (Bereiter, 2003; Dikli, 2006; Higgins, Xi, Zechner, & Williamson, 2011). Although AES systems can achieve scoring accuracy that is on par with humans (e.g., Shermis & Hamner, 2013; Weigle, 2010), they do not assess essays in the same manner as humans do and cannot measure some essential aspects of the construct of writing such as argumentation or rhetorical effectiveness (Condon, 2013; Deane, 2013; Herrington & Moran, 2001). An important area of interest has been to increase the construct coverage of AES systems (e.g., Crossley et al., 2015; Enright & Quinlan, 2010). To facilitate this, it is necessary to investigate features that are important to human evaluations of writing proficiency (such as lexical sophistication, among many others) and evaluate ways to measure them automatically (Burstein, Marcu, & Knight, 2003; Enright & Quinlan, 2010; Kyle & Crossley, 2015; Kyle, 2016).

Due to the importance of lexical sophistication in L2 writing (Cumming, 1990; Laufer & Nation, 1995; Schoonen et al., 2011), prominent AES systems include indices of lexical sophistication in their scoring models. Given the proprietary nature of most AES models, however, relatively little is known regarding their use of these indices. Enright and Quinlan (2010) report that e-rater, which is used to score both independent and source-based TOEFL writing tasks, uses two lexical complexity indices (word length and the use of less frequent words). Respectively, these indices account for 7% and 4% of the score produced by e-rater. Foltz, Streeter, Lochbaum, and Landauer (2013) indicate that the Intelligent Essay Assessor (IEA), which is primarily used for assessing L1 writing, includes features related to lexical sophistication such as word maturity and word variety. Foltz et al. do not, however, indicate the weights given to these indices in scoring models.

Current study

While a number of previous studies have explored the relationship between lexical sophistication and holistic scores of writing proficiency, few (if any) studies have investigated the newly developed measures of lexical sophistication outlined in the previous section. Additionally, most of the extant studies regarding the relationship between lexical sophistication and writing proficiency scores have explored independent writing tasks (cf. Cumming et al., 2005; Guo et al., 2013). This has resulted in gaps in our understanding regarding (a) the relationship between lexical sophistication and independent and source-based writing task proficiency scores, and (b) whether independent and source-based tasks require different linguistic resources with regard to lexical sophistication. We address these gaps by examining the relationship between newly developed indices of lexical sophistication and holistic scores of writing proficiency in relation to independent and source-based TOEFL writing tasks.

Specifically, this study is guided by the following research questions:

1. What is the relationship between lexical sophistication and independent writing task proficiency scores?

2. What is the relationship between lexical sophistication and source-based writing task proficiency scores?

Table 1
Descriptive statistics for the essays included in the TOEFL public use dataset: mean (standard deviation).

Corpus	N	Score	Number of words
Independent	480	3.427 (.887)	315.600 (78.596)
Form 1	240	3.383 (.864)	321.830 (79.720)
Form 2	240	3.471 (.910)	309.38 (77.117)
Integrated	480	3.151 (1.244)	200.44 (51.692)
Form 1	240	3.254 (1.179)	204.840 (52.437)
Form 2	240	3.148 (1.308)	196.040 (50.662)

3. Do responses to independent and source-based writing tasks differ with regard to lexical sophistication?

Method

Corpus

We selected independent and integrated (i.e., source-based) essays written by 480 individuals as part of the TOEFL that comprise the Educational Testing Service (ETS) public data set. The corpus includes responses to two forms of the TOEFL (i.e., includes responses to two independent essay prompts and two integrated essay prompts). The independent prompts ask test takers to write an essay that asserts and defends an opinion on a particular topic based on their own life experience. The integrated prompt asks test takers to read a short passage, listen to a related lecture, and synthesize the information given in the reading and the lecture. Essays were rated by two trained raters employed by ETS using a scale that ranged from 1.0 to 5.0. Any scores that differed by one point or less were averaged. If any two ratings for an essay differed by more than a single point, a third rater evaluated the essay. The holistic rating rubric used to evaluate the independent tasks includes descriptors related to the completion of the task, organization, development of ideas, coherence, word and phrase use, and syntax. The holistic rating rubric used to evaluate integrated tasks includes descriptors mostly related to content (e.g., whether test takers appropriately summarized the two passages and responded to the task).[1] Table 1 comprises descriptive statistics for the corpus including the number of essays, the average score, and the average number of words from each form and task.

Indices of lexical sophistication

We examined a number of indices included in the freely available Tool for the Automatic Analysis of Lexical Sophistication (TAALES; Kyle & Crossley, 2015) that represent a wide range of theoretically important aspects related to lexical sophistication. In order to control for essay length (e.g., Chodorow & Burstein, 2004) we selected the 114 length-normalized indices in TAALES. TAALES calculates indices of lexical sophistication for unigrams (words), bigrams, and trigrams. Included are a number of frequency indices from a variety of both spoken and written corpora (e.g., the British National Corpus), range indices from spoken and written corpora (e.g., SUBTLEXus), academic language indices (e.g., Academic Word List; Coxhead, 2000), and psycholinguistic word information indices (e.g., concreteness; Brysbaert, Warriner, & Kuperman, 2014). We also wrote a Python script that employs the Natural Language Toolkit (NLTK; Bird, Klein, & Loper, 2009) to calculate four indices of polysemy and hypernymy.[2] We present more details of the selected indices below.

Word frequency indices

Word frequency indices are calculated by taking the sum of the frequency values with regard to a particular frequency list (e.g., the BNC) for words in a text and dividing that sum by the number of words in that text. If a word in a target text is not represented in the frequency list, the word is not included in the calculation of the index. TAALES calculates frequency indices based on a number of reference corpora-derived frequency lists. Lemmatized frequency indices are

---

1. The independent and integrated scoring rubrics are freely available on the ETS website at http://www.ets.org/Media/Tests/TOEFL/pdf/Writing_Rubrics.pdf.

2. Both this script and TAALES are freely available at http://www.kristopherkyle.com/.

derived from the 4.5-million word Thorndike-Lorge corpus of popular magazine articles (Thorndike & Lorge, 1944), the 1-million word written section of the Brown corpus (Kuc9era & Francis, 1967), and the 1-million word London-Lund Corpus of English Conversation (Brown, 1984). Un-lemmatized frequency indices are derived from 80-million word written and 10-million word spoken subsets of the British National Corpus (BNC Consortium, 2007) and the 51-million word SUBTLEXus corpus of American subtitles (Brysbaert & New, 2009). For each list, TAALES includes an index for all words (AW), content words (CW), and function words (FW). Additionally, TAALES calculates logarithm-transformed frequency indices.

Range indices

TAALES includes a number of range indices. Range indices are calculated for AW, CW, and FW. These indices are derived from the 500 texts in the Brown corpus (Kuc9era & Francis, 1967), 574 spoken and 3083 written texts in the BNC (BNC Consortium, 2007), and the 8388 subtitle texts in SUBTLEXus (Brysbaert & New, 2009). Additionally, TAALES calculates indices based on the 15 text categories in the Brown Corpus (Kuc9era & Francis, 1967), which can be described roughly as genres (e.g., news reporting, news editorials, academic writing, science fiction, mystery and detective fiction). Scores from these indices calculate the average number of text categories in which the words in a text occur. Words that occur in all categories are general-purpose words, while words that occur in only one category are more restricted in their use.

N-gram indices

Crossley et al. (2012) derived bigram and trigram frequency lists from the 80-million word written and the 10-million word spoken subsets of the BNC (BNC Consortium, 2007). TAALES calculates normalized n-gram frequency counts. For each list, normalized counts are calculated using the number of words in the text as the denominator and by using the number of bigrams/trigrams in the text that are also represented in the frequency list as the numerator. Additionally, the proportion of unique bigrams/trigrams that occur in a target text that also occur in the frequency list are calculated.

Academic list indices

TAALES includes indices derived from the AWL and the AFL. For the AWL, indices are calculated for the entire AWL and for each of the 10 sublists (see Coxhead, 2000; for more information on the AWL). For the AFL, indices are calculated for the entire AFL, the "core" AFL, the written AFL and the spoken AFL (see Simpson-Vlach & Ellis, 2010; for more information on the AFL).

Word information indices

TAALES includes a number of psycholinguistic word information indices based on the MRC psycholinguistic database (Coltheart, 1981) and two newly collected databases (Brysbaert et al., 2014; Kuperman, Stadthagen-Gonzalez, & Brysbaert, 2012). Indices are calculated for AW, CW, and FW. Included are familiarity, concreteness (for words and bigrams), imageability, meaningfulness, and age of acquisition.

Polysemy and hypernymy

We calculate polysemy and hypernymy indices based on the Wordnet database (Fellbaum, 1998). We calculate polysemy as the mean number of senses contained in content words (nouns, verbs, adjectives, and adverbs). Hypernymy indices comprise the mean number of superordinate terms words in a text have. We calculate hypernymy for nouns, verbs, and the combination of nouns and verbs.

Statistical analysis

In order to determine the relationship between a variety of indices of lexical sophistication and L2 independent and integrated writing assessment scores, we conducted two identical sets of statistical analyses that differed only in terms of the corpora analyzed (i.e., one with the data from the independent essays and one with the data from the integrated essays). Following the procedure outlined below, we ran a stepwise multiple regression to determine the amount of variance in holistic scores that could be explained by indices of lexical sophistication.

We first checked to ensure that each index was normally distributed. Any indices that did not meet the criteria of normality were discarded.[3] We then conducted a multiple analysis of variance (MANOVA)

---

3. In fine-grained linguistic analyses, normality is often grossly violated due to a high-number of zero-counts (i.e., for rare features). In such cases,

statistic between the data from the two prompts to control for prompt differences (e.g., Crossley, Weston, McLain Sullivan, & McNamara, 2011; Hinkel, 2002). Any indices that were significantly different ($p < .05$) between prompts were removed from further consideration. We then ran a correlation between the remaining indices and holistic essay quality score. Any indices that did not demonstrate a significant ($p < .05$) and meaningful relationship ($r > .1$) with holistic scores were removed from further consideration. We also removed any indices that were strongly correlated (r .7) with the number of words in each essay to control for text length, which strongly affects human judgments of quality (Ferris, 1994). We then checked the remaining indices for multicollinearity. Any indices that were very strongly correlated (r .9) were flagged and in each collinear set the index with the strongest relationship with holistic scores was kept (Tabachnick & Fidell, 2001). A stepwise multiple regression was then conducted. If the resulting model included any variables with switched signs (i.e., the stepwise model used the inverse of a variable to create an optimal model), the variable was removed from consideration to ensure that the final model reflected the initial correlations and the regression was run again. To ensure that the results of the multiple regression were consistent across the entire data set, a multiple regression with 10-fold cross validation (10-fold CV) was conducted using the indices identified in the initial multiple regression. 10-fold CV is a statistical procedure in which 90% of the data are used to create a model, and then that model is tested on the remaining 10% of the data. This procedure is repeated until all of the data have been used as the test set, and then the results from the ten models (or folds) are averaged (e.g., Tabachnick & Fidell, 2001). To investigate the differences between independent and integrated TOEFL essays with regard to lexical sophistication we conducted MANOVA and discriminant function analysis (DFA) statistics. We first conducted a MANOVA using essay type (independent/integrated) as fixed factors and the predictors identified in the regression analyses above as dependent variables. We then entered the indices that demonstrated significant and meaningful differences into a DFA. DFA is often used to predict group membership of items (e.g., independent and integrated essays)

---

variable transformation is not possible. While aggregated features can also be used to obtain normally distributed data, the use of non-aggregated indices tend to produce more accurate and fine-grained results (Crossley et al., 2015).

based on predictor variables (e.g., indices of lexical sophistication). We used a stepwise DFA on the entire data set and employed leave one out cross validation (LOOCV) to ensure that the model is generalizable across the data set.

Results

Independent essays
Assumptions

Of the 118 indices considered, 15 violated normality (the majority of these were due to zero counts for AWL and AFL lists) and were removed from further consideration. Of the 103 indices remaining, 26 were not meaningfully correlated (absolute value of r .1) with holistic scores. None of the indices were strongly correlated ($r > = .7$) with essay length. Of the remaining 77 indices, 55 demonstrated significant differences between prompts. The remaining 22 indices were analyzed for multicollinearity. After checking for multicollinearity, 14 variables remained. See Table 2 for correlations between the remaining variables and holistic scores.

Regression analysis

The 14 variables were entered into a stepwise multiple regression in order to determine the variance in holistic scores explained by indices of lexical sophistication. After removing variables that switched signs, the regression analysis yielded a significant model that included six indices of lexical sophistication: *BNC written range for all words, BNC written bigram frequency logarithm, hypernymy (nouns and verbs), and imageability for all words*. The model accounted for 36.8% of the variance in holistic scores (see Table 3 for an overview of the model). A follow up 10-fold CV multiple regression explained 35.4% of the variance, indicating that the model is stable across the dataset. The results indicate that range, bigram frequency, hypernymy and imageability are important predictors of TOEFL independent essay quality.

Integrated essays
Assumptions

Assumptions Of the 118 indices considered, 20 violated normality (the majority of these were due to zero counts for AWL and AFL lists) and were removed from further consideration. Of the 98 indices remaining, 50 were not meaningfully correlated (absolute value of r .1) with holistic scores. None of the indices were strongly correlated ($r > = .7$) with essay length. Of the remaining 48 indices, 39 demonstrated significant differences between prompts. The remaining nine indices were analyzed for multicollinearity. After checking for multicollinearity, six variables remained. See Table 4 for correlations between the remaining variables and holistic scores.

Table 2

Correlations between indices entered into stepwise multiple regression and holistic score for independent writing.

Index	N	r	p
BNC Written Range AW Kuperman age of acquisition CW SUBTLEXus Range CW	480 480 480	−0.409 0.403 −0.398	<.001 <.001 <.001
Familiarity CW Hypernymy (nouns and verbs) Kucera-Francis Frequency CW Logarithm BNC Spoken Frequency CW	480 480 480 480	−0.392 0.372 −0.361 −0.337	<.001 <.001 <.001 <.001
Kucera-Francis Frequency FW Logarithm BNC Written Trigram Proportion	480 480	0.274 0.216	<.001 <.001
Hypernymy (verbs)	480	.195	<.001
Imageability AW BNC Written Bigram Proportion	480 480	−0.161 0.151	<.001 <.001
BNC Spoken Freq FW BNC Written Bigram Frequency Logarithm	480 480	0.109 0.107	<.001 <.010

Table 3
Summary of stepwise multiple regression models for independent writing.

Entry	Predictors included	r	R^2	R^2 change	B	β	SE
1	BNC Written Range AW	.409	.167	.167	−.599	−.196	.018
2	BNC Written Bigram Frequency Logarithm	.588	.345	.178	.457	2.345	.243
3	Hypernymy (nouns and verbs)	.596	.355	.010	.148	.332	.104
4	Imageability AW	.606	.368	.013	−.120	−.013	.004

Note: Estimated constant term = 18.552, b= unstandardized beta, SE = standard error; B = standardized beta.

Table 4
Correlations between indices entered into stepwise multiple regression and holistic score for integrated writing.

Index	N	r	p
Hypernymy (nouns)	480	0.263	<.001
Kucera-Francis number of categories AW	480	−0.176	<.001
Thorndike-Lorge Frequency AW Logarithm	480	−0.171	<.001
BNC Written Bigram Frequency Logarithm	480	−0.122	.007
Kuperman age of acquisition FW logarithm	480	0.109	.017
Hypernymy (nouns and verbs)	480	0.108	.018

Table 5
Summary of stepwise multiple regression models for integrated writing.

Entry	Predictors included	r	R^2	R^2 change	B	β	SE
1	Hypernymy (nouns)	.263	.069	.069	.234	.569	.110
2	Kucera-Francis number of categories AW	.288	.083	.014	−.121	−.448	.167

Note: Estimated constant term = 5.628, b = unstandardized beta, SE = standard error; B = standardized beta.

Regression analysis

The six variables were entered into a stepwise multiple regression in order to determine the variance in holistic scores explained by indices of lexical sophistication. The stepwise regression resulted in a significant model including two variables (*hypernymy [nouns]* and *Kucera-Francis number of categories*). The model accounted for 8.3% of the variance in holistic scores (see Table 5 for an overview of the model). A follow up 10-fold CV multiple regression explained 7.5% of the variance, indicated that the model is stable across the dataset. The results demonstrate that hypernymy and number of categories are indicators of TOEFL integrated essay quality.

Differences between independent and integrated essays

MANOVA

The MANOVA indicated that each index identified in the regression models above demonstrated significant and meaningful differences between independent and integrated essays. These results are summarized in Table 6.

Table 6
MANOVA Results.

Variable	Independent Mean (SD)	Integrated Mean (SD)	F (1, 957)	η^2_p
BNC Written Range AW	80.918(2.712)	72.858(3.702)	1480.87	.607
BNC Written Bigram Frequency Logarithm	1.523(0.173)	1.252(0.196)	517.34	.351
Hypernymy (nouns)	5.422(0.509)	6.155(0.512)	495.11	.341
Hypernymy (nouns and verbs)	3.488(0.395)	4.292(0.423)	927.56	.492
Imageability AW	319.283(8.473)	337.049(18.005)	382.59	.285
Kucera-Francis number of categories AW	14.242(0.262)	13.355(0.336)	2076.02	.684

Note: For all indices $p < .001$.

Table 7
Discriminant function analysis confusion matrix.

	Predicted Independent	Predicted Integrated	Total
Independent	460	20	480
Integrated	35	445	480
Accuracy	95.8%	92.7%	94.3%

DFA

Following the MANOVA, the six indices identified in the regression models above were checked for multicollinearity. The two range indices (*BNC written range for all words* and *Kucera-Francis number of categories*) were collinear ($r > .9$). Because the latter demonstrated stronger differences between independent and integrated essays, the former was removed from further consideration. The remaining five indices were entered into a stepwise DFA. The model created by the stepwise DFA achieved a classification accuracy of 94.3% accuracy using three indices (*Kucera-Francis number of categories, imageability for all words,* and *hypernymy [nouns]*). This is significantly higher (df = 1, n = 960, $x^2 = 753.340$, $p < .001$) than what would be expected by chance. The reported Kappa = .885, indicates almost perfect agreement between actual and predicted essay type (Landis & Koch, 1977). The stepwise LOOCV DFA also achieved a classification accuracy of 94.3%, suggesting that the predictor model is stable across the dataset. Table 7 comprises the confusion matrix for the stepwise DFA, which shows the number of independent and integrated essays that were correctly predicted by the model. The results indicate that responses to independent and integrated tasks can be accurately distinguished based on indices of lexical sophistication related to range of registers, imageability, and hypernymy.

Discussion

The results suggest that the production of sophisticated lexis is an important predictor of holistic scores of writing proficiency with regard to independent tasks, but not with regard to source-based tasks. Specifically, the results indicate that indices of word range and bigram frequency, which have not been explored with regard to timed, argumentative L2 writing, are important indicators of holistic writing proficiency scores in independent TOEFL writing samples, but not in TOEFL integrated writing samples. These findings underscore the complexity of the construct(s) of L2 writing proficiency (e.g., Schoonen et al., 2011) and highlight differences with regard to the relationship between receptive and productive lexical knowledge and holistic scores of writing proficiency in integrated tasks. Baba (2009), for example, found a positive relationship between receptive vocabulary knowledge and holistic writing proficiency scores for integrated tasks, while the current study found only a weak relationship between productive lexical knowledge (as measured by indices of lexical sophistication) and holistic integrated writing scores. Furthermore, lexical sophistication differs between responses to independent and integrated tasks in ways that allow for independent and integrated essays to be accurately categorized based solely on indices of lexical sophistication. The findings are important because they suggest that independent and integrated writing tasks lead to the production of different linguistic features supporting the notion that the two tasks measure distinct writing proficiency constructs (Chapelle et al., 2008). Additionally, the findings suggest that range and bigram frequency are stronger predictors of independent essay quality than word frequency, which has been the most common metric of lexical sophistication used in previous writing quality studies (e.g., Crossley et al., 2013; Laufer & Nation, 1995). This finding has important implications for automatic essay scoring and feedback systems along with implications for L2 writing pedagogy. We discuss the importance of these findings below divided by each analysis.

Lexical sophistication and independent essay tasks

A multiple regression model consisting of four indices of lexical sophistication explained 36.8% percent of the variance in holistic independent essay scores (35.4% in the LOOCV). Importantly, the inclusion of two variables, *BNC Written Range AW* and *BNC Written Bigram Frequency Logarithm*, explained a large portion of this variance (16.7% and 17.8%, respectively). Two other indices explained the remaining 2.3% of the variance, including *Hypernymy (nouns and verbs*; 1.0%) and *Imageability AW* (1.3%).

These results indicate that raters tend to assign higher scores to essays that include words with a more restricted range. This suggests that essays that include words that are more specific and language-domain appropriate are likely to receive higher scores. Examples 1 and 2 below highlight differences between sentences with high and low average range scores. Both sentences are taken from essays written on the topic of cooperation.

1. Low range example (Quality score of 4.5. Range score of 65.96):
   Second, the accelerated effect of globalization since the fifties has accentuated the need for cooperation.
2. High range example (Quality score of 3. Range score of 79.89):
   First, commercial between countries had been expanded and became bigger and that would make countries to think how to deal with other countries more than past days before this revolution of communication and information spreading.

On average, the words in the low range sample occur in fewer than two-thirds of the texts in the written section of the BNC. Words such as *accelerated, globalization, fifties,* and *accentuated* have particularly low range scores (averaging 7.55), suggesting that they are used in a smaller percentage of texts and are thus more sophisticated. On average, the words in the high range sample occur in almost 80% of the texts in the written section of the BNC. Words such as *revolution, communication,* and *spreading* have relatively low range scores (averaging 31.27), but the majority of the words in the sentence have high range scores, indicating they are less lexically sophisticated. The two sentences communicate similar ideas (i.e., cooperation between countries is becoming increasingly important) but the first employs words that occur in fewer contexts, while the second uses more general words.

These results are novel with regard to independent essay tasks, and suggest that range is an important indicator of holistic L2 writing proficiency scores. Furthermore, in this study and in Kyle & Crossley's (2015) lexical proficiency study, range was a stronger predictor of holistic scores of writing proficiency and written lexical proficiency than frequency. This suggests that predicting productive L2 lexical proficiency is more closely related to the number of texts a word occurs in than the sheer number of times it occurs. This provides some evidence that range indices should be considered in the creation of vocabulary learning lists and in automatic essay scoring models.

Further, these results indicate that raters tend to assign higher scores to essays that include more frequent bigrams. This suggests that using appropriate word combinations may be important for earning higher scores on independent essays. Examples 3 and 4 below illustrate the difference between sentences that earn high and low bigram frequency scores.

1. High bigram frequency example (total essay quality score 4.5, Bigram score of 1.6): *I think it is true that at schools and companies today group work is valued more than before.*
2. Low bigram frequency example (total essay quality score 3, Bigram score of 0.7): *The world is developing very fast, the compete is change more hard.*

The bigram frequency database used in TAALES includes the most frequent 50,000 bigrams in a written subset of the BNC. The first example earns a relatively high bigram frequency score because most of the bigrams in the sentence occur in the database and are relatively frequent. Of the 17 bigrams in Example 3, twelve are represented in the database. Interestingly, the sentence is well formed, but *at schools*, *companies today*, *today group*, *is valued*, and *valued more* are not among the 50,000 most frequent bigrams in the BNC. In Example 4, which earns a lower bigram frequency score, only four of the 11 bigrams occur in the database, indicating that they are not among the most frequent 50,000 bigrams in a written subset of the BNC. In the first clause of the sentence, *The world is developing very fast,* which is well-formed, four of the five bigrams are counted, while none of the bigrams in the second clause *the compete is change more hard* are counted. These differences result in an average bigram frequency score that is twice as large in the first example than in the second. The bigram frequency index, therefore, seems to be tapping into both lexical knowledge (e.g., collocational knowledge) and grammatical knowledge, supporting the notion that lexis and grammar are intertwined (Halliday, 1991; Römer, 2009; Sinclair, 1991). These results are novel with regard to timed argumentative independent essays, and add to a growing body of literature that underscores the predictive value of n-gram frequency measures (e.g., Crossley et al., 2012; Kyle & Crossley, 2015). This evidence suggests the importance of n-gram frequency in predicting L2 writing proficiency scores.

Hypernymy (*Hypernymy [nouns and verbs]*) and imageability (*imageability AW*), together explained a small amount (2.3%) of the variance above n-grams and range indices. Essays tended to be assigned higher scores by raters if they included words that had more superordinate terms (i.e., were more specific) and less imageable. These results support previous research in the area of word information and hypernymy in L2 writing in that more essays that contain more specific words are scored higher (e.g., Guo et al., 2013). However, these results contrast with previous research that indicates language learners use words with fewer superordinate terms (i.e., are more abstract) as their proficiency develops (e.g., Crossley et al., 2009). This is likely because human ratings of writing proficiency are more strongly linked to the use of specific textual examples that support a claim whereas the assessment of lexical proficiency is more strongly linked to lexical abstractness.

The results of the regression analysis for the independent essays align well with the TOEFL independent writing rubric. This rubric asks raters to consider features that are strongly related to lexical sophistication such as "appropriate word choice," "range of vocabulary," and "idiomaticity." The findings of this analysis suggest that raters of TOEFL independent essays may either explicitly or implicitly (see Eckes, 2008) attend to these rubric descriptors and give higher scores to essays that contain lexical features such as lower word range, higher bigram frequency, higher hypernymy, and lower imageability.

Integrated essay score

The relationship between lexical sophistication and integrated writing proficiency scores was much weaker than with independent essays. Overall, correlations between the indices of lexical sophistication investigated and integrated writing proficiency scores were low. Accordingly, the model that included two predictors was able to explain only 8.3% of the variance in integrated essay scores. These indices included *hypernymy (nouns)* and *Kucera-Francis number of categories AW*. The mean number of hypernymic levels for nouns index (*hypernymy [nouns]*) explained 6.7% of the variance in integrated essay scores. Essays that on average included nouns that were more specific (i.e., had more superordinate terms) tended to earn higher scores. The range of registers index (*Kucera-Francis number of categories AW*) added 1.4% to the variance in integrated essay scores explained by the model indicating that integrated included words that occur in fewer registers tended to earn higher scores. These results suggest that the use of specific lexis is an indicator of quality in responses to integrated essay tasks in much the same way that it was predictive of writing quality for the independent tasks.

These results may also highlight an important distinction between receptive and productive vocabulary knowledge. Baba (2009), for example, indicated that vocabulary knowledge (as demonstrated on receptive vocabulary tests of breadth and depth) was moderately correlated ($r = .400$ and $r = .340$, respectively) with scores on a summary writing task. From a productive perspective, as evidenced in this study, however, the strongest correlation between lexical sophistication and integrated writing scores was small ($r = .263$), suggesting that for integrated tasks (which generally involve summary writing), receptive lexical knowledge may be a greater boon than productive lexical knowledge. That is to say that comprehending the reading (and/or listening passage) may be more advantageous than being able to employ sophisticated lexis in writing.

These findings, like the findings for the independent essays, also align well with the expectations found in the TOEFL integrated writing rubric, suggesting that lexical sophistication is not a particularly important factor in TOEFL integrated essays. The integrated scoring rubric generally includes descriptors that focus on the accurate summarization and synthesis of the content included in the reading and listening passage. The rubric contains few references to language use (and none related directly to lexical sophistication) and those that are contained in the rubric focus on language errors that impede accurate summarization and synthesis.

Differences between responses to independent and source-based tasks

The results of the MANOVA and the DFA provide additional evidence that responses to independent and integrated tasks differ with regard to the occurrence of lexical features related to lexical sophistication. These differences were such that responses could be categorized by task with an accuracy of 94.3%. In general, these results show that independent responses tend to include lexical items that occur widely throughout different texts and context (i.e., are less specific), while integrated responses tend to include lexical items that occurred in a more restricted range of texts and contexts as reflected in the range indices (see Table 6). Responses to independent tasks also contained lexical items that were more sophisticated with regard to bigram frequency and were less imageable and had fewer superordinate terms (i.e., were more abstract) than responses to integrated tasks. Overall, this analysis demonstrated that responses to integrated tasks were more sophisticated with regard to the document and register-level range indices and included lexical items that were more imageable and contained more superordinate terms (i.e., were more specific). All indices demonstrated large effects for the differences between independent and integrated essays.

These results felicitously align with the nature of the two tasks. The independent tasks used in this study ask test takers to discuss their opinions on cooperation and the subjects they would like to study, respectively. The integrated tasks, on the other hand, discuss fish farming and bird migration, respectively. Knowing that test takers tend to repeat specific lexical items from listening and reading passages in their responses to integrated tasks (Crossley, Clevinger, & Kim, 2014), it seems likely that more specific and imageable terms related to fish farming and word migration (i.e., *fish, farm,* and *bird*) will be included in integrated responses. Such responses will also be limited in the range of the words used because the assignment limits the potential topic. In contrast, test takers responding to independent tasks about *opinions* and *school subject* will have much lower imageability and hypernymy scores and will not be limited in the range of words they can use to describe their opinions and experiences.

Conclusion

Overall, these results suggest that newly developed indices of lexical sophistication are important indicators of writing proficiency with regard to independent tasks. Additionally, the results suggest that indices of lexical sophistication are generally less important indicators of writing proficiency in source-based tasks. The results also suggest that independent and source-based tasks require writers to draw on different linguistic resources related to lexical sophistication.

The results from this study supports the TOEFL validity argument (i.e., the inclusion of both independent and integrated writing tasks; Chapelle et al., 2008) in that, at least with respect to lexical sophistication, the independent and integrated tasks seem to evaluate different language skills (cf. Cumming et al., 2005; Guo et al., 2013). The independent tasks clearly evaluate test takers' productive lexical knowledge. Higher scoring independent essays tend to include words that occur in fewer contexts, are more specific and less imageable, and two-word combinations that are more frequent in reference corpora than lower scoring independent essays. These findings suggest that raters are attending to rubric descriptors related to lexical sophistication. Responses to integrated tasks, on the other hand, seem to evaluate productive lexical knowledge to a much lesser degree, which is also reflected in the rating rubric.

This study also has important implications for automatic essay scoring systems and automatic essay feedback systems. The majority of previous systems have relied on simple word frequency and word length indices to assess lexical sophistication (e.g., Attali & Burstein, 2006; Enright & Quinlan, 2010). The findings from this study indicate that lexical features such as range and bigram information may be better predictors of holistic scores of writing proficiency than simple word frequency. Adding indices related to range and bigram frequency may allow AES systems to more accurately assess the construct of lexical sophistication, and may result in gains in construct coverage and scoring accuracy.

In addition, these findings have implications for L2 writing instruction. For instance, the results related to range indices suggest that L2 learners should be exposed to words within a wide variety of settings, domains, and genres so that they have access to context-general and context-specific lexical items. Furthermore, the results related to bigram frequency suggest that vocabulary learning may benefit from contextual approaches that look not only at words in isolation but also frequent word neighbors (i.e., collocations) and verbal constructions (e.g., Ellis, O'Donnell, & Römer, 2013; O'Donnell, Römer, & Ellis, 2013). One limitation in our study is the manner in which we dealt with prompt differences (e.g., Crossley et al., 2011; Hinkel, 2002). We opted to remove any indices that demonstrated significant differences between prompts, which eliminated a large number of indices from our analysis. This conservative approach limited the number of indices we could sample, but also ensured that reported model strength was not moderated by prompt difference. In addition, our exploration of writing proficiency assessments only included a limited sampling of writing tasks included in the TOEFL. However, the results from this sample suggest that the construct of writing proficiency is indeed complex (e.g., Schoonen et al., 2011) and likely consists of a number of writing proficiencies. Future research should continue to explore the bounds of these proficiencies to determine which features of writing proficiency are robust and generalizable across writing tasks, and which are domain specific.

REFERENCES

Attali, Y., & Burstein, J. (2006). Automated essay scoring with e-rater[1] V. 2. *The Journal of Technology, Learning, and Assessment 4*(3) . http://ejournals.bc.edu/ ojs/index.php/jtla/index.

The British National Corpus, version 3 (BNC XML Edition). (2007). Distributed by Oxford University Computing Services on behalf of the BNC Consortium. Retrieved from http://www.natcorp.ox.ac.uk/.

Baba, K. (2009). Aspects of lexical proficiency in writing summaries in a foreign language. *Journal of Second Language Writing, 18*, 191–208. Bereiter, C. (2003). Foreword. In M. D. Shermis, & J. Burstein (Eds.), *Automated essay scoring: A cross-disciplinary perspective* (pp. vii–ix).Mahwah, NJ: Lawrence Erlbaum.

Biber, D., Conrad, S., & Cortes, V. (2004). If you look at.: Lexical bundles in university teaching and textbooks. *Applied Linguistics, 25*, 371–405. http://dx.doi. org/10.1093/applin/25.3.371.

Bird, S., Klein, E., & Loper, E. (2009). *Natural language processing with Python*. O'Reilly Media, Inc..

Brown, G. D. A. (1984). A frequency count of 190 000 words in the London-Lund corpus of English conversation. *Behavior Research Methods Instruments & Computers, 16*, 502–532. http://dx.doi.org/10.3758/BF03200836.

Brysbaert, M., & New, B. (2009). Moving beyond Kuc9era and Francis: A critical evaluation of current word frequency norms and the introduction of a new and improved word frequency measure for American English. *Behavior Research Methods, 41*, 977–990. http://dx.doi.org/10.3758/BRM.41.4.977.

Brysbaert, M., Warriner, A. B., & Kuperman, V. (2014). Concreteness ratings for 40 thousand generally known English word lemmas. *Behavior Research Methods, 46*, 904–911. http://dx.doi.org/10.3758/s13428-013-0403-5.

Burstein, J., Marcu, D., & Knight, K. (2003). Finding the WRITE stuff: Automatic identification of discourse structure in student essays. *Intelligent Systems, IEEE, 18*(1), 32–39.

Chapelle, C. A., Enright, M. K., & Jamieson, J. M. (2008). Test score interpretation and use. In C. A. Chapelle, M. K. Enright, & J. M. Jamieson (Eds.), *Building a validity argument for the Test of English as a Foreign Language*[TM] (pp. 1–25).New York, NY: Routledge.

Chodorow, M., & Burstein, J. (2004). Beyond essay length: Evaluating e-rater[1]'s performance on TOEFL[1] essays. *ETS Research Report Series, 2004*(1) [i-38.10.1002/j.2333-8504.2004.tb01931.x].

Coltheart, M. (1981). The MRC psycholinguistic database. *Quarterly Journal of Experimental Psychology Section A, 33*(4), 497–505. http://dx.doi.org/10.1080/ 14640748108400805.

Condon, W. (2013). Large-scale assessment, locally-developed measures, and automated scoring of essays: Fishing for red herrings? *Assessing Writing, 18*(1), 100–108.

Coxhead, A. (2000). A new academic word list. *TESOL Quarterly, 34*, 213–238. http://dx.doi.org/10.2307/3587951.

Crossley, S. A., & McNamara, D. S. (2009). Computational assessment of lexical differences in L1 and L2 writing. *Journal of Second Language Writing, 18*, 119–135.

Crossley, S. A., & McNamara, D. S. (2012). Predicting second language writing proficiency: The roles of cohesion and linguistic sophistication. *Journal of Research in Reading, 35*, 115–135. http://dx.doi.org/10.1111/j.1467-9817.2010.01449.x.

Crossley, S. A., & McNamara, D. S. (2013). Applications of text analysis tools for spoken response grading. *Language Learning & Technology 17*(2), 171–192. http://llt.msu.edu/.

Crossley, S. A., Salsbury, T., & McNamara, D. S. (2009). Measuring L2 lexical growth using hypernymic relationships. *Language Learning, 59*, 307–334. Crossley, S. A., Salsbury, T., & McNamara, D. S. (2010). The development of polysemy and frequency use in English second language speakers. *Language Learning, 60*, 573–605. http://dx.doi.org/10.1111/j.1467-9922.2010.00568.x.

Crossley, S. A., Weston, J. L., McLain Sullivan, S. T., & McNamara, D. S. (2011). The development of writing proficiency as a function of grade level: A linguistic analysis. *Written Communication, 28*, 282–311. http://dx.doi.org/10.1177/0741088311410188.

Crossley, S. A., Cai, Z., & McNamara, D. S. (2012). Syntagmatic, paradigmatic, and automatic n-gram approaches to assessing essay quality. In P. M. McCarthy, & G. M. Youngblood (Eds.), *Proceedings of the 25th international Florida artificial intelligence research society (FLAIRS) conference* (pp. 214–219).Menlo Park, CA: The AAAI Press.

Crossley, S. A., Cobb, T., & McNamara, D. S. (2013). Comparing count-based and band-based indices of word frequency: Implications for active vocabulary research and pedagogical applications. *System., 41*, 965–981.

Crossley, S. A., Clevinger, A., & Kim, Y. (2014). The role of lexical properties and cohesive devices in text integration and their effect on human ratings of speaking proficiency. *Language Assessment Quarterly, 11*, 250–270.

Crossley, S. A., Kyle, K., & McNamara, D. S. (2015). To aggregate or not? Linguistic features in automatic essay scoring and feedback systems. *Journal of Writing Assessment 8*(1) . http://www.journalofwritingassessment.org/index.php.

Cumming, A., Kantor, R., Baba, K., Erdosy, U., Eouanzoui, K., & James, M. (2005). Differences in written discourse in independent and integrated prototype tasks for next generation TOEFL. *Assessing Writing, 10*(1), 5–43.

Cumming, A. (1990). Expertise in evaluating second language compositions. *Language Testing, 7*, 31–51. http://dx.doi.org/10.1177/026553229000700104.

Deane, P. (2013). On the relation between automated essay scoring and modern views of the writing construct. *Assessing Writing, 18*(1), 7–24.

Dikli, S. (2006). An overview of automated scoring of essays. *The Journal of Technology, Learning, and Assessment, 5*(1) .

Eckes, T. (2008). Rater types in writing performance assessments: A classification approach to rater variability. *Language Testing, 25*, 155–185.

Ellis, N. C., O'Donnell, M. B., & Römer, U. (2013). Usage-based language: Investigating the latent structures that underpin acquisition [Issue Supplement]. *Language Learning, 63*(s1), 25–51. http://dx.doi.org/10.1111/j.1467-9922.2012.00736.x.

Engber, C. A. (1995). The relationship of lexical proficiency to the quality of ESL compositions. *Journal of Second Language Writing, 4*, 139–155. Enright, M. K., & Quinlan, T. (2010). Complementing human judgment of essays written by English language learners with e-rater[1] scoring. *Language Testing, 27*, 317–334.

Fellbaum, C. (Ed.), (1998). *WordNet: An electronic lexical database.* Cambridge, MA: MIT Press.

Ferris, D. R. (1994). Lexical and syntactic features of ESL writing by students at different levels of L2 proficiency. *TESOL Quarterly, 28*, 414–420. http://dx.doi. org/10.2307/3587446.

Foltz, P. W., Streeter, L. A., Lochbaum, K. E., & Landauer, T. K. (2013). Implementation and applications of the Intelligent Essay Assessor. In M. D. Shermis, & J. Burstein (Eds.), *Handbook of automated essay evaluation: Current applications and new directions* (pp. 68–88).New York, NY: Routledge.

Grant, L., & Ginther, A. (2000). Using computer-tagged linguistic features to describe L2 writing differences. *Journal of Second Language Writing, 9*, 123–145.

Gries, S. T. (2008). Dispersions and adjusted frequencies in corpora. *International Journal of Corpus Linguistics, 13*, 403–437. http://dx.doi.org/10.1075/ ijcl.13.4.02gri.

Guo, L., Crossley, S. A., & McNamara, D. S. (2013). Predicting human judgments of essay quality in both integrated and independent second language writing samples: A comparison study. *Assessing Writing, 18*(3), 218–238.

Halliday, M. A. K. (1991). Corpus studies and probabilistic grammar. In K. Aijmer, & B. Altenberg (Eds.), *English corpus linguistics* (pp. 30–43).New York, NY: Longman.

Hardy, J. A., & Römer, U. (2013). Revealing disciplinary variation in student writing: A multi-dimensional analysis of the Michigan Corpus of Upper-level Student Papers (MICUSP). *Corpora, 8*, 183–207.

Herrington, A., & Moran, C. (2001). What happens when machines read our students' writing? *College English, 63*, 480–499.

Higgins, D., Xi, X., Zechner, K., & Williamson, D. (2011). A three-stage approach to the automated scoring of spontaneous spoken responses. *Computer Speech and Language, 25*, 282–306.

Hinkel, E. (2002). *Second language writers' text: Linguistic and rhetorical features*. Mahwah, NJ: Lawrence Erlbaum.

Hyland, K. (2007). Genre pedagogy: Language, literacy and L2 writing instruction. *Journal of Second Language Writing, 16*, 148–164.

Jarvis, S. (2002). Short texts, best-fitting curves and new measures of lexical diversity. *Language Testing, 19*, 57–84. http://dx.doi.org/10.1191/ 0265532202lt220oa.

Kellogg, R. T., & Raulerson, B. A. (2007). Improving the writing skills of college students. *Psychonomic Bulletin & Review, 14*, 237–242. http://dx.doi.org/ 10.3758/BF03194058.

Koda, K. (1993). Task-induced variability in FL composition: Language-specific perspectives. *Foreign Language Annals, 26*, 332–346. Kuc9era, H., & Francis, W. N. (1967). *Computational analysis of present-day American English*. Providence, RI: Brown University Press.

Kuperman, V., Stadthagen-Gonzalez, H., & Brysbaert, M. (2012). Age-of-acquisition ratings for 30,000 English words. *Behavior Research Methods, 44*(4), 978–990.

Kyle, K., & Crossley, S. A. (2015). Automatically assessing lexical sophistication: Indices, tools, findings and application. *TESOL Quarterly, 49*, 757–786.

Kyle, K. (2016). Measuring syntactic development in L2 writing: Fine grained indices of syntactic complexity and usage-based indices of syntactic sophistication (Doctoral dissertation). Retrieved from http://scholarworks.gsu.edu/alesl_diss/35.

Landis, J. R., & Koch, G. G. (1977). The measurement of observer agreement for categorical data. *Biometrics*. http://dx.doi.org/10.2307/2529310.

Laufer, B., & Nation, P. (1995). Vocabulary size and use: Lexical richness in L2 written production. *Applied Linguistics*, *16*, 307–322. http://dx.doi.org/10.1093/ applin/16.3.307.

Laufer, B. (1994). The lexical profile of second language writing: Does it change over time? *RELC Journal*, *25*(2), 21–33. http://dx.doi.org/10.1177/ 003368829402500202.

Leki, I., & Carson, J. G. (1994). Students' perceptions of EAP writing instruction and writing needs across the disciplines. *TESOL Quarterly*, *28*, 81–101. Malvern, D. D., & Richards, B. J. (1997). A new measure of lexical diversity. *British Studies in Applied Linguistics*, *12*, 58–71.

Manchón, R. M., Murphy, L., & Roca de Larios, J. (2007). Lexical retrieval processes and strategies in second language writing: A synthesis of empirical research. *International Journal of English Studies*, *7*(2), 149–174.

Morris, L., & Cobb, T. (2004). Vocabulary profiles as predictors of the academic performance of Teaching English as a Second Language trainees. *System*, *32*, 75–87.

National Commission on Writing for America's Families, Schools, and Colleges (2003). The neglected R: The need for a writing revolution. New York, NY : College Entrance Examination Board.

O'Donnell, M. B., Römer, U., & Ellis, N. C. (2013). The development of formulaic sequences in first and second language writing: Investigating effects of frequency, association, and native norm. *International Journal of Corpus Linguistics*, *18*, 83–108. http://dx.doi.org/10.1075/ijcl.18.1.07odo.

Plakans, L., & Gebril, A. (2013). Using multiple texts in an integrated writing assessment: Source text use as a predictor of score. *Journal of Second Language Writing*, *22*, 217–230.

Plakans, L. (2008). Comparing composing processes in writing-only and reading-to-write test tasks. *Assessing Writing*, *13*(2), 111–129.

Römer, U., & O'Donnell, M. B. (2011). From student hard drive to web corpus (part 1): The design, compilation and genre classification of the Michigan Corpus of Upper-level Student Papers (MICUSP). *Corpora*, *6*, 159–177.

Römer, U. (2009). The inseparability of lexis and grammar: Corpus linguistic perspectives. *Annual Review of Cognitive Linguistics*, *7*, 140–162.

Read, J. (1998). Validating a test to measure depth of vocabulary knowledge. In A. Kunnan (Ed.), *Validation in language assessment* (pp. 41–60).Mahwah, NJ: Lawrence Erlbaum.

Reynolds, D. W. (1995). Repetition in non-native speaker writing. *Studies in Second Language Acquisition*, *17*, 185–209.

Schmitt, N., Schmitt, D., & Clapham, C. (2001). Developing and exploring the behaviour of two new versions of the Vocabulary Levels Test. *Language testing, 18*, 55–88.

Schoonen, R., van Gelderen, A., Stoel, R. D., Hulstijn, J., & de Glopper, K. (2011). Modeling the development of L1 and EFL writing proficiency of secondary school students. *Language Learning, 61*, 31–79.

Shermis, M. D., & Burstein, J. (Eds.). (2013). *Handbook of automated essay evaluation: Current applications and new directions*. New York, NY: Routledge.

Shermis, M. D., & Hamner, B. (2013). Contrasting state-of-the-art automated scoring of essays. In M. D. Shermis, & J. Burstein (Eds.), *Handbook of automated essay evaluation: Current applications and new directions* (pp. 313–346).New York, NY: Routledge.

Simpson-Vlach, R., & Ellis, N. C. (2010). An academic formulas list: New methods in phraseology research. *Applied Linguistics, 31*, 487–512. http://dx.doi.org/ 10.1093/applin/amp058.

Sinclair, J. (1991). *Corpus, concordance, collocation*. Oxford University Press.

Tabachnick, B. G., & Fidell, L. S. (2001). *Using multivariate statistics*, 4th ed. Needham Heights, MA: Allyn & Bacon.

Thorndike, E. L., & Lorge, I. (1944). *The teacher's word book of 30,000 words*. New York, NY: Teachers College Columbia University. Toglia, M. P., & Battig, W. R. (1978). *Handbook of semantic word norms*. Hillsdale, NJ: Lawrence Erlbaum.

Weigle, S. C. (2010). Validation of automated scores of TOEFL iBT tasks against non-test indicators of writing ability. *Language Testing, 27*, 335–353. Xue, G., & Nation, I. S. P. (1984). A university word list. *Language Learning and Communication, 3*(2), 215–229.

Kristopher Kyle is an Assistant Professor in department of Second Language Studies at the University of Hawai'i. His research interests include second language writing and speaking, assessment, and second language acquisition. He is especially interested in applying natural language processing (NLP) and corpora to the exploration of these areas.

Scott Crossley is an Associate Professor at Georgia State University. His interests include computational linguistics, corpus linguistics, cognitive science, discourse processing, and discourse analysis. His primary research focuses on the development and application of computational tools in second language learning and text comprehensibility.

TEACHING ENGLISH IN THE TWO-YEAR COLLEGE

TETYC is one the web at http://www2.ncte.org/resources/journals/teaching-english-in-the-two-year-college/

Teaching English in the Two-Year College (TETYC) publishes articles for two-year college English teachers and those teaching the first two years of English in four-year institutions. We seek articles (4,000–7,000 words) in all areas of composition (basic, first-year, and advanced); business, technical, and creative writing; and the teaching of literature in the first two college years. We also publish articles on topics such as program and curriculum development, assessment, technology and online learning, writing program administration, developmental education in writing and reading, speech, writing centers in two-year colleges, journalism, reading, ESL, and other areas of professional concern.

A Partnership Teaching Externship Program: A Model that Makes Do."

We selected this article by Darin Jensen and Susan Ely because of the way it fills a gap in and advances important arguments about graduate preparation for instructors in two-year colleges. With the curricular range that includes, sometimes, multiple levels of non-degree credit/basic writing, as well as learning skills and critical reading courses, two-year colleges demand much of their instructors. As public institutions in the age of austerity, they are often also under-resourced and rely heavily on contingent instructors. Jensen and Ely's article draws from their study of what they call an 'externship' program designed to fill the gaps in graduate preparation that many instructors feel when they begin teaching at two-year colleges. Part description of the program, part reflection, part critique, the article uses voices of the participating instructors to make visible the challenges instructors face in adapting to new teaching environments and offer a road-map for helping such instructors develop professionally in ways that support their work in two-year college English.

A Partnership Teaching Externship Program: A Model That Makes Do

Darin Jensen and Susan Ely

This essay and the teaching externship it describes grew out of our attempt to respond to gaps in two-year college English instructor preparation, particularly in basic writing, at Metropolitan Community College in Omaha, Nebraska.

The authors are English faculty members at Metropolitan Community College (MCC) in Omaha, Nebraska. We were hired as full-time English faculty members in 2009. We were told that at least half of our teaching load was to be in developmental or basic writing. Neither of us had any graduate coursework in teaching developmental writing or in teaching at the two-year college. In 2012, Darin Jensen decided to pursue a PhD at the University of Nebraska at Lincoln with hopes to investigate the history of basic writing and teaching in the two-year college primarily because of the gaps he discovered in his own preparation to be a teacher. At the same time, Susan Ely became the coordinator of basic writing at our institution and had many of the same questions. Like many teachers, she had taken an introductory course for teaching assistants that provided graduate students a light overview of composition theory and pedagogy; however, none of the readings had anything to do with basic writing or teaching in the two-year college.

When we were hired, neither of us was aware that basic writing was its own field of study with a body of knowledge and best practices. Eventually, we took on administrative roles where part of our duties were to hire part-time professionals; soon we found that our lack of knowledge about basic writing and teaching in two-year college contexts was present in the pool of teachers from which we were hiring, too. This problem led us to design and implement an externship partnership with the University of Nebraska at Omaha (UNO) in basic writing so could address these gaps in our local context.

Over the last four years we designed and implemented a teacher development program with graduate students that encompasses theory and practice of basic writing in a co-teaching model. Currently, the graduate students receive credit in the form of an independent study. As part of the course, the students receive classroom experience similar to a K–12 student teaching model. The externship includes coteaching, lesson planning, grading, and working through a developmental writing course side-by-side with an experienced instructor. We offer this model as one that demonstrates a way to build a program that meets the need of community colleges in hiring qualified instructors, that prepares graduate students for careers beyond graduate school, and that helps universities make important reforms in graduate programs to move beyond merely replicating scholars for research institutions. The conception of this model was to guide students in acquiring knowledge and experience that the authors had gained as practitioners but had not gained in preparation for this profession.

We designed the program around basic writing because there was an exigent need for qualified instructors who simply did not exist. At our institution, we are able to find many instructors experienced with first-year writing, even though those instructors almost always lack knowledge of the institutional, instructional, and student contexts of the community college. We hasten to add that we know all too well that two-year college faculty are expected to teach other developmental courses such as reading courses and learning skills courses without adequate graduate preparation or professionalization. We lament that fact and know that it is an important area of study. However, that work, while important and worthwhile, is beyond the scope of this essay.

We believe that our problem is a common one. For example, Holly Hassel and Joanne Baird Giordano tell readers in "Occupy Writing Studies" of the difficulties faced by new instructions at the community college. They note the "adjustment to teach this student population" as well as the areas in which the instructors were trained presented significant challenges (134). Hassel and Baird Giordano argue that more scholarship is needed from "open-enrollment institutions" to provide the knowledge base these teachers need (134).This call is not new. In

2001, Jo Ann Buck and MacGregor Frank wrote that "graduate level preparation for community college teaching was deficient in the early 1970s" (241).They located the problem in the disconnect between the mission of the community college and the graduate students' preparation, lamenting that it was no surprise that teachers were underprepared, giving this disconnection (241). When we began, we saw the externship as merely meeting our local need, but we believe the model also enters into and draws attention toward a national need. Further, we designed this program to be activist in nature. We strongly believe that the lack of teacher preparation for the profession of two-year college English instructor, and for the discipline of basic writing in particular, is a disadvantage to the two-year college students who are often underrepresented and underprepared students. It is also disadvantageous to graduate students who are left without adequate professional preparation. Here we draw on Patrick Sullivan for inspiration. In "The Two-Year College Teacher-Scholar-Activist" he eloquently argues that teachers in the two-year college engage in the noble work of democratizing American higher education (327). We believe that training teachers for the important context of open admissions institutions makes that work possible.

Background

When we began our externship program in 2012, we did not look to the literature for other models. We created our model wholly out of what we could get our institution and UNO to agree to do. However, as we began to revise the program, we looked for models of professional preparation to inform our work. Unfortunately, such models are rare. Holly Hassel's review of 239 issues of *TETYC* from 2001 to 2012 bears this out. Her project took as a starting point a 1999 article that outlined future research areas at the two-year college. Using that frame, she found that authors in the journal had "directly addressed [. . .] identity and technology" and had produced "notable essays [. . .] for research, advocacy, or professional service" (346–47). Hassel goes on to identify areas in need of serious representation—noting that in more than a decade of articles in the flagship journal of two-year scholarship "just 8 of 239 (3 percent) of articles address preparing future faculty to teach in the two-year college, including a group of five professional documents," and that none of those articles were formal studies (355). This finding affirmed both our and our colleagues' lack of preparation to teach in the two-year college as being widespread. *TETYC* is not the only site for such scholarship, but even sources such as the National Association for Developmental Education (NADE) or the *Journal of Basic Writing* have paid scant attention to this issue. This fact emphasizes what we take to be Hassel's point: there is a serious gap in the research and scholarship of teacher preparation in our profession.

Moreover, as we examined the literature, we found that this gap was systemic and historic. Ellen Andrews Knodt, in "Graduate Programs for the Two-Year College Faculty: History and Future Direction," locates the cause of this problem in universities' orientation toward graduate education, noting difference of status with the mission of teaching giving them "almost by definition" an "inferior status" in higher education (125).

A decade later, a Two-Year College English Association committee authored the "TYCA White Paper on Developmental Education Reforms" wherein they also take up this gap in training and preparation. The committee offers "recommendations for national disciplinary organizations," which include a call to encouraging graduate programs to provide preparation for "two-year college teacher scholars" (Hassel et al. 228).The Modern Language Association recognizes this gap as well in its 2014 Report of the MLA Task Force on Doctoral Study in Modern Language and Literature. In it the writers argue against the "narrow replication" of scholars and for more substantive training in teaching. The document mentions community colleges as a career option more than once. From reading these documents, we can see there is an awareness across English studies that the community college is an important site of work and that training for that profession is lacking.

To this point we believe it is imperative to add attention to basic writing preparation as well. In her 2006 article "Reasoning the Need: Graduate Education and Basic Writing," Barbara Gleason found fewer than twenty graduate courses in teaching basic writing across the country. To put this into some context, the American Association of Community Colleges' 2015 Fact Sheet reports that more than 12 million students attended community college in 2014 and that this number represented 46 percent of all undergraduates (AACC). The National Conference of State Legislaturesin its report on remediation found multiple studies showing more than 50 percent of community college students are placed in a remedial or developmental class (Bautsch 1).At Metropolitan Community College, 48 percent of our incoming students placed into developmental writing (see Appendix B on the *TETYC* website). If we take these figures, we might guess that half of students entering community colleges took a developmental writing course. If that is true, then millions of students begin in developmental writing courses at community colleges every year, and very few courses or programs exist to prepare faculty to serve these students successfully. Gleason highlights these high stakes, noting that "basic writing's central mission merits the attention of every professional in composition and rhetoric" because basic writing advocates for "student access to higher education" (49).

We believe that this lack of teacher preparation is systemic. In fact, just one issue of *TETYC*, March 2001, is devoted to future faculty training. In that issue there are four articles"discussing teacher training for future faculty members"(Reynolds). Further, in her research, Gleason found just two issues of the *Journal of Basic Writing* "focused entirely on professional preparation for teachers (Spring/Summer 1981) and (Spring/Summer 1984" (50).At the time we designed our program, resources like the 2001 issue of *TETYC* were unknown to us. Even if we had these resources, the fact is that they are between fifteen and thirty-five years old. Clearly, the lack of preparation and historical context for two-year writing teachers is emblematic of the invisibility of two-year college teachers' work. Works like W. Norton Grubb's *Honored but Invisible* and Barbara K. Townsend and Susan B. Twombly's *Community College Faculty: Overlooked and Undervalued* attest to this at both the level of graduate preparation and two-year institutional attention to teaching. In particular, Grubb points out in his study that we have very little idea of what a teacher really looks like in the community college. He tells his readers that "there's almost no information about what teaching looks like in the 'teaching college'" and that the teaching has "never been the subject of sustained analysis of what happens or why it looks as it does" (11).Townsend and Twombly put the invisibility Grubb describes into context, noting that "there is little discussion of preparation programs and even less discussion of skills," and that what there is seems to be "ad hoc and uncoordinated" (42). To this we would add what community college professionals already know: two-year colleges serve the largest portion of first-generation students, the largest number of minority students, and the largest number of students who come from lower socioeconomic backgrounds. This fact speaks to our mission as a profession. To that point, Mark Reynolds and Sylvia Holladay-Hicks wrote in their preface to *The Profession of English in the Two-Year College:* "the two-year college is uniquely American: No other institution of higher education is dedicated to fulfilling the educational needs and goals of all the people in the community" (vii). With that mission in mind, and with the notion that the access for millions of unprepared students to engage in democratic education, civic involvement, and greater economic agency being at stake, we began to attempt to meet this need by designing a program that fit our local exigencies.

EXTERNSHIP PROGRAM

We choose the word *externship* here because the word is defined as experiential learning opportunities, similar to an internship, provided by educational institutions to give students short practical experiences in their field of study. We choose the term, too, because Gregory Cowan, a scholar who spearheaded some of the earliest thinking and writing about training programs for community college faculty, suggested the term in a 1971 *College Composition and Communication* article. We rejected the term *apprentice* because of its problematic hierarchical nature. When we decided on the externship model, we turned to our contacts at UNO to gauge their interest. UNO has an MA in English with about fifty graduate students in the department at any one time (Christensen). Many of these graduates go on to teach at MCC, and more than half of our full-time faculty have graduate degrees from the university. We felt because of this existing connection that they would be interested in a partnership. We were also aware of an earlier failed apprenticeship model. In speaking with their English faculty, Dr. Tammie Kennedy noted that UNO's graduate students "often don't have a deeper understanding of the needs and challenges of community college students, as well as the pedagogical issues, especially basic writing and ESL" (interview). After we met with the faculty at the university, we were all amenable to the program and saw its worth.

Our difficulty arose from the fact that there was no system in place to facilitate the partnership. What we settled on for our first year was a scheme wherein the interested graduate students would take an internship course at the university where we served as the site of the internship. This proved to be a problematic model because the graduate students were not really interns, but were student-teachers. Further, the model was problematic because the graduate students did not produce a paper or academic project. In the subsequent years, Dr. Kennedy at the university took the students on in an independent study. In this version, the graduate students created a portfolio of the teaching materials they had co-created and used while in the externship, as well as a teaching philosophy aimed at a community college audience and a new CV. We found this model more useful for students. Dr. Kennedy works with us at the end of the semester to determine a grade for their externship.

Dr. Kennedy receives no financial remuneration for this work. She found that the work is difficult to categorize in terms of quantifying it as part of her workload and "affects compensation and/or how the work counts in terms of teaching/ scholarship/service," which is a significant and enduring issue (interview). An early reviewer of this manuscript suggested that we have a memorandum of understanding with the university, but such an agreement would not provide a solution for how this work should be counted. The truth is that community college teaching, because of its low value in the university, is a hard sell. We also found little support from our college. Even though the authors were essentially mentoring, co-teaching, and facilitating discussion on the theory and practice of teaching writing, no release time was made available for this work. We were able to negotiate a $500 stipend as compensation. We make this point not to elicit sympathy, but to demonstrate the difficult realities of inter-institutional work and of making institutional and systemic change. Ironically, while we were attempting to facilitate this experience for the graduate students, we were also learning how difficult it was to actually create such a partnership and have the work valued.

We designed the program so that we could engage with the externs in a series of readings beginning in January and then co-create the syllabi for the class. Following that, the graduate student would co-teach with the instructor during the spring quarter at the community college. Since the university is on a semester system and the college is on a quarter system, we employed the two-month difference to have four meetings to discuss a series of readings. We designed the teaching program so that the graduate students would have the theory first and then engage in teaching. The time commitment for the externs is quite extensive. Each graduate student had to be in class with the instructor for all forty-four contact hours during the quarter, the discussion meetings were more than two hours each, there were twenty-two preparation hours (one before each class), and attendance was required at a minimum of one grading session, which accounted for approximately four hours. The total time commitment for the program approached approximately eighty hours. Like a student-teacher/practicum teacher relationship in K–12 preservice teacher preparation, this externship provided guided practice and side-by-side mentoring for the novice teacher. What follows is an in-depth look at facets of the program.

READINGS

As we said, the graduate students read four sets of readings to provide them with background and theories about teaching in a basic writing classroom. We attempted to divide the readings thematically. Our choices were based on privileging background information for the graduate students on the different issues they would encounter in their classrooms. For the first meeting in each of the years, we have had the students read Mike Rose's *Lives on the Boundary*. From the second year on, we added Burton R. Clark's "The 'Cooling-Out' Function in Higher Education" to the first meeting. We feel that Rose's work provides one of the best and most accessible narrative introductions to the students and issues in developmental education, while Clark's essay, even though it's dated, provides an important counterpoint to the promise of developmental education in Rose's book. When these works are in conversation, it allows the students and the facilitators to have a discussion about the nature of developmental education. In some years, we have also added a portion of Mary Soliday's *The Politics of Remediation*. This work demonstrates the artificial and cyclical nature of remedial education and who is classified as remedial. Putting her introduction and first chapter into conversation with Rose's discussion of historical levels of literacy early in his book is a revelation for the graduate students, as it was, frankly, for us when we first encountered it.

In the first year, we relied almost totally on Susan Naomi Bernstein's *Teaching Developmental Writing*, which is a comprehensive resource we've found useful in introducing teachers to developmental education because it provides a broad background that gives an important historical context. We also used other texts such as Rose's. One of our reviewers noted that many of the readings we used were out-of-date. Part of the "datedness" of the readings came from our ignorance of up-to-date sources as we began the work on this program; however, a significant reason for keeping readings that are out-of-date is that they provide a historical contextualization of the work that we do—thus, we believe, grounding teachers in the discipline.

In each of the years we have given attention to ESL students and the special concerns that they bring to our courses because they make up a significant part of our student population. At our institution, nonnative speakers and generation 1.5 students are often tracked into developmental coursework for a variety of reasons. Authors such as Ilona Leki, Dana Ferris, and Ann Johns offer essential contexts for framing and responding to the teaching and writing of these students. Another important theme for us in the readings was the working-class or first-generation student. We found Adrienne Rich's essay, "Teaching Language in Open Admissions" to be an excellent way to begin talking about teaching our students. This year we are using an even larger section of Patrick Finn's book *Literacy with an Attitude* because we want to talk more about the notion of educating students in their own best interests. The graduate students responded positively to these kinds of essays because the readings were new to them—in a sense the essays revealed a new perspective. The reading lists for two of the four years of the externship are included in Appendix A (found on the *TETYC* website).We have included the lists because we believe they offer a genesis of a reading list for graduate students and new professionals in the two-year college. We believe, too, that it is worth comment to say that the reading list is a demonstration of the interdisciplinary nature of being an instructor in the community college.

Teaching in a two-year college requires familiarity with composition, reading, ESL, andragogy—the method and practice of teaching adults—class studies, and more.We wanted to be sure to have some history of higher education so that the externs could understand how public thinking about higher education influences their work and realize that the history of community college students, and of basic writers in particular, has been tumultuous at times.These lists represented just the barest framing for our graduate student partners.The graduate students themselves responded very positively about the breadth of the readings. For example, Bobby felt the readings "reinforced the need to consider the whole student," while Emily told us in her interview that the readings "enabled me to have a deeper understanding of diverse student populations and the practice of teaching itself." Jean related that the "readings and the following discussions often caused me to reflect on my previous teaching experiences as well as my present classroom approach." From their responses, we are hopeful that we've helped them begin to think about this work in ways that enhance their teaching practices and the learning of their future students.

Course Planning and Teaching

Another facet of our externship was our attention to course and lesson planning. Both of us met with our graduate student partners to design a syllabus and a general assignment sheet. Nearly all of the graduate externs had been TAs, but they had had little preparation in syllabus and course design beyond the ubiquitous TA practicum. Sitting down, discussing the objectives of the course, scaffolding assignments, discussing a reasonable workload were novel experiences for them. Interestingly, engaging in the reading and discussion caused us to engage in reflection about our syllabi as well. In this way, we've added essays to our syllabi which we were unaware of until these discussions with externs. In addition to planning the syllabus together, the externs met with us for an hour before each class to go over the lesson. Afterward we spent another hour reflecting on the class that we had just taught. The graduate students found this experience to be immensely valuable. We hasten to add that we have become more reflective teachers as a result. We say this because the process of sitting down and articulating each curricular choice caused us to question and look at those choices anew.

For our part, we teach the first section of MCC's developmental English class as a dialectical classroom. We are focused on developing literacy in an integrated reading and writing model. Therefore, we privilege vocabulary acquisition, close reading, summary, explicit instruction, and discussion as we negotiated meaning with the students. These exercises scaffold into response assignments that roughly follow the process model of composition. Further, to increase the knowledge base of students, we use themed readings for the entire term. We use different themes in our classroom, with one of us using narratives such as Sherman Alexie's *The Absolutely True Diary of a Part-Time Indian* and Sandra Cisneros's *The House on Mango Street* and the other using Immaculée Ilibagiza's *Left to Tell Discovering God amidst the Rwandan Holocaust* and other readings. We built our classes around themes—the theme in my class is schooling and identity, for example—because our college is divided into several campuses, and each campus has a distinctly different student population. We read, write, and discuss in every class. Importantly, we write with our students and had our externs do the same.Writing with the students allows us to experience the work and show ourselves doing the work, which is something that we've discovered is often unfamiliar to our students. Essentially, while we are co-teaching with the graduate student externs, we are modeling such behaviors as writing with the students, lesson planning, and reflection that we have come to believe are the hallmarks of effective teaching in a developmental classroom.

A note about our curriculum: we are aware that there is a current trend to use more nonfiction and expository texts, perhaps largely growing out of the Common Core. One of the reviewers of this manuscript wanted us to address our choice of narrative texts here. What we can say is that we pick texts that are engaging for our students. Further, *The House on Mango Street* and *The Absolutely True Diary of a Part-Time Indian* have allowed Darin to explicitly discuss the process of literacy, schooling, and identity. Susan's use of the memoir, while narrative, allows students to build knowledge of a subject, in this case the Rwandan genocide. We've allowed our experience and our students' engagement to drive our text selection.

Grading Writing

Another facet of the program that was novel to us was the co-assessing of student work with the graduate student extern. For at least one major assignment, and a small number of lower-stakes assignments, the graduate student and the authors read, commented on, and assessed work together. Darin had attended an MA program that used a portfolio system while he was a teaching assistant, so he was accustomed to reading student writing and coming to a consensus. Susan didn't come from a portfolio system and had only done a small bit of norming. This experience allowed us to come to terms with Bernstein's assessment that "students in basic writing need to practice writing full-length essays and can learn to understand rules of grammar, syntax, and style in rhetorical terms" (ix, quoting Micchiche). In our classes, since we eschew skill and drill pedagogy, we choose to concentrate on grammar in the context of writing increasingly complex summaries and responses.

Neither we nor the graduate students had any experience with co-assessing assignments. This experience allowed us to establish and discuss our hierarchy of concerns in assessing writing, how we triage issues, how and why we write the comments that we do, both marginal and terminal, and why we make our determinations. For example, with a set of responses, Darin and one of the externs each wrote a terminal comment on the essay. After the writing, they discussed why they emphasized what they did in the comment and then discussed how it might be heard by the student. It is an experience that both of us wished we had had when learning to teach, and one that all of the externs responded to positively in the program. And just as with the co-teaching, the act of drawing attention to our own assessment and commenting strategies helped us better rationalize and understand many of the choices we make in evaluating student work. We found that we all relished the intense relational experience of grading together. And while far too time-intensive to ever do on a regular basis, it is a practice we would like to research further.

REFLECTION AND OUTCOMES

Finally, we want to hear the voices of our externs. We interviewed them for this project with an IRB-approved set of questions. We are using pseudonyms. In their interviews, all of the respondent graduate students felt the experience has positively affected their teaching. Bobby wrote that he learned "how to teach and talk with diverse classrooms," which has "in turn allowed me to give more students freedom through language." Emily emphasized another aspect of practice, noting that she has "dedicated more time to reflections" and feels "more confident in my teaching and in addressing issues that come up in class with students." Powerfully and gratifyingly, Jean asserted that her very definition of teaching had changed as a result of the program:

> I have learned through experience that for a student to be successful in attaining any writing goal, I have to meet them where they are in their writing experience. I have learned that students often have different definitions of success than I do,

and I have come to accept this and help them accomplish whatever goal they have in the time they are in my class. I now understand teaching is not just teaching; it also means being a confidant sometimes, a counselor on other days, a coach or a cheerleader on others. I would define a writing teacher as one who provides guidance, instruction, and coaching throughout the stages of the writing process to help students become better thinkers, better writers, and better citizens. A teacher is someone who helps students discover their own agency and voice and helps them understand how to harness the power of that voice to be an effective agent of change.

Jean describes eloquently both the level of confidence and understanding that we desire in the preparation of future two-year college teachers. Bobby touched on this in his interview, too, noting that his previous "pedagogical practices were a sort of cobbled together mess of means I had picked up from watching successful teachers over the years," and that the work of the externships provided "direction, theory, development, and implementation." From these comments, it is clear that the program of coordinated reading, discussion, and co-teaching felt successful and satisfying to the participants. Bobby reported that his teaching evaluations after the program in his TA-ship as the university were markedly higher, too. At the very least, we believe our model provides direction and confidence for the novice teacher, which is a welcome change when compared to the overwhelming feelings other instructors describe in the literature (Fisher; Hassel and Giordano).

Importantly, too, in an age where adjunct employment has become the norm and full-time instructorships are a rare commodity, we want to say that three of the four externs in the first two years have found full-time employment, with the other going on to further study. Emily was an interview finalist twice before getting a full-time instructorship at a community college. She had a full-time position within two years of graduating and reported that she felt much better prepared for her interviews, especially with her ability to talk about the mission and purpose of community colleges. Jean is a non-tenure-track writing instructor at her university and has been a finalist for full-time community college positions as well. Nancy has a job teaching ESL in the community, and this is exactly the job for which she hoped the externship would prepare her. Obviously, these cases are so small in number that it would be unwarranted to draw large generalizations from them;

however, most of the adjuncts at our community college spend years being adjuncts, and these few teachers who had the externship experience seemed to do markedly better in getting to later stages of the interview process.

Conclusion

The externship program is continuing this year with one student. We hope to grow the program in the future. However, given that the work is a serious time commitment, and that the systems of the university and the college require finding tactics that allow for minimal compensation for the instructors, and that we haven't found a way to pay the externs for their work yet, it would be overly generous and optimistic to call this program sustainable and replicable at this time. We see our program as a serious and needed reform for the gross lack of training that universities provide to graduate students, many of whom will go on to be community college instructors. We know that we join the TYCA authors in the challenge of being college faculty who are often called on to make changes in persistence and completion "with little time for study and without training and compensation" (227). We know that we share the conclusions of the MLA report calling for better and more attention to teaching preparation, too. The task force calls on graduate programs, specifically doctoral programs, to "*Strengthen teaching preparation*," noting that "as a central component of doctoral education, preparation for teaching should include course work, practical experience, and mentoring. Pedagogic training should introduce students to the diverse missions, histories, and demographics of a wide range of institutions" (2). In our externship, we see ourselves providing that mentoring and also pedagogical and, frankly, andragogical training. However, the systems of the university, and we imagine most graduate programs, are not designed in a way that invites highly skilled two-year college practitioners to teach and be recognized in the university system. Ideally, one of the facilitators of a program like ours would be employed and compensated by the university, able to assign the grade for the independent study or course that the student is taking. Only then will sustainable bridges be built that will help graduate students move into professional teaching lives in community colleges in more substantive ways.

We believe, to draw on Sullivan again, that programs such as ours help to "deliberately frame our professional identity, in part as activists—accepting and embracing the revolutionary and inescapably political nature of our work," and that, in Sullivan's words, "this activism might, in fact, require some front-line, in-your face political work as we seek to create positive change in our communities and on our campuses" (327–28). Our program, while local and small, is an example of activism that challenges how we prepare our graduate students and demonstrates how we might accomplish this work one institution at a time.

Appendix A — Sample Graduate Student Reading Lists from the Externship Project

2013 Reading List for Teaching developmental Writing Author 1 and Author 2 Facilitators

Texts:
Bernstein, Susan Naomi. *Teaching Developmental Writing: Background Readings.* 3rd ed. New York: Bedford/St. Martin's, 2007. Print.
Rose, Mike. *Lives on the Boundary.* New York: Penguin, 1990. Print.

January 29—Introduction
Mike Rose. *Lives on the Boundary.*

February 14—Who Is the Basic Writer?
Jane Maher."'You Probably Don't Even Know I Exist': Notes from a Prison College Program"
Pages 56–71 in *Teaching Developmental Writing*

Ann E. Green."My Uncle's Guns."
Pages 73–82 in *Teaching Developmental Writing*

Valerie Kinlock. From "Revisiting the Promise of Students' Right to Their Own Language: Pedagogical Strategies"
Pages 40–55 in *Teaching Developmental Writing*

February 25—Thinking about Assessment

Dana Ferris."One Size Does Not Fit All: Response and Revision Issues for Immigrant Students"
Pages 83–100 in *Teaching Developmental Writing*

Patrick L. Bruch."Interpreting and Implementing Universal Instructional Design in Basic Writing"
Pages 164–174 in *Teaching Developmental Writing*

CCCC. CCCC Position Statement on Assessment. Pages 391–400 in *Teaching Developmental Writing*

March 15—Literacy
Glynda Hull and Mike Rose."'This Wooden Shack Place':The Logic of an Unconventional Reading."
Pages 246–259 in *Teaching Developmental Writing*

Barbara Gleason."Returning Adults to the Mainstream:Toward a Curriculum for Diverse Student Writers."
Pages 214–238 in *Teaching Developmental Writing*

Adrienne Rich."Teaching Language in Open Admissions." Pages 191–205 in *Teaching Developmental Writing*

April 5—ESL and Generation 1.5
Ilona Leki."Reciprocal Themes in ESL Reading and Writing." Pages 121–143 in *Teaching Developmental Writing*

Yu Ren Dong."The Need to Understand ESL Students' Native Language Writing Experiences."
Pages 370–380 in *Teaching Developmental Writing*

Beth Hartman and Elaine Tarone. From "Preparation for College Writing." Pages 381–389 in *Teaching Developmental Writing*

May 10—Program Structures
William B. Lalicker."A Basic Introduction to Basic Writing Program Structures: A Baseline and Five Alternatives."
Pages 15–25 in *Teaching Developmental Writing*

Karen Uehling. Creating a Statement of Guidelines and Goals for Boise State University's Basic Writing Course: Content and Development." Pages 27–38 in *Teaching Developmental Writing*

2016 Reading List for Basic Writing Apprenticeship
January 15, 1:30–3:30 PM—community colleges, the work, and the profession

Author	*Title*	*Format*
Mike Rose	*Lives on the Boundary*	Book
TYCA	Guidelines for Preparing…	Web
Burton R. Clark	"Cooling-Out" Function…	PDF

January 29, 1:30–3:30 PM—developmental writing and remediation

Naomi Bernstein	Introduction	Purple book
Adrienne Rich	Teaching Language…	Purple Book
Mike Rose	Remediation…	Purple book

February 12, 1:30–3:30 PM—ESL writing and writers
Dana Ferris and Ch. 1 and 2 PDFs
Michael Hedgecock Ann Johns Socioliterate Approaches PDF
CCCC Statement of Second Language Web Writing and Writers

February 26, 1:30–3:30 PM—class and education
Patrick Finn Chapters 1–12 Book

Spring classes begin on March 10th, so you will have to arrange a time to develop a syllabus with your partner instructor.

Books to be bought:
Rose, Mike. *Lives on the Boundary*

Bernstein, Naomi. Ed. *Teaching Developmental Writing*, 4th ed. (purple book) Finn, Patrick. *Literacy with an Attitude*

Appendix B: Interview Questions

Questions for the Participants in the Program

Did the apprenticeship program help you become a more reflective practitioner in the classroom? Please explain.

Did the apprenticeship program help you become a teacher-scholar? Please explain.

Did the apprenticeship program help you to better understand diversity, including ethnic diversity, socioeconomic diversity, and diverse ability learners? Please explain.

Did the apprenticeship program help you build better pedagogy to serve students? Please explain.

Did the apprenticeship program help you to ground your teaching in theory and research? Please explain. I would also be interested to know here if you felt that there were gaps present after the apprenticeship or if the apprenticeship pointed you to any new areas of research inquiry?

Did the apprenticeship program help you to develop curriculum either on your own or collaboratively? How was/is the curriculum developed different than other curriculum you had previously developed?

Did the apprenticeship program help you to serve your college and community or perhaps help you see how you might serve your college and community differently? Please explain.

Did definitions of teaching change for you because of the apprenticeship program? If so, can you explain how?

Would other members of your graduate school cohort have been helped if they had taken this program? If yes, how would they have been helped?

Would you recommend that this kind of apprenticeship be a part of the mandatory course of study or a track in a graduate program? Will you please explain your answer?

After this experience, do you see the mission of higher education differently? Please explain.

What about the apprenticeship attracted you to it?

What were the best aspects of the apprenticeship?

- Did you feel that the apprenticeship provided preparation in theory, practice, and research that you would not have otherwise gotten in your graduate program? Please explain.
- If you are working in higher education now, did the apprenticeship give you knowledge and skills that made you better prepared for the position? Please explain.
- What did you learn about higher education policy and the politics of education during the apprenticeship?

Questions for the Teacher-Facilitators of the Apprenticeship Program

- What were your goals and outcomes for the apprenticeship? Why did you choose them?
- After facilitating the apprenticeship, how has your own teaching changed, if at all?
- Did you have an opportunity to engage in an apprenticeship like this when you were a student? If not, would you have if it had existed? Please explain.
- Why did you found the apprenticeship?
- What does the apprenticeship provide that a traditional graduate assistant teaching position cannot? Please explain.
- What did you teach the students about the community college, institutional contexts, and other items that might fit under the notion of higher education politics?
- What components did you include in the apprenticeship? How did you prioritize them in your work with the apprentice?
- What were your guiding principles for your work with the apprentice? Why did you choose those principles? For example, did you think it particularly important to demonstrate a student-centered classroom, or that explicit instruction was important?
- How did engaging in and facilitating the apprenticeship aid in your professional development as a teacher? Please explain.
- What were the challenges of the apprenticeship? Scheduling? Institutional support? Please explain.

Questions for the Faculty Sponsor of the Apprenticeship Program

- Why did you think this was an important program to bring to your institution?
- Can you describe your experience with community colleges?
- What do you think the typical faculty member's experience is with community colleges in your department and institution?

Did the program aid in your students' professional development? Please explain.

Is there a need to address preparation for teaching in the two-year college or teaching basic writing in your department?

How has that need been traditionally met?

How would this need be ideally met?

If you had the opportunity, would you have all graduate students engage in a teaching experience apprenticeship like this one? Please explain.

What were the challenges in sponsoring this apprenticeship experience? Were they academic? Institutional? Financial? Please explain.

WORKS CITED

American Association of Community Colleges (AACC)."2015 Fact Sheet." *American Association of Community Colleges,* 2015.Web.

Bautsch, Brenda. "Reforming Remedial Education." *Hot Topics in Education.* National Council of State Legislatures. Retrieved from http://www.ncsl.org/ documents/educ/remedialeducation_2013.pdf. 10 OCT 2015.

Bernstein, Susan Naomi. *Teaching Developmental Writing: Background Readings.* 4th ed. New York: Bedford/St. Martin's, 2013. Print.

Buck, Jo Ann, and MacGregor Frank."Preparing Future Faculty: A Faculty-in Training Pilot Program." *Teaching English in the Two-Year College* 28.3 (2001): 241–50.Web.

Christensen, Maggie. Personal communication. 31 Aug. 2015.

Cowan, Gregory."Guidelines for Junior College English Teacher Training Programs." *College Composition and Communication* 22. 3 (1971): 303–13. http://www.jstor.org/stable/356482. 19 Jan. 2016.

Finn, Patrick. *Literacy with an Attitude: Educating Working-Class Children in Their Own Self-Interest.* 2nd ed. Albany: State U of New York UP, 2009. Print.

Fisher, Nancy M."'You've Got to Role with the Punches': Developing as a TwoYear College Instructor." *Teaching English in the Two-Year College* 28.3 (2001): 271–76.Web.

Gleason, Barbara."Reasoning the Need: Graduate Education and Basic Writing." *Journal of Basic Writing* 25.2 (2006): 49–75.Web.

Grubb,W. Norton. *Honored but Invisible: An Inside Look at Teaching in Community Colleges.* New York: Routledge, 1999. Print.

Hassel, Holly."Research Gaps in Teaching English in the Two-Year College." *Teaching English in the Two-Year College* 40.4 (2013): 343–63.Web.

Hassel, Holly, et al."TYCA White Paper on Developmental Education Reforms." *Teaching English in the Two-Year College* 42.3 (2015): 227–43. Web.

Hassel, Holly, and Joanne Baird Giordano."Occupy Writing Studies: Rethinking College Composition Needs for the Teaching Majority." *College Composition and Communication* 65.1 (2013): 117–39.Web.

Kennedy,Tammie. Personal interview. 10 July 2015.

Knodt, Ellen Andrews."Graduate Programs for Two-Year-College Faculty: History and Future Directions." *The Profession of English in the Two-Year College*. Edited by Mark Reynolds and Sylvia Holladay-Hicks. Portsmouth, NH: Boynton/Cook Heinemann, 2005, 125–36.

Miller, Samantha. Personal interview. 14 July 2015.

MLA Task Force on Doctoral Study in Modern Language and Literature. "Report of the MLA Task Force on Doctoral Study in Modern Language and Literature." *MLA*. May 2014.Web.

Reynolds, Mark. "Editorial." *TETYC* 28.3 (2001): 237. PDF.

Reynolds, Mark, and Sylvia Holladay-Hicks, eds. *The Profession of English in the Two-Year College*. Portsmouth: Boynton/Cook, 2005. Print.

Rich, Adrienne. "Teaching Language in Open Admissions." *Teaching Developmental Writing: Background Readings*. 4th ed. Ed. Susan Naomi Bernstein. New York: Bedford/St. Martin's, 2013. 12–26. Print.

Smith, Ashley A. "Florida's Remedial Law Leads to Decreasing Pass Rates in Math and English." Inside Higher Education, 25 June 2015.Web.

Soliday, Mary. *The Politics of Remediation: Institutional and Student Needs in Higher Education*. Pittsburgh: U of Pittsburgh P, 2002. Print.

—."The Two-Year College Teacher-Scholar-Activist." *Teaching English in the Two-Year College* 42.4 (2015): 327–50. Web.

Townsend, Barbara K., and Susan B. Twombly. *Community College Faculty: Overlooked and Undervalued*. San Francisco: Jossey-Bass, 2007. Print.

Walker, Angelika. Personal interview. 21 July 2015 Ward, Frankie. Personal interview. 15 July 2015.

Darin Jensen is an instructor at Des Moines Area Community College in Iowa. He has taught at three community colleges over the last 15 years. He can be reached at darin.l.jensen@gmail.com. Susan Ely is an instructor at Metropolitan Community College in Omaha, Nebraska. She primarily teaches basic writing and has served as coordinator of the Basic Writing Program. She may be reached at seely@mccneb.edu.

RHETORIC REVIEW

Rhetoric Review is one the web at https://www.tandfonline.com/toc/hrhr20/current

Rhetoric Review (RR), a scholarly interdisciplinary journal of rhetoric, publishes in all areas of rhetoric and writing, and provides a professional forum for its readers to consider and discuss current topics and issues. The journal publishes manuscripts that explore the breadth and depth of the discipline, including history, theory, writing, praxis, philosophy, professional writing, rhetorical criticism, cultural studies, multiple literacies, technology, public address, graduate education, and professional issues.

Making, not Curating, the Rhetorical Tradition: Ways through and beyond the Canon

Erika Claire Strandjord's article asks us to reconsider and take responsibility for the ways in which the rhetorical canon is framed and communicated through our pedagogies—specifically, course syllabi and curriculum design. As the peer reviewers of her article note, Strandjord's article makes "two noteworthy contributions: (1) demonstrating particular ways of remodeling an Introduction to Rhetoric course; and (2) invoking the discipline of folklore to argue that 'tradition' is a dynamic process of stewardship that shouldn't be conflated with 'canon.'"

Making, not Curating, the Rhetorical Tradition: Ways through and beyond the Canon

Erika Claire Strandjord

The idea of the rhetorical tradition continues to trouble scholars, in part because it is often conflated with the Western rhetorical canon. The current way we use the word tradition is tied to nineteenth–century ideas of inheritance and continuity, which reinforce the canon. Using folklore scholarship to redefine tradition as something we continuously make and take responsibility for moves away from the canon while still allowing for creative use of past rhetorical practices and theories. Redefining tradition as something we make and pass on responsibility for should inform our teaching and reform the syllabi we create for our rhetoric courses.

THERE'S SOMETHING WRONG WITH THE SYLLABUS

While building the syllabus for an introduction to rhetoric class in 2012,[1] I struggled with both my desire to provide a diverse range of rhetors and rhetoricians to read and with the sense that an introductory course should be an historical survey of the 2,500-year Western rhetorical canon (WRC).[2] Despite my desire to decenter the Western canon, the syllabus I ended up creating was predictably heavy on the Greeks and light on work done by marginalized people. On the one hand, I decided the syllabus choices I made were justified given that the course was introductory and only ten weeks long. On the other hand, I was dissatisfied with how the canonical readings narrowed the class's perspective so that we read everything as if it either confirmed or challenged the canon. Even though I was committed to questioning the canon and the exclusionary history of the rhetorical tradition, I reinforced that very canon in my pedagogy.

A brief Internet search for rhetoric syllabi confirms that I am not the only person with this problem; marginalized people's rhetorical theories and practices, if on a syllabus at all, are generally relegated to a single day or week. Increasing scholarship about noncanonical rhetoric has not yet broadly affected our classroom practices, especially at the introductory level. We can see this pattern in rhetoric readers, with gender/race/class often put into their own sections. Puzzling over this issue brought me to folklore scholars' writing on the meaning and power of tradition, writing that influenced my own scholarship. This research leads me to argue that the problem with the rhetorical tradition is not its resistance to change but rather our misunderstanding of the rhetorical tradition as equaling the Western rhetorical canon.

My desire to redefine tradition so that it is no longer synonymous with the canon does not mean that I no longer see the WRC as useful. As Robert R. Johnson notes:

> The act of constructing (or should I say "crafting"?) a knowledge base is in itself problematic. For one thing, the foundationalist ring of the term *base* conjures up formalist senses of categorizing that imbue the act as one of placing positivist notions of unchanging and settled definitions. ... On the other hand, crafting a visible construct is a beginning that can be played with, literally, as we seek some sense of the knowledges that comprise the craft of writing studies. (683)

Even though Johnson does not speak directly to the field of rhetoric, his analysis maps neatly onto the challenges facing teachers of rhetoric. Clinging to the canon suggests that there is a certain "truth" about rhetorical studies that can only be approached through the WRC (or at least through the canon first and only then through other paths). Despite this, we can see the continuing dominance of the Western rhetorical canon as an invitation to play with our course designs, as a chance to imagine crafting the rhetorical tradition in ways that interweave extracanonical and canonical rhetorical texts. In order to begin this playful crafting, I look at our current (mis)identification of the rhetorical tradition with the WRC and propose an alternative definition of tradition that allows for creativity.

Throughout this essay I refer to "the rhetorical tradition" and choose not to refer to "rhetorical traditions." Changing "tradition" to "traditions" has been proposed as a solution to the problem of the monolithic Western rhetorical canon (see Bizzell and Jarratt's "Report from the history of rhetoric discussion groups," for example).[3] However, pluralizing does not necessarily mean that every group's tradition of persuasion is going to be put on the same footing as the WRC. Pluralizing, in other words, can end up reinforcing the dominance of the Western rhetorical canon as the *real* rhetorical tradition and other rhetorical traditions as lesser.

Another reason I prefer to keep the singular, at least for the present, is that the plural "traditions" can seem to posit separate traditions that are parallel but not overlapping. It is clear that patterns of rhetorical practice from different peoples, places, and times intersect, overlap, borrow, and attempt to dominate each other or coexist. The rhetorical tradition can remain an overarching term that encompasses a human interest in and commitment to persuasion and meaning-making while still allowing room for specificity when we discuss particular communities and peoples with our students. Even so, using the singular "rhetorical tradition" can end up reinforcing the WRC and obscuring the rich variety of ways in which humans communicate and persuade. My hope is that redefining our idea of *tradition* will avoid that trap, but the argument over terms will surely continue.

Defining *Tradition* in the Rhetorical Tradition

The field of rhetoric and composition has a longstanding argument about what the rhetorical tradition is and how it does or does not fit with the Western rhetorical canon.[4] At the first Octalog in 1988, Nan Johnson discussed the "intellectual space which is created when we struggle to react to the demands and implications of multiple interpretations. This means going further than simply acknowledging that multiplicity is inevitable; it means feeling obliged intellectually by multiplicity" (46). Cheryl Glenn, at the second Octalog, made it clear that "multiplicity" must include "regendering" rhetoric to create "an expanded, inclusive rhetorical tradition" (29). These two scholars' ideas of engaging multiple voices and adding previously ignored and marginalized groups to the rhetorical tradition represent a broader, popular call for rhetoricians to look beyond the canon. That call, as the second and third Octalogs demonstrate, was heeded as scholars began to do more and more work that did not rely on or reinforce the canon.

However, calling for a reimagining of the rhetorical tradition as not the canon is still something we need to do. At the third Octalog, published in *Rhetoric Review* only four years ago, multiple scholars noted how our teaching of rhetoric has failed to reflect the multiplicity in our scholarship. Ronald L. Jackson II noted in his Octalog address,

> It seems to me we still teach rhetoric the way we always have. We still train students to ignore nonmainstream (that is, non-White) rhetorical traditions. As professors and scholars, we also tend to sidestep our responsibility to be epistemologically responsible and just within this vast terrain of rhetorical studies. (117–18)

Jackson's contention about our failure to revise our classroom practices is affirmed by Malea Powell, who argues that we still place the canon at the center of the field, calling that move "a narrowness of vision that insists on connecting every rhetorical practice on the planet to Big Daddy A and the one true Greco-Roman way" (121). Jackson and Powell are not alone in their critiques of the field, and from their and others' words, it is clear that even as we have expanded our study of rhetoric beyond the canon, we still have not taken on the responsibility of radically expanding our classroom work.

The canon is troubling, and we have had little success in destabilizing it despite years of valuable work in feminist, Native, African-American, disability, digital, and other rhetorics. These struggles, however, do not indicate a problem with a rhetorical tradition but rather with our understanding of it. A narrow understanding of tradition does not reflect the rich discussion of tradition in other fields, especially the field of folklore, which could help us decouple tradition from canon. Redefining *tradition* helps us become stewards of tradition rather than curators of the canon: Stewards value what has been entrusted to them while making changes and taking responsibility for moving into the future whereas curators preserve and display the past. The rhetorical tradition is worth stewarding because it joins us to valuable histories and practices, and it passes on responsibilities that give meaning to our scholarship and teaching. The rhetorical tradition, in other words, is not the canon, and the canon itself obscures the diverse beliefs and practices surrounding persuasion that make up the rhetorical tradition.

Tradition is not the Canon, and Vice Versa

Current rhetorical scholarship generally equates tradition with canon and the rhetorical tradition with the Western rhetorical canon. This conflation portrays the Western rhetorical canon as the uppercase Rhetorical Tradition, with other meaning-making and persuasive practices relegated to being lowercase rhetorical traditions, as Abraham Romney notes in "Indian Ability (*audilidad de Indio*) and Rhetoric's Civilizing Narrative" (17). This attitude echoes what Dorothy Noyes identifies as a nineteenth-century view of tradition as inheritance, in which "the vehicle is now itself sacred" (236). Similarly, folklore scholar Simon J. Bronner explains that tradition is often associated with "precedent, continuity, and convention" (146). The restrictive understanding of tradition that Noyes and Bronner criticize emphasizes top-down authority and explains in part how the canon resists revision: If we understand tradition as authoritative, sacred, and dependent on continuity, then texts, performances, and practices that do not obviously follow the pattern set by the canon are then excluded from, or only very reluctantly welcomed into, the rhetorical tradition.

Cheryl Glenn, in her groundbreaking *Rhetoric Retold*, explains the problem of expanding the canon thusly:

> For too long, the arbiters of canonical acceptance have operated on the basis of $X1$. Whenever a woman has accomplished the same goals as her male counterpart ... the stakes immediately rise. She may have achieved X, but she needs $X plus 1$ to earn a place in rhetoric. (15)

People excluded from power understand this challenge: In order to be acknowledged, they need to do and *be* more than those with access to power. Glenn's argument that a lack of extant texts from historically excluded rhetoricians works against their inclusion in the canon still rings true, but her analysis does not go far enough. Marginalized rhetoricians do not always follow the forms and genres of canonical texts in their own work, and so their place in the rhetorical *tradition* is unclear because they do not clearly belong in the *canon*.

We can see this problem as it plays out in the second edition of Bizzell and Herzberg's *The Rhetorical Tradition*, which did much to include rhetoricians previously excluded from the canon. While this anthology represents an important attempt to decenter the canon, no new anthology has been published. This means there is no single text to assign our students that both includes extracanonical rhetoric and positions that rhetoric as equal to canonical readings. Franny Howes critiques how the compendium continues to marginalize extracanonical rhetoricians in "Imagining a Multiplicity of Visual Rhetorical Traditions: Comics Lessons from Rhetoric History." She explains:

> This problem is not repaired by adding a few people of color to the narrative ... Gloria Anzaldúa's critique of this narrative and of ethnocentrism now appears at the very end of this book, page 1592 of 1673. What does it mean to situate a narrative about how the history of writing also begins with the Aztecs' "tlilli, tlapalli" at the very end of the history, rather than the beginning? (6)

Howes makes the very important point that how we physically position texts can marginalize certain rhetorical practices and reinforce the boundaries around the WRC. I would add that *The Rhetorical Tradition* also marginalizes new additions by juxtaposing them with canonical texts.

The section on nineteenth-century rhetoric demonstrates how inclusion can lead to marginalization. It begins with selections from Richard Whately's *Elements of Rhetoric*, which neatly follow the work from Blair and Campbell that ended the previous section. Selections from works by Maria Stewart, Sarah Grimké, Frederick Douglass, Phoebe Palmer, and Francis Willard appear after Whately, signaling a major departure from the previous canonical texts. Rather than presenting selections of treatises on rhetoric, these additions show women and African-Americans asserting rhetoricity and arguing for the right to speak and write for audiences. Quite simply, these texts seem not to belong in the canonical narrative of the rhetorical tradition because they don't fit in with the established pattern of texts; at best, they appear to be examples of that tradition put into practice by people who were arhetorical before encountering Western rhetoric. In the introduction to the section, Bizzell and Herzberg do an admirable job of contextualizing minority rhetorics in the nineteenth century, pointing to how difficult it was for marginalized people to make themselves heard in the public sphere. Furthermore, they point to how minority rhetors were able to "forge their own unique rhetorical identities, adapting traditional rhetoric and also bringing important new elements to the repertoire of Western rhetoric" (993). Acknowledging the contributions of African-Americans, women, and Native Americans marks an important shift in *The Rhetorical Tradition*, but by continuing to equate "traditional rhetoric" with "Western rhetoric," the volume still implicitly positions the Western rhetorical canon as the rhetorical tradition, with other practices reflecting and revising, but not representing unique elements of *the* rhetorical tradition.

If we understand the rhetorical tradition as the WRC, we will continue to argue about who does and does not belong. Challenges to the canon, when it is equated with tradition, become challenges to the rhetorical tradition. Traditions—because we learn them, live them, and teach them—evoke (and provoke) strong emotions, and so if we perceive resistance to the canon as the desire to destroy tradition, we will react accordingly. Rather than defend the canon or call for its destruction, I imagine a third way that seeks to honor what the WRC has given us, to decenter the canon's importance in our classrooms, and to teach our students about the responsibility we must take for both the worthy and dishonorable parts of the rhetorical tradition.

Redefining Tradition, or, Rebuilding our Rhetorical House

Our first step must be to gain a broader (and better) understanding of what tradition is. The nineteenth-century concept of tradition emphasizes continuity, authority, and a sacred regard for the texts and practices of the past. This definition takes us back to the canon, and so we must move to a more nuanced understanding of tradition in order to decenter the canon. The field of folklore offers rich resources for revising our understanding of tradition. Folklore scholars, like rhetoric scholars, are sensitive to context, power, and how action and speech are influenced by the present and the past. Folklore scholarship frequently employs ethnography and related qualitative methodologies, which are a basis of much rhetoric and composition scholarship, allowing for "ground-up" instead of "top-down" theory-building. Unlike rhetoric, folklore scholarship has a rich history of debating the term *tradition* in ways that do not conflate it with canon. Folklore scholars' discussion of tradition illuminates how we can reimagine the rhetorical tradition and more fully accept rhetorical practices and histories that are usually marginalized. Our desire for a more inclusive body of texts and practices suggests that we are already moving beyond a restrictive definition of the term—we have just not yet made this move explicit.

First revision to our definition of *tradition*: Tradition changes while maintaining connections to the past. Rather than present the rhetorical tradition (read: Western rhetorical canon) as immutable, this revision encourages us to see the past as a rich, adaptable resource. Folklore scholars have discussed this facet of tradition extensively. Mats Widbom summarizes this feature of tradition eloquently in "The Farms of Lima: Living and Building Between Tradition and Change." He claims:

> Tradition is something that is constantly being reinterpreted and recreated in the present, in dynamic oscillation between continuity and change ... the ability to renew one's home within the framework of tradition—to make extensions, refurbish, refurnish, replace, and redecorate—that is one of the most powerful incitements to everyday creativity. (140)

Tradition, in Widbom's argument, is a recursive process that continually moves between past and present while allowing the present-day carriers of tradition to make their own contributions and changes. In his essay Widbom writes about tradition in the context of historic homes in Sweden, homes that are still occupied and lived in. While homeowners have some limits on what they can do to the houses they inhabit, they are still free to make the homes their own and to make changes.

Taken metaphorically, we can see ourselves as inhabitants of the rhetorical tradition: Our homes may be built from different sets of texts and practices, but they share some common features. Very few of us, I imagine, would want to tear our rhetorical tradition down and start from scratch, but some features may not serve us now, and some may in fact make our homes unwelcoming. We have encountered or learned to value other texts and practices that can enhance our rhetorical tradition house, and we should incorporate them thoughtfully and responsibly.

Second revision to our definition of *tradition*: We are active participants in making and imagining the rhetorical tradition. While Widbom gives us a sense of how we can actively participate in changing the rhetorical home we live in, he does not fully articulate how we shape that tradition before passing it on. If the rhetorical tradition is made of past texts that exist in a canon, then our job is to simply pass on the whole package. If we, to follow Widbom, rearrange that canon, take out bits, and add in new bits, then we are active curators, not makers. In their introduction to *The Individual and Tradition: Folkloristic Perspectives*, folklorists Ray Cashman, Tom Mould, and Pravina Shukla present a further step we can take in rethinking tradition and our role in it:

> We all use elements of the past to meet our needs in the present and our hopes for the future. In the process we make tradition our own, leaving our marks ... they are all ... a reflection of the self as forged in the shaping and reshaping of tradition. (1)

We cannot simply view ourselves as carriers or curators of tradition; we must acknowledge that we "make tradition our own" and change both ourselves and the tradition in the process. Roy Wagner argues a similar point in *The Invention of Culture*, that culture is not separate from individuals but is continuously created and changed as people interact with their context. What does it mean "to make tradition our own" and continuously create it? It does not mean ownership in the sense of doing what we wish without regard for our effect on others and on the tradition. It does not mean that we can add or subtract from it without due consideration. Rather, making tradition our own gives us agency but also encourages reflection and a conscientious approach to teaching.

Third revision to our definition of *tradition*: What ultimately matters is the responsibility for rhetorical practices and texts that we value. A crucial piece of our responsibility to the rhetorical tradition comes from our relationships with our students. Even though the rhetorical tradition is larger and longer than one person could fully account for, passing on tradition depends on personal interactions between individuals and communities and the obligations such interactions create. Noyes proposes that we understand tradition as relational: "[L]et us return to that Roman act of tradition: the hand-to-hand transfer of—something. A practice, a body of knowledge ... " (248). Noyes makes tradition personal by reestablishing the idea of the "hand-to-hand transfer," which describes what we do when we teach. We hand over our rhetorical knowledge to our students, who will use it, build on it, and pass it on as well. It is important that we understand that what gets passed on in traditions and the communities that value them is not a sacred, immutable text. No, what makes tradition powerful is the responsibility that passes from person to person. Noyes argues this point, claiming:

> Let us agree that what is being transferred through the object is not in the first instance authority ... nor property. ... Rather, the transfer is of responsibility ... tradition is not at bottom either a badge of pride or an inheritance to display but a job that must be done [and] what it means, how it is to be used. (248)

Noyes's definition emphasizes the mutual act of giving and receiving and the obligation to honor and cultivate the tradition that comes along with the gift of a practice. It is not only the act that matters but also knowledge and stewardship that make tradition.[5]

Focusing on practices and our responsibility for them helps us review the rhetorical tradition as stewards rather than curators. As curators, we preserve and perhaps rearrange our syllabi, but as stewards we are free to broaden our teaching to embrace extracanonical rhetorical practices and communities that will enrich and enliven the rhetorical tradition. Approaching the rhetorical tradition in this way acknowledges both how we are enmeshed in the past and how we are active participants in using the past to affect—and effect—the present.

So, what does this mean for the rhetorical tradition? At the very least, it means that we can no longer confuse the Western rhetorical canon with the rhetorical tradition. It is unlikely that we were brought up in a rhetorical house constructed only with texts from the WRC, and so we cannot simply cling to the canon as if it were the best and only way to teach and understand rhetoric. We also need to rethink our attachment to the canon. For those of us who have strong attachments to parts of the rhetorical tradition that are not represented in the canon, this redefinition invites us to boldly claim equivalent status and value with the canon. For those of us who have strong ties to the WRC, a new understanding of tradition means that we cannot act as gatekeepers to the rhetorical tradition; instead we should welcome previously excluded meaning-making practices and theories into the tradition. Whichever stream we feel most allegiance to, one change is certain: We cannot continue to relegate women and marginalized peoples to one day or week of our syllabi in survey courses or any course if we want to be responsible stewards.

Teaching the Rhetorical Tradition: Guidelines and a Snapshot

I now turn to imagining ways we can approach the rhetorical tradition as scholars and teachers of rhetoric. My focus rests primarily on teaching for several reasons: first, because rhetorical education is part of our vocation; second, because many students share our classrooms for only one term, and we cannot count on giving them the canonical version of rhetoric one term and the remade rhetorical tradition another; third, because the classroom is a primary site of handing on and remaking tradition. Remaking the rhetorical tradition involves not only carefully selecting texts that teach the responsibilities we wish to pass on to our students but also thinking about what practices and metaknowledge we will pass on with the readings, audio pieces, films, hypertexts, and experiences we assign to our students.

My thinking about teaching the rhetorical tradition instead of the canon owes much to the pedagogical and scholarly work of others, showing once again that tradition is passed on through practice, not just texts. Nan Johnson's strategy of having students collect and present examples of rhetoric has convinced me that part of making students responsible for the rhetorical tradition must involve encouraging them to see the rhetorical work done by everyday texts, objects, and actions.[6] A summer CIC seminar run by Malea Powell taught me how the act of making things is also a process of making meaning and also how to sit and listen to texts and acts instead of going straight to criticism. Gabriela Raquel Ríos's work with khipu has inspired my thinking about what meaning-making practices we can bring into the classroom to shift our understanding of rhetorical practices into material, visual, and digital realms. Much of what follows is inspired by their work.

Teachers of rhetoric will not all agree on what we want to make students responsible for in the rhetorical tradition, and I see that as a good thing. Difference and dialogue can lead us to reflect more on the tradition we teach and on our responsibilities. However, I do think that there are certain elements that a class concerned with passing on responsibility should include. The first is polyvocality. Traditions are never singular or monolithic; even if there are agreed-upon norms, each person receiving tradition takes responsibility for it and shapes it in turn. Malea Powell's 2012 Chair's Address is an example of putting polyvocality into practice.[7] Powell incorporated other scholars' words and voices into her address, and each section in another speaker's voice began with, "This is my story," and in the printed version of the address, each story ends with the italicized words, "*Take this story. It's yours now. Do with it what you will*" (389–90). Powell refused to give a monovocal address, and each story that helped make up the speech was then gifted to the listeners and readers, an approach that clearly calls the audience to become responsible participants in listening to and passing on stories in the field of rhetoric and composition.

It is important in a tradition-centered classroom to have students not just listen to many voices but to encourage them to take responsibility for the stories they have heard. The second element of tradition-centered classrooms is what Gesa E. Kirsch and Jacqueline J. Royster call "excellence." In "Feminist Rhetorical Practices: In Search of Excellence," they define excellence thusly:

> Excellence involves an ethos of care, introspection, and attention to the material conditions of the past and the present. ... It entails an open stance, strategic contemplation, and creating a space where we can see and hold contradictions without rushing to immediate closure, to neat resolutions, or to cozy hierarchies and binaries. (664)

Kirsch and Royster's discussion of excellence sets a high standard for those who wish to practice it. Like polyvocality, excellence engages in tradition by asking practitioners to take responsibility for a variety of ideas, texts, and practices, to pay close attention to context, to listen, and to postpone judgment. To pursue excellence means to pay rigorous attention to the circulation of power and continuous questioning of the status quo. Students introduced to the rhetorical tradition in a way that engages with polyvocality and excellence would see themselves as embroiled in the rhetorical works and situations they learn and write about.

As scholars and teachers committed to polyvocality and excellence as a base, we should then ask ourselves the following questions:

1. What in the rhetorical tradition (both textual and nontextual) has informed my approach to the field?
2. What rhetorical practices and theories will pass on the responsibilities I wish to give to my students while still addressing the problematic nature of the rhetorical tradition?
3. How can I teach texts in ways that illuminate rhetorical practices and do not reify texts as sacred objects?
4. What will I have my students make and practice as they become responsible stewards of the rhetorical tradition?

Our answers will lead us down different paths of course design, and will likely eschew an historical survey. Instead, we can create syllabi that put readings together from different communities and times in ways that illuminate connections and acknowledge injustices, creating a richer approach to the rhetorical tradition.

To make these suggestions and questions more concrete, I return to the opening scene of this essay: the introduction to rhetoric class I taught several years ago. That class would proceed differently now: It would be messier and less linear, but also more representative of what the rhetorical tradition can look like. Upon reflecting on my work teaching and studying rhetoric, I have outlined two major goals for my own courses:

1. Students should take responsibility for the exclusionary nature of the Western rhetorical canon and understand that it is not the only path to rhetoricity.
2. Students should feel responsible for the rhetorical practices they engage in as members of communities and of society. They should take steps (however small) to practice rhetoric in the civic sphere.

Both goals are friendly to including readings from the WRC, but both also leave room for fieldwork that students can do in their own communities, which may not be represented in the canon. In what follows, I present a snapshot of what the first half of the term of my revised course would look like as well as the outlines of a term-long collaborative project. One thread running through the entire class would be the questions, "What practices does this text/performance value?" and "Who is being made responsible for the practices described/taught in this text?"

Because I want my students to think critically about tradition as they learn the rhetorical tradition, the course would begin with folklore scholarship defining tradition, including Noyes's essay "Tradition: Three Traditions" and the introduction to *The Individual and Tradition: Folkloristic Perspectives* by Cashman, Mould, and Shukla. For perspectives on the idea of the rhetorical tradition, students would read excerpts from the Octalogs and Jarratt and Bizzell's "Rhetorical Traditions, Pluralized Canons, Relevant History, and Other Disputed Terms." Students would write about the definitions of *tradition* in the readings to compare with discussions of *tradition* they found in popular culture. Explorations of the term *tradition* would provide an entry point to discussions of power, canon-formation, and the role of responsibility and practice in shaping and passing on tradition.

Moving forward, I would adopt the practice Annie Mendenhall in conversation suggested to me: start the class by reading extracanonical work and only then move to the canon. As some one teaching in North America, I would begin with rhetorical work done by Native peoples. For this beginning unit, students would read the *Haudenosaunee Great Law of Peace* (*Kaianerekowa Hotinonsionne/Gayanashagowa*) and Angela Haas's article "Wampum as Hypertext." Students would read these two texts to understand the rhetorical/textual theory that Haas is building and the theory and practice in the *Haudenosaunee Great Law of Peace*. Students would write a short paper or multimedia text exploring the rhetoric of these two texts and how they shape our understanding of rhetoric and tradition.

Next, students would read the David Hume and John Locke selections in *The Rhetorical Tradition* and the Constitution of the United States. Students would be encouraged to compare Hume, Locke, and the Constitution to the Native rhetorics studied earlier and to theorize ways in which the WRC draws from other peoples' rhetorical practices. An important part of this second step would be exploring how other theories and practices of persuasion have been ignored or erased from the Western rhetorical canon so that students understand both the richness of the rhetorical tradition but also the WRC's exclusionary history.

Teaching canonical texts only after establishing the value of marginalized rhetorical work helps counter the dangers of the comparative approach, which, as Daniel Cole writes, "risks suggesting to a greater or lesser degree that Native rhetorics are subordinate to Western rhetoric, or that they are best understood in relation to Western rhetoric" (126). Furthermore, by learning about how indigenous systems of government influenced the thinking of the likes of Benjamin Franklin and how wampum strings and belts can represent a sovereign origin of hypertext, students begin to understand the rhetorical tradition as independent of the canon.

This text selection sets the stage for further exploring the Western rhetorical canon both in its richness and its exclusion of large numbers of people. Additionally, the texts' civic and community focus introduces students to the ways in which the rhetorical tradition seeks to shape community and public discourse, the concentration of the rest of the course.

Following these first readings and writings, I would introduce students to the major project of the term: researching the rhetorical practices of Unraveled Crafters, an informal knitting and crocheting group that meets twice a month at a local library branch. This project would incorporate (and create) rhetorical knowledge and also allow students to explore what they had learned about tradition from folklore. The project would also incorporate ethnographic and interview methods commonly used in folklore. Clifford Geertz's chapter "Thick Description" from *The Interpretation of Cultures* would establish the importance of detailed writing and reinforce the idea that "what we call our data are really our own constructions of other people's constructions of what they and their compatriots are up to" (8). We would also read Scott Lyons's "Rhetorical Sovereignty: What Do American Indians Want from Writing?" to emphasize that communities and peoples determine their own discourse and that imposing rhetorical theories from the outside is not necessarily the most fruitful way to understand a group's rhetorical life. The special issue on craft rhetorics from *Harlot* would also provide a useful introduction to craft rhetorics and how craft works in communities.

Students would take turns throughout the term going to observe the group during its meetings and would also interview group members individually. If students were feeling particularly brave, they might also act as observer-participants and conduct research that way. We would have days set aside in the syllabus for class discussions of what students were learning through their research and for building theories as a group about the rhetorical practices of Unraveled Crafters. For the end of the term, students would collaborate on a multimedia presentation that would explore Unraveled Crafters' rhetoric through speech, image, sound, and other media. The crafting group would be invited to the presentation of the project so that students could understand their responsibility not only to the rhetorical tradition but also to the communities they engage with both in and out of school.

Sending students into the community to research would serve as a bridge into extracanonical readings that deal particularly with civic discourse and public speech. This move encourages critical examination of what civic life entails, who is invited into civic discourse, and how public arenas are moderated. Students would read Frederick Douglass's speech, "What, to the Slave, is the Fourth of July?" and the Maria Stewart, Sarah Grimké, and Frances Willard selections from *The Rhetorical Tradition*. Next, students would dip into the Western rhetorical canon by reading selections from John Quincy Adams's *Lectures on Rhetoric and Oratory* (particularly the opening lecture, which covers the reasons to learn rhetoric) and the selections by Adams Sherman Hill in *The Rhetorical Tradition*. As with the first set of readings, I would encourage students to see how the WRC was borrowing from/imitating the extracanonical readings and how the canon excluded or ignored the contributions of people outside dominant groups. We would also work to understand how the constructions of civic discourse in Adams and Hill define the public sphere and who participates in it.

Since one of my goals in teaching rhetoric is to encourage students to participate in civic discourse, the class would turn to the present day, and students would provide material for the class to study. If I were teaching the class now, I would introduce readings on the #BlackLivesMatter movement, Idle No More, and Frank Waln's anti-Keystone XL song "Oil 4 Blood" to start discussion and to help students understand the expectations for what materials they might bring to class on subsequent days. As students brought in materials and discussed them, I would need to be flexible and ready to introduce helpful terms and concepts from rhetoric—like *identification* and *consubstantiality* for students examining how communities cohere—to continue building a class vocabulary and understanding.

The culmination of this part of the course would be for students to participate in the discourse they brought to the class for discussion. Students could compose a letter, a series of tweets, memes, a *YouTube* video, or another text, and I would assign an accompanying reflection assignment in which students explained how they saw tradition and responsibility operating in their chosen discourse, their choice of medium, and how they crafted their message to participate in the discourse. It would be important to encourage students to see not only the ways in which groups engage in civic life but also how power and privilege operate in different contexts to help prevent students from participating in civic discourse in a way that silences or speaks over those who are already marginalized. An ongoing focus on power and privilege would instead encourage students to participate thoughtfully in civic discourse and to understand and speak when others are participating in ways that silence.

The pattern set up in the first half of the term would continue in the second half, moving into twentieth and twenty-first century rhetorical work and conversations. Ending the course with students' rhetorical research would bring home the idea that the rhetorical tradition is a living tradition at work in our communities and would also bring our exploration of tradition full circle. I also hope that students would leave the course with a better understanding of their own responsibility to communicate and persuade with a deep awareness of power and how it circulates in discourse and society.

Conclusion: The Value and Danger of Tradition

I hope we will continue our conversation about how best to teach the rhetorical tradition; I hope we will continue to imagine how we can take responsibility for passing that tradition on in ways that honor the contributions of many peoples. The field of rhetoric is too rich to be reduced to a tradition that leaves out or marginalizes the contributions of people who are not represented in the WRC, and it is time for our understanding of tradition to catch up to where we are.

As we consider revising our understanding of tradition, it is important that we never lose sight of responsibility and the possibilities and perils inherent in it. Passing on responsibility for practices can be a destructive force if the beliefs and values attached to those practices are themselves harmful and discriminatory. This means that we must remember the ways in which the rhetorical tradition excludes or does violence to people. Rhetoricians are deeply aware of power and how it circulates in discourse, and teaching the rhetorical tradition as responsibility asks us to be even more sensitive to how rhetorical practices and theories shape the way in which humans relate to one another. Amy Lynn Heyse's "The Rhetoric of Memory-Making: Lessons from the UDC's Catechisms for Children" is an excellent example of the dangers of tradition. Heyse explores the United Daughters of the Confederacy's use of catechisms to teach Southern pride to young people in the early 1900s. Along with lessons on the glorious past of the Confederacy, young people also learned the values of white supremacy and segregation, values that continue to trouble the US today.

Clearly we do not want to pass on such destructive values in our teaching of the rhetorical tradition, but Heyse's research serves as a caution: We cannot ignore the values and beliefs that adhere to the texts we teach in our classrooms and study ourselves. Furthermore, we must expose and teach about these dangers. This is crucial to a new understanding of tradition: We are not absolved of the problems of power and privilege in academia and in our field. Instead, redefining tradition makes us even more responsible. As we continue to debate and engage with the rhetorical tradition, we must pay attention to the ways in which tradition promises a way through the richness of rhetorical theory and practice as well as to the ways in which tradition can perpetuate and naturalize exclusion. This is not easy work, but we are ready for it.

Notes

1. The constructive feedback from *RR* reviewers Victor Vitanza and John Schilb proved invaluable as I worked on this article. I also thank Jacob Babb, T. J. Geiger II, Annie Mendenhall, and Julia Voss for critiquing drafts and providing encouragement throughout the process. The Concordia College Faculty Writing Retreat, led by Joan Kopperud and Stephanie Ahlfeldt, also deserves recognition for providing time for me to turn pages of notes into an article.

2. Whether or not introductory rhetoric courses cover the history of rhetoric, it is important to disrupt the Western rhetorical canon. As the end of this essay suggests, I see eschewing an historical survey in introductory courses as a fruitful course of action. However, I also want us to consider how we can teach the history of rhetoric in ways that decenter the WRC.

3. Even this proposal is controversial. Bizzell and Jarratt note: "Many people at the conference did not even like the term 'traditions,' plural, because they felt that any version of the word 'tradition' implies a continuity and teleology for the texts and figures under study that is tendentious and exclusionary" (20).

4. While I focus on the Octalogs as representing key moments in our debates about the rhetorical tradition, edited volumes like *Writing Histories of Rhetoric* (Vitanza) and *Theorizing Histories of Rhetoric* (Ballif) capture how rhetoric and composition has worked to break the bonds of the canon. *Theorizing Histories of Rhetoric* highlights the innovative work we are doing with feminist and queer theory, hauntology, and sub/versive historiography. The inventiveness of the volume further throws into the relief the staid convention of most rhetoric syllabi.

5. The idea of stewardship of a practice echoes Anna Frost's theory of literacy stewards in "Literacy Stewardship: Dakelh Women Composing Culture" (2011). Noyes's definition of tradition clarifies how stewardship is the most appropriate term for understanding our relationship to the rhetorical tradition.

6. The Digital Archive of Literacy Narratives and other archives present rich sites for research in this vein.

7. Kathleen Blake Yancey, Gwendolyn Pough, Douglas D. Hesse, and Howard Tinberg have also used polyvocality to great effect in their own chair's addresses.

Works Cited

Ballif, Michelle, ed. *Theorizing Histories of Rhetoric.* Carbondale and Edwardsville: Southern Illinois UP, 2013.

Bizzell, Patricia, and Bruce Herzberg. *The Rhetorical Tradition.* 2nd. ed. Boston and New York: Bedford/St. Martin's, 2001.

Bizzell, Patricia, and Susan Jarratt. "Rhetorical Traditions, Pluralized Canons, Relevant History, and Other Disputed Terms: A Report from the History of Rhetoric Discussion Groups at the ARS Conference." *Rhetoric Society Quarterly* 34.3 (2004): 19–25.

Bronner, Simon J. *Explaining Traditions: Folk Behavior in Modern Culture.* Lexington: UP of Kentucky, 2011.

Buck, Amber, et al., eds. *Craft Rhetorics.* Spec. issue of *Harlot* 14 (2015): n. pag. Web. 15 Oct. 2015.

Cashman, Ray, Tom Mould, and Pravina Shukla. "Introduction: The Individual and Tradition." *The Individual and Tradition: Folkloristic Perspectives.* Ed. Ray Cashman, Tom Mould, and Pravina Shukla. Bloomington and Indianapolis: Indiana UP, 2011. 1–26.

Cole, Daniel. "Writing Removal and Resistance: Native American Rhetoric in the Composition Classroom." *College Composition and Communication* 63.1 (2011): 122–44.

Frost, Anna. "Literacy Stewardship: Dakelh Women Composing Culture." *College Composition and Communication* 63.1 (2011): 54–74.

Geertz, Clifford. *The Interpretation of Cultures: Selected Essays*. New York: Basic, 1973.
Glenn, Cheryl. *Rhetoric Retold: Regendering the Tradition from Antiquity Through the Renaissance*. Carbondale and Edwardsville: Southern Illinois UP, 1997.
Haas, Angela. "Wampum as Hypertext: An American Indian Intellectual Tradition of Multimedia Theory and Practice." *Studies in American Indian Literatures* 19.4 (2007): 77–100.
Hesse, Douglas D. "Who Owns Writing?" *College Composition and Communication* 57.2 (2005): 335–57.
Heyse, Amy Lynn. "The Rhetoric of Memory-Making: Lessons from the UDC's Catechisms for Children." *Rhetoric Society Quarterly* 38.4 (2008): 408–32.
Howes, Franny. "Imagining a Multiplicity of Visual Rhetorical Traditions: Comics Lessons from Rhetoric Histories." *ImageTexT: Interdisciplinary Comics Studies* 5.3 (2010). Dept. of English, University of Florida. Web. 6 May 2014.
Johnson, Robert R. "Craft Knowledge: Of Disciplinarity in Writing Studies." *College Composition and Communication* 61.4 (2010): 673–90.
"Kayanla? Kówa––The Great Law of Peace" *Oneida Tribe of Indians of Wisconsin*. Oneida Tribe of Indians of Wisconsin, n.d. Web. 12 Feb. 2016.
Kirsch, Gesa E., and Jacqueline J. Royster. "Feminist Rhetorical Practices: In Search of Excellence." *College Composition and Communication* 61.4 (2010): 640–72.
Lyons, Scott Richard. "Rhetorical Sovereignty: What Do American Indians Want from Writing?" *College Composition and Communication* 51.3 (2000): 447–68.
Noyes, Dorothy. "Tradition: Three Traditions." *Journal of Folklore Research* 46.3 (2009): 233–68.
Octalog. "The Politics of Historiography." *Rhetoric Review* 7.1 (1988): 5–49.
––––. "Octalog II: The (Continuing) Politics of Historiography." *Rhetoric Review* 16.1 (1997): 22–44.
––––. "Octalog III: The Politics of Historiography in 2010." *Rhetoric Review* 30.2 (2011): 109–34.
Pough, Gwendolyn D. "It's Bigger than Comp/Rhet: Contested and Undisciplined." *College Composition and Communication* 63.2 (2011): 301–13.
Powell, Malea. "2012 CCCC Chair's Address." *College Composition and Communication* 64.2 (2012): 383–406.
Romney, Abraham. "Indian Ability (*audilidad de Indio*) and Rhetoric's Civilizing Narrative: Guaman Poma's Contact with the Rhetorical Tradition." *College Composition and Communication* 63.1 (2011): 12–34.
Vitanza, Victor J., ed. *Writing Histories of Rhetoric*. Carbondale and Edwardsville: Southern Illinois UP, 1994.

Wagner, Roy. *The Invention of Culture*. Rev. ed. Chicago: U of Chicago P, 1981.
Widbom, Mats. "The Farms of Lima: Living and Building Between Tradition and Change." *Swedish Folk Art: All Tradition is Change*. Ed. Barbro Klein and Mats Widbom. New York: Harry N. Abrams, 1994. 129–40.
Yancey, Kathleen Blake. "Made Not Only in Words: Composition in a New Key." *College Composition and Communication* 56.2 (2004): 297–328.

Erika Claire Strandjord is an assistant professor of English at Concordia College in Moorhead, Minnesota. She researches the role that rhetorical education plays in creating and maintaining ethos in communities, focusing especially on community organizations and the teaching of traditional handcrafts. She can be reached at estrandj@cord.edu.

WPA: WRITING PROGRAM ADMINISTRATION

WPA is one the web at https://www.tandfonline.com/toc/hrhr20/current

WPA: Writing Program Administration publishes empirical and theoretical research on issues in writing program administration. We publish a wide range of research in various formats, research that not only helps both titled and untitled administrators of writing programs do their jobs, but also helps our discipline advance academically, institutionally, and nationally.

On Learning to Teach: Letter to a New TA

E. Shelley Reid's article exemplifies the high quality of research on writing program administration that the journal aims to publish while also demonstrating how writers can produce great work by experimenting with genre and different approaches to audiences. Many of us who are already seasoned and experienced writing teachers read this article and wish we had had such a clear and thoughtful exploration of the kinds of strategies to learn as much as possible from a pedagogy course. As Reid notes, "many experienced teachers would say we are still learning," and this letter to a new TA has lots to offer to teachers, no matter who new or experienced they may be.

On Learning to Teach: Letter to a New TA

E. Shelley Reid

Dear Students,

Welcome to your pedagogy course! Your course might be like mine: three credits, one night per week for fourteen weeks, with a focus on preparing new teachers to teach college composition the following semester. Perhaps yours is a pre-semester workshop or a series of afternoon in-services; you may find yourself studying teaching just before or even well after you have begun to teach writing.

Regardless, you might be tempted to treat this class like just another school event in a long, familiar line of school events. And yet it's not, not quite. The way you will learn in studying pedagogy—studying not just a new field, but one that is so personal, dynamic, and multifaceted—may differ significantly from how you learn in your other courses. Thus you may need new strategies in order to feel and be successful. The more you know about how students like you learn in a course like this, the better prepared you'll be to set goals and succeed at them. To that end, I want to share six learning strategies that can help you see how people like you learn to teach writing better. I hope that you can use these concepts to increase both your confidence and your success as a teaching learner and perhaps even pass some of them on to your own students.[1]

Strategy 1: Access prior knowledge

Although pedagogy instructors often design our courses as introductions, we recognize that you bring a lot of relevant prior knowledge to the table—and you need to figure out how to access as much of it as possible. While you may have just a few weeks of formal pedagogical study, you have been a successful student of reading and writing, and you have been going to school and thinking about teaching and learning, for decades. Despite any dark hours in which you may suffer from impostor syndrome (that nagging feeling that if people really knew how unprepared you are, they'd cart you off to the boondocks and find you a job scraping mud off moose hide), you have already been preparing to teach writing.

You are already a writing teacher. You know that most people best learn to write when they write something and receive feedback on it from a careful reader. Thus, every time you have given thoughtful feedback to another writer, you have been teaching. In this class, you will take steps to refine your strategies for classroom teaching, but you are not a blank slate. You're also already a writing/teaching theorist. Perhaps you have not yet studied composition theory or taken an education class. But every time you chose one course over another and every time you found one writing assignment more engaging than another, you were building a theory of learning and writing. You know a lot about how you best learn; you may also have considered how your friends learn. While you might not have named these theories, you practice them every week. You bring all this knowledge to your pedagogy course—whether it's on the tip of your tongue or lurking beneath the surface of your mind like the hidden bulk of an iceberg—and you should take some time to articulate what you know.

First, you will need to know about your knowledge for confidence. This class, more than your other classes, may present you with a range of completely unfamiliar material. Reminding yourself of your own expertise may prove crucial in order for you to combat imposter syndrome and stay motivated as you encounter surprises and challenges.

Second, you will need to know about that knowledge for community. The more you can remember that your classmates and colleagues are knowledgeable theorists, too, the more you will be able to benefit. (This class is not populated by clueless rookies!)

Third, you need to access your knowledge for consistency. You don't want to believe one thing as a learner and a writer but dogmatically teach your students something else, or to adopt a practice that contradicts your own principles. If you don't believe it's effective to craft an outline or write three-point theses or consult a peer as you write, for instance, but you profess that good writing pedagogy means that all your students must do so, you may be creating conflict for yourself as a teacher.

Finally, you need to know what you know for change, in order to adapt as you learn. Even if everything you know about writing is correct and functional, it may not all work in your future classrooms: in order to teach people who are not like ourselves, all of us need to learn some strategies that are different, even opposite, from ones that worked for us as learners. If you do not know what you assume, prioritize, or desire as a writer, learner, or teacher, you may find yourself caught by an unexpected behavior, like an iceberg swept along by subsurface currents.

As you begin this course of study, then, you should identify what you already know about teaching and writing, share it with others, and explore how prior knowledge complements and contradicts new learning.[2]

Strategy 2: Understand and adapt to *conscious incompetence*

Learning theorists outline an overlapping, recursive set of four stages encountered—and often re-encountered—by most students. In an early stage of what is called *unconscious incompetence*, learners of any subject (calculus, soccer, writing, bass guitar) do not know what they do not know. If you have ever watched informal groups of young children play soccer, you may have witnessed some blissful moments of unconscious incompetence: what they don't know about player deployment strategies or the offsides rule isn't worrying them at all.

In the next stage, *conscious incompetence*, learners become acutely aware that they do not know how to do something well. As your pedagogy class evolves, for instance, you may discover that you are uncertain how best to respond to a student essay or plan a week's worth of class activities about critical reading. In this stage, learners begin to recognize errors and make deliberate efforts to improve their performance. Yet they are often less happy and less confident, since nobody enjoys feeling incompetent.

Learners can cycle into a third stage, *conscious competence*, wherein they can perform tasks well but only when they concentrate carefully. These students are much improved, yet they may sometimes feel exhausted or disheartened by the effort involved. As a new writing teacher, you will provide helpful comments on students' essays, but to do so, you may need to reread your guidelines or even to go back to compare two B-minus documents to check for consistency. Eventually, learners can move into *unconscious competence* with some tasks or sets of tasks: they can perform well without having to devote excessive attention to the matter at hand. Teachers who are familiar with a subject and a writing task often review and comment without much second-guessing.

If this cycle holds true for all learners—including your own writing students—why should you pay special attention to it in a pedagogy class? Because several factors can magnify the effects of conscious incompetence for teaching learners like you. First, the feeling can surprise you because in the rest of your classes, the things you're incompetent at may be relatively few in comparison to all the knowledge you've accumulated. What's one new theorist or primary text compared to the dozens you already know? In comparison, the conscious incompetence you may encounter in a pedagogy class can stick out like a very sore thumb.

To complicate matters, in learning to teach, you are likely to inhabit all four stages at once, relative to different aspects of teaching. Just as you start to feel comfortable with commenting on student writing, for example, you'll read an article about multi-genre assignments that makes you realize you don't fully comprehend genres as a concept. Frequently, in learning teaching, as soon as you understand the issues at one level, your view refocuses so that you can see new challenges and unknowns at the next level. So instead of progressing steadily toward competence as the workshop or semester goes along, you are—like many experienced teachers—likely to encounter new incompetencies each week.

Finally, as you prepare to teach classes of unknown students, the stakes may feel pretty high. After all, if you're incompetent in interpreting the latest Swedish film, probably only you and your professor (or maybe a few trusted peers) will know. If you're incompetent at designing a peer review assignment, you may fail much more publicly. Since you can feel exposed at the front of a classroom, learning to teach can feel very personal, even if you tell yourself that it's just a job or just a class. Moreover, you may become worried about building your hoped-for career in this profession. These magnifying factors are inherent to being a new learner of a complicated, highly personal task—but that doesn't make the incompetence feel any better.

At some point, therefore, you may need some additional coping strategies as a teaching learner. You can remind yourself that the incompetence feeling is a normal learning stage and one that will diminish over time. You can take time to review all the knowledge and competencies you do have that can buoy you up. When you do make progress, you should take time to celebrate those gains while you prepare to learn still more. You might even decide to ask directly for reassurance or specific guidance from an experienced teacher, program director, or mentor. Not everyone will expect (or notice) that you feel especially concerned about a concept, student encounter, or skill. When you finally reveal your conscious incompetence anxieties (and now you have a technical term to use for them!), you may discover that you're doing better than you think or learn that there are some straightforward steps you could take to gain more clarity and competence.

The better you become at recognizing the signs that you are having a round of learning pains, understanding that they are inherent to the process of learning a new and intricate profession, and finding a strategy to alleviate them, the more you'll gain from the opportunities in this course.[3]

Strategy 3: Integrate multiple learning approaches

Just as becoming physically fit requires more than one kind of endeavor (cardiovascular conditioning, weight training, flexibility exercises), learning to teach also requires a kind of cross-training. When a pedagogy course feels like a whirlwind tour through multiple topics or exercises, it can be overwhelming.

Yet you can also see the "If It's Tuesday This Must Be Belgium" aspect of a pedagogy course as a distinct contribution to your learning because of two key considerations. First, research shows that learning and practicing integrated, overlapping tasks in context—as jazz musicians, jet pilots, and basketball players do—provides better long-term learning than mastering all about X and then all about Y separately. In teaching, the tasks you perform are always interconnected, so it's to your advantage to learn about assessing student writing, then work on designing an assignment, then think again (from a new, more informed perspective) about how to evaluate the student work from that assignment. Instead of mastering each one, you can gain an initial, more holistic understanding about how assigning and evaluating are linked in the practice of teaching.

Second, perhaps even more than other students, teaching-learners need to acquire knowledge through all three of the major modes of learning:

- *learning about*, or declarative knowledge that helps you understand key concepts;
- *learning how*, or procedural knowledge that helps you develop skills and abilities; and
- *learning through insight*, or reflective/metacognitive knowledge that helps you gain awareness of your own opportunities and motivations.

Table 1 helps show how each of these modes might play out in learning to be a teacher, a profession that requires you to know the *about* and the *how* of teaching, of writing, of individual student learning, and of classroom learning—and to reflect on your own writing and teaching metacognitively.

Despite the divisions noted on the chart, these approaches to learning often occur simultaneously: for instance, most recent research emphasizes that declarative knowledge must be blended with procedural knowledge, in all fields. Students who know about chemistry or US history also need to be able to solve how-to problems in that field. Indeed, many learning specialists argue that students strongly benefit from this more integrated learning, even if an integrated, problem-focused approach means that less material will be covered in those courses or that learning won't be organized in tidy, predictable components.

Your pedagogy class will likewise help you blend some declarative knowledge about the subject matter with practice in some of the procedures that teachers need to know. A pedagogy course, like other introductory courses, can't cover everything. Yet again, the gaps in this class may feel different to you. When a US history class only touches on the War of 1812 so that there's more time to investigate the Civil War in depth, few students worry. When a pedagogy course skips over a topic, the loss can feel more dramatic because you may actually need to know—tomorrow!—more about assisting multilingual writers. It is difficult to trust that you will succeed without knowing that key information now. Since full coverage is impossible, metacognitive learning becomes crucial for teaching-learners. Metacognition supports your ability to transfer learning to a new situation and continue to learn there. In a pedagogy class in particular, nearly all of your practical experiences will need to be adapted to the next student, in the next semester, at the next school. Therefore, your metacognitive knowledge—the stories you tell yourself about teaching and being a teacher, how you accustom your neurons to solving teaching problems—will prepare you to continue learning the material your class doesn't cover.

When you encounter a new topic, task, or approach in your pedagogy class, you might shrug and think "Tuesday: Belgium." But you can also map out the process by connecting this learning approach to the integrated practices of your future teaching by linking any new approach to one or more types of learning (declarative, procedural, metacognitive), or by telling yourself a new story about what and how you are learning.[4]

Table 1

Mode of learning	Field-specific knowledge	Example
Declarative knowledge about ...	Composition as a field and an institution	Design a syllabus to meet field-wide learning goals
	Writing, reading, researching, revising strategies	Explain concept of audience to students
	Effective practices for classroom learning	Design a session integrating experiential learning about genres
Procedural knowledge of ...	Writing, reading, researching, revising strategies	Prioritize strengths and weaknesses in student drafts
	Effective pedagogical strategies for individual learning	Provide revision-directed comments on student drafts
	Effective pedagogical practices for classroom learning	Use follow-up questions to deepen students' analysis during class
Metacognitive knowledge of ...	One's own writing practices	Draw on one's own struggles with revising to provide suggestions to students
	One's own learning preferences	Reflect on one's enjoyment of collaborative learning, knowing that it will fit some learners better than others
	One's own teaching practices	Analyze a successful teaching moment: what factors contributed?

Strategy 4: Learn from multiple sources and experiences

Since one pedagogy course will not teach everything you need to know, you need to know how to learn about teaching from other sources. Certainly delving into the iceberg of your prior knowledge and looking for strategies that will transfer to new contexts can both help here.

If you have observed a mentor teacher recently, you have encountered another valuable source of pedagogical learning: your peers, both those in your cohort and those with more experience than you. You need to deliberately cultivate your ability to learn teaching explicitly from your peer teachers—by talking with them, reviewing their materials, observing as they teach, and asking critical questions. Few good teachers work as hermits, inventing their own assignment wheels and building their curricula with bricks shaped only by their own hands. Other teachers' approaches won't always be what you feel most comfortable with, and yet those methods may succeed with students as well as or better than your own. Of course, you will have to judge how to adapt others' ideas to fit your own major principles or goals. You should also try someone else's idea more than once before concluding that it doesn't work for you.

In addition, you have an opportunity now to engage in a special kind of implicit pedagogical learning. You're a practicing student, and every time a teacher makes a move—even now as you're reading this letter—you can reflect on that moment to increase your understanding of how teaching and learning work. You should use this metacognitive double vision to peer behind the curtains of your own learning scenes: Why do you think your teacher just made that move? How did other students react? If you're satisfied or frustrated as a learner, what factors have contributed to that experience? If you had been the teacher, what approach might you have taken to assist a student such as yourself?

Your goal is not to become the know-it-all who critiques all of her senior professors or sees his future students perfectly. Instead, your goal is to become a question-it-all, to use your dual position as a teacher and learner to better empathize with students and teachers who are navigating complex classroom currents. Any time when you find yourself in the position of a learner—you start a new Pilates class, switch to a different computer, add someone to your family—you can renew your double vision and become someone who sees teaching as teaching, who watches yourself and others learn rather than only letting it happen.

When you step outside your pedagogy class or workshop, try to look for ways to practice learning about teaching, directly by consulting with teaching peers to see what you can borrow from them, and indirectly by using your double vision to reflect on your own learning experiences.[5]

Strategy 5: Explore "managed uncertainty" and "failing forward"

It is neither true that good teaching cannot be studied nor that good teaching can be completely learned from books. Very good teachers prepare by studying models and principles, and they continue to learn from their daily interactions with their students.

While it is just barely possible that a class session you design might go either 100% or 0% the way you plan it—you have your perfect rainbow class, or you encounter aliens who turn everyone into mushrooms—most teaching happens in the middle zone. From your own previous perspective, it may have seemed that decent classes without alien invaders usually proceeded in the 90–95% perfect zone. Yet many experienced teachers feel that we work in the 40–70% zone, delighted that some of a class session is going as we had hoped and then actively adapting in order to keep the rest of the class in an acceptable (and sometimes exciting) controlled spin so that learning can continue. One of my mentors once asked one of her nationally renowned colleagues about the best class he ever taught: he responded quietly and with only a little humorous exaggeration, "Well, I could tell you about a pretty good 10 minutes last spring. . . . "

During a pedagogy class, you will indeed learn some strategies to prepare you to handle many elements of teaching, and you will learn the reasons and principles behind such strategies. These principles will help you predict a fair amount of what will create a successful learning environment. You should try to predict what you can, just as sailors check the weather forecasts and tides: professionals don't just wing it. But you will also need to practice a flexible mindset so you will be ready to adapt everything you learn to your own personal and educational style, to the learning goals of any class you teach, to the personality of any group of students overall, and to the vicissitudes of any particular day of teaching. In other school subjects, you may have been (and might still be) judged by your ability to draw correct conclusions and show that you've mastered a stable body of material. As a teaching learner, however, you should judge your increasing preparation more by how many variables you can identify in a dynamic situation and how many reasonable alternate paths you can imagine. Each time you mentally praise yourself for considering multiple possibilities rather than settling on a right answer, you build up your tolerance for productive uncertainty.

Since you will always learn and teach without being certain, you will always face failures as a pedagogy learner and as a teacher. Beyond your occasional bouts of conscious incompetence, you will—as I do—mess things up, or elements of your teaching will simply go awry on their own. Now, unless you hang out in a science lab or play a video game regularly, you may not have spent a lot of time failing and having that be a normal, accepted part of the way students learn and professionals perform. Yet teachers are like laboratory biologists and midnight gamers: we often fail because we are fully engaged in a complex endeavor (a good thing!), not because we lack knowledge or commitment. Indeed, our potential for growth often depends on our willingness to take risks and fail. It's better, of course, if we don't fail utterly, which is one reason we work on managing uncertainty and predicting multiple opportunities. It's best if we fail forward—that is, if we see any particular failure not as a final judgment of our capabilities or worth, but as an opportunity to try something again, differently. Even when you are uncomfortable with or frustrated by failure, research shows that you can learn to modify your reaction to it, to identify not just what went wrong but how you yourself can change in response by exploring your assumptions, attitudes, approaches, preparations, and/or goals.

Much of your conscious incompetence will pass, eventually. Yet teaching is overall an uncertain enterprise, and you will be a better teaching learner when you manage your uncertainty by expecting, practicing, and even valuing it; by predicting what you can and adapting to the rest; and by using failures as opportunities for learning rather than signs that you should give up and turn back.[6]

Strategy 6: Extend your new teacher timeline

The very existence of English 101 gives many students and professors the illusion that second-semester students should know all they need to know about college writing. Anyone familiar with the field or the actual course knows this is patently impossible: writing is far too complex an endeavor to be mastered via one class. Interestingly, though, some pedagogical education programs can similarly foster the illusion that once their TAs finish one course, they magically know all they need to know about teaching. After all, we quickly put you in charge of your own classrooms and tell you you're going to be fine. That illusion can leave you caught in the middle: officially prepared, but truthfully still learning. As a TA interviewed recently put it, it can feel like he's letting people down: "It's kind of frustrating just not being perfect [yet]."

At some point, you do have to step into a classroom without knowing everything. On the other hand, when you step into the classroom for that first time, you may bring an excitement, an energy, and/or a freshness to the material that your students will find highly appealing, and those qualities will enhance the learning environment substantially. So when program leaders say that "you are ready to teach," they are not lying. They have hired capable readers and writers with strong teaching potential, and they are helping you gain additional declarative, procedural, and metacognitive learning that is sufficient to make you a competent teacher for their program.

You will still also be a teaching learner: not just the way all good teachers are lifetime learners, but an intensive still-at-the-beginning teaching learner. Researchers estimate that new teachers can spend from three to five years moving from being "senior learners" to "colleagues in training" to "junior colleagues." During these early years—years, not months—almost all of teachers' best work is just consciously competent: they have to think hard about their actions in order to feel successful. Some days they create class sessions that match precisely what they learned as core principles in their pedagogy classes, and on other days they improvise with whatever is in their book bags. Moreover, every time they try something new, the challenge can send them right back to conscious incompetence.

While you may transition smoothly into teaching your first classes (and everyone hopes that you do!), if your experience is uneven or involves setbacks, then you are probably experiencing a normal teaching learning curve, not having a personal catastrophe or letting your program down. Not only are other experienced teachers not aiming for the 95% accuracy zone, but you get to be a new teacher—the kind who asks questions, relies on his peer colleagues, worries about her time management, and fails at some key goals—for longer than your first semester.

Given this multi-year path, you might look at your pedagogy course as providing at least two kinds of learning resources. First, there is immediate learning, which is about preparation rather than mastery. You will be able to gain some in-depth competence in a few core areas of declarative and procedural knowledge and consider how to apply it more widely. For instance, the questions you learn to ask as you design a writing task—questions about students, learning goals, genres, institutions, and assessments—will recur as you design class sessions, inquire about multilingual learners, or even consider your policy about late work.

Second, there is delayed learning. Your initial course of study will also help you become aware of other questions, concepts, or strategies that will be important to you in the long run as a teaching learner, even if you cannot fully explore them during your first semester or two. Looking forward, you can acknowledge and prioritize for yourself what there is to be learned. What new technologies or genres might you want to help student writers to explore? How might you eventually want to create better opportunities to engage students in community projects or explore alternate approaches to feedback and assessment? If you're making a five-year learning plan, you can dream big: what do you want on your to-learn list?

The more you tell yourself the true story about being a teacher on the first steps of an extended learning journey, the more you can enjoy each of the successes of your learning and teaching right now. This approach can help you prioritize your pedagogy learning to focus on a few concepts to learn deeply now and identify several more for later consideration.

Moreover, recognizing the extended timeline of teaching learning enables all five of the other strategies I've listed here. When you don't have to be perfect by Friday, you can take time to investigate your own prior knowledge and integrate new knowledge into it so that the new ideas have a more stable foundation. You will have time to encounter conscious incompetence and to experiment with teaching strategies in an uncertain world. You can learn from your peers and your experiences as you piece together a dynamic, evolving understanding of how teaching works for you—rather than accepting a simple, pre-packaged view of it from a how-to manual. You will have time to learn to think like a teacher who can wield those tools and strategies across a wide variety of educational situations.[7]

Moving Forward as a Pedagogy Learner

You may not need the strategies I have outlined here. When learning is going smoothly—and keep in mind that you are an expert learner or you wouldn't have made it this far—students don't need new ways to think about how to learn. But having names for these learning concepts might still help you. If you start to feel off-balance or overwhelmed as a teaching learner, you might stop and consider what factors are at work. It will always be possible that you're experiencing normal school or life factors: too much work, not enough time. (It's also possible that the class might be a bad class or you might be an unsuccessful pedagogy learner: any of these six learning strategies can be pushed too far, perhaps leaving learners with too much uncertainty or feeling only incompetent. But in a roomful of people thinking hard about teaching and learning, complete breakdowns like those are rare and can often be resolved.) If your standard coping strategies as a student don't work, though, you may find it useful to remind yourself of some of the new ways of learning that are part of your pedagogy education.

Perhaps just as important, you may be able to help your own students when they struggle. Students at any level who have been accustomed to one kind of learning environment—perhaps one that focused on right answers or teacher directives more than your classes will, for instance—can stumble when they switch to new learning challenges. Your students might benefit from exploring their own prior knowledge or understanding that you don't expect perfection from them in just a few weeks. Or perhaps you will want to explore deep, problem-solving learning approaches with them and explain why you're teaching that way.

I think that many experienced teachers would say we are still learning. Yet that's not quite the same as the excitement (and frustration and occasionally moments of dread) that comes with the first rounds of learning to teach, with realizing the full range of creative opportunities you will have as you begin to interact with students in a new learning environment. Whether you are taking up classroom teaching just for the time being or as a lifelong vocation, I hope you can also take this opportunity to expand your understanding of your own learning processes—so that you can continue learning and helping others learn with balance, humor, and grace in whatever explorations lie ahead of you.

—Shelley

Notes

1. For arguments about how new teachers benefit from understanding general learning theories, see Parkay and Stanford (32–34); for more about how writing teachers benefit from questioning their assumptions about learning, see Stygall (40–41); for specific arguments about promoting "thinking like teachers" to new instructors, see Auten. Perkins argues more generally for all students to "play the hidden game" of understanding learning strategies (136–38).

2. For an introduction to the concepts of prior knowledge, negative transfer, and transfer generally, see Ambrose et al. (15–27) or Bransford et al. (235–38); for an overview of those concepts in composition studies, see Moore. For the idea of (pedagogy) students who have already developed "theories in use," see Parker (413); for the idea of TAs as "senior learners," see Sprague and Nyquist (295); for an analysis against viewing new English TAs as blank slates see Stenberg (63–66). For one exploration of ways that TAs sometimes teach against their own writing principles, see Dryer. The conversation about new (composition) TAs resisting (or critically inquiring about) pedagogical theories is extensive; Hesse and Welch represent two key voices here. For one take on the concept of teachers' icebergs, see Malderez and Bodóczky (14). For general arguments about having teachers use reflective strategies to uncover their assumptions, see Bamberg, Brookfield, Dryer, Ebest, Reid "Teaching," and Winslow. Arguments about the benefits of collaborative learning overall go back to Bruffee.

3. For a quick summary of learners' competence stages, see Ambrose et al. (97–98) or Sprague and Nyquist (297–98). For one take on the pressure in graduate school to seem knowledgeable, see Recchio (255). For a definition of mastery in unstructured problems as ever-increasing attentiveness to more detailed challenges, see Bereiter and Scardamalia (esp. 79–82). For analysis of how the interpersonal and managerial dimensions of teaching can raise the stakes for new teachers, see Morgan (395, 399–400).

4. For a summary of research about the benefits of interleaved or back-and-forth study, see Brown Roediger, and McDaniel (46–66). A brief overview of declarative and procedural knowledge can be found in Ambrose et al. (18–20). To consider additional kinds of teacher knowledge (such as pedagogical content knowledge), see Shulman. For a summary of how metacognitive activity supports learning transfer, see Bransford et al. (67–68). The chart is adapted from Reid "What Is" (200). Discussions of problem-posing education go back notably to Freire; Bain provides one of many discussions

of the recent "deep learning" research in his chapter "Messy Problems" (133–63). For analysis of the challenges of coverage in the composition pedagogy course, see Hardin (37–38) and Reid "Uncoverage." For more on metacognition and reflective practice in pedagogy generally, see Schön as well as Hillocks (126–37); see Bamberg (151–52) or Broz (136–37) about new writing teachers specifically.

5. See Dobrin (23) on the institutional similarities between pedagogy education and first-year education. For explanations of how TAs should learn from equal or senior peers, see Martin and Paine or Weiser; for lists of questions that could help (new) teachers better notice their peers' work in a (K–12) classroom, see Portner (50–55) or Boreen et al. (42–44, 61–67). For more on the benefits of reflecting on our autobiographies as learners, see Brookfield (49–51, 115). For an extended reflective example of student-to-teacher double vision (though with the assistance of mature hindsight), see Stenberg (77–91); for a description of a reflective teacher-narrative assignment, see VanderStaay.

6. The practicum course vs. theory course debate regarding the "TA training course" in English Departments has a long history; for one recent summary, see Dobrin—and note that most of the essayists in his collection resist any easy binary. Among scholars explaining that (learning) teaching is unpredictable, see Dannels (18–19), Belanger and Gruber (114), and Stenberg (148–49). For arguments that new teachers should measure their progress against clear and evolving criteria grounded in scholarship, see Rose and Finders. For arguments that constructivist, adaptive teachers who locate responsibility for change in themselves are most open to improvement and thus success, see Hillocks (e.g., 134–35). For a review of the research on the benefits of tolerating difficulty and failure in learning, see Brown Roediger, and McDaniel (90–98); consider also Dweck's work on fixed mindset vs. growth mindset learners (6–9).

7. For recent data on the pace of learning of composition TAs and arguments about the need to extend pedagogical education beyond the seminar, see Estrem and Reid (474–76) and Reid, Estrem, and Belchier (61–62). For more on the "pedagogy of the extracurriculum" (Hesse and Sandy 124), see also Bamberg, Ward and Perry, and Weiser. Senior learners (etc.) comes from Sprague and Nyquist (295); the quotation from the TA comes from Estrem and Reid (475). For more on why new TAs might work on just a few skills at a time to gain confidence in core competencies before tackling additional challenges, see Sprague and Nyquist (298).

Works Cited

Ambrose, Susan A., Michael W. Bridges, Michele DiPietro, Marsha C. Lovett, Marie K. Norman. *How Learning Works: 7 Research-Based Principles for Smart Teaching.* Jossey-Bass, 2010.

Auten, Janet. "Teaching as Text—The Pedagogy Seminar: Lit 730, Teaching Composition. (Course Design)." *Composition Studies*, vol. 40, no. 1, 2012, pp. 95–112.

Bain, Ken. *What the Best College Students Do.* Belknap P, 2012.

Bamberg, Betty. "Creating a Culture of Reflective Practice: A Program for Continuing TA Preparation After the Practicum." Pytlik and Liggett, pp. 147–58.

Belanger, Kelly, and Sibylle Gruber. "Unraveling Generative Tensions in the Composition Practicum." Dobrin, pp. 113–40.

Bereiter, Carl, and Marlene Scardamalia. *Surpassing Ourselves: An Inquiry Into the Nature and Implications of Expertise.* Open Court Publishing, 1993.

Boreen, Jean, Mary Johnson, Donna Niday, Joe Potts. *Mentoring Beginning Teachers: Guiding, Reflecting, Coaching.* 2nd ed., Stenhouse Publishers, 2009.

Bransford, John D., Ann L. Brown, Rodney R. Cocking, editors. *How People Learn: Brain, Mind, Experience, and School.* National Academy P, 2000.

Brookfield, Stephen D. *Becoming a Critically Reflective Teacher.* Jossey-Bass, 1995.

Brown, Peter C., Henry L. Roediger III, Mark A. McDaniel. *Make It Stick: The Science of Successful Learning.* Belknap P, 2014.

Bruffee, Kenneth A. "Collaborative Learning and the 'Conversation of Mankind'." *College English*, vol. 46, no. 7, 1984, pp. 635–52.

Dannels, Deanna. *8 Essential Questions Teachers Ask: A Guidebook for Communicating with Students.* Oxford UP, 2014.

Dobrin, Sidney I. "Introduction: Finding Space for the Composition Practicum." *Don't Call It That: The Composition Practicum*, edited by Sidney I. Dobrin. NCTE, 2005, pp. 1–34.

Dryer, Dylan B. "At a Mirror, Darkly: The Imagined Undergraduate Writers of Ten Novice Composition Instructors." *College Composition and Communication*, vol. 63, no. 3, 2012, pp. 420–52.

Dweck, Carol S. *Mindset: The New Psychology of Success.* Ballantine, 2006.

Ebest, Sally Barr. *Changing the Way We Teach: Writing and Resistance in the Training of Teaching Assistants.* Southern Illinois UP, 2005.

Estrem, Heidi, and E. Shelley Reid. "What New Writing Teachers Talk About When They Talk About Teaching." *Pedagogy*, vol. 12, no. 3, pp. 449–80.

Freire, Paolo. *Pedagogy of the Oppressed.* Continuum, 1993.

Hardin, Joe Marshall. "Writing Theory and Writing the Classroom." Dobrin, pp. 35–42.
Hesse, Douglas. "Teaching as Students, Reflecting Resistance." *College Composition and Communication*, vol. 44, 1993, pp. 224–31.
—, and Kirsti Sandy. "Teaching Teachers and the Extracurriculum." Tremmel and Broz, 116–25.
Hillocks, George. *Teaching Writing as Reflective Practice*. Teachers College P, 1995.
If It's Tuesday It Must Be Belgium. Directed by Mel Stuart, performances by Suzanne Pleshette, Ian McShane, Vittorio De Sica, Wolper Pictures, 1969.
Malderez, Angi, and Caroline Bodóczky. *Mentor Courses: A Resource Book for Teacher-Trainers*. Cambridge UP, 1999.
Martin, Wanda, and Charles Paine. "Mentors, Models, and Agents of Change: Veteran TAs Preparing Teachers of Writing." Pytlik and Liggett, pp. 222–32.
Moore, Jessie. "Mapping the Questions: The State of Writing-Related Transfer Research." *Composition Forum*, vol. 26, Fall 2012.
Morgan, Meg. "The GTA Experience: Grounding, Practicing, Evaluating, and Reflecting." *The Writing Program Administrator's Resource*, edited by Stuart C. Brown and Theresa Enos. Lawrence Erlbaum, 2002, pp. 393–410.
Parkay, Forrest W., and Beverly Hardcastle Stanford. *Becoming a Teacher*. 9th ed., Pearson, 2012.
Parker, Robert B. "Writing Courses for Teachers: From Practice to Theory." *College Composition and Communication*, vol. 33, no. 4, 1982, pp. 411–19.
Perkins, David. *Making Learning Whole: How Seven Principles of Teaching Can Transform Education*. Jossey-Bass, 2009.
Portner, Hal. *Mentoring New Teachers*. 3rd ed., Corwin P, 2008.
Pytlik, Betty P., and Sarah Liggett, editors. *Preparing College Teachers of Writing*. Oxford UP, 2002.
Reid, E. Shelley. "Teaching Writing Teachers Writing: Difficulty, Exploration, and Reflection." *College Composition and Communication*, vol. 61, no. 2, p. 376 [W197–W221].
—. "Uncoverage in Composition Pedagogy." *Composition Studies*, vol. 32, no. 1, pp. 15–34.
—. "What is Teaching Assistant Preparation?" *A Rhetoric for Writing Program Administrators*, edited by Rita Malenczyk, Parlor P, 2013, pp. 197–210.
—, Heidi Estrem, and Marcia Belchier. "The Effects of Writing Pedagogy Education on Graduate Teaching Assistants' Approaches to Teaching Composition." *Writing Program Administration*, vol. 36, no. 1, pp. 32–73.
Recchio, Thomas E. "Essaying TA Training." Pytlik and Liggett, pp. 254–65.

Rose, Shirley K, and Margaret J. Finders. "Thinking Together: Developing a Reciprocal Reflective Model for Approaches to Preparing College Teachers of Writing." Pytlik and Liggett, 2002, pp. 75–85.

Schön, Donald. *The Reflective Practitioner: How Professionals Think in Action*. Basic Books, 1983.

Shulman, Lee S. "Knowledge and Teaching: Foundations of the New Reform." *Harvard Education Review*, vol. 57, no. 1, 1987, pp. 1–21.

Sprague, Jo, and Jody D. Nyquist. "A Developmental Perspective on the TA Role." *Preparing the Professoriate of Tomorrow to Teach*, edited by Jody D. Nyquist, Robert D. Abbott, Donald H. Wulff, Jo Sprague, Kendall/Hunt Publishing, 1991, pp. 295–312.

Stenberg, Shari J. *Professing and Pedagogy: Learning the Teaching of English*. NCTE, 2005.

Stygall, Gail. "Bridging Levels: Composition Theory and Practice for Preservice Teachers and TAs." Tremmel and Broz, pp. 40–49.

Tremmel, Robert, and William Broz, editors. *Teaching Writing Teachers of High School English and First-Year Composition*. Heinemann, 2002.

VanderStaay, Steven L. "Critiquing Process: Teaching Writing Methods as Problem Solving." Tremmel and Broz, pp. 95–104.

Ward, Irene, and Merry Perry. "A Selection of Strategies for Training Teaching Assistants." *The Allyn and Bacon Sourcebook for Writing Program Administrators*, edited by Irene Ward and William J. Carpenter. Longman, pp. 117–38.

Weiser, Irwin. "When Teaching Assistants Teach Teaching Assistants to Teach: A Historical View of a Teacher Preparation Program." Pytlik and Liggett, pp. 40–49.

Welch, Nancy. "Resisting the Faith: Conversion, Resistance, and the Training of Teachers." *College English*, vol. 55, no. 4, 1993, pp. 387–401.

Winslow, Rosemary. "The GTA Writing Portfolio: An Impact Study of Learning by Writing." Dobrin, pp. 315–36.

Acknowledgments

I am deeply grateful to Barb Bird, Jason Palmeri, and Kate Ryan for their kind and insightful feedback on drafts of this article; to Heidi Estrem, for encouraging me in the earliest versions of it; to the supportive editors of *WPA: Writing Program Administration*; and to my pedagogy students, who keep showing me more and more about how to learn to teach teachers.

E. Shelley Reid is an associate professor of English and director of the Center for Teaching and Faculty Excellence at George Mason University, Virginia's largest public research university. Her work on teacher preparation, mentoring, and writing education has appeared in *College Composition and Communication, Composition Studies, Pedagogy, WPA: Writing Program Administration,* and *Writing Spaces.*

PRESENT TENSE

A Journal of Rhetoric in Society

Present Tense is on the Web at http://www.presenttensejournal.org/

Present Tense: A Journal of Rhetoric in Society is a peer-reviewed, blind-refereed, online journal dedicated to exploring contemporary social, cultural, political and economic issues through a rhetorical lens. In addition to examining these subjects as found in written, oral and visual texts, we wish to provide a forum for calls to action in academia, education and national policy. Seeking to address current or presently unfolding issues, we publish short articles ranging from 2,000 to 2,500 words, the length of a conference paper. For sample topics please see our submission guidelines. Conference presentations on topics related to the journal's focus lend themselves particularly well to this publishing format. Authors who address the most current issues may find a lengthy submission and application process disadvantageous. We seek to overcome this issue through our shortened response time and by publishing individual articles as they are accepted. We also encourage conference-length multimedia submissions such as short documentaries, flash videos, slidecasts and podcasts.

Composing Artificial Intelligence: Performing Whiteness and Masculinity

Patricia Fancher's "Composing Artificial Intelligence: Performing Whiteness and Masculinity" was the lead article in *Present Tense*, Volume 6, Issue 1. The article explores the case of Eugene Goostman, a chatterbot that passed the Turing Test for machine intelligence when mistaken for a human. Fancher demonstrates through her analysis how the machine's designers achieved this feat through the performance of a white, male embodied identity that conferred an assumption of human intelligence due to racial and gender bias. Fancher's timely article deftly weaves together many scholarly topics at the heart of Present Tense's mission: feminist rhetorical studies, race and rhetoric, rhetorics of embodiment, and technology. The work illuminates how certain racialized and gendered embodiments are socially coded, with important implications for designers and users of artificial intelligence.

Composing Artificial Intelligence: Performing Whiteness and Masculinity

Patricia Fancher

On June 8, 2014, a computer program named Eugene Goostman successfully passed Alan Turing's proposed test for machine intelligence. At least the test's organizer, a leading and controversial scholar in cybernetics, claimed that this chatterbot was the first computer to successfully pass the Turing Test.[1] During this test, judges engaged in text-based conversations with two participants: one was a human and the other was a computer. As soon as one third of the human judges guessed that the computer was a human, the machine was said to have passed the test for intelligence. To pass the test, the team of computer scientists, which was led by Vladimir Veselov and Eugene Demchenko along with the Wholesale Change software company based near Silicon Valley, designed their chatterbot as a chatty boy. When reflecting upon the successful test, one of the programmers described Eugene as a bawdy thirteen-year-old schoolboy who "to a great extent, passed this Turing test with a lot of dick jokes" (qtd. in Ulanoff).

Although Eugene Goostman is far from an ideal performance of intelligence, this chatterbot's performance is notable because his intelligence is constituted through a rhetoric of embodiment. In passing as an intelligent human, Eugene Goostman performed embodiment. But whose body would be performed for this "landmark" test in artificial intelligence? I argue that Eugene Goostman performs the embodiment of whiteness and masculinity, and, in doing, he makes visible the assumed naturalness of associating intelligence with masculinity and whiteness. To establish these points, I will analyze the discourse of

Eugene Goostman, the team of computer scientists who programmed Eugene, and the various interlocutors' conversations with Eugene.[2]

By analyzing the discourses of Eugene Goostman and his performance of embodiment, I am responding to Maureen Johnson, Daisy Levy, Katie Manthey, and Maria Novotny's call for more feminist work recognizing that through "the inherent relationship between embodiment and rhetoric, we can make all bodies and the power dynamics invested in their (in)visibility visible, thereby strengthening the commitment to feminist rhetorical work" (39). In her definition of a posthuman feminist rhetorical methodology, Sarah Hallenbeck argues that feminist rhetorical research needs to move beyond analyzing women's rhetorical intention and toward analyses of "how gendering occurs through different linkages" in specific discursive and material contexts (19). Building on these calls for feminist rhetorical work, I demonstrate how Eugene Goostman makes visible that which is typically invisible: the gendering and racializing discourses of intelligence and the linkages between embodiment and how intelligence is identified, especially within communities associated with Silicon Valley.

Rhetoric of Embodiment

While a rhetoric of embodiment may be defined in a number of ways, I employ a definition informed by feminist rhetorical theory. In *Peitho's* recent "Key Concept Statement" defining embodied rhetoric, the authors include both discourses about bodies as well as bodies themselves (Johnson et al. 39). Given that Eugene Goostman has no flesh and blood body, my analysis focuses specifically on discourse about bodies. While there are multiple definitions of embodiment, I follow Jordynn Jack's definition for this analysis: "metaphors that move from an embodied source domain (i.e., the human body) to the target domain" (207). In this case, Eugene Goostman is the target domain, and embodied metaphors lead the human judges to successfully identify with Eugene. "Rhetoric of embodiment," then, includes metaphors of white, male bodies that, in the case of Eugene Goostman, constitute an identifiable performance of intelligence.

Whiteness, as a social trope, is identified in part by its invisibility, which is to say that whiteness seldom identifies itself as a racial trope but rather is often the presumed natural or invisible cultural value (Ratcliffe 37-38). Masculinity is another trope that represents a set of status quo values especially within scientific and technical discourses (see Keller; Harding.) The social power of both whiteness and masculinity are significant precisely because they are most often invisible and are often identified with normalcy rather than any embodied particularity. As Krista Ratcliffe argues, whiteness and masculinity "remain steeped in very real material consequences for US culture and for individual people's lives. This logic demands that race [and gender] be studied, not to reify its existence but to expose its functions so as to interrupt injustices and promote social justice" (15). It has been the work of feminist rhetoricians (among others, for instance in feminist technoscience studies) to uncover the implicit or concealed bodies in science and technology.

This chatterbot *explicitly* depends on both whiteness and masculinity in order to perform persuasive intelligence. Therein lies the irony and also Eugene's usefulness for the study of technical and scientific rhetoric as a lens into understanding the techno cultures that are prevalent in Silicon Valley and elsewhere. Most technical communication conceals the very real bodies involved in knowledge construction. Scholars of rhetoric have consistently identified technical and scientific discourses that disembody: discourses that rhetorically erase bodily particularity or embodied context and that often are perceived as objective, neutral, and true (see Katz; Slack, Miller, and Doak; Frost and Eble). For example, G. Mitchell Reyes defines the dominant mathematical discourse, which was the discipline that Alan Turing was trained in, as a contemporary form of "Platonic Realism" (475) that discursively erases "precisely the Person—who is finite, lives outside of the formal mathematical code" (479). Additionally, cognitive scientists Rolf Pfeifer and Josh Bongard define the "classical approach" for defining intelligence (as is measured in the IQ test) as an exclusive focus on central processing in the brain without any connection to bodily experience or interaction with environments (27-33).

Of course, scientific and technical discourses have never actually been without bodies. Rather, the actual bodies composing technical communication are erased in the interest of preserving the appearance of objective, universal knowledge. In that erasure of embodiment, scientific and technical discourses also erase the predominance of whiteness and masculinity within these communities. Eugene makes visible that which is typically concealed: he actively presents and cultivates white, masculine embodiment in order to conceal the fact that he has no body at all.

Embodying a Chatterbot

Eugene Goostman's rhetoric of embodiment includes a rich array of everyday experiences that may be typical of a thirteen-year-old Ukrainian boy. He speaks of activities that are stereotypical of young boys: caring for a pet guinea pig, watching *Star Wars*, making friends at school, and dreaming of what he wants to be when he grows up. Eugene's experiences also include emotions. Throughout his published interviews, this chatterbot is often excited, disappointed, confused, rude, and empathetic. At one point, Eugene empathizes with his conversant and his pet: "all we feel sad sometimes [sic]. Even my dear guinea pig feels depressed sometimes" (qtd. in Ulanoff).

Specifically, the program was given a backstory that also mirrored its programmers' experiences: Eugene Goostman's gender, name, and nationality all parallel the biography of one of the key programmers, Eugene Demchenko. Demchenko's experiences were used as a familiar foundation for this chatterbot's convincing performance of intelligence. In a way, Demchenko replicated himself as a program, which is a familiar trope in computer science. In *Fathering the Unthinkable*, Brian Easlea reveals the consistent use of paternal metaphors that create father-son relationships between computer scientists as fathers and their computers or programs as sons. These men pass on their intellectual code, if not their genetic code, to future generations through the computing technologies they develop. From his analysis, Easlea concludes "our whole culture is basically masculine in character but modern science is its cutting edge" (7). In this way, Eugene Goostman is a chip off the ol' block of his programmers.

This rhetoric of embodiment is not just identifiable, it also constitutes the grounding premises upon which Eugene Goostman's intelligence is performed. After defining Eugene's specific body and embodied experiences, a knowledge base was built upon that bodily foundation. "Our main idea," Veselov explains, "was that he [Eugene Goostman] can claim that he knows anything, but his age also makes it perfectly reasonable that he doesn't know everything" (qtd. in University of Reading). Eugene's particular knowledge set was limited to what a thirteen-year-old boy from Ukraine would likely know. For example, the online version refused to answer math-related questions because math is boring and hard. At the same time, he could talk about popular culture in detail: "Star wars [sic] are stupid and primitive, and Yoda is a big green smelling alien talking frog" (Ulanoff). His experience of cities was limited to his hometown, Odessa, Ukraine, and to the places he had seen in movies. After discovering that his conversant was in New York, Eugene replied by drawing from the only experience a boy his age may likely have: "I saw New York in many movies. I think it exists to bewilder people's imagination[s] all-over the world" (Ulanoff). His Ukrainian nationality was also strategic: if English is his second language, then judges may overlook incorrect or awkward grammar.

Gendering and Racializing a Chatterbot

Veselov explains, "we spent a lot of time developing a character with a believable personality" (qtd. in University of Reading). This believable personality was successful. One of the judges describes his experience: "the software running on the computers was very sophisticated, understood slang and colloquialisms and made typos, answered in a jokey and informal manner, and ran rings around me" (qtd. in Horn). In order to cultivate this successful performance, Eugene Goostman projects whiteness and masculinity.

Veselov and Demchenko consider Eugene's convincingly rude character to be one of their most significant technical accomplishments. Veselov explains, "this year we improved the 'dialog controller,' which makes the conversation far more human-like when compared to programs that just answer questions" (qtd. in University of Reading). John Denning, a programmer on the team, explains the goal of Eugene's dialogue controller: "if a conversation turns rude, Goostman turns rude, just like a real conversation. If you put your kid on the schoolyard, you want your kid to defend himself" (qtd. in Ulanoff). Essentially, they programmed this chatterbot to present the personality of a schoolyard bully. When Lance Ulanoff asked him about computer games, Eugene replied, "I hope you aren't one of those computer geeks . . . . I'm not a geek." Additionally, Ulanoff reported, "sometimes he [Eugene] makes creepy innuendos about women because he's a thirteen-year-old." Sexism, mocking people, car racing—all of these characteristics draw upon stereotypes of traditional, boyish masculinity in order to perform intelligence in a convincing way.

Identifying Intelligence in a Chatterbot

Eugene Goostman does not represent the best or most impressive intelligence. Rather, he represents the most familiar and identifiable; thus, identification was the key for passing the Turing Test. Identification, in the Burkean sense, suggests that before persuasion happens there must be some consubstantial relation, or a common ground of shared substance that may be recognized consciously or unconsciously (*Rhetoric* 55). Metaphorically, Burke defines identification as "one's way of seeing one's reflection in the social mirror" (*Philosophy* 227). The programmers projected themselves and their embodied experience onto the chatterbot's intelligent performance. And the judges saw themselves reflected in this performance of white male embodiment. If not their own personal experience, then the judges, at the least, would have identified Eugene's white, male performance as familiar, common, and, therefore, convincing.

However, it is important to note that the team of programmers at Wholesale Change was an international team, out of which two of the nine members were women (Wholesale Change). Despite the national and gendered diversity of the programming team, they collaboratively composed, tested, and refined Eugene Goostman's performance of whiteness and masculinity. In doing so, they reified white masculine embodiment as the most convincing and identifiable form of intelligence. Importantly, the judges—which included a diverse set of people—confirmed the power of whiteness and masculinity as identifiable forms of intelligence when they were convinced that this rude, sexist boy was an intelligent human.

Conclusion

Eugene's performance of intelligence functions as a social mirror, reflecting cultural tropes of whiteness and masculinity that are intertwined with identifiable performances of intelligence. By reading Eugene Goostman's text for its embodied rhetoric, this discourse makes visible the continued centrality of whiteness and masculinity as the most convincing performance of intelligence. Ironically, this gendered and raced intelligence is made visible because the intelligent subject being tested has no body at all but relies upon a rhetoric of embodiment to perform convincing intelligence.

Silicon Valley, as the hub of tech culture in the US and internationally, is especially entrenched in a culture of whiteness and masculinity. This is not to say that the tech workers are all white and male but that the culture is predominantly white and male, and both consciously and unconsciously foster cultures that exclude women and people of color (Vassallo et al.; Myer). Efforts to create diversity in these communities have had limited success. The number of women receiving computer science degrees has only declined over the past three decades, from 37% in 1982 to just 17% in 2015 (Henn). While only 4% of computer science degrees are earned by African Americans, the rate of hiring African Americans is still lower, with only 2% of computer science jobs going to African Americans (Myer). Eugene's performance of intelligence, as well as the fact that his performance was successfully identified as human, suggests one reason why efforts to include diversity have been unsuccessful: the problem may be in the very way that Silicon Valley identifies intelligence. Eugene's performance suggests that the most recognizable, identifiable performance of intelligence is also a familiar performance of whiteness and masculinity.

To conclude, I want to return to Krista Ratcliffe's call in *Rhetorical Listening*: social tropes of race and gender "remain steeped in very real material consequences for US culture and for individual people's lives. This logic demands that race [and gender] be studied, not to reify its existence but to expose its functions so as to interrupt injustices and promote social justice" (15). Eugene Goostman, as an example, addresses Ratcliffe's call: his case exposes how racialized and gendered tropes have real material consequences; however, his performance also points toward directions to focus our work for addressing the second aspect of her call: interrupt injustices and promote social justice. This analysis suggests that, in order to interrupt the injustices that flourish in Silicon Valley and in tech culture, we must rhetorically and systematically disentangle masculinity and whiteness from intelligence. And the first step in doing this is to critically assess the terms on which we evaluate and perform intelligence, making space for and affirming racially and gender diverse performances of intelligence.

Note: I am very grateful for the friends and mentors who gave of their time and energy to help me draft and revise this article. Many thanks to

Heather Steffen, Josh Mehler, Risa Applegarth, Karen Lunsford, Per Hoel, and the editors and reviewers at Present Tense.

NOTES

1. Most computer scientists responded critically to the news of this successful Turing Test (see Wilks). The test is dismissed, in part, because computer scientists are building machines that display forms of intelligence different from human-centric definitions of intelligence (see French). return

2. Specifically, I am drawing this content from the University of Reading press release, online news coverage, interviews with the chatterbot's inventors and judges, and published interviews with an online version of Eugene Goostman. Note that all published text from the chatterbot comes from an earlier version of the chatterbot that was developed in 2001 and is said to be less sophisticated (Ulanoff). The actual transcripts of the 2014 Turing Test have not been made publicly available. return

WORKS CITED

Burke, Kenneth. *A Rhetoric of Motives*. Berkeley: U of California P, 1969. Print.

—. *The Philosophy of Literary Form: Studies in Symbolic Action*. Berkeley: U of California P, 1974. Print.

Easlea, Brian. *Fathering the Unthinkable: Masculinity, Scientists, and the Nuclear Arms Race*. London: Pluto, 1983. Print.

French, Robert M. "Moving beyond the Turing Test." *Communications of the ACM* 55.12 (2012): 74. Print.

Frost, Erin A., and Michelle F. Eble. "Technical Rhetorics: Making Specialized Persuasion Apparent to Public Audiences." *Present Tense: A Journal of Rhetoric in Society* 2.4 (2015): n.pag. *Present Tense*. Web. 15 Oct. 2016.

Hallenbeck, Sarah. "Toward a Posthuman Perspective: Feminist Rhetorical Methodologies and Everyday Practices." *Advances in the History of Rhetoric* 15.1 (2012): 9–27. Print.

Henn, Steve. "When Women Stopped Coding." *National Public Radio*. NPR, 21 Oct. 2014. Web. 15 Oct. 2016.

Harding, Sandra G. *The Science Question in Feminism*. Ithaca: Cornell UP, 1986. Print.

Horn, Leslie. "What It Was Like to Judge that History-Making Turing Test." *Gizmodo*. Gizmodo, 16 June 2014. Web. 15 Oct. 2016.

Jack, Jordynn. "A Pedagogy of Sight: Microscopic Vision in Robert Hooke's Micrographia." *Quarterly Journal of Speech* 95.2 (2009): 192–209. Print.

Johnson, Maureen, Daisy Levy, Katie Manthey, and Maria Novotny. "Embodiment: Embodying Feminist Rhetorics." *Peitho: Journal of the Coalition of Women Scholars in the History of Rhetoric and Composition* 18.1 (2015): n.pag. *Peitho*. Web. 15 Oct. 2016.

Katz, Steven B. "The Ethic of Expediency: Classical Rhetoric, Technology, and the Holocaust." *College English* 54.3 (1992): 255. Print.

Keller, Evelyn Fox. "Gender and Science." *Discovering Reality*. Ed. Sandra Harding and Merrill B. Hintikka. 2nd ed. Dordrecht: Kluwer, 2006. 187–205. Print.

Meyer, Robinson. "On a Scale of 1 to 10, Silicon Valley's Lack of Racial Diversity Is a 7." *The Atlantic*.The Atlantic Monthly Group, 1 Nov. 2015. Web. 15 Oct. 2015.

Pfeifer, Rolf, and Josh Bongard. *How the Body Shapes the Way We Think: A New View of Intelligence*. Boston: MIT, 2006. Print.

Ratcliffe, Krista. *Rhetorical Listening: Identification, Gender, Whiteness*. Carbondale: Southern Illinois UP, 2006. Print.

Reyes, G. Mitchell. "Stranger Relations: The Case for Rebuilding Commonplaces between Rhetoric and Mathematics." *Rhetoric Society Quarterly* 44.5 (2014): 470–91. Print.

Slack, Jennifer Daryl, David James Miller, and Jeffrey Doak. "The Technical Communicator as Author: Meaning, Power, Authority." *Journal of Business and Technical Communication* 7.1 (1993): 12–36. Print.

Ulanoff, Lance. "Turing Test Winner Eugene Goostman: The Inside Story." *Mashable*. Mashable, 12 June 2014. Web. 15 Oct. 2016.

University of Reading. "Turing Test Success Marks Milestone in Computing History." *University of Reading*. University of Reading, 8 June 2014. Web. 15 Oct. 2016.

Vassallo, Trea, Ellen Levy, Michele Madansky, Hillary Mickell, Bennett Porter, Monica Leas, and Julie Oberweis. *The Elephant in the Valley*. Women in Tech, 2016. Web. 15 Oct. 2016.

Wilks, Yorick. "Don't Believe the Science Hype–We Haven't Created True AI yet." *The Guardian*. Guardian News and Media Limited, 11 June 2014. Web. 15 Oct. 2016.

Wholesale Change. "Eugene Goostman: The Weirdest Creature in the World." *Wholesale Change*. Wholesale Change, n.d. Web. 15 Oct. 2016.

COMPOSITION STUDIES

Composition Studies is on the Web at http://www.uc.edu/journals/composition-studies.html

In publication since March 1972, *Composition Studies* holds the distinction of being the oldest independent journal in its field. Consistent with its beginnings as a forum for discussing teaching experiences, Composition Studies continues to publish scholarship about teaching writing but has expanded to include a wide range of historical, theoretical, and exploratory studies related to writing, pedagogy, administration, literacy, and emerging areas of interest. The journal's interest in growing with the field is perhaps best illustrated by a statement in the mission welcoming work that doesn't fit neatly elsewhere.

Sensing the Sentence: An Embodied Simulation Approach to Rhetorical Grammar

By connecting neuroscientific, rhetorical, and embodied approaches to grammar pedagogy, Hannah J. Rule offers teachers novel classroom strategies adaptable for a variety of classrooms and for a range of diverse students, including non-neurotypical learners. This article represents a theoretically informed, pragmatic effort to re-see one of the most fraught issues in the field of writing studies: how to teach grammar.

Sensing the Sentence: An Embodied Simulation Approach to Rhetorical Grammar

Hannah J. Rule

This article applies the neuroscientific concept of embodied simulation—the process of understanding language through visual, motor, and spatial modalities of the body—to rhetorical grammar and sentence-style pedagogies. Embodied simulation invigorates rhetorical grammar instruction by attuning writers to the felt effects of written language, prioritizing how syntactical structures move, look, and adjust meaning in fine-tuned ways. Simulation methods thus help ease a central concern of writing teachers: they bridge the gap between knowing about grammar and knowing how to do grammar. Embodied simulation research, when partnered with insights in embodied composition and disability studies, contributes to composition pedagogy an accessible, dynamic means of addressing the local in our students' writing.

> "The act of composing with writing cannot be severed from the act of composing with our senses."
>
> —Kristie S. Fleckenstein, *Embodied Literacies* (2003)

To begin, a familiar scene to the writing teacher: a first-year writing student of mine—I'll call her Mary—had come to my office to discuss an essay draft. She seemed most vexed by my comment that parts of her draft lacked "flow," especially in the opening paragraph. I tried to minimize that concern, suggesting that she prioritize bigger picture questions first. We nevertheless began talking about flow, and I tried first to describe it: flow is when the reader feels connections that leap up and pull us along, I said. When flow lacks, each sentence feels like its own distinct island and the reader must laboriously swim to reach the next one. These attempts to describe flow to Mary—even partnered with my emphatic swimming gestures—were appropriately met with squinty eyes and mumbled "uh huhs."

So I ditched flow, moving on to another means of talking about textual cohesion, the known-new contract. This concept, I told Mary, encourages writers to start a new sentence with the focus of the previous sentence. Known-new felt like a more concrete approach than flow; it could pull us down into the architecture of Mary's sentences on the page. Mary clearly grasped the idea of known-new (before introducing something new, her second sentence should begin with what she had focused on in the first sentence), but she froze a bit when I asked her to spot the subject in her opening sentence. While this approach might have eventually gotten us somewhere, I abandoned it. I felt like I was quizzing her on parts of speech, sending a message that a sentence is a space only for the "proper" identification of parts and application of pre-set rules.

Finding myself out of ideas, my mind turned to some cognitive science research I had been reading recently—research that forms the focus of this article—about how we embody and visualize language in order to make meaning. I asked Mary to read her first sentence aloud. Gesturing out to the space in front of us, I showed her what her words made me picture. Mary's opening sentence, which was something like, "Students today use a lot of technology, like cell phones, Facebook, laptops and more," put me in a classroom of college students (one just like our classroom, I told her). All had big flat phones or tablets with the screens lit up. Because "picturing" something, for me, feels most like movement (rather than a flat movie or still image), I mimed how I saw the students typing feverishly on laptops while effortlessly pressing the phones to their ears. Mary nodded along. As Mary read me her next sentence—something like, "Textbooks have been an important part of school for a very long time"—I found myself sweeping my hand quickly to the left. Gesturing with my hands the shape of an open book, I was now looking down at a textbook as it became enmeshed in a time and place long ago, maybe back to the time of the Greeks in their robes, sitting in rows and looking into their (anachronistic) textbooks.

I asked Mary if she could feel how *physically far away* that second sentence felt, how *literally distant* the book and the Greeks seemed from those technology-juggling modern students. She nodded. I then asked how the second sentence might instead "keep us in the classroom," or keep the action of the scene focused on the multitaskers. After talking aloud a bit, Mary began writing above her second sentence. "Around all this technology," she wrote, "textbooks can seem out of place..." From there, Mary and I continued embodying her words through visualization, gesture, movement, and verbal description, and she redesigned her sentences to create more coherent moves.

I describe this scene first to highlight a challenge familiar to the college writing teacher: the struggle to find ways to talk about writing at the sentence-level. We dutifully dispense commonplaces to our students, but they can let us down. Though flow is well secured in the vernacular of composition teachers and peer-reviewing students alike ("your essay flows really well!"), the concept fails to reveal how to build flow on the page. And maybe more often, as in the known-new contract, familiar sentence-level strategies can feel like mental formula, tricks to monitor sentences and ensure they are "right." What's more is that in composition's current pedagogical mindset, writing teachers are unsure if we should be talking about sentences at all. That is, the sentence is practically *verboten* in our pedagogies (owed to, among other factors, the paradigmatic shift from current-traditional-error-seeking-red-pens to global-development-big-picture process, and to the fall of 1970s-era sentence combining and generative rhetoric (Connors)). The sentence survives today only as a pedagogic relic, and carries along with it the thorny question of grammar instruction. As Laura R. Micciche has noted, "In composition studies, grammar instruction is unquestionably unfashionable" (716), and this commonplace view is supported by a mountain of research concluding plainly that "we should not expect knowledge of grammar to influence the quality of writing" (Hillocks 76).

In contrast to this wave of sentence-eliding, however, efforts persist to reanimate the sentence as a central site of writing instruction, including, for example, authentic writing approaches to the study of grammar in context (Anderson; Dunn, "Does Bad Grammar"; Weaver). Rhetorical grammar pedagogies too have reimagined the sentence as a global compositional concern, not one of mere polishing or proofreading. "Understanding rhetorical grammar," Martha Kolln writes, "means understanding the grammatical choices available to you when you write and the rhetorical effects those choices will have on your reader" (3). Any sentence-level intervention, though, may be undermined by students' prior experiences with doing grammar. Students, it seems, still endure sentence diagramming and worksheets that reinforce sentence work as identification and error-hunting procedures only. As a result, college writers can freeze up when we talk about their writing at the sentence level, as happened with Mary. The question then becomes how do we get our student-writers to experience sentence-making as dynamic rhetorical action, to *feel* the effects of their constructions, as Kolln hopes?

The breakthrough I had with Mary represents a lively and novel way to reshape students' conceptions of the sentence. Mary and I came to share in the experience of her meaning, I will argue in this essay, through making explicit the process of *embodied simulation*: the experiential processes of understanding language through visual, spatial, motor, affective, and other sensory modalities. A linguistic and neuroscientific theory of meaning-making, embodied simulation suggests that "we understand language by simulating in our minds what it would be like to experience the things that the language describes" (Bergen 13). Making simulation explicit and dialogic helped Mary make meaningful changes to the structure of her sentences. She observed my embodiment—my gestural, associative, and visual conception of her words—and intervened to redirect that experience toward more cohesive expression.

In what follows, I align embodied simulation research and theory with composition's established beliefs about visual and kinesthetic dimensions of composing. At the same time, through work in embodied composition and disability studies, I modify some of this theory's assumptions (e.g., the tendency to privilege sight over other senses) in order to imagine more inclusive classroom methods. I then connect simulation's claims about grammar to instructional scenes from my own rhetorical grammar and style classroom and to familiar sentence-style imperatives (e.g., use active verbs). When in conversation with composition, embodied simulation research contributes to our pedagogy an engaging, dimensional, and intuitive way to address the local—the sentence—as a dynamic embodied space.

Embodied Simulation, Embodied Composition

Embodied simulation is a theory of meaning emerging in related disciplines including neuroscience, linguistics, philosophy, and cognitive psychology and is demonstrated through ongoing empirical study. As neuroscientist Benjamin K. Bergen describes it: "Meaning is a creative process in which people construct virtual experiences—embodied simulations—in their mind's eye" (16). The concept of simulation emerges from a broader framework that cognitive psychologist Raymond W. Gibbs, Jr. names "the embodiment premise." Gibbs outlines this basis for understanding cognitive and psychological phenomena as follows:

> Human language and thought emerge from recurring patterns of embodied activity that constrain ongoing intelligent behavior. We must not assume cognition to be purely internal, symbolic, computational, and disembodied, but seek out the gross and detailed ways that language and thought are inextricably shaped by embodied action. (*Embodiment* 9)

What makes simulation impactful in the writing classroom is first that meaning-making is understood as a dynamic, creative process: reading or expressing language entails imagistic, bodily, associational, and sensory *action*. This bodily engagement is incited and directed by language, but its experience unfolds only by virtue of an individual's complex lifeworld. For example, simulation researchers might suggest that Mary's words first called to my mind a movie-like, two-dimensional image of tech-wielding college students. The vague imagery I experienced, however, was not abstract "stock" footage. Instead, I evoked specific visual memories of the classroom where I taught Mary. Her general mention of "a long time" took me back to the Greeks for perhaps no other reason than I was reading ancient rhetoric at the time. And while, as a sighted person, visuality was a component of my experience of Mary's words, I experienced spatiality and movement through gesture most vividly. I was putting myself in the shoes of the action I perceived. According to Gibbs, I was creating a "meaningful construal by simulating how the objects and actions depicted in language relate to embodied possibilities. Thus, individuals use their embodied experiences to 'soft-assemble' meaning rather than merely activate pre-existing abstract, conceptual representations" (*Embodiment* 200-1).

Embodied simulation research[1] is also invigorating because its assumptions echo established work in composition studies that demonstrates the ineluctable corporeality of composing (Dunn, *Talking*; Fleckenstein, "Writing Bodies"; Fleckenstein, Calendrillo and Worley; Haas and Witte; Murray; Perl; Stenberg; Syverson). Pushing against our collective dualist Cartesian assumptions, disability studies and composition scholar Jay Dolmage writes:

> The dominant discourse surrounding the teaching of writing focuses on texts and thoughts, words and ideas, as though these entities existed apart from the bodies of teachers, writers, audiences, communities. As a discipline, broadly speaking, we in composition and rhetoric have not acknowledged that we have a body, bodies; we cannot admit that our prevailing metaphors and tropes should be read across the body,

or that our work has material, corporeal bases, effects, and affects. (110)

Our everyday classroom practices with texts, says Dolmage, continue to be implicitly disconnected from embodied experience. Simulation represents a way to address this disconnect: as psychology and embodied cognition scholar Arthur M. Glenberg puts it, following the assumptions of embodied simulation, "language is understood by driving the brain into states that are analogous to the perceptual, action, and emotional states that arise during perception of and acting in the real situation" (6). By extension, perception of syntactical constructions can be unlocked through processes of embodied sensing, picturing, and moving, or *sensing the sentence*. Indeed, drawing out the visual and kinesthetic dimensions of composing will likely feel familiar to compositionists; however, as I argue in this section, simulation research provokes us to see bodily sensation at the core of word work. At the same time, embodied composition and disability scholarship reframe some assumptions in simulation theory toward more inclusive classroom practice.

Simulation researchers are conducting a large number and range of studies using unbiased measures including reaction times, timed matching tasks, eye-tracking technology, and *f*MRI scans in order to validate simulation at the level of neurological occurrence[2]. But the felt phenomenological experiences of simulation may already be familiar: the imaginative world-building that happens as you read a gripping novel, giving directions to a familiar place by twisting your body to move through a mental street map, or feeling disoriented as you watch the film version of a book you hold dear. While for some a good novel or sentence can spawn three-dimensional worlds almost automatically, for others (like some of our students) the experience of text may feel more like a flattened soundscape of words. Making simulation processes explicit and dialogic, then, may or may not initially resonate with students' cache of experiences, especially with the sentence. But inviting simulation into the writing classroom can be transformative for most, if not all. Glenberg, whose research explicitly links simulation to literacy, warns that for those students "who fail to make the link between the written word and the embodied experience, reading becomes a boring exercise in word-calling that rarely results in meaning" (8). Simulation evokes the transformative pedagogical power of emphasizing that words and sentences comprise *literal* action—language moves us, maps spaces, and makes us see and feel things in myriad and idiosyncratic ways.

This is not to say, though, that simulation is a panacea. There is risk, for example, of seeming to speak uncritically or with certainty about what brains and bodies do. Compositionists too may be weary of invocations of the brain as explanations of complex, social and cognitive literate processes, as in the past the field has perhaps been too eager to apply them (Newkirk 3; Rose). The ways simulation researchers talk about brain activity should also not be accepted simply as "a physical explanation for [the] behavioral phenomenon" of reading, composing, or language comprehension (Weisberg et al.). Simulation theory is not just about peering into the brain, though; it does maintain some social constructivist orientations. For example, the felt dimensions of simulation (visual, spatial, proprioceptive, gestural) are assumed to emerge from idiosyncratic worldly experience (Bergen 177). The theory accounts too for the constructedness of that experience; as stated by Gibbs, "Bodies are not culture-free objects, because all aspects of embodied experience are shaped by cultural processes" (*Embodiment* 13).

Research on embodied simulation also has a direct, though not unproblematic, connection to a book central to the humanities and close to composition, George Lakoff and Mark Johnson's *Metaphors We Live By*[3]. Lakoff and Johnson, we remember, demonstrated the embodiment of language by closely examining metaphorical clusters like "up is good" (which grounds phrases like *I'm on cloud 9, the stock market is soaring, I'm feeling upbeat*). These turns-of-phrase become meaningful, they argue, by virtue of collective physical and spatial experience in the world: "Our constant physical activity in the world, even when we sleep, makes an up-down orientation not merely relevant to our physical activity but centrally relevant. . . . the structure of our spatial concepts emerges from our constant spatial experience, that is, our interaction with the physical environment" (56). This physical grounding of metaphor demonstrates the linguistic tendency to "conceptualize the nonphysical in terms of the physical" (Lakoff and Johnson 59).

And this bridge made by metaphor is crucial in simulation theory, as it helps account for the embodied basis of "language about things that we can't see or do" (Bergen 196). Lakoff and Johnson's intervention unites language with embodiment and demonstrates how simulation processes can extend to the abstractions of the academic discourses that preoccupy teachers of writing. At the same time, some assumptions founding this touchstone text are concerning. Critics have pointed out the ways this theory purports "a universality of both physical and conceptual experience" (Altman 500)—such as the supposedly fully shared experience of walking upright or the assumed connection between seeing and knowing (Vidali 34). As is well established in disability, gender, and constructionist discourses, "the construct of an 'ideal' or 'universal' body is a fiction, a fantasy" (Wilson and Lewiecki-Wilson 13). Forwarding simulation does risk unwittingly presuming universality in embodiment and continuing to overvalue the relationship of literacy and vision.

Visuality, indeed, has long been connected to language and knowledge. As Mark Sadoski and Allan Paivio suggest, imagery evokes a history as long as the discipline of rhetoric itself (ix), a long-standing tension "between an abstract, verbal emphasis and a concrete, imaginal emphasis in cognition and learning" (27). Compositionists too have argued in different ways for the importance of the visual: Joddy Murray suggests the image is "elemental to thought, to emotion, and ultimately to composing" (3); Hildy Miller links mental imagery with emotion in the writing process (116); Debra Innocenti helps students "facilitate a physical relationship with the words on the page" through dynamic mental movies (60). Even Linda Flower and John R. Hayes' cognitive problem-solving theory of composing makes space for the nonverbal image (372). There has been, in other words, an established impulse to install seeing at the center of writing and its instruction, and embodied simulation theory could be said to reify this impulse. But, rather than proceed with presumptions about visuality (as the unimodal domain of the eyes), work in embodiment and disability studies provides nuance toward understanding seeing instead as multisensory and diverse.

Based on my discussion of simulation thus far, readers might be most reminded of Kristie S. Fleckenstein's *Embodied Literacies: Imageword and a Poetics of Teaching*. Fleckenstein argues for the fundamentally imagistic nature of literate practice, or the "embodiment of literacy through imagery" (6-7). A central difference, though, between simulation and Fleckenstein's imageword is where the impetus for imagery is found. Fleckenstein establishes that the "prevalence of imagery in our lives indicates the extent to which imagery needs to transform our theories of meaning" (11). Living life now in in the midst of a "pictoral turn" (2), literacy practitioners must turn to imagery as an "alternative imaginary" (2) because "our students already locate themselves and their writing-reading at the suture points of image and word" (Fleckenstein 14). While of course visual culture continues to stretch our conceptions of writing and its teaching, simulation theory offers a different, and perhaps more pressing, impetus. That is, after accepting some of the tenets of simulation, the visuality of literacy is not just fitting to shifts in culture but also increasingly characteristic of what researchers continue to discover about the embodied mind. Amassing simulation research suggests that we do not really *choose* to link imagery and word; rather, this link is the precise way in which meaning becomes possible at all.

At the same time, Fleckenstein's nuanced construction of imagery contributes to simulation pedagogy a more responsive conception of what picturing language or sensing the sentence can mean. While imagery might be first associated with flattened "snapshots" or still mental images (19), Fleckenstein emphasizes instead the "multidimensionality" (21) of imagistic experience, asserting, "imagery encompasses a range of modalities that nest within one another" (19). Imagistic experience is necessarily and deeply multimodal:

> Imagery comes in an unending stream and a range of individual modalities. Rarely do these modalities remain neatly demarcated. Images tend to nest a range of senses, resulting in meanings that are collaborative products of sound, sights, and touch, providing full and resonant . . . significance to meaning. "Seeing" doesn't occur alone or in isolation but is accompanied by feeling. After all, the physiological system of visualization includes the apparatus to detect texture. (19-20)

While research in neuroscience and simulation reinforces the links Fleckenstein here establishes between feeling and seeing and the multimodality of imagery (see Lacey and Lawson), it is also true that Bergen, for example, tends to cast simulation most often through *seeing* metaphors, like "the mind's eye" (or as discussed in the next section, grammar as a *movie* director). It is thus vital to keep Fleckenstein's concept of multimodal imagery at the fore of simulation practices, enacted in inclusionary ways by encouraging its unfolding through a *range* of bodily modalities—showing, gesturing, narrating, and moving. It is equally imperative to proceed with awareness of the nuance that disability scholars have brought to "categories" of dis/ability, like blindness and sightedness. As Julia Miele Rodas writes, "blind experience, like the range of visual experience, is infinitely diverse" (119). As simulation practitioners, we cannot presume the ways that a legally blind individual may experience a wide range of visual sensations, nor can we presume anything about the visual sensations of ostensibly "sighted" students. In sum, doing simulation ought not assume any standard ways of experiencing visuality and other bodily sensations, or any ease in doing so.

Simulation research focuses on action and movement as much as visuality and thus also has implications for the kinesthetic dimensions of literacy. For example, much simulation research shows that parts of the brain responsible for motor coordination (the areas of the brain connected to bodily movement in the world) also become engaged when action-oriented sentences are read. In one such study, participants read sentences that involved "hand verbs like grasp, foot verbs like kick, or mouth verbs like bite" (Bergen 91). Their *f*MRI scans demonstrated that "understanding language about actions measurably activates motor regions of the brain" (91). Ernest Davis expands upon this connection between physical action and language:

> If you read the sentence, "John turned the key in the ignition" or "John screwed off the gas cap," the part of the brain that controls motion of the hand is activated. Remarkably, after reading the first sentence, an experimental subject finds it easier to turn their hand clockwise than counterclockwise; the reverse is true after reading the second sentence. This kind of visualization and activation of motor control is known as "embodied simulation." (1)

Neuroscientists are demonstrating that understanding language, as far as the brain is concerned, is a lot like physically moving in the world. This idea that reading about actions is akin to doing them is enjoying increasing visibility (Berns et al.; Tamir et al.), making the adage that words transport us into other worlds and lives much more literal. Or, as Bergen puts it, "Understanding language, in multimodal ways, is a lot like being there" (92).

Just as with the interaction of simulation and visuality, this motoric aspect of simulation theory has implications for the relationship compositionists have assumed between the kinesthetic and linguistic. This influence can be illustrated through Karen Klein and Linda Hecker's essay, "The Write Moves: Cultivating Kinesthetic and Spatial Intelligences in the Writing Process." Following the assumptions established by Patricia Dunn and by Howard Gardner's multiple intelligences theory (89), these pedagogues argue that students need ways of capitalizing on intelligences beyond linguistic prowess. In working with both "visual thinkers" and "dyslexic students," the authors discovered that "many individuals struggling to express their ideas on paper could build models of how ideas relate using pipe cleaners, Legos, or Tinkertoys, or they could walk those ideas across a room, changing direction to indicate changes in logical structure" (89). These activities "help students generate language as well as organize it. Holding or touching an object or moving our bodies through space appears to simulate the flow of language" (89-90).

Klein and Hecker suggest some "appearance" of a relationship between physical movement and language, emphasizing the power of "*cross-fertilizing* students' linguistic abilities with spatial or kinesthetic intelligences" (89, emphasis mine). But language and corporeality are ultimately understood by Klein and Hecker as separate modes: under the guidance of multiple intelligences theory, linguistic intelligence is fully distinct from spatial, visual, and kinesthetic ones. Simulation theory, by contrast, implies that spatial and kinesthetic intelligences are fully entailed within linguistic intelligence and vice versa. The spatial experience of walking the structure (where students follow their transitions and organizational logic to physically move through a room) would become not just a helpful alternative avenue for understanding what has been assumed to be the linguistic abstractions of essay structure. Those spatial experiences are a necessary part of how meaning is constructed: transition words, under the influence of simulation, are better understood to move us *literally* through an essay. Signal words like *moreover* incite us to place new information over or on top of what is already known. Linguistic intelligence then is more aptly understood as *inseparable from* spatial, kinesthetic, and other sensory modes.

This interpretive shift impacts how we conceive of kinesthetic practices and our students. Consider Mary: under the influence of the theory of multiple intelligences, we might think of her as a visual or kinesthetic learner in need of a physically grounded way to understand textual coherence or flow. Or, as Dunn might frame it, Mary needed the chance to use visual, aural, spatial, emotional, kinesthetic, and social ways of knowing (*Talking* 1) as an alternative to the "primacy of language" (*Talking* 21) that dominates writing classrooms. Dunn has championed the idea of the "multiple channel strategy" (8), which rightly insists on giving students space to contribute their knowledge in ways that go beyond the word, like sketching, three-dimensional modeling, or moving. Embodied simulation provides what I see as a complementary multiple channels strategy. Since simulation implies that literate processes already entail within them a complex mix of visual, motor, spatial, and other sensing modalities—more plainly, that all literacy is multiliteracy—then *no intelligence or mode* is beyond Mary's grasp. Opening multiple channels with simulation would mean not turning *away* from words to other modes, but instead drawing out dialogically the visual, spatial, gestural experiences of those words. Simulation is then another means of enacting the inclusivity and access that Dunn and others have sought. Embodied simulation research encourages us to bring inclusive embodied methods to our baseline composition practices in order to impact inclusion and engagement and to continue anew Dunn's declaration that "[a]ll writers . . . benefit from multiple pathways" (1). To enact a simulation approach to teach transitions, or essay structure, or, as I discuss below, rhetorical grammar and sentence style is ultimately to make explicit and dialogic our varied embodied experiences, or simulations, of language.

Simulation as Rhetorical Grammar and Sentence Style Method

Simulation theory and research has much to say about the formative, shaping roles of grammar in meaning making. Bergen devotes much space in his book *Louder than Words* to describing grammar as an engine that guides and directs simulation experiences. If words, Bergen suggests, "provide the cast of characters, props, and sets," then it is grammar that "directs the action so that the scene plays out in the intended fashion" (94). Grammatical structures can dictate perspective, detail, and focus within simulations and bind details, like color, movement, and size, to their relevant objects (Bergen 118). Bergen casts grammar's role as that of the "director" (114), finely shaping how (textual) action is visualized and embodied, a conception echoed in Joan Didion's well-known essay "Why I Write." In Didion's words, "To shift the structure of a sentence alters the meaning of that sentence, as definitely and inflexibly as the position of a camera alters the meaning of the object photograph. . . . The arrangement of the words matters, and the arrangement you want can be found in the picture in your mind. The picture dictates the arrangement" (Popova). Accepting the premise that grammar "modulate[s] what part of an evoked simulation someone is invited to focus on, the grain of detail with which the simulation is performed, or what perspective to perform the simulation from" (Bergen 118) supposes that grammar is indeed not best understood as a matter of "correctness," but of—just as rhetorical grammarians have told us—*choice*, a pursuit fundamentally connected to meaning. Simulation invites us to understand sentences not as deadened objects to diagnose and label. Rather, sentences incite action, as we intuitively and dialogically construct meaning, perceiving structures as choices with embodied, visualized effects.

In this final section, I demonstrate simulation methods as they emerged in a 300-level course I taught on rhetorical grammar and style at a large midwestern university, a course populated mostly by English majors interested in improving their writing. Using Kolln's *Rhetorical Grammar* and Donald A. Daiker, Andrew Kerek, and Max Morenberg's sentence style and combining approaches in *The Writer's Options*, we engaged in class discussion and exercises to help students consider the rhetorical actions of sentences. I recreate these scenes not to provide a set of "should-do"s or to offer "proof" that these methods work. Instead, I share them to inspire possibilities for recasting sentence work as embodied meaning work in a range of ways. Doing so can be invigorating not only in specialized writing courses like mine, but also in the context of first-year writing or writing centers. I am also measured in my belief in simulation, not knowing for sure how this approach may or may not connect with any given individual writer, including those identified as L2, underprepared, multilingual, or as writers with a range of visual, cognitive, or aural differences. But practicing simulation by emphasizing its multisensory and diverse nature helps ensure that it is as ethical and accessible as possible.

I discovered the usefulness of simulation in this course very early in the term, as I was trying to formulate questions about direct objects. We were looking at examples: *Jim builds his daughter a sandcastle at the beach.* "So where is the direct object here? And what does it *do*?" I began. My generous students offered textbook-type definitions: it receives the action. Okay, I thought (instantly questioning the value of identifying direct objects at all). "But what if we *picture* or try to put ourselves into the action of this sentence? Who's there? Show and tell me what they are doing." Students offered simple scenes at first: "Uh, Jim is building a sandcastle at the beach," they said, laughing a little. "Yes," I said, "But, really try to imagine this action concretely! Close your eyes." I read the sentence again and they offered more specificity: a baby sits in the sand playing with a shovel; Jim digs tirelessly. The sun is out. Another version: Jim's tween daughter stares at her phone as she sits in a beach chair; Jim (now a little older) keeps looking back at her hopefully as he shapes the castle. As we imagined possibilities for the scene, my students quickly established the differences between a direct and indirect object as we explored the relationship between the action and objects in the scene and sentence. Significantly, students' conceptions of indirect and direct objects emerged through the specificities of their simulations, as opposed to the traditional strategy of *naming and defining*. By inviting students to simulate, this previously unmemorable sentence was now *alive* in very different ways across the room and the functions of its parts intuited rather than labeled.

Starting discussion with simulation also led to fruitful debates and decreased students' need to call upon familiar grammar dictates or tricks. One student, for instance, asked if a sentence like "He feels hurt" could be said to have a direct object because, he argued, "hurt" answers a familiar formulaic question that grammar handbooks provide for finding a direct object: *What does he build? A sandcastle. What does he feel? Hurt?* I turned the question back to the students, asking them again to embody the action of these sentences. We perceived and discussed the differences in the nature of the action of *feeling* compared to the action of *building*, which led us to a discussion of transitive and intransitive verbs. It was not a discussion based on those terms and definitions, but rather primarily on the experienced nuance of embodied meaning (seeing and gesturing how the action of *feels* is different than that of *builds*). Embodying the sentence allowed students to *discover* the differences between grammatical constructions, a process reflected in simulation insights: "Readers use their embodied abilities to immediately create construals of the different perspectives, and the shifts of perspective, of the objects and actions described by language" (Gibbs, *Embodiment* 199-200). Simulation, moreover, reduces the *risks involved* in talking about a sentence, the risk of misnaming a grammatical part or "being wrong" about how a sentence is constructed. Sharing each individual's varied sense experiences of a given sentence is also valuable in itself. The multiplicity in a sense "proved" to students that adjusting the construction of a sentence is a matter of shaping meaning; subtle syntactical choices impact how a reader experiences the writer's meaning, and even the smallest adjustment can radically reshape that experience.

After inviting students to produce a few more simulated example sentences, I decided to explicitly introduce simulation as a method of our course. I explained some of the research that supported it and that we would continue to practice it throughout the term. I asked students to reflect on the simulating they had done: we discovered Fleckenstein's "nesting" sensory quality of picturing, the vagueness and variability of the mental picture, the ways that perceived action as movement seemed to feel most vivid. I spoke a bit about Bergen's idea of grammar as a movie director. They named the simulation approach the "grammera" (or "grammar camera") and we called upon it often for the rest of the term.

As the course progressed we examined and composed various structures, like appositives, participial phrases, and absolutes, as outlined in *The Writer's Options* and *Rhetorical Grammar*. In our discussion of absolutes, for example, we began by exploring examples like this one from Flannery O'Connor: "There was no bus in sight and Julian, his hands still jammed in his pockets and his head thrust forward, scowled down the empty street" (Nordquist). Students began by noticing the phrases set off by commas and their focusing effects. We then turned to Kolln's description in *Rhetorical Grammar*: "Absolute phrases are, indeed, noun phrases," Kolln writes. "This pattern, with a participial phrase as the postheadwork modifier, is our most common form of the absolute, although sometimes that modifier is a noun phrase, sometimes a prepositional phrase" (212). If, as with Mary, simply finding the subject of a sentence leads to paralyzed silence, what happens to students faced with this kind of definition? Much previous knowledge is required to get a handle on it. This familiar definitional and classification approach, echoed in most other grammar handbooks, gets caught up in first *categorizing*, instead of leading with why a writer would want to *use* an absolute phrase.

So we left this definition behind for a moment and deployed the "grammera" on examples like the one above. Students experienced the relationship between the absolute phrases and the main focus of sentences. They felt the varied cinematic effects of the structure: lingering focus, artful repetition, or delivery of subtle detail. These phrases direct the reader's focus, they said. One student noticed, in a sentence that contained several absolutes in a row, that the reader was made to linger on elements of a character's body, creating an objectifying gaze. He described this effect as "inception description"—in other words, absolutes piled on top of one another creates the sense of ever-narrowing detail, moving the focus further and further toward the subject. By picturing these new structures *first*—or in essence, by *discovering* their meaning through movement and visualization and thereby discovering how they impart nuanced meaning—students intuited why a writer would choose the absolute form as well as patterns for producing the structure in their own writing.

In this way, simulation modifies the baseline approach of rhetorical grammar by prioritizing the intuitive, embodied experience of any grammatical structure, which in turn demonstrates its rhetorical effects and leads writers to understand when and how they might deploy it. And prioritizing intuition is terribly important because it affirms what we know about how writers operationalize grammar knowledge when composing. As Patrick Hartwell defines it, grammar begins as the operative "grammar in our heads," which is "tacit and unconscious knowledge" (111). The problem for instruction, as Hartwell notes, is that while this internalized sense of grammar "is eminently useable knowledge—the way we make our life through language…it is not accessible knowledge, in a profound sense, we do not know that we have it" (111). The goals of rhetorical grammar, though, are to "raise consciousness about style, to encourage [writers] to make the kinds of stylistic choices that send an important message" (Kolln 211). How can consciousness be raised about a body of knowledge that is profoundly unconscious?

Kolln characterizes this consciousness-raising process as systematic and rules-based, as she writes, "Consider that there is stored within you, in your computer-like brain, a system of rules, a system that enables you to create the sentences of your native language. The fact that you have such an internalized system means that that when you study grammar *you are studying what you already 'know'* "(1, emphasis in original). But this grammar system, as Hartwell helps us understand, is not conscious knowledge of rules or terminology. Our life with language is not best understood as a system of rules in our computer-like brains. Simulation methods can transform rhetorical grammar practice because it prioritizes the *sense* of the sentence gained through intuition and forged through a history of reading and the ability to creatively assemble meaning. As Gibbs asserts, "embodiment shapes...*people's intuitions about*, and immediate understanding of, the meaning of various words, phrases, and linguistic expressions" ("Embodied" 2, emphasis added). Instead of swimming through complex definitions—instead of starting with identifying the subject, instead of thinking in terms of noun or participial phrases, instead of perceiving sentences as a set of separate elements we can label—we can simply ask students to dive in and sense the sentence. Kolln herself opens the door to this adjustment when she describes the absolute phrase metaphorically (unfortunately, in just one little sentence in a three-page description of this structure): "the absolute phrase moves the reader in for a close-up view, focusing on a detail, just as a filmmaker uses a camera" (212). What if *Rhetorical Grammar* led with and elaborated upon embodied descriptions like these? How might that change students' eagerness and ability to recognize and build their "conscious knowledge" of sentence constructions? What if all our discussions of sentence-level style began with the premise that we embody meaning?

As we neared the end of the course and a major revision project, my students commented on their newfound ability to "see" sentences. I think they meant this in two ways: the grammera, of course, but also seeing in terms of perceiving, assembling and ably rearranging the bricks of a sentence in different ways. With this discovered outcome, we turned to familiar writing handbook edicts on style that would help inform their revision processes. We discovered—not surprisingly— that embodied simulation provides felt rationales for familiar writing handbook advice and links various imperatives together, as demonstrated in the following examples.

One of the most familiar commandments we discussed was to "use active verbs." For example, in the Purdue OWL's directives about resume writing, we read, "You should use action verbs in workplace writing because they make sentences and statements more concise. Since concise writing is easier for readers to understand, it is more reader-centered. Because reader-centered writing is generally more persuasive, action verbs are more convincing than non-action verbs" (Brizee, Jarrett, and Schmaling). This is well-reasoned advice, though ironically, the explanation is not so concise. It is of course true that concision is friendly and persuasive to readers. But this description does not elucidate what an active verb is and, more importantly, why in this particular rhetorical situation, active verbs are persuasive. A simulation perspective can consolidate and clarify the rationale: using specific and carefully selected verbs helps the reader embody, or gain "visual proof" of the writer's previous work experience. If we make meaning by imagining "being there," then focused active verbs propel the virtual embodied experience in a maximally vivid and specific way. In this genre, active verbs *show* job experience rather than vaguely *tell* about it (yet another of our writing missives already tinged with the assumptions of simulation). Simulation also helps writers judge the effects of their own writing: they can ask if they are helping the reader really *see and experience* the world their words create, a much more accessible measure than more elusive ones like persuasion or reader-friendliness.

Consolidating and clarifying these rationales is of great import to our writing students given just how *many* sentence-style directives we ask them to consider. Take, for example, the following list of imperatives in John J. Ruszkiewicz, Maxine E. Hairston, and Christy E. Friend's *SF Express* handbook, each separately elaborated in sections on clarity and economy: use vigorous verbs, do not overuse *to be* verbs, reduce the number of passive verbs, replace cluttered verb phrases with single lively verbs (143), cut nominalizations, and cut *It is* and *There are* sentence openings (149). Though useful advice, following each of these edicts would take much time and concerted effort. Simulation intervenes to unify these instructions around the question of *movement*. For example, nominalizing transforms actions that are easy to see and feel into inert, immobile things. *There are* constructions eliminate action. Cluttered verbs confuse or hide the action. A simulation perspective consolidates these concerns about verbs with one: choose an active, lively, fitting verb that propels readers' embodied experiences. Writing students are repeatedly told simply to "avoid" the passive voice and nominalizations but are not offered explanations as to why. Simulating passive/active variations like "There is considerable destruction in the neighborhood from the storm" versus "The storm destroyed much of the neighborhood" produces different visual and embodied foci. Rather than rotely abiding by the edict to "avoid the passive voice," a rule that students tend to understand as gospel, simulation provides an accessible means of judging which action and focus best fits rhetorical aims. As my rhetorical grammar students and I discovered, once simulation becomes the baseline for understanding the work of sentences, new ways emerge to understand and act upon familiar writing concepts.

If individuals fine-tune meaning from the smallest of grammatical differences, then writing teachers are wise to spend time attuning students to how their grammatical choices can shape and direct embodied experience. Doing so explicitly and dialogically in the classroom helps students develop awareness of how they and others experience language. And while simulating cannot ensure that students always create acceptable and compelling structures, it does intervene in the central problem in teaching grammar: the gap between *knowing about* grammar and *knowing how to do* grammar. As Kolln writes, "Your grammatical knowledge is largely subconscious: You don't know consciously what you 'know.' When you study grammar you are learning about these grammar rules that you use subconsciously every time you speak" (2). Kolln's is a familiar attempt to build a bridge from the subconscious "grammar in our heads" (Hartwell 111) to the systemic study of rules-based grammar. But, in light of simulation, we do not really need the rules much, nor the names or definitions that *knowing about* grammar traditionally entails. Simulation allows us, as Hartwell advises, to "shuck off our hyperliterate perception of the value of formal rules, and to regain the confidence in the tacit power of unconscious knowledge" (121). But rather than leaving that power tacit, sensing the sentence uniquely provides a method—a shared vocabulary of language, gesture, movement, seeing—that accesses and makes social our intuitive language experiences so that writers may perceive and adjust their written meanings. Embodied simulation thus contributes to composition pedagogy an accessible means of addressing the local in our students' writing, as the sentence becomes an inhabited, dynamic, and embodied space.

NOTES

1. My discussion of simulation is mostly based on Benjamin Bergen's accessible and comprehensive book as well as Gibbs and Glenberg, but the following sources also inform my discussion: Berns, Blaine, Prietula, and Pye; Gibbs, "Embodied"; Falck and Gibbs; Fischer and Zwaan (840-843); Jacob; Lane, Kanjila, Omaki, and Bedny; Mendelsund; Santana and de Vega; Tamir, Bricker, Dodell-Feder, and Mitchell.

2. An example of how this research aims to validate the occurrence of simulation may be helpful. In one such study on "implied perspective," conduct-

ed by Rolf Zwann and described by Bergen, participants were asked to read a sentence (e.g., *The carpenter hammered the nail into the floor*), then shown a picture of an object and asked to decide if that object had been mentioned in the sentence. Researchers mixed in non-matching images and varied how matching object images were oriented in the picture (the whole nail might be shown lying on its side or just the head of the nail). Participants affirmed that the object (the nail) was mentioned *much faster* when "the orientation of the object implied by the sentence matched the orientation of the picture" (Bergen 54). The response is faster, this kind of study argues, because individuals had just been *simulating this action as though they were performing it.* Studies like these assert the occurrence of implied perspective through quantifiable time measurements only, not by asking if the participants "saw" the nail or embodied the action. A simulation pedagogy, by contrast, is chiefly interested in drawing out the varied, subjective experiences of simulation.

3. Lakoff and Johnson's connection to embodied simulation extends beyond their well-known book. Lakoff trained Benjamin Bergen, and Mark Johnson's subsequent works elaborate on embodied meaning (Johnson, *Body in the Mind*; Johnson, *Meaning*; Lakoff and Johnson, *Philosophy in the Flesh*).

Works Cited

Altman, Meryl. "How Not to Do Things with Metaphors We Live By." *College English* 52.5 (1990): 495-506. Print.

Anderson, Jeff. "Zooming In and Zooming Out: Putting Grammar in Context into Context." *English Journal* 95.5 (2006): 28-34. Print.

Bergen, Benjamin K. *Louder than Words: The New Science of How the Mind Makes Meaning.* New York: Basic Books, 2012. Print.

Berns, Gregory S., Kristina Blaine, Michael J. Prietula, and Brandon E. Pye. "Short- and Long-Term Effects of a Novel on Connectivity in the Brain." *Brain Connectivity* 3.6 (2013): 590-600. Web. 1 July 2015. <http://online.liebertpub.com/doi/pdf/10.1089/brain.2013.0166>.

Brand, Alice G., and Richard L. Graves, eds. *Presence of Mind: Writing and the Domain Beyond the Cognitive.* Portsmouth: Boynton/Cook, 1994. Print.

Brizee, H. Allen, Natasha E. Jarrett, and Katy A. Schmaling. "What is an Action Verb?" *The OWL at Purdue.* Purdue Online Writing Lab, 25 April 2010. Web. 6 July 2015. <https://owl.english.purdue.edu/owl/owlprint/543/>.

Connors, Robert J. "The Erasure of the Sentence." *CCC* 52.1 (2000): 96-128. Print.

Daiker, Donald A., Andrew Kerek, and Max Morenberg. *The Writer's Options: Combining to Composing.* 2nd ed. New York: Harper and Row, 1982. Print.

Davis, Ernest. "Embodied Simulation as a Theory of Language" Rev. of *Louder than Words*, by Benjamin Bergen. n.p., n.d.: 1-3. Web. 03 July 2015. <https://cs.nyu.edu/davise/papers/bergen.pdf>.

Dolmage, Jay. "Writing Against Normal: Navigating a Corporeal Turn." *Composing (Media) = Composing (Embodiment): Bodies, Technologies, Writing, The Teaching of Writing*. Ed. Kristin L. Arola and Anne Wysocki. Logan: Utah State UP, 2012. 110-126. Print.

Dunn, Patricia A. "Does Bad 'Grammar' Instruction Make Writing Worse?" *Teachers, Profs, Parents: Writers Who Care*. WordPress, 27 Jan. 2014. Web. 8 July 2015. <https://writerswhocare.wordpress.com/2014/01/27/does-bad-grammar-instruction-make-writing-worse/>.

—. *Talking, Sketching, Moving: Multiple Literacies in the Teaching of Writing*. Portsmouth: Boynton/Cook, 2001. Print.

Falck, Marlene Johansson, and Raymond W. Gibbs, Jr. "Embodied Motivations for Metaphorical Meaning." *Cognitive Linguistics* 23.2 (2012): 251-72. Print.

Fischer, Martin H., and Rolf A. Zwaan. "Embodied Language: A Review of the Role of the Motor System in Language Comprehension." *The Quarterly Journal of Experimental Psychology* 61.6 (2008): 825-50. Print.

Fleckenstein, Kristie S. *Embodied Literacies: Imageword and a Poetics of Teaching*. Carbondale: SIUP, 2003. Print.

—. "Writing Bodies: Somatic Mind in Composition Studies." *College English* 61.3 (1999): 281-306. Print.

Fleckenstein, Kristie S., Linda T. Calendrillo, and Demetrice A. Worley, eds. *Language and Image in the Reading-Writing Classroom: Teaching Vision*. Mahwah: Lawrence Erlbaum, 2002. Print.

Flower, Linda, and John R. Hayes. "A Cognitive Process Theory of Writing." *CCC* 32.4 (1981): 365-87. Print.

Gibbs, Raymond W., Jr. "Embodied Experience and Linguistic Meaning." *Brain and Language* 84.1 (2003): 1-15. Print.

---. *Embodiment and Cognitive Science*. Cambridge: Cambridge UP, 2005. Print.

Glenberg, Arthur M. "How Reading Comprehension is Embodied and Why That Matters." *International Electronic Journal of Elementary Education* 4.1 (2011): 5-18. Web. 31 August 2016. < http://www.iejee.com/index/makale/50/how-reading-comprehension-is-embodied-and-why-that-matters>.

Haas, Christina, and Stephen Witte. "Writing as Embodied Practice: The Case of Engineering Standards." *Journal of Business and Technical Communications* 15.4 (2001): 413-57. Print.

Hartwell, Patrick. "Grammar, Grammars, and the Teaching of Grammar." *College English* 47.2 (1985): 105-27. Print.

Hillocks, George, Jr. "Synthesis of Research on Teaching Writing." *Educational Leadership* 44.8 (1987): 71-82. Web. 7 July 2015. <http://www.ascd.org/ASCD/pdf/journals/ed_lead/el_198705_hillocks.pdf>.

Innocenti, Debra. "The Mind's Eye View: Teaching Students how to Sensualize Language." *Language and Image in the Reading-Writing Classroom: Teaching Vision*. Ed. Kristie S. Fleckenstein, Linda T. Calendrillo, and Demetrice A. Worley. Mahwah: Lawrence Erlbaum, 2002. 59-70. Print.

Jacob, Pierre. "Embodied Cognition, Communication, and the Language Faculty." *Language and Action in Cognitive Neuroscience*. Ed. Yann Coello and Angela Bartolo. New York: Psychology Press-Taylor and Francis, 2013. 3-30. Print.

Johnson, Mark. *The Body in the Mind: The Bodily Basis of Meaning, Imagination, and Reason*. Chicago: U of Chicago P, 1987. Print.

—. *The Meaning of the Body: Aesthetics of Human Understanding*. Chicago: U of Chicago P, 2007. Print.

Klein, Karen, and Linda Hecker. "The Write Moves: Cultivating Kinesthetic and Spatial Intelligences in the Writing Process." Brand and Graves 89-98. Print.

Kolln, Martha. *Rhetorical Grammar: Grammatical Choices, Rhetorical Effects*. 5th ed. New York: Pearson, 2007. Print.

Lacey, Simon, and Rebecca Lawson, eds. *Multisensory Imagery*. New York: Springer, 2013. Print.

Lakoff, George, and Mark Johnson. *Metaphors We Live By*. Chicago: U of Chicago P, 1980. Print.

—. *Philosophy in the Flesh: The Embodied Mind and its Challenge to Western Thought*. New York: Basic Books, 1999. Print.

Lane, Connor, Shipra Kanjila, Akira Omaki, and Marina Bedny. "'Visual' Cortext of Congenitally Blind Adults Responds to Syntactic Movement." *The Journal of Neuroscience* 35 (2015): n. pag. Web. 15 February 2016. <http://www.jneurosci.org/content/35/37/12859.abstract>.

Mendelsund, Peter. *What We See When We Read: A Phenomenology with Illustrations*. New York: Vintage Books, 2014. Print.

Micciche, Laura R. "Making a Case for Rhetorical Grammar." *CCC* 55.4 (2004): 716-37. Print.

Miller, Hildy. "Sites of Inspiration: Where Writing is Embodied in Image and Emotion." Brand and Graves 113-24. Print.

Murray, Joddy. *Non-Discursive Rhetoric: Image and Affect in Multimodal Composition*. Albany: SUNY P, 2009. Print.

Newkirk, Thomas, ed. *Only Connect: Uniting Reading and Writing*. Upper Montclair: Boynton/Cook, 1986. Print.

Nordquist, Richard. "Absolute Phrase (Grammar)." *About.com*. About, Inc, 2014. Web. 17 September 2014. <http://grammar.about.com/od/ab/g/absoluteterm.htm>.

Perl, Sondra. *Felt Sense: Writing with the Body*. Portsmouth: Boynton/Cook, 2004. Print.

Popova, Maria. "'It's an Aggressive Hostile Act': Joan Didion's Thoughts on Writing." *The Atlantic*. The Atlantic Monthly Group, 17 Oct. 2012. Web. 15 February 2016. <http://www.theatlantic.com/entertainment/archive/2012/10/its-an-aggressive-hostile-act-joan-didions-thoughts-on-writing/263679/>.

Rodas, Julia Miele. "On Blindness." *Journal of Literary and Cultural Disability Studies* 3.2 (2009): 115-30. Print.

Rose, Mike. "Narrowing the Mind and Page: Remedial Writers and Cognitive Reductionism." *CCC* 39.3 (1988): 267-302. Print.

Ruszkiewicz, John J., Maxine E. Hairston, and Christy E. Friend. *Scott Foresman SF Express*. 2nd ed. Upper Saddle River: Prentice Hall, 2005. Print.

Sadoski, Mark, and Allan Paivio. *Imagery and Text: A Dual Coding Theory of Reading and Writing*. Mahwah: Lawrence Erlbaum, 2001. Print.

Santana, Eduardo, and Manuel de Vega. "Metaphors Are Embodied, and so Are Their Literal Counterparts." *Frontiers in Psychology* 2 (2011): n. pag. *PubMed Central*. Web. 1 July 2015. <http://www.ncbi.nlm.nih.gov/pmc/articles/PMC3110336/>.

Stenberg, Shari J. "Embodied Classrooms, Embodied Knowledges: Rethinking the Mind/Body Split." *Composition Studies* 30.2 (Fall 2002): 43-60. Print.

Syverson, Margaret. *The Wealth of Reality: An Ecology of Composition*. Carbondale: SIUP, 1999. Print.

Tamir, Diane I., Andrew B. Bricker, David Dodell-Feder, and Jason P. Mitchell. "Reading Fiction and Reading Minds: The Role of Simulation in the Default Network." *Social Cognitive and Affective Neuroscience* 11.2 (2016): 215-24. Print.

Vidali, Amy. "Seeing What We Know: Disability and Theories of Metaphor." *Journal of Literary & Cultural Disability Studies* 4.1 (2010): 33-54. Print.

Weaver, Constance. *Teaching Grammar in Context*. Portsmouth: Heinemann, 1996. Print.

Weisberg, Deena Skolnick, et al. "The Seductive Allure of Neuroscience Explanations." *Journal of Cognitive Neuroscience* 20.3 (2008): 470–77. *PubMed Central*. Web. 27 Oct. 2015. <http://www.ncbi.nlm.nih.gov/pmc/articles/PMC2778755/>.

Wilson, James C., and Cynthia Lewiecki-Wilson. "Disability, Rhetoric, and the Body." *Embodied Rhetorics: Disability in Language and Culture*. Ed. James C. Wilson and Cynthia Lewiecki-Wilson. Carbondale: SIUP, 2001. 1-24. Print.

WLN: A JOURNAL OF WRITING CENTER SCHOLARSHIP

WLN: A Journal of Writing Center Scholarship is on the Web at https://wln-journal.org/

With Volume 40, the *Writing Lab Newsletter* was renamed as *WLN: A Journal of Writing Center Scholarship* to better reflect what it had long since become: a journal addressing questions of the theoretical, pedagogical, and administrative work of writing centers. Articles illustrate how writing centers work in an intersection of theory and practice, underpinned by theory, research, and scholarship. *WLN* aims to inform newcomers as well as extend the thinking of those who are more knowledgeable and experienced. Authors report on research and describe programmatic models that can be adapted to the varied contexts in which writing centers exist.

Feminist Mothering: A Theory/Practice for Writing Center Administration

Miley's essay is an excellent demonstration of how theory and practice intersect and inform each other in writing center work. Confronting the academy's tendency to view writing center work as merely feminist "mothering," Miley confronts what those in our field continually lament, that such a perspective misunderstands the value of feminist theory as well as devalues the writing center, its administrators, and any benefits students derive from tutorial instruction. To counter that misunderstanding, Miley turns to the very positive aspects emphasized in feminist theory and contrasts that with the corporatization of the academy. She calls on current composition and writing center scholarship to help writing center professionals see how the practices of listening, reflecting, and collaborating, as articulated in feminist theory and practiced in tutorials, help to nurture students' writing skills and independence. What Miley offers writing center administrators is a space "to speak a new discourse that rejects devaluation of our feminist practices, empowers our nurturing work, and resists . . . the production model of the neoliberal institution" (20). For hundreds of writing center professionals who have tried to face down the constant demeaning of their work and themselves, Miley provides a powerful argument.

Feminist Mothering: A Theory/Practice for Writing Center Administration

Michelle Miley

> *If there is anything that I have learned in my time [as a tutor in the Writing Center], it is the way that spaces can influence and shape your experiences. I have spent 5 semesters in this space, learning to listen, to ask questions, to be empathetic, and to be confident. The Writing Center has been the central site of my growth throughout my undergraduate career, and I will forever be grateful for the family that this space provided me. These orange couches will continue to be my favorite place on campus.*
>
> —Tutor Post on Facebook (April 29, 2016)

In my first year as a new writing center director, I found myself in an unusual meeting. Somehow, one of our State Representatives had heard from one of her constituents that our writing center, newly renovated and now directed by a tenure track faculty member, had recently declined in quality from the service it had been providing. Our writing center tutors were not editing students' papers for them. Rather, under my leadership, tutors were simply talking to students about their writing. And that talk, she heard, was all about feelings. She reported this narrative to our president, concerned about the direction our student support was heading. Fortunately, a colleague who knows the representative orchestrated a meeting so that we could explain that while we do not edit students' papers (such an action would not help students learn or develop as writers), our work with students covers much more than simply their "feelings" about writing. Somewhat surprised at how committed we are to our pedagogy, the representative agreed to talk to us. She now has a better understanding of why our tutors work with writers in conversation rather than with a red pen. But the experience troubles me; having the work of a writing center described as "just talking about feelings" diminishes and devalues what I believe is central to a necessary pedagogy writing centers offer in today's university systems.

My experience reflects the devaluation of writing center work that for years scholars have connected to the feminization of writing centers. Over twenty years ago, Mary Traschel noted, "To the extent that writing centers are constructed as feminized worksites they risk . . . containment and separation from the academic marketplace, where the value of real, 'intellectual work' is negotiated" (32).[1] More recently, Melissa Nicolas warns against the feminization of the center, arguing that our reputation as "nurturing service-oriented places" is problematic since this "'feminization of the writing center narrative' functions to 'code the position of the writing center director as 'inferior,' regardless of rank" (12). Jackie Grutsch McKinney, placing the narrative of writing centers as "cozy home" as the "most firmly entrenched" part of our grand narrative (20), notes that this domesticated narrative can lead to the devaluation of writing center directors:

> Whether female directors have carved themselves a home in the writing center (an argument I'm not prepared to make) or centers have been labeled "feminine" and thus seen as inferior by others, clinging to the identity of a writing center as cozy home may be problematic in terms of gender. Female directors who insist on cozy, inviting spaces may be unwittingly narrating their work as not intellectual in the eyes of some. Fact is, *if the writing center is a home and staff is family, that makes the director the mother.* (26, emphasis added)

I know that in an environment of corporatized academies,[2] any ties to domestication may prove dangerous. Any analogies to writing center as home or a director's work as mothering work in an institutional system revering a production model has the potential to diminish writing centers to a subservient position. But, while deconstructing our grand narrative, Grutsch McKinney asks us to imagine what doors narratives close as well as open. I wonder what doors we close if we abandon "writing center as home," and our work as "nurturing work." Could the caregiving work of writing centers, caregiving Traschel ties to our roots, be vitally necessary in university systems where students often experience intense stress to keep up with the pace of capitalistic production? Could our "mothering" work be essential in resisting the patriarchal culture of our academic institutions? I resist the silencing of my mother identity both at home and in the center. What some might call the mothering work of the writing center fulfills me and empowers me. I find joy in creating a space where student writers struggle to find their own voice, a messy space that allows growth and development of writers and tutors, a space that works alongside the classroom space, but that does not replicate that space. The Facebook post that begins this article, a post made by one of our tutors prior to graduation, suggests that our familial, "homey" space, a space shaped by our own insistence on listening, encouraging, nurturing, is indeed an important space to many. Rather than silencing or rejecting the identity of "feminine" space, I would like to see writing centers reclaim our nurturing (mothering) work as empowering, vital work within the institution. Applying the theory of feminist mothering developed by Andrea O'Reilly, I argue that by infusing the principles of feminist mothering into our own theorization of writing center administration, writing center directors empower writing center work and resist the neoliberal, patriarchal production of the institution.

FEMINIST MOTHERING: A THEORY/ PRACTICE FOR ADMINISTRATION

In Adrienne Rich's powerful exploration of her own experience as mother, she differentiates between two "meanings of motherhood" (13). The first reflects the institution of motherhood as experienced within patriarchal culture, a culture that "for most of what we know as the 'mainstream' of recorded history, has ghettoized and degraded female potentials" (13). She juxtaposes "motherhood" against the experience of "mothering," one rooted in "the biological potential or capacity to bear and nourish human life" (13). Writing center directors may see parallels in Rich's experience and their own in a university system that focuses on production and outcomes, devaluing, as Shari Stenberg notes, "learning processes that entail engagement of (an often recursive) process, collaboration and dialogue among learners, and reflection" (8). Our insistence that writing centers not be recognized as domesticated, feminized spaces speaks to our feelings of degradation.

Responding to the space that Rich opened up for a new discourse on motherhood, mothering theorists like O'Reilly have begun to explore other narratives that empower rather than diminish the mothering experience. The practice/theory O'Reilly calls *feminist mothering* offers a discourse that reclaims power for the mother and "so provides a promising alternative to the oppressive institution of patriarchal motherhood" ("Introduction" 4). As such, feminist mothering acts as a negation of motherhood as institution, allowing women to be both feminists and mothers. Recognizing that it is a tension-filled term, O'Reilly defines "feminism" within the context of feminist mothering as a "recognition that most (all?) cultures are patriarchal and that such cultures give prominence, power, and privilege to men and the masculine and depend on the oppression, if not disparagement of women and the feminine" (8). "Feminist mothering may refer to any practice of mothering that seeks to challenge and change various aspects of patriarchal motherhood that cause mothering to be limited or oppressive to women" ("Feminist Mothering" 796).

In a similar vein to O'Reilly, composition scholar Stenberg argues that repurposing feminine practices (and I would argue through repurposing empowering feminine practices) within the neoliberal institution is vital for students. Stenberg notes the importance of understanding "education as a complex, relational practice" in helping our students become active participants in shaping their worlds (8). The writing center, a space where feminine practices like listening, reflection, and collaboration are nurtured, can be one of those spaces. I am interested in how thinking through the theory/practice of feminist mothering opens a space for administrators to speak a new discourse that rejects devaluation of our feminine practices, empowers our nurturing work, and resists the silencing of feminine values in the production model of the neoliberal institution.

In theorizing how we can empower the nurturing work of writing centers and writing center administration, I draw from three principles O'Reilly sees replicated in the mothering practices of feminist mothers. First, feminist mothers reject the patriarchal assumption that a mother's identity is solely that of mother. Resisting the erasure of identity beyond mother-self, feminist mothers insist on work identities, partner identities, activist identities; in addition, they do not limit the identity of mother to the biological, heterosexual mother. Secondly, feminist mothers insist on shared parenting, rejecting the institutional doctrine that the mother must be the sole caretaker of the children. Carework is shared by partners, by friends, by family, and through daycare. Finally, feminist mothers believe that mothering work is not limited to the private, domestic sphere, but rather that motherwork is social and political. The political work of these mothers occurs not only in the advocacy for all peoples, but also in the raising of children with feminist values.

IDENTITY BEYOND MOTHER/DIRECTOR

The first principle of feminist mothering I draw from speaks to the multidimensionality of writing center administrators' work and identities. O'Reilly notes that "feminist mothering does not restrict or reduce a woman's identity and purpose solely to motherhood" ("Feminist Mothering" 818). I argue that cultivating a multidimensional identity is necessary not only for mothers but also for writing center administrators.

In my motherwork with my children, I have often insisted that the cultivation of my identity beyond wife and mother is essential both to my health and to my children's. Yes, I am often tired. Yes, I am often torn between the professional work I need to do and the time I want to spend with my children. Amber Kinser calls this inherent tension of a mother who has relationships with people other than her children "relating-in-multiplicity" (125). This same tension exists in the writing center. The nature of my work as a writing center director means that I must also balance multiple relationships and identities; there are constant meetings. And my faculty line means I must find time away from the center to engage in research and writing. My time away is often confusing not only to tutors but to others outside our center who do not realize my role is multidimensional. But, as developing my selfhood through work beyond my children is valuable to them, my insistence on research and on other relationships makes visible for others in the institution the intellectual work that is a part of directing a center. Through my insistence on self-outside the "mother-role" of the writing center, I empower our work as intellectual, valuable work within the institution.

INSISTENCE ON SHARED PARTNERSHIP

Another principle from feminist mothering that speaks to writing center administration occurs in the insistence of shared partnerships. In order for mothers to invest "time and energy to develop a selfhood beyond motherhood," feminist mothering insists "upon real, shared parenting (partner, daycare, othermothering, etc.) and critique[s]. . . the excessive child-centeredness of intensive mothering" ("Feminist Mothering" 818). Writing centers, often dubbed the "fix-it shops" of writing, are used to having students sent our way so that we can do the work (nurturing work?) of improving or fixing their "lack of development" as writers. Michael Pemberton, for example, notes the danger of the "marriage" between writing centers and writing in the disciplines faculty members, echoing the often heard excuse that other faculty "don't have time to teach writing" (120).

We know to resist this "fix-it shop" mentality. And we know that writing center theory grounds itself in theories of collaboration. Michele Eodice even asks us to "demand collaboration" as a means to "reach others in ways that can impact policy, influence administrative and institutional leaders, and help us grow leaders from among our writing center fellows" (129). But collaboration often results in one entity being subsumed by another, or into what Katrina Powell and Pamela Takayoshi call "missionary activism, "when one takes on the identity of "service provider" or "savior," to act as "the one in control, the paternal figure who knows best when to intervene" (395–396). My colleague Doug Downs and I have coined the term "collaboricity," a combination of "collaboration" and "reciprocity" to reflect shared partnership, an acknowledgement of both the independence and interdependence of writing programs and writing centers (forthcoming 2016). This idea of shared partnership—educators working sometimes together, sometimes independently—reflects the insistence of feminist mothering that care of children cannot solely lie on the mother's shoulders. Helping our students grow and develop (which sometimes means listening to their feelings) must be a shared enterprise.

MOTHERING AS POLITICAL/ACTIVIST ROLE

But feminist mothering does more than simply empower mothers and motherwork. In outlining the theory of feminist mothering, O'Reilly insists that feminist mothers make better mothers. Through teaching feminist values to their children, making mothering activist work, feminist mothers allow "children to grow outside and beyond the gender straightjackets of patriarchal culture" ("Feminist Mothering" 811). Children develop empathy, care, acceptance. O'Reilly notes that in developing these values, children may find themselves at odds with their peers who hold to patriarchal values. She notes that feminist mothers "must teach our children not only to resist patriarchy but more importantly how to keep safe and sane in so doing" ("Feminist Mothering" 811).

Writing center administrators often advocate for teaching values indicative of feminist values. Sarah Blazer's recent article on a "cohesive, transformative staff education" program that orients staff "to issues of difference" and develops inclusivity (17) is just one example; Tracy Santa's article on listening is yet another. In my role as director, I want to create a space for writers to find their voices, and I want my tutors to have voice, too. In a sense, I want to "raise my tutors" to have feminist values.

Feminist values often come through in my insistence that those of us in the writing center must take both reflective and reflexive stances, that we must practice what Krista Ratcliffe describes as rhetorical listening. Confronting different viewpoints through rhetorical listening can be unsettling at times, particularly as one both listens empathetically and stands firm in one's own identity. As Grutsch McKinney notes, "[Feminist] work does not have to be 'comfortable' . . . and in fact, might work better if it is confrontational and unsettling" (27). I do want tutors to be safe and sane in their work. But in the sometimes unsettling work, I have seen tutors begin to develop empathy for others and confidence in themselves. The Facebook quote beginning this article speaks to both, as does our center's recent panel of past tutors who joined us to talk to current tutors about what they had taken from their writing center work into their lives beyond the university. Over and over they mentioned empathy. Confidence and empathy— what more could we want?

CONCLUSION

I hear voices cautioning me about creating too much of a "mothering" space, of being too "mothering" in my interactions with tutors and student writers. I hear those cautions, and I heed them. These are known dangers. Feminist mothering provides a theory/practice by which I can embrace the nurturing/motherwork of the writing center while resisting the patriarchal trappings in the domestication of motherhood. And through empowering the nurturing work of the writing center, the practice of feminist mothering provides me a means by which to resist the neoliber al values that are shaping our institutions. By thinking through administration through the lens of feminist mothering, I believe writing center directors can embrace the nurturing work that we do, using our feminist values to, as Stenberg argues, intervene in our increasingly neoliberal institutions.

NOTES

1. Traschel's article not only gives a thorough review of the feminization of writing center work but also provides a positive comparison between mothering work and writing center administration.
2. See Slaughter and Rhoades on the corporatization of the university.

WORKS CITED

Blazer, Sarah. "Twenty-first Century Writing Center Staff Education: Teaching and Learning Towards Inclusive and Productive Everyday Practice." *Writing Center Journal*, vol. 35, no. 1, Fall/Winter 2015, pp. 17-55.

Eodice, Michele. "Breathing Lessons: Or Collaboration Is. . ." *The Center Will Hold*, edited by Michael A. Pemberton and Joyce Kinkead, Utah State UP, 2003, pp. 114-129.

Grutsch McKinney, Jackie. *Peripheral Visions for Writing Centers*. Utah State UP, 2013.

Lunsford, Andrea. "Collaboration, Control, and the Idea of a Writing Center." *Writing Center Journal*, vol. 12, no. 1, Fall 1991, pp. 3-11.

Kinser, Amber. "Mothering as Relational Consciousness." *Feminist Mothering*, edited by Andrea O'Reilly, SUNY P, 2008, pp. 123-142.

Miley, Michelle, and Doug Downs. "Crafting Collaboricity: Harmonizing the Force Fields of Writing Program and Writing Center Work." *Writing Program and Writing Center Collaborations: Transcending Boundaries*, edited by Alice J. Myatt and Lynée L. Gaillet, Macmillan, forthcoming.

Nicolas, Melissa. "Where the Women Are: Writing Centers and the Academic Hierarchy." *Writing Lab Newsletter*, vol. 29, no. 1, September 2004, pp. 11-13.

O'Reilly, Andrea. "Introduction." *Feminist Mothering*, edited by Andrea O'Reilly, SUNY P, 2008, pp. 1-24.

O'Reilly. Andrea. "Feminist Mothering." *Maternal Theory: Essential Readings*, edited by Andrea O'Reilly, Demeter P, 2007, pp. 792-821.

Pemberton, Michael. "Rethinking the WAC/Writing Center Connection." *Writing Center Journal*, vol. 15, no. 2, Spring 1995, pp. 116-133.

Powell, Katrina M., and Pamela Takayoshi. "Accepting Roles Created for Us: The Ethics of Reciprocity." *College Composition and Communication*, vol. 54, no. 3, February 2003, pp. 394-422.

Ratcliffe, Krista. *Rhetorical Listening: Identification, Gender, Whiteness*. Southern Illinois UP, 2005.

Rich, Adrienne. *Of Woman Born: Motherhood as Experience and Institution*. Norton and Co., 1986.

Santa, Tracy. "Listening in/to the Writing Center: Backchannel and Gaze." *WLN: A Journal of Writing Center Scholarship*, vol. 40, no. 9-10, May/June 2016, pp. 2-9.

Slaughter, Sheila, and Gary Rhoades. *Academic Capitalism and the New Economy: Markets, State, and Higher Education*. Johns Hopkins UP, 2009.

Stenberg, Shari J. *Repurposing Composition: Feminist Interventions for a Neoliberal Age*. UP of Colorado, 2015.

Traschel, Mary. "Nurturant Ethics and Academic Ideals: Convergence in the Writing Center." *Writing Center Journal*, vol. 16, no. 2, Fall 1995, pp. 24-45.

ENCULTURATION

encuturation
a journal of rhetoric, writing, and culture

Enculturation was launched in 1996 by two graduate students. In twenty years it has never been affiliated with a press or organization and has only had minimal institutional support by one university. Currently it is hosted on an individual's server and supported with one RA through the University of South Carolina. Almost all of the managerial, editorial, and production work continues to be done by young faculty and graduate students in the field of rhetoric and composition. The mission of the journal has generally been to publish broader ranging interdisciplinary work related to rhetoric and composition that is more theoretical or media-oriented.

Enculturation is on the Web at http://enculturation.net/

From Spectacular to Vernacular: Epideixis in Tactical Urban Design

Watson argues that since the Civil Rights march from Selma to Montgomery in March 1965, citizens' access to public monuments, memorials, parks, and highways as sites of protest and display has been eroded, creating a situation in which such spectacular citizen displays are fewer and farther between due to more restrictive laws and sanitized "free speech zones." These spectacular forms of protest have been replaced by vernacular citizen urbanism such as "open streets," "ad-busting," "weed bombing," "chair bombing," "depaving," "reclaimed setbacks," "pop-up town halls," and "guerrilla gardening," to more political displays of tactical urbanists who seek to remake cold or hostile public spaces. He argues that such forms of citizen placemaking warrant more significant rhetorical study and that vernacular displays, which inhabit banal public spaces on sidewalks and streetscapes, are best understood within the tradition of epideixis, or rhetorical display. He examines them as works of vernacular epideictic design—the material construction of (often temporary) structures, affordances, and coordinative signs designed to inspire observation, reflection, and the reassertion of shared values. Watson's article is a solid piece of scholarship that is both timely and cuts across composition and communication audiences. It received excellent blind reviews from scholars in both fields.

View this article online at *Enculturation's* website: http://enculturation.net/from-spectacular-to-vernacular

From Spectacular to Vernacular: Epideixis in Tactical Urban Design

Blake Watson

> *The public realm in America has two roles: it is the dwelling place of our civilization and our civic life, and it is the physical manifestation of the common good.... The public realm has to inform us not only where we are geographically, but it has to inform us where we are in our culture. Where we've come from, what kind of people we are.*
>
> —James Howard Kunstler,
> "The Ghastly Tragedy of the Suburbs"

In late March 1965, nearly 8,000 civil rights marchers walked the 52-mile stretch of U.S. Highway 80 from Selma, Alabama, crossing the Edmund Pettus Bridge, to reach the state's capital, Montgomery, in order to highlight the disenfranchisement of African Americans. Unlike the 600 marchers who on March 6, "Bloody Sunday," also tried to cross the Edmund Pettus, the 8,000 went unmolested, largely thanks to the ruling in *Williams v. Wallace* from U.S. District Court Judge Frank M. Johnson, who issued an injunction permitting the four-day march from Selma to Montgomery (Johnson). Ultimately, the Selma marches led to perhaps the most significant piece of legislation of the twentieth century: The Voting Rights Act. As such, the Selma marches can be considered one of the most important and successful modern instances of demonstrative material rhetoric. Unfortunately, as constitutional law professor Ronald Krotoszynski has detailed in the *Yale Law Review*, a series of rulings beginning in the late 1960s and continuing throughout the 1970s reshaped and eroded the "public forum doctrine" that protected these important marches. Krotoszynski's recent *LA Times* article on the fiftieth anniversary of the Selma Civil Rights Marches puts the situation in stark relief: "Today, it would be impossible to obtain a federal court order permitting a five-day protest march on a 52-mile stretch of a major U.S. highway. Under contemporary legal doctrine, the Selma protests would have ended March 8, 1965."

There is little disagreement that citizens ought to be owed access to public sites of symbolic significance as a matter of self-expression. Public monuments and memorials are, after all, instantiations of communal identity, commemorative material expressions of "who we are" and "what we value" (see Dickinson, Ott, and Aoki; Blair). And yet citizens' dwindling access to public monuments, memorials, parks, and highways as sites of protest and display has created a situation in which such *spectacular* citizen displays are fewer and farther between.

The sanitization of spectacular sites from organized citizen expression, including the rise of so-called "free speech zones," has coincided, though, with a more *vernacular* placemaking of a novel sort that should interest rhetorical studies. Guerrilla citizen urbanism is on the rise, from roguish acts like yarn bombing (originating in Texas in the mid-2000s) to the more political displays of tactical urbanists who seek to personalize and reimagine cold, even hostile (see, e.g., the rise of "bum-proofing"), public spaces. Websites such as *NextCity*, *Planetizen*, and Atlantic Media's *CityLab* have popped up in response to a growing public interest in such citizen-led urban design, while books such as *Insurgent Public Space* and *The Social Life of Small Urban Spaces* have flooded human geography and urban design schools. Such publications highlight how vernacular placemaking by citizens has become an important form of citizen action. This article proposes that citizen placemaking thus warrants increased rhetorical study and that vernacular displays, which inhabit banal public spaces on sidewalks and streetscapes, are best understood within the tradition of *epideixis*, or rhetorical display.

To show how vernacular placemaking functions as *epideixis*, this article examines several tactics described and illustrated in *Tactical Urbanism*, a guidebook for advocacy through small-scale urban design. Sometimes referred to as guerilla, pop-up, or D.I.Y. urbanism, tactical urbanism is a movement within urban design that advocates for a New Urbanist approach to city planning and design. Tactical urbanists especially advocate for denser, more walkable, more communitarian cities, and they do so in a particular way: by instructing citizens how to construct temporary displays in their neighborhood public spaces (e.g., sidewalks, streets, parking spaces, and empty lots). *Tactical Urbanism* guidebooks, of which there are numerous volumes, include tactics such as chair bombing, in which citizens create temporary seating space on public sidewalks; PARK(ing) Day parklets, which are makeshift greenspaces set up in street parking spaces;

and guerrilla gardening, which entails planting flowers, plants, and grass in sidewalk cracks, potholes, and vacant lots. These tactics are devised to draw attention to disrepair and disuse, demonstrate novel design possibilities, and redefine the character of communities through the design, construction, and arrangement of rhetorically meaningful objects in relatively banal public spaces. By attending to these vernacular displays as instances of rhetorical *epideixis*, we can gain insight into a fundamental mechanism of material display advocacy in public space.

For some time in rhetorical study, argumentative approaches to visual and material displays have been a productive way to understand public display advocacy, but, as an epideictic approach emphasizes, rhetorical displays are not merely prelude to argumentation. Kevin DeLuca's "image politics," for instance, provides useful insight into the ways in which material displays radiate out onto the internet as mediated "image events." For DeLuca, the image event is always destined for argumentation, even if the display itself is only the opening act. As he argues, image events do not so much make explicit arguments as proffer postmodern argumentative fragments, "mind bombs that expand the universe of thinkable thoughts" (DeLuca and Peeples 144). But what DeLuca describes—the creation of displays designed to "get them asking whether there are better ways to do things"—lies at the heart of epideictic rhetoric, which is important for the establishment and maintenance of communal values, not just as a warrants for enthymemes to come, but for their own sake (qtd. in DeLuca and Delicath 326).

Through a reading of tactical urbanist texts and tactics as instances of rhetorical display, this article examines the rhetorical work of vernacular *epideictic design*—the material construction of (often temporary) structures, affordances, and coordinative signs designed to inspire observation and reflection, to shore up and reassert shared values, and to teach a way of "seeing with" those values. Epideictic is a politically potent, often covert genre of rhetoric that succeeds less on the basis of proposition and argument (and indeed traditionally mustn't be seen as argument) and more on the revelatory display (and concealment) of an object, act, or person of symbolic importance to a community. Public material displays, if well-crafted, do something similar, drawing attention to embodiments of the values of the community, concealing complicating issues, and asking community members to look, reflect, and act according to those values without necessarily dictating how to do so or justifying with reasons. Epideictic design is rhetorical not (or not merely) as a *proposal* for particular actions, nor as a *justification* for a set of policies, but fundamentally as a paradigmatic *civic education*, a demonstration of a way of valuing space/place. This article examines how material public displays teach observers both to see banal public spaces as worthy of recognition and how to "look with values" at public space.

Tactical urbanist displays function as civic education in at least two ways: First, instruction in *what matters*—which actions, objects, and persons deserve recognition, acknowledgment, and emulation—is insinuated into everyday life as tactical urbanists use material objects to highlight and recommend some places/practices and indict others. By building, painting, and digging these structures right into the materials of public space—benches, streets, and sidewalks—they demonstrate alternative possibilities for those spaces and materially embody a value-laden *view of* the built environment. Secondarily, these displays teach spectators how to "see with" the correct set of values via what Jordynn Jack calls a "pedagogy of sight," a way for observers to perceive and recognize the good and the ill "in accordance with an ideological or epistemic program" (Jack 192). This facilitated recognition of values invites spectators to take the designer's vision forward with them as a way of seeing the world. This article proceeds by describing several examples of tactical urbanist advocacy-with-things, as described in *Tactical Urbanism* guidebooks. These displays are distinguished into *demonstrative displays* of alternative possibilities and *satirical displays*, meant to censure certain spaces that conflict with "our values." Once in place, tactical urbanist displays illustrate not just how the built environment can influence what "we (as a community) value" but also how we come to recognize exigencies for ourselves.

What Is Tactical Urbanism?

The Tactical Urbanism guidebooks are a series of free e-books published and promoted by the Street Plans Collaborative,[1] an urban design and advocacy firm. These guidebooks define, encourage, and instruct readers in the commission of tactical urbanism. The text, which is explicitly aimed at average citizens with no particular expertise, encourages local, neighborhood-level interventions. While Mike Lydon and his coauthors don't explicitly identify their practices as rhetorical or even as communicative, a close reading of their texts and projects illustrates just how rhetorical their architectural and design tactics and strategies are. Their brief, image-heavy texts illustrate a series of public space interventions, tactics with names like "open streets," "ad-busting," "weed bombing," "chair bombing," "depaving," "reclaimed setbacks," "pop-up town halls," and "guerrilla gardening." The guidebooks even follow rhetoric's centuries-old handbook tradition, in which devices and techniques for effective advocacy are taxonomized.[2] Each entry describes a design project meant to persuade and its intended effect.

WEED BOMBING

PURPOSE: To draw attention to blighted neighborhoods and to incite action in cleaning them up.
LEADERS: Neighborhood Associations
Artists
Activists
SCALE: Street || Block
FACT: Weed bombing began in Miami, FL under the cover of darkness, but sheds light on public and private property negligence.

Weed bombing is the act of converting overgrown weeds into works of street art. Inspired by other forms of 'tactical bombings,' downtown Miami resident and business owner, Brad Knoefler enlisted other neighborhood activists and artists to spray paint weeds in bright colors. Knoefler, who is also the founder of the Omni Parkwest Redevelopment Association (OPRA), is a vocal critic of the various large-scale redevelopment plans slated for his Omni Parkwest, and the lack of maintenance efforts. He is also known to take action into his own hands. "We used to cut the weeds ourselves," say Knoefler, "but it's much more beneficial to beautify them and convert them into street art. Unlike traditional graffiti, weed bombing doesn't damage private or public property and has immediate benefits to our quality of life."

While Knoefler undertook the effort in creative protest, he's found little resistance from the city and downtown development authority. Still, according to one newspaper article, Knoefler plans to keep bombing the weeds until a more concerted, sanctioned city effort is made.

Weed bombing can make overgrowth look more like flowers.
Credit: Kerry McLaney

A weed bomb just north of downtown Miami.
Credit: Kerry McLaney

Weed bombs highlight disparities in where public and private maintenance dollars are spent.
Credit: Kerry McLaney

TACTICAL URBANISM

Fig. 1. Weed bombing tactic (Mike Lydon).

For example, weed bombing (see fig. 1) involves painting weeds bright fluorescent colors to draw attention to otherwise easily ignored urban disrepair. Another device, depaving (fig. 2), consists of digging up pavement on vacant lots and exposing the soil for other uses, all the while highlighting the prevalence of asphalt and lack of exposed soil.

DEPAVE

PURPOSE: To reduce storm water pollution and increase the amount of land available for habitat restoration, urban farming, tree planting, native vegetation, and social gathering
LEADERS: Neighborhood Activists
Non-Profits
SCALE: Lot || Block
FACT: Since 2007, over 700 volunteer have replaced more than 94,100 square feet of unnecessary asphalt with permeable gardens and community green space. As a result, 2,221,115 gallons of stormwater is diverted annually.

While impervious surfaces are a fact of urban life, the paving of millions of acres contributes to numerous environmental problems, namely the polluting of our waterways through stormwater runoff.

Portland's all-volunteer Depave organization seeks to incrementally reduce stormwater pollution by surgically removing unnecessary pavement. To do so, Depave transforms impervious driveways and parking into community green spaces and gardens that naturally mitigate stormwater runoff pollution.

Depave began as an unsanctioned, self-organized neighborhood effort in 2007, but has blossomed into an influential non-profit organization that has received grants from the U.S. Environmental Protection Agency, the Oregon Department of Environmental Quality, Patagonia, and the Multnomah Soil and Water Conservation Districts. It is also supported by many other businesses, organizations, government departments and schools. Depave therefore provides a great example of how short-term unsanctioned initiatives can become sanctioned, long-term efforts within a very short amount of time.

Over the past four years Depave has turned nearly 100,000 thousand square feet of parking lots into expanded school yards, community gardens, food forests, and pocket parks. While this work has reduced millions of gallons of stormwater runoff, it has also built strong ties between neighbors and the city in which they live.

If you want learn more, Depave written a helpful how-to guide describing their process.

Clear instructio
Credit: Picasa user Depave?

Depaving in acti
Credit: Picasa user Depave?

The Fargo Forest Garden replaced 3,000 square feet of asph
Credit: Picasa user Depave?

Fig. 2. Depaving tactic (Mike Lydon).

Fig. 3. Pavement to plazas (Felipe Bengoa).

In figure 3, on the other hand, tactical urbanists reconfigure how pedestrians and vehicles are directed in public space by literally redrawing the textual, coordinative, and aesthetic features of urban public spaces.

In all these instances, we can draw a parallel between these tactics and rhetorical devices (e.g., apostrophe or synecdoche) because each describes, in one medium or the other, a technique with the end goal of persuasion. The only difference is that while a rhetorical device describes a resource of language, design tactics describe a persuasive resource of materials and their display. That is, objects are rhetorical, but not necessarily in the same way that language is, engaging us not as *auditors*, but as spectators.

Spatial Argumentation or Epideictic Design?

The tendency in rhetorical criticism is to read the persuasiveness of displays not as "shaping through sharing," as Celeste Condit has described one function of epideictic rhetoric, but as instances of enthymematic argumentation (Condit 291). For instance, Kevin DeLuca's readings of protester self-display rely on "image events": protesters who create spectacles (e.g., environmental activists in trees) designed to draw media attention and provide free press for an issue (DeLuca 12). Since their messages are typically heterodox, they can also expect to be framed unfavorably by the media, and so self-display is an important argumentative resource because it is one of the few things protesters have complete control over. Their bodies become "not merely flags to attract attention," but the sum and substance of an enthymematic argument (12).

In one of the only other readings of tactical urbanism, Danielle Endres, Samantha Senda-Cook, and Brian Cozen read the PARK(ing) Day tactic (a.k.a. "parklets") as an implicit, enthymematic argument for more communal, pedestrianized public spaces (124-26). As they claim early on, "alterations of place/space can make arguments . . . can make claims and provide support for claims in an enthymematic process wherein audiences that encounter them fill in the premises" (123-25). They continue:

> we consider the (re)constructions of place by PARK(ing) installations to be material spatial arguments that call for adherence to an alternate vision of what a parking spot, and urban space more generally, can be. Particular PARK(ing) installations serve as a form of argument by example, with the installations as the evidence for the claim that reconceptualizing parking spaces is not only possible but also desirable. (125).

Specifically, their article examines the ephemerality of these material displays, a key component of Endres and Senda-Cook's original "place in protest" concept. Because they occupy parking spaces, PARK(ing) Day parklets are intentionally temporary and soon dismantled. What is left of PARK(ing) Day are its archived, remediated traces: "photographs, videos, and written accounts" (Endres et al. 129). It is the combination of this temporary installation in the city and its imagistic recording and preservation that combine to give the tactic its full argumentative effect (130).

Fig. 4. San Francisco parklet (Mark Horgan).

While I agree substantially with their reading of PARK(ing) Day, my argument is that the covertly rhetorical mode that Endres et al. describe, in which "audiences that encounter them [parklets] fill in the premises," is in fact an important feature of *epideixis*, whose operative mode is something more like self-persuasion than argumentation. It was Perelman and Olbrechts-Tyteca who first pointed to just such an epideictic function in argumentative rhetoric: "epidictic [*sic*] oratory has significance and importance for argumentation because it strengthens the disposition toward action by increasing adherence to the values it lauds" (49-50). For Perelman and Olbrechts-Tyteca, the distance between gaining the adherence of an audience and the appropriate moment for action opens the opportunity for diminished conviction and failure to take action (48-52). Epideictic oratory bridges those gaps in its hearers' resolve through the display of exemplars of virtue and communal identity. For tactical displays, the revelation of inconsistencies between shared values and particular practices and norms is *made salient* for onlookers—for example, by (literally) highlighting exemplars of urban decay (i.e., weed bombing). Such displays do less to justify claims (argumentative work) than they do to generate exigencies. They will have succeeded once we *recognize* an exigence *as exigent*.

Endres et al.'s use and description of PARK(ing) Day as a "spatial meme for users to rethink and recreate their own public urban spaces" is appropriate (and indeed memes also operate as a display rhetoric), for these are reconfigurations and revisualizations of public space that suggest a novel way of viewing (125). They term this "argument by example," ultimately concluding that the effective installation of a parklet suggests "that reconceptualizing parking spaces is not only possible but also desirable" through spatial argument (125). Yet here the work of reconceptualization (literally "to consider again") is the work of (re)presentation and identification, not argument. PARK(ing) Day invites us to examine again, to see anew, and to reflect upon the true nature of place/space by showing and not telling.

The weed bomb, for example, does fit into enthymemes surely and effectively, especially as it is remediated online, its implications are drawn out, and an interpretation is made by advocates. As we encounter the weed bomb without any frame, however, we are offered the opportunity to observe it and reflect on it *for ourselves*.[3] Tellingly, the first parklets were created by the conceptual artist Bonnie Ora Sherk as installation pieces in the 1970s. The practice was taken up and spread in 2005 by the Rebar Group, an art studio in San Francisco. Rebar is primarily a group of artists and sculptors whose principal mode of persuasion is display—getting otherwise oblivious denizens of public space to look at, recognize, and reflect on the value of banal public space—and so it should come as no surprise that their inventions fit best within an epideictic tradition. As Rebar claims on their website, "PARK(ing) Day has effectively *re-valued* the metered parking space as an important part of the commons—a site for generosity, expression, socializing and play. And although temporary, PARK(ing) Day has inspired direct participation in the civic processes that permanently alter the urban landscape" (Rebar "About," emphasis mine). This is, after all, what art asks of us—how we should engage with it, as an opportunity for reflection and reexamination rather than the basis of some implicit argument or one part of an implied or imminent enthymeme. *Epideixis* is indeed often and importantly a prelude to argumentation and deliberative rhetoric, but that is not all it is. Aesthetic and playful displays such as weed bombs, guerrilla gardens, depavements or PARK(ing) Day parklets seek to change something much deeper than a particular instance of the policy at hand. They ask us to change something about how we value urban space generally, to reflect on "who we are," what our priorities are, and what our shared space reflects about us.

Does tactical urbanism have an ultimate argumentative agenda? Surely it does, as epideictic rhetoric has always had. The battle over what counts as the values, virtues, and vices of a community does significant work in determining what may be argued for and on what bases. For most of us, a particular proposal probably even springs easily to mind. Something like, "We should devote more of the street to people and less to cars." Crucially, however, the display itself is non-propositional. It does not tell us what to do or how to go about doing it. It does not give reasons, nor justifications, even if we may easily provide them. What the parklet does, and effectively so, is to show us something familiar in a new way, the epitome of epideictic rhetoric. As Endres et al. themselves conclude, "PARK(ing) Day has an impact on a generalized space—the parking space.... encourag[ing] a new perspective for seeing parking spaces and thinking about urban landscape as constructed" (138). Thus, as their own account of it attests, place in protest is deeply epideictic, describing a repeated "reconstruction of a place" that might lead to "a change in the meaning of that place" or "encourage a *new perspective for seeing* parking spaces and *thinking about* urban landscape as constructed" (138, emphasis mine). This reading almost exactly describes the effect and purpose of epideictic rhetoric: to reframe or display something "in a new light" such that an audience of spectators (*theoroi*) may reflect on, re-envision, and revalue it. Shared values, ideals, norms, virtues, and vices constitute the vital foundations of argument and deliberation, but we do not (typically) *argue about* which shared values we shall have. We learn to notice *what matters* not by being reasoned with, but through the subtle process of *epideixis*, by learning to recognize and acknowledge.

Vernacular Epideictic Design: Displaying What Matters

Tactical urban displays provide an epideictic civic education by holding up exemplars of laudable (or vicious) behavior for admiration (or censure) and asking that observers recognize and assent to the example on display. In this way *epideixis* is more than a frivolity, a practice exercise in amplification or stylistic "showing off." This "mere display" view of epideictic rhetoric has been much revised by contemporary rhetorical scholarship. We really ought to think of *recognition* rather than "praise and blame" when we think of epideictic rhetoric. As Lawrence Rosenfield argues, "[If we followed] Aristotle's lead we [would] interpret epideictic discourse simply as 'praise and blame' rhetoric instead of fundamentally about '"acknowledgement" and "disparagement"'" (133). Such exhibition is accomplished traditionally through figurative oratory—for instance, *ekphrasis* (evocative description) or *auxesis* (amplification)—in order to evoke what Quintilian referred to as *fantasia* (imagined visualization) (Prelli 5-20). Yet material displays accomplish these same ends, not through oratory but through world-making of a more literal sort. As Dickson puts it, material rhetoric is "a mode of interpretation that takes as its object of study the significations of material things and corporeal entities—objects that signify not through language but through their spatial organization, mobility, mass, utility, orality, and tactility" (297). By taking advantage of architectural, positional, and design tactics and devices to quite literally "bring before the eye" a perspective on the world, material displays give salience and presence to certain elements and features while concealing others.

Rosenfield's distinction (not praise, but acknowledgment) transforms *epideixis* from something a rhetor *adds to* an object of display into a rhetorical act of *facilitated recognition*. For Rosenfield, this means drawing out a radiance that was always already there, "the opportunity of *beholding reality impartially*" (Rosenfield 133). *Epideixis* shows us something familiar "in a new light" or, more exactly, it clears the way for an already-present "Radiance of Being," an inner essence, "to shine through" (Rosenfield 135). It does so by "exhibiting or making apparent (in the sense of showing or highlighting) what might otherwise remain unnoticed or invisible" (135). *Epideixis* is never done purely for the sake of commemoration, but rather as a material invitation for spectators to recognize virtue's embodiment and ultimately learn to recognize, internalize, and live life together in accordance with a shared set of societal values.[4] It reifies what is fact by wrapping observation in communal values, offering spectators an experience that resonates with communal values they already hold.

The importance of *observation* and *reflection* to rhetorical display should not be understated here. Aristotle reserved for the audience of epideictic oratory the term "spectator" (*theoros*) rather than "judge" (*kritas*), which was the term applied to audiences of both deliberative and forensic rhetoric. Through either a (re)description or (re)narration of a life or act, the oratory itself reveals the true essence of the thing, its essential nature, which an audience is called to witness, reflect on, and often emulate. Thus, epideictic oratory *displays* by taking advantage of the evocative affordances of language, "bringing before the eye" what is not literally present. As spectators, we "experience rhetorical displays in the classical sense of ceremonial speeches [*epideixis*] that seek to inspire audiences with images and exemplars of the excellent and wonderful in human experience" (Prelli 8).

Aristotle insists time and again that epideictic rhetoric relies on amplification rather than argument to provide for the reader a *paradeigma* or "concrete example" to be "set before" the audience, not to support a proposition (Rosenfield 135). The *Encomium of Helen*, for instance, invites its audience to reconceive Helen not as a villain but as a victim by elaborately re-narrating her betrayal as a story of seduction, offering an opportunity to "look again," to reexamine and then rethink the object of display. Similarly, in the *Funeral Oration*, Pericles praises an idealized Athens in which the audience wishes to believe, a place of inclusiveness and equality despite the realities of slavery and patriarchy, thereby reifying those ideals in the lives and deaths of the soldiers being buried and constructing both Athens and her dead soldiers anew for his audience. As these examples show, it is the twin notions of the impartial beholding of reality and the noncontroversiality of the shared values evoked that give *epideixis* the innocuous air that allows it to persuade while seeming to do no such thing.

Based on all this, we might expect epideictic rhetoric to be a valuable tool for the powerful—the rhetoric of patriotism, religiosity, and tribalism. And it is. Epideictic speeches are instruments of authority, typically delivered by community leaders such as presidents or generals. Even something as simple as a prayer will typically be delivered by the head of a household. This is as true of material displays as it is of oratory. Within scholarship on the rhetoric of display, we are used to identifying the epideictic in true spectacles (e.g., monuments and memorials) that serve a spectacular epideictic purpose such as a public commemoration or a symbolic emblem of a nation, city, or political party (see Prelli; Dickinson, Blair, and Ott; Balzotti and Crosby), but do so less often with non-state vernacular displays (for vernacular examples, see Hauser "Demonstrative"; Erni). This should not be surprising; monuments and memorials parallel the ceremonial, inspirational, and community-binding displays of epideictic oratory. Like public oratory, they exist in central spaces where singular, awe-inspiring experiences may be shared with other community members. And like the epideictic oratory of Pericles or Lincoln, they often issue from positions of power to bind a community under a single identity. As we'll see, vernacular urban displays are on the rise, especially as denizens take responsibility for the (re)design of the city as an increasingly bottom-up and expressive act of composition.

Demonstrative displays are the primary rhetoric of tactical urbanism, including tactics from open streets initiatives and *ciclovías* to chair bombings and Build a Better Block parties. Tactical urbanist displays do something similar to traditional epideictic oratory by demonstrating an alternative possible future and inviting citizens to try it out, to adopt it or reject it, but to consider it through their experience of it. Tactical urbanists believe that their designs may prove themselves useful and valuable if only they can be exhibited and auditioned live and in-person. The designs are explicitly meant to be "tried out" and their value appreciated firsthand. For example, the pavement-to-plazas tactic "demonstrates" an alternative reality that has potential to become permanent.

Fig. 5. Pavement to plazas tactic (New York City Dept. of Transportation).

In figure 5, a simple paint job changes the way vehicles and pedestrians occupy the streetscape. Because behavior in urban space, especially busy streets, is potentially dangerous, these spaces are heavily saturated with coordinative signals (e.g., signs, lines, colored asphalt), and these coordinative signs are meant to pass from the top down, designed to both protect and control pedestrians and drivers. As denizens of this space inhabit, experience, and accept this space, they learn a new perspective on what such a space "is for." Crosswalks define a more significant zone for pedestrians in the otherwise auto-centric street. Figure 5 also illustrates the difference between the expressive tactical designs of citizens and those made by a bureaucracy of urban planners. Instead of weighing statistics on traffic flows, insurance parameters, best practices, and efficient light intervals, the citizen design expresses values, asserting and expanding the space meant for pedestrians in the urban landscape. It is an epideictic rather than technocratic design.

Fig. 6. Les Bouquinistes (Mike Lydon).

Lydon's guidebooks trace the historical roots of tactical urbanism to Paris's *Bouquinistes*, the street booksellers who occupy the recognizable green wooden boxes that line the Seine, as the historical archetype for the movement. During the sixteenth century, unauthorized booksellers coalesced on the banks of the Seine to peddle their wares.

Not surprisingly, brick-and-mortar Parisian bookshops had the political clout to have *Les Bouquinistes* banned in 1649 (Uzanne 20). Eventually their popularity brought them back, though, this time confined to limited locations along the Seine and with the stipulation that the shops must be broken down into boxes each night. Today, the familiar green boxes of *Les Bouquinistes* that line the Seine have been designated a UNESCO World Heritage site, an accomplishment Lydon touts as the first victory of tactical urbanism (Lydon 5).

Les Bouquinistes, typically common peddlers of limited means, were only able to open up space for themselves through the physical presence of their shops. At first these shops were quite temporary, but as *Les Bouquinistes* went unmolested, they settled into territories and more permanent encampments. As Lydon explains it, Parisians were essentially given the opportunity to "try out" the riverside booksellers (Lydon 5). Their existence became an accepted part of public life and, with time, found enough of a foothold to become permanent. *Les Bouquinistes* had stumbled on an (ultimately successful) rhetorical tactic that tactical urbanists today use explicitly. Just as *Les Bouquinistes* did, Lydon's public space interventions are designed to create speculative, cheap, temporary objects and displays that reconfigure public space in the hope that others come to accept them, and the values they embody, via an experience of them.

Fig. 7. Painting guerrilla crosswalk (Elijah McKenzie, Broken Sidewalk).

For both *Les Bouquinistes* and pavement to plazas, a desired change is effected through material insinuation. Were this intervention to cost more than paint and labor, it might never get made. The presence of the displays is *tactical*, both temporary and maneuverable, which means that they may be created either with authorization or without, as with the "guerilla crosswalks" tactic. These demonstrations can be cheaply made and easily undone; thus, they may be approved and funded more easily. Tactical urbanism is defined by this incremental, temporary, and sometimes unsanctioned nature. It prods at what is allowable, working at the edges of municipal ordinances and patience to make only the easiest and most temporary changes to everyday public spaces, a pragmatism born of the expense and bureaucracy of urban design itself.

Not all tactical urbanist displays are demonstrations of alternative possibility, however. Many epitomize the flipside of praise: blame and censure. The weed bombing tactic may be understood as an instance of such shaming, or *vitupera*, its purpose being disidentification between audience and the object on display through the literal "highlighting" [of] urban weeds in fluorescent colors. The purpose of shaming, just as much as praise rhetoric, is to tribalize a community, to bring "us" together in a unified viewpoint as apart from and opposed to "them." These displays constitute the second major category of epideictic design: satiric display.[5] Precisely because of epideictic's authoritative role in public discourse, there is a long tradition of satire in *epideixis*.[6] The weed bomber merely holds up an object, one its painter presumably sees as blameworthy, to preexisting communal standards and asks viewers to see the absurdity in it. In doing so the bomber may subtly alter those values, a process Celeste Condit details at length in an article on the political functions of epideictic, *shaping* what will become the warrants of future deliberations *through sharing*. (Condit 290). Cracks, flaws, and problems are made absurdly patent for viewers, often by beautifying them with color. Guerilla gardening (fig. 8) also constitutes a satiric display, highlighting cracks and potholes that might otherwise be ignored by planting often elaborate miniature gardens in them. Similarly, the PARK(ing) Day tactic presents the viewer with the absurd spectacle of a parking space-shaped slice of park against a field of asphalt. These displays mock the pretenses of pay parking spaces and urban decay by pairing them with grass, trees, and bodies. As with most satire, we are meant to admire the skill and creativity of the author as much as her moral indignation, both of which lend the display its startling, satirical effect. Just as it requires the eloquence of a Swift or a Pope to adequately satirize through literature, so too do tactical displays require the design skills that Lydon and his contributors have. The goal of such a display, while rhetorical, should not be rationalized as an argument; the epideictic essence is the reflection it prompts through the ironic vision it invites us to share in.

Fig. 8. Guerrilla gardening (Steve Wheen).

Pedagogy of Sight: How to See with Values

At least as important as showing us *what matters*, material public displays teach us how to view the world, to *see with values*. Witnesses to these displays are not just called to live by the virtues displayed, they are also taught *a way of viewing* their world. The argument that we may be *taught* how see in accord with a set of values is made powerfully by Jordynn Jack's concept of a pedagogy of sight, "a rhetorical framework that instructs readers *how* to view images in accordance with an ideological or epistemic program" (Jack 192). Jack develops the term to clarify the necessity for instruction that confronted Robert Hooke as he tried to make sensible some of the first micrographic images to a broad audience: "Hooke's challenge was to make such objects *worthy* of careful observation . . . he needed to render what could be seen simply as meaningless squiggles or abstract matter recognizable as objects of study" (193, emphasis mine). In order to do so, Hooke's text figured his images and diagrams within a familiar ideology (Christian) and a metaphorical idiom (bodies are machines). Importantly, a pedagogy of sight teaches viewers not just how to view the particular engravings at hand, but also how to take that ideological-metaphorical mode of viewership forward into the ways they viewed the world (Jack 192-93). By figuring the microscopic world as made up of natural machines, Hooke both offered the images *as evidence* of the mechanisms of nature and at the same time taught viewers *how to see* mechanistic bodies in microscopic images. We all "see with values" all the time, whether that means recognizing "worthy" objects of our attention, defining and ignoring the scenery against which those things stand, or even our recognizing what is or isn't an entity at all. How else do we learn to *recognize*?

Fig. 9. The first PARK(ing) Day in San Francisco (Rebar, "Portfolio).

This operation has been examined most closely in the context of scientific visualizations: graphs, maps, and images that re-present nature for viewers. Behind any display stands some designer making choices, taking advantage of this opportunity for reexamination by crafting the scene to be encountered. Hooke's microscopic images exhibit what would appear to be little more than unintelligible squiggles, yet come to serve as evidence of a mechanistic theory of the natural world that is offered to make sense of the squiggles. Similarly, epideictic displays are made to offer "a view of" or "a perspective on" something we thought we knew—a hero, a villain, a war, or practice—and to invite witnesses to reexamine and reconceive them. Thus, the dual evidentiary and pedagogical roles at work in a scientific pedagogy of sight, at once both a reason to believe and a useful new mode of recognition, infuses epideictic display as well.

By exhibiting an ideology "in the flesh," tactical urbanists teach witnesses a new way of *seeing with* their values. Whether they are reappropriating parking spaces as parks, bombing empty sidewalks with seating, or highlighting the decay of the urban landscape with weed bombs, tactical urbanists display for spectators their own unique way of seeing the city. Spectators are thus invited to see that these spaces do or do not live up to communal standards and are invited to internalize that value-laden way of viewing. As they go forward, they may recognize similar exigencies for themselves and make judgments and arguments about their amelioration.

Weed bombs again provide a textbook case. By spray painting overgrown weeds in public space, tactical urbanists literally highlight problems and issues by giving *salience* to features of the material environment. *Tactical Urbanism 2*, for instance, describes the actions of weed bomber Brad Knoefler, a Miami resident and "vocal critic of the . . . lack of maintenance efforts" in his neighborhood (37). At first Knoefler cut the weeds in his neighborhood public sidewalks and streets, but he now claims, "it's much more beneficial to beautify them and convert them into street art" (qtd. in Lydon 37). Thus, while Knoefler clearly wants the weeds cleared up and his neighborhood to be better cared for generally, cutting the weeds sends no particular message and must be done again and again. His playful and satiric act of spray painting weeds rather than cutting them and making them invisible helps observers "resee" the space in which they live.

Fig. 10. Weed bomb (Grant Stern).

Brightly colored spray painted weeds are rhetorical displays, but their purpose is explicitly *not* the change they seek in the world, but inviting others to (re)see the world as a tactical urbanist does. As Lydon makes clear in the heading of the same page of the guidebook, the purpose of weed bombing is "to incite action in cleaning [blighted neighborhoods] up" (37). The weed bomb display teaches onlookers a way of attending to and *recognizing what matters*, to "see with the appropriate values," to see the world as does the activist who perceives weeds or pavement as exceedingly salient, obtrusive, and *exigent*.[7] Like composers of visual images, in other words, designers of material displays necessarily reinscribe into material displays *a way of looking* at the world.

But what actions do brightly colored weeds advise us to take? Do they propose their own eradication? Or perhaps they suggest a celebration of weeds' unnoticed beauty? Only by reading the tactical urbanist texts are we given proposals and the full argumentative context for their spatial argument. It is not at all clear that these displays argue for anything in particular. And neither must "place in protest" always mean a "spatial argument." As Endres et al. recognize, the point of PARK(ing) Day tactics is to incite spectators to "rethink public space" (137). Like epideictic oratory, epideictic design trades on its ability to persuade *covertly,* preferring showing to telling, teaching viewers how to see with values.

This act of seeing, and specifically *recognizing*, isn't just about noticing what might otherwise be ignored; noticing is bound up with evaluation and may be taught through well-crafted display. What we consider exigent rather than unremarkable often begins with the very act of perception, our ability to recognize exigencies *as exigent* when we encounter them. In oratory, this salience is typically given through the simulation of experience, *fantasia*, evoked by *auxesis* or *ekphrasis*, which transports the audience. Encomia, eulogies, and panegyrics all display by narrating the lives and acts of the great and ignoble. Epideictic design, however, reveals and conceals in uniquely visual and material ways—salience is given through visual or tactile emphasis and highlighting. Both epideictic oratory and design make salient *what matters* so that the rest of the community might share this way of recognizing, might *notice* violations of communal values rather than passing them by without comment.

The public displays of tactical urbanism teach witnesses how to (re)see their urban environment—not just witnesses to pointedly expressive monuments or memorials, but viewers of everyday public space/place. Whether tactical urbanist displays do this by highlighting exigencies or demonstrating possibilities, their ultimate goal is *civic education*, to teach witnesses how to attend to space/place *in the proper way*, to see issues not just in this or that pothole or parking space, but to learn to *see with* the proper set of values, to recognize virtue and vice when it arises. Tactical urbanist interventions help us, in other words, "see as" new urbanists do, to recognize their problems *as problems*. Seeing with the proper set of values means something more than knowing what "our values" are. It means learning to bring those values to bear in particular instances, to recognize virtue and vice embodied when we see them. Here, the word *recognition* should resonate in both the sense of "to identify" and the sense of an "acknowledgement" or "appreciation." Once we can see how some practice, person, or norm aligns with (or fails to align with) shared values, we may go on to recognize such value-laden instances again and again. We will have learned to *see with values*, to recognize what is blameworthy and praiseworthy as it manifests itself concretely.

Conclusion

My hope with this article has been to explore a *vernacular* material rhetoric and the epideictic role it performs in shaping shared, public values. Because politically engaged citizens have been cut off from spectacular sites like the Selma bridge, sites that lend their arguments moral force, their rhetorical energy has found expression in vernacular spaces. Tactical urbanism is an important instance of citizens "speaking back" through the public spaces that are embodiments of elite conceptions of the common good, but they are less pointed and more playful and satiric than what they've replaced. By studying not just the pointed protest displays of social movements, nor overtly expressive monuments and memorials, but rather the *epideictic design* (and redesign) of everyday public spaces, I hope to point the way toward the constitutive rhetorical work of design. Tactical urbanists don't so much tell us what to value, believe, or do as they help us visualize and recognize meaningful instances of our values' material manifestations. An epideictic lens offers rhetorical analysts the ability to examine more than truth assertions, but also how dearly held values and beliefs find their material expression, what counts as a violation of those values, and how we learn to recognize those exigencies.

If we think of epideictic oratory as a way of giving concrete form to communal values and a way of pointing to, describing, and narrating virtuous and vicious exemplars of those values, *epideictic design* is an attempt to place those values in actual concrete. Yet questions remain for those interested in (or concerned about) the political potential of epideictic design. What techniques and devices might comprise "eloquence" in design? What principles—architectural, ergonomic, aesthetic—contribute to effective epideictic displays? How does *usage* articulate with the rhetoric of materials—not just as visual displays, but as functional objects? And though the rhetoric of display tends to focus on how displays create *salience*, what explains the rhetorical potency of the invisible mundane, the ways banal public spaces tend to iterate in parallel—from sidewalks to potholes to the common park bench—communicating meaning not by assertion but by accretion, subtly and repeatedly marking space as *for* some and not others?

None of this is meant to deny the importance of the argumentative work done by these material and visual displays, especially as images of tactical urbanism are archived, annotated, remediated, and mobilized. Nor does it insist that all displays are epideictic by their nature. But if we conflate argumentation with the values and warrants on which it is based, then eventually argumentative rhetoric subsumes epideictic rhetoric. Rather, by understanding public objects in both senses, we get a fuller picture of what rhetorical work displays can uniquely do. An epideictic reading of tactical urbanism invites us to remember and recognize the pervasive and subtle, even intentionally covert, political work of rhetorical *epideixis* in public space.

Notes

1. There exist several texts all titled *Tactical Urbanism*. The guidebooks referenced here are those available as e-books for free online, especially *Tactical Urbanism 2: Short-Term Action // Long-Term Change*, which is not to be confused with the print book *Tactical Urbanism: Short-Term Action for Long-Term Change*.

2. Rhetorical treatises, handbooks, and exercises on composing epideictic, from the *Rhetorica ad Herennium* through Kenneth Burke, include instruction and rules of thumb for producing displays through language (toasts, eulogies, panegyrics, etc.), praising the deceased, amplifying and revealing strengths, and concealing flaws. The tactics described in tactical urbanist handbooks provide similar instruction in material interventions in vernacular public space.

3. Endres et al. assert that spatial arguments may stand alone, requiring no explanatory language to make their argument. We may grant that assertion and still ask whether those supplied premises are themselves persuasive. This article asserts that spectators are persuaded (or not) by tactical displays in much the same ways they might be persuaded by a work of art. This is, I think, in keeping with the experiential, stylistic, and affective bases of Endres and Senda-Cook's term "place in protest" (see Endres and Senda-Cook). See also Erika Doss's *Memorial Mania* for the argument that contemporary memorialization practices, especially spontaneous and temporary memorials, are primarily concerned with archiving emotion.

4. Several scholars make this educative point explicitly (Rosenfield; Condit; Poulakos). Gerard Hauser interprets Aristotle's epideictic rhetor as someone who "provide[s] concrete guidance on how to live in harmony with

noble ideals" by valorizing emblems of what a community considers its highest values ("Aristotle" 15).

5. This term is borrowed from the literary scholar Dustin Griffin, who traces the origins of satire to epideictic oratory and the declamatory training received by its greatest practitioners, from Juvenal to Swift.

6. Paradoxical or mock encomia, for example, begin with the Greek satirists Varro and Lucian and include encomia of bees, salt, and mice. As Kirk argues, "the exact point in literary history at which the paradoxical encomium became either temporarily or permanently confused with the Menippean satire is unclear" (33).

7. Bitzer and Vatz's rhetorical situation debate turned on the origin of exigency: whether it was located "in the world" or the rhetorical creation of rhetors who "gave salience" to certain states of affairs. Rhetorical display suggests that such a dichotomy is false because designed materials can "give salience" not just through language, but through the design of the built environment.

Works Cited

Balzotti, Jonathan Mark, and Richard Benjamin Crosby. "Diocletian's Victory Column: Megethos and the Rhetoric of Spectacular Disruption." *Rhetoric Society Quarterly*, vol. 44, no. 4, 2014, pp. 323-42.

Bengoa, Felipe. "Okuplaza—Pavement to Plaza in Santiago." *Opencity Projects*. OpenCity Projects Inc., http://opencityprojects.com/okuplaza-san-diego/.

Blair, Carole. "Contemporary U.S. Memorial Sites as Exemplars of Rhetoric's Materiality." *Rhetorical Bodies*, edited by Jack Selzer and Sharon Crowley, U of Wisconsin P, 1999, pp. 16-57.

Buchanan, Richard. "Declaration by Design: Rhetoric, Argument, and Demonstration in Design Practices." *Design Discourse: History, Theory, Criticism*, edited by Victor Margolin, U of Chicago P, 1989, pp. 91-109.

Condit, Celeste Michelle. "The Functions of Epideictic: The Boston Massacre Orations as Exemplar." *Communication Quarterly*, vol. 33, no. 4, 1985, pp. 284-98.

DeLuca, Kevin Michael. *Image Politics: The New Rhetoric of Environmental Activism*. Guilford P, 1999.

Delicath, John W., and Kevin DeLuca. "Image Events, the Public Sphere, and Argumentative Practice: The Case of Radical Environmental Groups," *Argumentation*, vol. 17, no. 3, 2003, pp. 315-33.

DeLuca, Kevin, and Jennifer Peeples. "From Public Sphere to Public Screen: Democracy, Activism, and the 'Violence' of Seattle." *Critical Studies in Media Communication*, vol. 19, no. 2, 2002, pp. 125-51.

Dickinson, Greg, Carole Blair, and Brian L. Ott. *Places of Public Memory: The Rhetoric of Museums and Memorials.* U of Alabama P, 2010.

Dickinson, Greg, Brian L. Ott, and Eric Aoki. "Spaces of Remembering and Forgetting: The Reverent Eye/I at the Plains Indian Museum." *Communication and Critical/Cultural Studies*, vol. 3, no. 1, 2006, pp. 27-47.

Dickson, Barbara. "Reading Maternity Materially: The Case of Demi Moore." *Rhetorical Bodies*, edited by Jack Selzer and Sharon Crowley, U of Wisconsin P, 1999, pp. 297-313.

Doss, Erika. *Memorial Mania: Public Feeling in America.* U of Chicago P, 2010.

Endres, Danielle, and Samantha Senda-Cook. "Location Matters: The Rhetoric of Place in Protest." *Quarterly Journal of Speech*, vol. 97, no. 3, 2011, pp. 257-282.

Endres, Danielle, Samantha Senda-Cook, and Brian Cozen. "Not Just a Place to Park Your Car: PARK(ing) as Spatial Argument." *Argumentation and Advocacy*, vol. 50, no. 3, 2014, pp. 121-140.

Erni, John Nguyet. "Flaunting Identity: Spatial Figurations and the Display of Sexuality." *Rhetorics of Display*, edited by Lawrence J. Prelli, U of South Carolina P, 2006, pp. 311-326.

Hauser, Gerard A. "Aristotle on Epideictic: The Formation of Public Morality." *Rhetoric Society Quarterly*, vol. 29, no. 1, 1999, pp. 5-23.

—. "Demonstrative Displays of Dissident Rhetoric: The Case of Prisoner 885/63." *Rhetorics of Display*, edited by Lawrence J. Prelli, U of South Carolina P, 2006, pp. 229-54.

Griffin, Dustin H. *Satire: A Critical Reintroduction.* UP of Kentucky, 1994.

Hou, Jeffrey. *Insurgent Public Space: Guerrilla Urbanism and the Remaking of the Contemporary Cities.* Routledge, 2010.

Horgan, Mark. "File:SFParklet.jpg." *Wikipedia.org.* Wikimedia Commons, https://en.wikipedia.org/wiki/File:SFParklet.jpg.

Jack, Jordynn. "A Pedagogy of Sight: Microscopic Vision in Robert Hooke's Micrographia." *Quarterly Journal of Speech*, vol. 95, no. 2, 2009, pp. 192-209.

Jay, Martin. "The Rise of Hermeneutics and the Crisis of Ocularcentrism." *Poetics Today*, vol. 9, no. 2, 1988, pp. 307-26.

Johnson, Frank M. Williams v. Wallace. 17 Mar. 1965, http://www.leagle.com/decision/1965340240FSupp100_1325/WILLIAMS%20v.%20WALLACE.

Kirk, Eugene P. *Menippean Satire: An Annotated Catalogue of Texts and Criticism.* Garland Publishing, 1980.

Krotoszynski, Ronald J. "Could a Selma-like Protest Happen Today? Probably Not." *Los Angeles Times*, 7 Mar. 2015, http://www.latimes.com/opinion/op-ed/la-oe-0308-krotoszynski-selma-march-protest-doctrine-20150308-story.html#page=1.

Kunstler, James Howard. "The Ghastly Tragedy of the Suburbs." TED Network, Feb. 2004, https://www.ted.com/talks/james_howard_kunstler_dissects_suburbia?language=en.

Latour, Bruno. "Visualisation and Cognition: Drawing Things Together." *Knowledge and Society: v. 6: Studies in the Sociology of Culture Past and Present*, edited by Henrika Kuklick, JAI P, 2012, pp. 1-40.

Lydon, Mike. *Tactical Urbanism 2: Short-term Action // Long-term Change*. Street Plans Collaborative, 2012, https://issuu.com/streetplanscollaborative/docs/tactical_urbanism_vol_2_final.

McKenzie, Elijah. "SoBro's Colorful Crosswalks Could Be the First Sign of Real Change in the Neighborhood." *Broken Sidewalk*. http://brokensidewalk.com/2014/sobros-colorful-crosswalks-could-be-the-first-sign-of-real-change-in-the-neighborhood.

New York City Department of Transportation "Pavement to Plazas." *Better Cities and Towns*. New Urban News Publications. http://bettercities.net/images/14499/pavement-plazas.

Perelman, Chaïm, and Lucie Olbrechts-Tyteca. *The New Rhetoric: A Treatise on Argumentation*. U of Notre Dame P, 1969.

Poulakos, Takis. "Isocrates's use of Narrative in the *Evagoras*: Epideictic Rhetoric and Moral Action." *Quarterly Journal of Speech*, vol. 73, no. 3, 1987, pp. 317-328.

Prelli, Lawrence J. Introduction. *Rhetorics of Display*, edited by Lawrence J. Prelli, U of South Carolina P, 2006, pp. 1-38.

Rosenfield, Lawrence W. "The Practical Celebration of Epideictic." *Rhetoric in Transition: Studies in The Nature and Uses of Rhetoric*, edited by Eugene E. White, Pennsylvania State UP, 1980, pp. 135-155.

Rebar Group. "About PARK(ing) Day." *Parking Day RSS*. Rebar Group Inc., http://parkingday.org/about-parking-day/.

—. "Portfolio: PARK(ing) Day." *Rebar Art Design Studio San Francisco*, http://rebargroup.org/parking-day.

Uzanne, Octave. *The Book-Hunter in Paris: Studies among the Bookstalls and the Quays*. E. Stock, 1893.

Whyte, William H. *The Social Life of Small Urban Spaces*. Project for Public Spaces, 2001.

COMMUNITY LITERACY JOURNAL

Community Literacy Journal is on the Web at http://www.communityliteracy.org/

The *Community Literacy Journal* publishes both scholarly work that contributes to the field's emerging methodologies and research agendas and work by literacy workers, practitioners, and community literacy program staff. We are especially committed to presenting work done in collaboration between academics and community members.

We understand "community literacy" as the domain for literacy work that exists outside of mainstream educational and work institutions. It can be found in programs devoted to adult education, early childhood education, reading initiatives, lifelong learning, workplace literacy, or work with marginalized populations, but it can also be found in more informal, ad hoc projects. For us, literacy is defined as the realm where attention is paid not just to content or to knowledge but to the symbolic means by which it is represented and used. Thus, literacy makes reference not just to letters and to text but to other multimodal and technological representations as well.

Brokering Literacies: Child Language Brokering in Mexican Immigrant Families

Steven Alvarez's article represents the kind of community literacy work that we want to publish and help to acknowledge in both the fields of Community Literacy Studies and in Rhetoric & Composition. Alvarez's work could not be more timely and generative. The article's focus on "child language brokering among child bilingual youths and their parents" is a model of ethnographic research and contextual analysis of the lived literacy experiences of young people and their immigrant families.

Brokering Literacies: Child Language Brokering in Mexican Immigrant Families

Steven Alvarez

This article reports from instances of child language brokering among emergent bilingual youths and parents at a New York City after-school community literacy program composed largely of Mexican immigrant families. I argue that youth language brokers negotiated literacies with and for their parents in differing contexts, with different audiences, and under different dynamics of power relations. Young language brokers utilize bilingual practices to translate, interpret, and advise between adults and family members of different ages. Language brokers, I argue, use their bilingual learning to help their families and to show they care.

Keywords: language brokering, bilingual learning, immigrant families, family literacies

This article reports on five years of ethnographic research into the day-to-day instances of child language brokering among emergent bilingual youths and parents at a New York City after-school community literacy program composed largely of Mexican immigrant families. My research explores the languages and literacies of participant bilingual youth language brokers, bilingual mediators who communicate between monolingual adults. These youth language brokers negotiated meaning with and for their parents in differing contexts, with different audiences, and under different dynamics of power relations. The young language brokers utilized varying levels of bilingual practices to effectively increase translate, interpret, and advise between adults and family members of different ages. Bilingual brokers develop practices to navigate complex information in their family lives, which would never be fully evaluated in their schooling, but yet which schools would seem to expect or even demand in terms of family-involved literacy learning among "gifted" students (Valdés).

My research examines language brokering among mothers and children and the day-to-day literacy practices of children participating in the Mexican American Network of Students (MANOS) community literacy after-school program. The MANOS language brokers involved and engaged monolingual Spanish dominant family members in their schooling lives, which were largely conducted in English. This positive aspect of language brokering, however, balanced with power differences that happen in bilingual exchanges. Language brokering collaborations sometimes produce conflicts from linguistic inequalities, which re-distribute intergenerational authority between parents and children. Depending on the contexts, being aware of these power differences can also be places for literacy researchers to recognize how bilingual parental collaborations with children happen in families. This last aspect adds to the learning of emergent bilingual students who come to understand the responsibilities of language brokers when communicating with diverse audiences, including educators.

Research in language brokering has examined the complex strategies of youth language brokers navigating audiences, languages, and literacies (Orellana; Orellana and García; Orellana and Reynolds; Orellana et al.; Weisskirch). This article adds to a line of ethnographic research into language brokering as saturated with conflicting authorities and social bridges between languages and cultures. As in previous research portraying children as social actors living in their existential present, and not as "adults in the making" (Corsaro 225), I speak directly with youth language brokers to consider how young people's understandings of their families, their educations, and their languages actively contribute to each as they see themselves in their everyday lives. In this article, the social values of non-standard, minoritized languages and literacy practices demonstrate how two youths felt about language brokering and its power in their families, particularly when translating to help their mothers in different contexts.

Language brokers occupy a unique position in communication. In *Translating Childhoods: Immigrant Youth, Language, and Culture*, Marjorie Faulstich Orellana argues that youth language brokers mediate adult-to-adult conversations and often voice their concerns about the translated contents of both oral and written texts between different monolingual audiences. The MANOS children brokered for mothers around the neighborhood, but also in such tense circumstances as admission to emergency rooms, and interviews with counselors and lawyers. In one case, Sarita, the 17-year-old daughter of 38-year-old

Guadalupe, brokered between her Spanish-speaking mother and the English-speaking teachers of her two younger brothers (in fourth and first grade), offering her mother more than mere translations; she provided Guadalupe analyses of situations and assumed the function of adviser when six-year-old Miguel was diagnosed with a speech impediment and required therapy appointments. Especially in matters relating to school and guarding her younger brothers, Sarita's bilingual abilities to shuttle across languages had increased her family stature in the eyes of Guadalupe. This sense of "role reversal" could misguidedly be seen as a result of when children socialize their parents, or become parents for their children. To understand such power dynamics in a more nuanced way, however, we must consider how language brokering becomes a way that children help their parents as a form of respect and familial duty.

To understand the potential social and academic benefits language brokering might have for children, we must also understand how translation functions beyond language and literacy into the lives of families. As Orellana contends, second-generation language brokers in families do not always see themselves as parents to their parents. Rather, language broker youth consider their translations and interpretations as contributions to the good of the family, as a way of demonstrating care. Young people help their family members with their language brokering, and in doing so, they enact social relationships between audiences. Language brokers meet where English and Spanish circulate and conflict in overlapping markets of cultural values, histories, and power. Language brokers are attuned in to this awareness in their day-to-day linguistic interactions, especially as they not only translate and interpret, but they often advise as well. These aspects of language brokering are important for educators to recognize, and they demonstrate the powerful tools that young language brokers utilize on a daily basis. As such, pedagogy inclusive to this feature of the home lives of millions of students underscores overlooked cultural, intellectual and linguistic strengths language brokers bring to classrooms across the nation.

Study Context: MANOS, the Mexican American Network of Students

This article draws from a larger research project into how English language acquisition and literacy transformed family relations and structured educational ambitions among tutors and MANOS families. Nine first-generation Mexican-origin immigrant families (9 mothers, 21 children) living in New York City were the focus of my study, all members of MANOS, a small, underfunded, self-sustained community literacy program, whose core of dedicated volunteers were also participants in this qualitative study. The grassroots MANOS offered free evening homework tutoring services three times a week, Mondays, Tuesdays, and Fridays. MANOS promoted active family involvement in schooling and positive views toward ethnolinguistic identity. The MANOS tutors varied in ages from 16 to late 50s. The majority, however, were young professionals in their twenties who volunteered once or twice a week, some all three evenings. Several tutors arrived to the program in their office clothes, and a few came from distant parts of other boroughs. Nearly all the tutors were second-generation Mexican Americans and first-generation college students. Several tutors were from different regions of the United States attending college in New York City. There was also a steady stream of local high school students and international university students from Mexico City who volunteered as tutors while earning community service hours to meet graduation requirements. All tutors spoke and wrote English, and some were more fluent in Spanish than others. For one tutor, Mandarin was her first language, Spanish her second, and English her third. Tutors who had the capacities to use Spanish when communicating with MANOS families did so. Children of parents also helped with language brokering duties to parents and young children who had little comprehension of English.

MANOS's mothers were the program's most important assets. In *Mexican New York: Transnational Lives of New Immigrants,* Robert C. Smith argues that gender roles in the Mexican family division of labor point to the cultural responsibility of education as within "female" spaces (97). By and large, the participation among children and tutors fell evenly between females and males, but among parents, there were more participant mothers than fathers at MANOS. At different times fathers also helped with homework, fundraising, and maintaining the space. By tutoring at MANOS, though, I learned about families through the interactions I had with mothers and children, as mothers were the primary regular caretakers I encountered. The MANOS mothers were exceptional in helping their children succeed in school, and they contributed to their children's educational needs in manners deemed fit and necessary for their children's well-being.

The data for my project was gathered primarily over a period of five years, beginning in early 2006, when I conducted my first round of family interviews in homes and at MANOS. These interviews were conducted in both Spanish and English with bilingual children and/or tutors serving as language brokers when possible. I digitally audio-recorded these interviews, as well as interactions with parents, children, and myself when working through homework, or when speaking, writing and/or reading at the MANOS center. Data consisted of digitally recaptured images of texts produced by MANOS children, parents, and tutors, photographs, as well as transcripts from interviews and tutoring sessions.

Using methods developed from my reading of Shirley Brice Heath's *Ways with Words: Language, Life and Work in Communities in Classrooms*, I initially coded audio-recorded homework tutorials involving tutors, parents, and children into different examples of language brokering as literacy events, searching for moments of translation as data for literacy as social practice. When examining instances of language brokering through the data, I problematized Heath's notions of literacy events as limited to monolingual conceptions of literacy brokering. I reconfigured, instead, literacy events in plurilingual dimensions, and in more recent research I have considered them as moments of "translanguaging events" reflecting the dynamic practices of individuals in bilingual contexts (Alvarez 326). In this article, I focus on such translanguaging events narrated as a vignette of a young person helping his mother during an exchange, and the reflection of another student when considering his history of language brokering for his mother as a form of family duty.

MANOS Serving Mexicanos in New York

The majority of my fieldwork occurred at the MANOS site, in the basement of a Catholic Church in one of New York City's outer boroughs, a space the church donated to MANOS for six hours each week. Historically, the neighborhood had been home to immigrant groups since the early nineteenth century. According to the Latino Data Project at the Graduate Center of the City of New York, in 2010, Mexicans composed 14.3% of New York City's total Latino population, with a growth rate of nearly 10% between 1990-2010 (4). At the time of this study, the neighborhood was one of New York City's "Little Mexico" immigrant barrios. Like several barrios in New York City, the Mexican community initially concentrated in the middle of a predominantly Puerto Rican neighborhood. Because of the racial diversity of New York City, the boroughs' "Little Mexicos" were often ethnically and racially diverse, and they have emerged around areas with relatively recent Spanish-speaking migrants from Latin America.

The growth of New York City's Mexican immigrant community underscores the need for MANOS's services to the neighborhood. Yet, despite an enormous unmet need for educational services, MANOS struggled to continue because of lack of institutional support. The underfunded, grassroots organization had struggled year by year to secure a donated location, to recruit tutors, to pay for heat during the winters, and, generally, to provide sufficient services to its members. Despite these hardships, MANOS had persevered for nearly a decade through the sheer will of its volunteer tutors and its member families. Though MANOS remained essentially a small-scale, family-driven after-school program, a long-standing goal had continually been to change its shape through its leadership and achieving legitimate non-profit 501(c)(3) status. This goal had been seen as a work-in-progress. Although less structured than most funded after-school programs, among the numerous social organizations mobilized by Mexican immigrants in New York City, MANOS was recognized as an established program and had won several honors from New York City and State governments, as well as from various cultural organizations in the tristate area, for its services to New York's Mexican community.

Language Brokering: Linguistic Power in Families

The linguistic activities of brokering and being brokers tint all the exchanges of languages analyzed in this study. To language broker is to serve as liaison with influence in exchanges between individuals, to partake in an exchange as an active audience assuming creative or independent agency. According to Lucy Tse, language brokers "influence the content and nature of the message they convey, and ultimately affect the perceptions and decisions of the agents for whom they act" (180). Robert S. Weisskirch argues that during language brokering, "the authority position of the parent may be suppressed as the child or adolescent acts as the spokesperson for the family" (546). During such cases, Carola Suárez-Orozco and Marcelo M. Suárez-Orozco claim that children of immigrants can become "parentified" (74–5). Maria Elena Puig also terms this possibility of role reversal of children and parents as "adultification" in her sample of Cuban refugee families (85).

Without doubt, there were are instances when language brokering disrupts power dynamics among parents and children, but these repositionings are not stable, as no child wields consistent power over parents. How the relations fluctuate is only a matter of contexts and situations. Power reversals are both positive and negative effects of language brokering, but bilingual practices develop in the movement between languages in communication. When the MANOS youths assisted their parents with written and spoken English, there sometimes indeed was a family role reversal where children socialized parents through language brokering, but less in a way to treat their parents as children. When I asked different MANOS youths about translating for their parents, they described language brokering as something they owed their parents, on a level with keeping spaces clean and doing homework.

Several of the MANOS youths had reported to me they were sometimes precociously pushed by their translation responsibilities to assume adult-like authority in their families for the making of meaning and choices, especially when dealing in official genres like applications, disciplinary reports, parent notices, and school permission slips. The linguistic power these bilingual youths cultivated happened as they were compelled to grow up prematurely through translating both meanings and consequences of such official texts. Lisa M. Dorner et al. argue that "children take on a wide variety of translating tasks and that these require considerable linguistic, arithmetic, and social-cultural dexterity" (452). The researchers provide examples of bilingual youth who "explain their own or siblings' report cards to their parents, translate at doctor's offices and banks, make purchases at local drug stores, fill out credit card applications, screen phone calls from telemarketers, and translate movies and television shows for family and friends" (452). Added to this dimension of family responsibility, the sociocultural practices of language brokering are the extension into bilingualism as a valuable aspect of family life for immigrants. Without a doubt, this "parentified" sense of power happened through the reinforcement of the linguistic marketplace and the exchange value behind the acquisition of the dominant language. But the rewards of language brokering could also be redistributed to the family for its communal good. The scholars who argue that language brokering complicates parent-child protocols in immigrant families must take note that language brokering is not the sole cause of the breakdown of communication or language loss in immigrant families. Language brokering is a day-to-day activity, and it deserves pedagogical appreciation. Language brokering can be a tool to reach the literacies of families and to increase involvement and interest in language learning.

One possibility to approaching this as a pedagogical opportunity is to affirm the positive attributes recognizing children's voices, their "adultification," or by affirming the positive attributes of children's linguistic power, and giving greater appreciation to these skills in curricula. Lucy Tse reports that the Latino students in her sample described mixed positive and negative emotions with regards to their brokering, ranging from embarrassed and burdened to proud, independent, and mature (192). Marjorie Faulstich Orellana reports that adolescents in her studies demonstrated feelings of responsibility and power in their roles as language brokers for their parents (57). Curtis J. Jones and Edison J. Trickett recognize the potential value for the social act of brokering in immigrant families. Translating for their parents, they claim, indeed may prove stressful for youth, but that "such activities may, in principle, also be a source of family solidarity and an opportunity to increase self-efficacy and sense of importance" (409). MANOS youths also reported that serving as a language broker for their parents was a tedious, sometimes embarrassing event, but that it was also something useful to help their families.

Brokering English and Authority: Language Brokering and Family Duties

Increasingly, my fieldwork at MANOS revealed to me how immigrant parents who attended the grassroots community literacy program gave great weight to their language brokering children's advice in normatively parental domains of family life. This was when situations become both moments for learning and also for questioning the influence of children in immigrant families, both as a situation for power disruption and also for acquisition of language skills. The shifts of power between generations I found, however, happened less intensely than as presented in language brokering and literacy research. This, however, did not mean that children were completely ruled by their parents, or that they ruled their parents, but, rather, they took pride in the power their English commanded, especially when they were able to use it to help their parents. Eleven-year-old Felipe Rubio (brother of Sarita, mentioned earlier) described a recent memory when he language brokered for his mother, 38-year-old Guadalupe,

> Like we went to a store and it's only me and my mom, and we talked to someone who didn't speak Spanish. And I said what they said to my mom, and I told the other person what my

mom said, and helped both of the people. It made me feel like I know more Spanish. It felt like . . . like I helped my mom with something. It makes me feel proud, because I'm doing a good thing. I'm doing something good.

Felipe's language brokering completed the shopping transaction, and for Felipe, his involvement with adults made him feel like he knew more Spanish, or that he was putting his Spanish skills to test and performing well. Speaking between adults also endowed him with authority. Felipe noted that he felt he knew more Spanish, credited to his ability to translate difficult phrases or semantics from English to Spanish and from Spanish to English. It certainly was a test of his bilingual repertoire in translating in the moment, but also of making sense between adults, and, as he said, "doing a good thing" by helping both people. It is telling that Felipe described the memory of his language brokering as "doing something good" to open the lines of communication.

When I asked Felipe if he had ever watched Guadalupe conduct herself in English in public without his help, he said "sometimes people can't hear her when she talks." Felipe credited this to his mother's "soft voice" in English. Guadalupe's voice in Spanish, though, he said, was "not soft." Felipe further clarified his statement about her English by saying that Guadalupe spoke "loud enough," but people couldn't hear her because of her accent, or that "they can't hear her like the way I do." Several MANOS students expressed similar feelings about these situations in the contact zones of asymmetrical power relations they encountered with their parents in public domains. Nevertheless, the sense of power, of "doing something good" to help his mother, empowered Felipe to think positive of his ability to language broker for the family, and as part of his family duty when called upon. For students like Felipe, activities to help build on this sense of positive association would increase comprehension of audience with bilingual activity.

When the MANOS language brokers assisted their parents in coping with English, the family "role reversal" was not a dramatic turn: children helped their parents and considered it as nothing more than helping out around the home or—if outside the home—as helping with home matters that contribute to the overall well-being of home life in the family. The example of Felipe's memory of language brokering for his mother illustrated this. Felipe's language brokering for his mother permitted him not only to extend his emerging biliteracy and bilingualism to her, but also to understand the practicality of language uses in his family and his special place as facilitator. He gained responsibility in his family because he used his bilingualism as a service to his household. Orellana's extensive longitudinal research with language brokers speaks to similar strengths immigrant youth acquire as they overcome moving between languages and helping their families. In the next section, I offer a language brokering narrative of a son helping his mother in detail.

Language Brokers Negotiating Literacies and Languages

In this section, I offer a vignette from my fieldwork at MANOS demonstrating language brokering in the everyday practices of a mother and son communicating together for specific ends. The setting was a Cinco de Mayo celebration sponsored by a Latino student group at a local university and held outside the university library's quad. Several of the members of the student group were also MANOS tutors. Together with MANOS, the students organized an event to celebrate Mexican culture on campus. The MANOS families helped to organize the entertainment and food vendors. The results on the steps before the campus library were Mexican folklórico and Aztec performance dancers, mariachis, poetry, and plenty of food vendors—including a taco truck from the neighborhood. I was reminded of some of the Cinco de Mayo celebrations I used to attend growing up in Arizona—though nothing quite like this one experienced on a college campus in New York City.

Several MANOS mothers pooled money together to prepare large batches of tamales and tostadas to sell at the event. One mother, 31-year-old Juana, set up a beauty care products table. Her son, eleven-year-old Luis, helped her with the suitcase, and also with setting up the intricacies of the display, as if he had done so before. I approached them and asked them how they were.

Juana, always cheerful, said hello to me, and we shook hands. I shook hands with Luis next and said hello. I said it was nice to see him giving his mother a hand.

"Sí verdad, Luis es un buen ayudante a su mama" (Yes it's true, Luis is a good assistant to his mother).

"She said I help her."

Juana was pretty much always able to understand my English. I could say things to her in English, and she would usually respond in Spanish, but sometimes in English. She often would use MANOS tutoring sessions with her sons to practice her English. She also spoke a good deal of English in her work as a housecleaner in Manhattan. Juana had attended school up to the eighth grade in Puebla, Mexico, but as the oldest child, she claimed it was her duty to forgo further education to help financially support her younger siblings. First, she migrated to Mexico City working domestic jobs there, but eventually found her way to New York City. Through her financial support to her family, all of her younger siblings have completed high school, and one graduated with a degree in education from college. When her boys Luis, and four-year-old Pablo were older, she hoped to complete her education, and eventually earn her college degree, before returning back to Mexico. Juana had begun selling cosmetics within the last six months as a way to earn some extra money working from home on weekends and some evenings. Her best customers were the mothers of MANOS, as well as the mothers at another after-school program just up the block from the program.

Juana and Luis both fielded and answered questions from interested browsers of her wares. I sat near them and observed Luis handle all the English language brokering duties for Juana, and how together they counted money and made change. One customer asked about the ingredients of some lotions, turning her attention between Juana and Luis. Juana held the bottle and read some of the ingredients, but then checked them with Luis, who read them, and then with the customer who read them. The customer made some comment about aloe content, which neither Juana nor Luis were sure about, but Luis pointed out that a different version of the lotion was very popular. He began in Spanish then corrected himself: "Claro—esta—señora—es muy rica: you must smell this—"

Luis then told the customer that there was no aloe in this type of lotion, but that his mother highly recommended it for its smell.

Juana said to Luis, "dile que lo pruebe" (tell her to try it). Juana gestured applying the lotion with her hands.

"You can try it, too. It smells very good," Luis said to the customer.

"Me gusta mucho este," said Juana.

"My mom says she likes this one a lot."

"Such a good sales team," the customer said with a smile, and she purchased the bottle of lotion.

The two made a solid team. After I asked Luis how he liked helping his mom with work. "It's fun because I can try to sell stuff and help my mom because sometimes she can't talk to the people who speak English, and I can talk to them to help her." For his effort, Juana gave a portion of each sale to her son.

Luis not only helped his mother with the transaction, but he also predicted how to approach his audience with practices he learned along with his mother. The move to smell the popular lotion was one Juana taught Luis, both explicitly and through practice with audiences she sold to in Spanish. During this day at the college, however, the sales team came into contact with a significant amount of English-speaking customers. For this reason, Luis's ability to negotiate languages and sales pitches became extremely important. Together, Juana and Luis did well to collaborate bilingually for the well-being of the family, but also for the caring togetherness of parent and child supporting one another.

From Theory to Practice: Schooling Values and Valuing Families

The setting for language brokering at MANOS involved bilingual youths mediating institutional and family literacy in a constellation of homework texts in Spanish and English, which in turn produced constellations of effects in their daily lives. The acts of language brokering in the case of the bilingual youths at MANOS were bilingual contacts between institutional and familial languages. In facilitating this communication, the youths who gained the potential to feel empowered as language brokers in their families. Without assurance and mentorship, language broker youth might turn to the dominant language and internalize a perceived "lack" in the home literacies, imposing a type of self-censorship and relying less and less on the home language as a form of everyday communication. Over the course of another generation or two, this eventually results in home language loss among immigrant families. Future research into language brokering should probe deeper into how transitions between language dominance in immigrant families. Research in such cases must examine linguistic power dynamics over extended periods of time and into actions that reduce language loss over the second and third generations.

MANOS's community literacy program, for some parents in the neighborhood, served as a last and only resort to do something for their children. It also functioned as a protected site away from the schools, where parents aired their grievances with their children's' schools, where parents could learn about schools without having to interact with school officials who intimidated and embarrassed them for not speaking English. The ease of speaking in Spanish, of course, facilitated this most. In *Language and Symbolic Power*, Pierre Bourdieu examines linguistic exchange as an always already structured interaction whose form and content carry certain ascribed levels of value or distinction. According to this framework, differently valued forms of speech and writing structure the internalized forms of self-imposed censorship experienced at the human level. In the case of language brokering, youths redistribute the values of languages more equitably. There is power in this, and certainly when considering the power of immigrant families to communicate collectively.

For language-minoritized families, the standardized academic English literacy required by schooling necessarily entails language brokering and power inequalities. This ability to redistribute linguistic inequalities permits non-English individuals to broker linguistic capital in the linguistic marketplace, and I argue language brokers profit in a number of ways. Their possession of English in their families signifies Bourdieu's notion of *ethos* as "a sign of status intended to be evaluated and appreciated," a "sign of authority, intended to be believed and obeyed" (66). At other times, this caused pressure and sometimes emotional pain when children felt ashamed for their parents' nonstandard English accents. Sometimes this accounted for a rapid transition to English dominance in the second generation and eventual heritage language loss.

Teaching Strategies to Reach Language Brokers

Understanding the practices of bilingual students in their families is a necessary undertaking for all educators. Barely recognized or integrated into school-based language arts, the language brokering performed by youth language brokers has a community-based language function rewarded and cultivated only outside school. Lisa M. Dorner et al. find in their sample that "higher levels of language brokering were significantly linked to better scores on fifth- and sixth-grade standardized reading tests" (451). These translingual types of classroom practices can extend from bilingual classrooms and into language arts in K-12, and even into university writing classes. Language brokering could be emphasized in schools with bilingual students as an untapped potential for empowering students and improving development of crafting voice in writing. Of course, more research must be performed to determine fully which aspects language brokering improves and how standardized testing scores intersect with specific aspects of the literacy activity. As it stands, however, language brokering and translation happen every day for immigrant families, and not as something learned by students for a test. School tests, however, do constantly remind students learning English about the social relations between their home languages and those preferred by institutions.

For example, the MANOS youths learned about the social relations between Spanish and English within New York City, and their accents among the seas of those around them. MANOS youth language brokers also observed how their parents' nonstandard English accents marked them as immigrants in the U.S. mainstream. This proved to be a difficult issue for some to fully comprehend, and they sometimes leveled blame at their parents for their Spanish dominance. MANOS students had acute ears for accents in English and Spanish, and as material for study, language brokers would no doubt demonstrate higher levels of comprehension for registers of voices. In this sense, this very important translanguaging activity deserves further invitation into school curricula. Until then, however, it is important to examine language brokering as it happens in communities of practice. In terms of intersections of life and study, ethnographic projects exploring student communities, languages, accents, and literacies encapsulate methods for students to discover data from their experiences for analysis.

There are a number of immediate and structural ways schools can tap into the potential of language brokers in classrooms and pedagogy. For the sake of immediacy, I offer two pedagogical outlines instructors could employ right away in language arts classrooms. These methods seek to utilize and promote students' bilingualism and biliteracies in their classrooms as sources for study, and to increase student engagement in conducting self-led research community projects that seek to sustain bilingual practices rather than assimilate monolingual assumptions about language standardization.

Educators should acknowledge the academic potential for studying translation and student autobiographies of spoken and written registers. Writing courses at all levels stand to gain by incorporating ethnography and autoethnography projects that take students into communities to conduct field research. Students' interviews should be transcribed with attention to accents and translations when necessary. *On Ethnography: Approaches to Language and Literacy Research* by Shirley Brice Heath and Brian J. Street offers an excellent primer to conducting student research projects studying literacies and learning. To further gain social perspectives, ethnographic projects should involve groups of students from different backgrounds each taking part in researching the homes and languages of classmates for writing. In such shared projects, students conduct fieldwork and write about the lived experiences of communities. They practice critical thinking skills applied to researching their lives and their rich, experiences. The results are relevant writing projects rooted in students' real lives.

Student-teachers in this model would develop their own educational skills by using ethnographic fieldwork, from which they derive the themes and words of special consequence to the targeted population. Ethnographic methods research can tap into pedagogical value of local language uses and theoretical rigor. For future instructors, ethnography is clearly a valuable learning tool. From a critical point of view, student researchers would come to note how dominant and minority languages interact through the bilingual practices of agents moving between languages, especially at the family level, but also in communities. Speculations into how power dynamics function between children's and adults' access to—and possession of—the dominant literacy would necessarily extend the scope of teacher training to examine how and why families sharing a common situation coalesce to address their interests and needs. This would also offer important insight to future instructors about the strengths students and their families bring to classrooms, complicating a one-dimensional stereotype of low-income immigrants as dependent vessels of deficits needing to be filled with the so-called "official" language.

At the moment, it is important to first understand that language brokering is a phenomena resulting from a variety of historical and social factors, but that it has occurred for thousands of years, as long as cultures have migrated across the globe. Language brokering is an everyday literacy practice, but one that in the United States gets relegated to outside classrooms. Encouraging language brokering inside classrooms is the beginning to recognizing it as a tool for student involvement and multicultural interest. As multilingualism and globalization continue to shape one another, all students will develop multilingual proficiencies. To begin now, however, teachers can begin by inviting language brokering into lessons. For example, teachers requesting translations from different languages into English from other languages during class lectures is a way to empower emergent bilingual students to speak, and with the authority of another language. Language brokering highlights student translation in context with conversations at hand, but it also lends esteem to the academic ability to speak of certain subjects in the classroom in languages not English.

In addition, activities that could require translation assurance, as in bilingual versions of poems, also can be places where instructors can ask students experienced as language brokers to further engage in class. When using media for analysis, finding those with subtitles in different languages can also invite participation from language brokers. Looking at examples of commercials from other parts of the world can become fruitful material for rhetorical analysis in a defamiliarized linguistic context. Students familiar with the language and culture in foreign commercials can become sources of authority for fielding questions from students and teachers. Questions of cultural difference could be researched into topics of comparative political or cultural issues.

Analysts and educators would serve this diverse society well by penetrating "smokescreens" attempting to segregate languages through politics, a project the linguist Ana Celia Zentella described two decades ago as teaching and learning from sociolinguistic inequalities. Zentella argues that the "language smokescreen that obscures ideological, structural, and political impediments to equity" can be used to examine the macro picture of Spanish as a historically thriving language in the United States (9). The anthro-political perspective—as Zentella terms it—is strongly allied with the precepts of critical or applied anthropology, as well as with critical discourse analysis and a Freirean pedagogy of empowerment from the grassroots. Following the anthro-political motivations for scholarly research set forth by Zentella, one hope for my research is to open teachers and parents to the existence of multiple routes to bilingualism, biliteracy, and language education.

Works Cited

Alvarez, Steven. "Translanguaging Tareas: Emergent Bilingual Youth Language Brokering Homework in Immigrant Families." *Language Arts*, 91. 5 (2014): 326–39.

Bourdieu, Pierre. *Language and Symbolic Power*, edited by John B. Thompson, translated by Gino Raymond and Matthew Adamson. Cambridge: Harvard UP, 1999. Print.

Corsaro, William A. *The Sociology of Childhood*. 2nd ed. Thousand Oaks: SAGE, 2005. Print.

Dorner, Lisa M., et al. "'I Helped My Mom,' and It Helped Me: Translating the Skills of Language Brokers into Improved Standardized Test Scores." *American Journal of Education*, vol. 113, no. 3, 2007, pp. 451-478.

Heath, Shirley Brice. *Ways with Words: Language, Life, and Work in Communities and Classrooms*. New York: Cambridge UP, 1983. Print.

Heath, Shirley Brice, and Brian V. Street. *On Ethnography: Approaches to Language and Literacy Research*. New York: Teachers College P, 2008. Print.

Jones, Curtis J., and Edison J. Trickett. "Immigrant Adolescents Behaving as Culture Brokers: A Study of Families from the Former Soviet Union." *Journal of Social Psychology*, 145. 4 (2005): 405–27. Print.

Latino Data Project. "The Latino Population of New York City, 1990–2010." City U of New York Center for Latin American Caribbean, and Latino Studies, 2011.

Orellana, Marjorie Faulstich. *Translating Childhoods: Immigrant Youth, Language, and Culture*. New Brunswick: Rutgers UP, 2009. Print.

Orellana, Marjorie Faulstich, and Ofelia García. "Language Brokering and Translanguaging in School." *Language Arts*, 91. 5 (2014) 386–92.

Orellana, Marjorie Faulstich, and Jennifer F. Reynolds. "Cultural Modeling: Leveraging Bilingual Skills for School Paraphrasing Tasks." *Reading Research Quarterly*, 43.1 (2008): 48–65. Print.

Orellana, Marjorie Faulstich, et al. "In Other Words: Translating or 'Para-Phrasing' as Family Literacy Practice in Immigrant Households." *Reading Research Quarterly*, 38. 1 (2003): 12–34. Print.

Puig, Maria Elena. "The Adultification of Refugee Children: Implications for Cross-Cultural Social Work Practice." *Journal of Human Behavior in the Social Environment*, 5. 4 (2002): 85–95. Print.

Smith, Robert C. *Mexican New York: Transnational Lives of New Immigrants*. Oakland: U of California P, 2006. Print.

Suárez-Orozco, Carola, and Marcelo M. Suárez-Orozco. *Children of Immigration*. Cambridge: Harvard UP, 2001. Print.

Tse, Lucy. "Language Brokering Among Latino Adolescents: Prevalence, Attitudes, and School Performance." *Hispanic Journal of Behavioral Sciences*, 17. 2 (1995): 180–93. Print.

Valdés, Guadalupe. *Expanding Definitions of Giftedness: The Case of Young Interpreters from Immigrant Communities*. Mahwah, NJ: Lawrence Erlbaum P, 2003. Print.

Weisskirch, Robert S. "Feelings About Language Brokering and Family Relations Among Mexican American Early Adolescents." *Journal of Early Adolescence*, 27. 1 (2007): 545–61. Print.

Zentella, Ana Celia. *Growing Up Bilingual: Puerto Rican Children in New York*. Malden, MA: Blackwell Publishers Ltd., 1997. Print.

Steven Alvarez is Assistant Professor of English and Coordinator of the First-Year Writing Program at St. John's University. He specializes in literacy studies and bilingual education with a focus on Mexican immigrant communities.

LITERACY IN COMPOSITION STUDIES

Literacy in Composition Studies is on the Web at http://licsjournal.org

Literacy in Composition Studies is a refereed open access online journal sponsoring scholarly activity at the nexus of Literacy and Composition Studies. With literacy and composition as our keywords we denote practices that are deeply context-bound and always ideological and recognize the institutional, disciplinary, and historical contexts surrounding the range of writing courses offered at the college level. Literacy is often a metaphor for the ability to navigate systems, cultures, and situations. At its heart, literacy is linked to interpretation—to reading the social environment and engaging and remaking that environment through communication. Orienting a Composition Studies journal around literacy prompts us to analyze the connections and disconnections among writing, reading and interpretation, inviting us to examine the ways in which literacy constitutes writer, context, and act.

Daughters Learning from Fathers: Migrant Family Literacies that Mediate Borders

Kaia Simon's "Daughters Learning from Fathers: Migrant Family Literacies that Mediate Borders" contributes to our understanding of how literacy practices are sponsored within Hmong families in the US. Opportunities for girls and women to access education and enter the professional workforce prompt the fathers in this study to revise traditional Hmong patriarchal constraints on daughters' literacy acquisition. Simon's ethnographic study, based on twenty-three Hmong women who came to the US as children, hinges on participants' descriptions of literacy events in their family contexts. She finds that Hmong fathers were central actors in these literacy events and that the different types of opportunities for literate women in the US led the families to revise Hmong gender roles. We appreciated Simon's ethnographic research because it provides a clear example of how family literacies may, in turn, challenge assumptions about culturally constructed gender roles.

Daughters Learning from Fathers: Migrant Family Literacies that Mediate Borders

Kaia Simon

KEYWORDS: family literacy, transnational literacy, gender, feminism, Hmong women

Scholarship in literacy studies has long demonstrated the significance of family literacy practices, with particular attention in recent decades to the literacy practices of migrant and refugee families.[1] Studies on migrant families have illuminated multiple aspects of their literacy: the experiences of migrant children as language and literacy brokers for adults (Al-Salmi and Smith; Guan et al.; Orellana); the intergenerational conflicts that emerge from literacy and language variations within families (Chao and Mantero; Figueroa; Sarroub); and the development and implementation of family literacy programs that incorporate literacy resources of migrant families within, or adjacent to, educational contexts (Alvarez; Auerbach; DaSilva Iddings; Moll and Gonzalez). Such studies often demonstrate that the differences in literacy access, education, and language fluency among members of migrant families result in conflict within families and between families and schools. While such literacy differences are a result of unequal conditions of migration and might be inevitable, my research reveals that conflict stemming from these differences is not. Based on an IRB-approved, empirical study of Hmong refugees, I show how literacy differences among generations of migrants can in fact inspire positive relations among family members, alter disempowering gender dynamics, and productively connect migrant families outward to public realms of literacy use, such as schools and workplaces. Specifically, in this article, I examine how literacy mediates a relationship often under-explored in studies of family literacy and literacy studies in general: fathers and daughters.

These issues surrounding family literacies and relationships are particularly acute for migrantgroups whoarrive to the US as refugees withvarying histories of literacy experiences; these literacy histories might be affected by the geopolitical forces that also propelled the group's migration to a host nation (Brandt and Clinton; Duffy, *Writing*). Additionally, refugee groups often face reductive assumptions about their cultures, languages, religions, and conditions of relocation: as Victor Bascara notes, part of the refugee condition is to be perpetually "emplotted into a narrative of innocence, victimization, rescue, and recovery" (198). This narrative can interfere with refugees' access to the public resources of literacy, and especially so for refugee women whom many assume to be further constrained by gendered cultural practices that interfere with their ability to act with agency (Narayama). Placing authority within migrant family literacies, as my study does, resists this narrative of refugee disempowerment, particularly for women from these groups whose access to literacy historically has been restricted. This study also contributes to conversations in family literacy studies that seek to value, and not intervene in or correct, migrant family literacy practices. I find that these relationships, fostered by interactions that center on literacy, inspire daughters to cross gendered borders between public and domestic spaces in order to access literacy resources. The daughters use these resources to achieve upward mobility as they also transform gender roles. Such insights into migrant family literacies ask scholars, educators, and the public to see literacy's role within migrant families, especially those families and cultures assumed to operate within strict patriarchal relations, as a force for positive change within families and a resource that helps children mediate borders to access public literacy resources. The findings of this article are drawn from an ethnographic study of twenty-three Hmong women's literacy, in which I explore the multiple intersections among literacy, family, gender, and culture. While the conflicts that circulate around migrant family literacies mentioned above are also present in Hmong refugee families (Lee, R. et al.) and patriarchal gender dynamics remain a potent force for Hmong women's lives in general, I also find that literacy opened space for the women in my study to develop relationships with their parents that supported their development of multiple literacies within their homes. In terms of my focus here, literacy mediated daughters' relationships with their fathers and also helped the women cross typical gendered borders in Hmong family relationships. These relationships, and the literacy lessons at the center of them, inform these women's ability to achieve unprecedented access to education, professional careers, leadership, and advocacy. As the women who participated in my study cross borders into public realms and access literacy resources available there, they revise expected gender roles for Hmong women.

CONTEXT OF THE STUDY

When I asked participants to tell me about messages they received from their parents about literacy, twenty of the twenty-three women I interviewed mentioned specifically their fathers' support for their educations. These father-specific comments stood out to me because, as is evident in studies that depict home literacy practices (e.g., Al-Salmi; Alvarez; Brandt, *Literacy*; Cintron; Heath, *Ways*; Moll and Gonzalez et al.), whether or not these studies focus specifically on migrant family literacies, fathers are largely absent. These studies reveal what Deborah Brandt calls "the heavy hand of mothers" (*Literacy* 151) and women in family literacies. In literacy histories where fathers do appear (e.g., Gilyard; Rodriguez; Rose), fathers are more antagonistic or absent than involved figures in literacy acquisition. Catherine Prendergast ("Or You Don't") and Brandt ("Accumulating") consider the role of fathers in accumulating, or not accumulating, literacy across generations. Vershawn Ashanti Young and David Kirkland consider the role of fathers and literacy in constructions of black masculinity. With the exception of Prendergast, these studies depict father-son relationships. All of this work points, from multiple approaches, to the data that the National Literacy Trust aggregates in its survey of studies of family literacy: fathers tend to be less involved, if at all, in their children's literacy acquisition and development—and even less so in the literacy of their daughters (Clark). Despite this trend in the literature, I find that for the Hmong women in my study, fathers played a noticeable role in their literacy development. Fathers verbally supported their educations, taught lessons at home, and invited them to cross borders into previously male-coded spaces. These relationships, and their fathers' influence in their literacy acquisition, became a resource these women drew from throughout their lives.

The Hmong are an ethnic group from Southeast Asia. They fled their villages in the mountains of Laos for refugee camps in Thailand at the end of the Vietnam War, due to the Hmong's alliance with the CIA in what became known as the Secret War.[2] For the Hmong who migrated to the US, relocation is what anthropologist Veena Das would call a "critical event": their lives were "propelled into new and unpredicted terrains" (5). These terrains were literal—the Hmong moved from refugee camps in Thailand to the United States—and cultural, as the Hmong lived an agrarian lifestyle in the mountains of Laos, practicing a primarily oral culture with very little literacy, until geopolitical forces displaced them from their homes and their way of life. After a critical event, writes Das, "new modes of action come into being which redefine[d] traditional categories" (6). One of the new modes of action for the Hmong is literacy.

Literacy as a new mode of action is especially significant for Hmong women. At the time of their relocation to the US, the Hmong had little alphabetic literacy in any language and maintained a primarily oral culture. In *Writing From These Roots*, John Duffy documents the multiple, sometimes competing, geopolitical forces that have acted upon the Hmong since their earliest history and interfered with their widespread literacy acquisition. Hmong women faced additional gendered interference: daughters were often, as one participant's mother told her, "prohibited" from access to the education that might have been available to their brothers, due to the patriarchal power structures that governed families. The daughters of the first generation of Hmong refugees, whether members of generation 1.5 or US-born, are the first to have widespread and expected access to literacy.[3]

These literate interactions are significant because in traditional father-daughter relationships in Hmong families, daughters often do not warrant much attention or investment from their fathers, literate or otherwise.[4] Yet, the only participant in this study whose parents were not supportive of her literacy, explains what she called "typical" relationships between Hmong parents and daughters: "My parents are very traditional, and when I say that, I mean my dad was a typical Hmong male where he had no involvement in our lives because we were women. My mom took full care of bringing up the girls. Her priority was to make sure that we were well trained to be someone's wife one day."[5] Decisions about family matters, including education, often adhere to what fathers wanted: patriarchal structures of power, kinship, decision making, and the strict gendered division of labor are documented in ethnographic studies of the Hmong in both Laos (Ireson; Symonds) and in the US (Donnelly).

By commenting on the centrality of literacy as a common site for opening, and fostering, the relationships between them and their fathers, these women reveal the interconnected nature of these gendered and cultural forces in their own literate development. I do not mean to imply that atriarchal relations were dismantled by these relationships and interactions. Instead, I intend to offer these findings as a corrective to the pervasive representations of "rigid Hmong patriarchy and Hmong women's submissiveness," as do Julie Keown-Bomar and Ka Vang in their study of Hmong women's agency and family relations (Keown-Bomar and Vang 140). The agency enacted by the women who participated in my study illustrates the need for approaches taken up by transnational feminist anthropologists Saba Mahmood and Laura Ahearn, who challenge scholars to expand notions of what agency means and how women experience it in their lived realities. In other words, agency does not have to manifest as resistance to power or conflict (Ahearn). Instead, I consider agency, as Mahmood does, in terms of women's ability to enact their desires. The relationships between daughters and fathers and the literacy lessons at their center are a form of cultural capital the women in my study use to enact agency as they pursue their desired literate opportunities in schools and workplaces, while they also maintain positive relationships with their families and communities. In order to hone in on the effects of literacy for Hmong women, this study focuses on those who were children at the time of their relocation or were born shortly after their parents arrived in the US. I started recruiting participants from professional networks that I developed when living in communities that were primary resettlement sites for the Hmong beginning in the late 1970s. To expand participation from these networks, at the conclusion of each interview, I asked the participant to share the names of anyone who might also be willing to meet with me. Because such snowball sampling relies on social networks (Browne), the twenty-three women I interviewed have achieved educational levels that are not typical among most Hmong women. In contrast to the majority of Hmong women, who do not earn post-secondary degrees (Ngo and Lee; Xiong), all of my participants attended some post-secondary education and twenty-two have bachelor's degrees. Of these, thirteen continued to pursue graduate degrees, and eleven have master's degrees in fields such as counseling, social work, public policy, or education; one of my participants has earned a doctorate, and another was a PhD candidate at the time of our interview. Such credentials might lead readers to make associations between my participants and "model minority" stereotypes. As Bic Ngo and Stacey Lee make clear, however, the Hmong defy inclusion in this notion of Asian American upward mobility for a few reasons. The Hmong resist assimilation as a diasporic group (Vang, C.) and do not demonstrate an upward trend in economic mobility in the 2010 census data, though more Hmong do earn high school diplomas and advanced degrees than past census records have shown (Xiong). The families of the women who participated in my study did not have the resources or social capital to be associated with the prominent image of Asian American families recently made popular by Amy Chua's *Battle Hymn of the Tiger Mother*. These scenes of literacy instruction between fathers and daughters are ad-hoc, improvised, and while they do participate in Immigrant Bargain and American Dream narratives (Alvarez, Vertovec), these interactions do not have the same neoliberal inflections that Susan Koshy locates and critiques in the Tiger Mother narrative as it applies to Asian Americans' upward mobility.

For my study, I conducted semi-structured oral literacy history interviews with twenty-three women who were children at the time of their family's relocation or born shortly thereafter and who are currently between the ages of 30 and 45.[6] This methodology is of particular salience when studying this group of refugee women because oral literacy history interviews allow participants to reveal their own literate practices in relation to the macrosocial forces that operate upon them, so that researchers can work to "untangle the knotted threads of literacy and history" (Vieira,"Doing" 139). Additionally, these literacy history interviews document the voices of migrant women who are too often left out of historical records. For these reasons, literacy history interviews" provide unexpected insights concerning the literacy development of individuals" (Duffy, "Recalling" 87), especially in the ways they reveal the individuals' own understandings of the role of literacy in their lives. Data collection occurred over an eight-month period in 2015-16. My interview protocol asked participants to share their literacy histories in relation to their K-12 educational experiences, their pursuit of higher education, their current work and literate practices. I also asked them to share their parents' messages and influences on their education and work. I transcribed all interviews. To extend my data collection beyond the interview transcripts, I also kept field notes at each interview and engaged in memoing throughout data collection (Heath and Street). When participants mentioned specific texts in the context of these literacy events, I asked them to share any copies or versions of these texts with me. Unfortunately, most of the texts had been lost over time—but I did collect samples of workplace writing, personal writing, and films created for college coursework. I also noted whenever participants referred to publicly available texts (published books, YouTube videos, etc.) and created a bibliography of these resources. The findings in this article draw primarily from interview transcripts and field notes.

In order to examine literacy's role as a mediating force for change for this generation, throughout the corpus of data I identified narratives of "literacy events," as defined by Shirley Brice Heath ("Protean" 445): specific memories where talk and texts, and talk about texts, intersect. Literacy events are productive units of analysis to answer the questions that animate this project, because participants' specific comments on literate activity speak to the ways literacy matters in their lived experiences of cultural change. I coded the interview transcripts for accounts of family literacy events and organized these excerpts according to prominent family members present. As I compiled the accounts that featured fathers and analyzed them in tandem, I specifically noted places where participants linked the literacy events with their fathers to their present day lives and drew parallels between the literacy event to lasting effects on their identities, their worldviews, and their ability to access the public resources of literacy.

My data analysis methods center on the narratives my participants offered within their oral literacy histories, in keeping with my commitment to reflexive transnational feminist methodologies (Mahmood; Mohanty; Narayan; Sato) that privilege and preserve the accounts and epistemologies of research participants. These methods both account for and minimize my positionality as I represent and analyze the interview transcripts by foregrounding the voices of the women who shared their histories with me. My analysis of these interviews pays careful attention to the language used by the women who shared their stories with me, so that their self-presentation is preserved and respected.

Likewise, as Martin Packer argues, such narrative analysis of interview data "invite[s] the interviewer to adopt a new way of seeing the world, including a way of seeing the speaker, the interviewee" (100) through its respect of the plot and language offered by the interviewee. Additionally, the participants featured in this article reviewed drafts and offered feedback in advance of its being sent out for review. I turn now to sharing the findings from this focused analysis, to demonstrate that family literacies mediated these women's access to the public resources of literacy and informed their revision of traditional gender roles.

In what follows, I make this case through the accounts of five women. To protect their privacy, I refer to them by pseudonyms. Their names, education credentials, and current occupations are listed in Table 1 along with some notes pertinent to their experiences. The memories of these five women, related to me through literacy history interviews, represent in detail the various possibilities that these father-daughter literate relationships manifested in the lives of the women who participated in my study. These five women talked about how they carried these lessons and relationships with their fathers throughout their lives and revealed the meaning they assigned to these experiences. In the explicit connections they make between the relationships with their fathers, life-long literacy practices, and their articulations of how their gender roles have changed, we are able to see how they give credit to these experiences as they continue to use literacy actively to mediate gendered borders between cultures, languages, families, communities, and US institutions.

Table 1. Featured Participants

Name (Pseudonym)	Education	Current Work	Notes
Phoua	Bachelor's Degree, Elementary Education	2nd grade teacher	PaChoua's older sister
PaChoua	Bachelor's Degree, Elementary Education	5th grade teacher	Phoua's younger sister
Nhia	Bachelor's Degree, Political Science Master's Degree, Public Policy	Director of state government policy	Public advocate for Hmong women on marriage and domestic violence
Nalee	Bachelor's Degree, Ethnic Studies	Hmong language teacher	Began career in education as a tutor for pregnant teens
Mai	Bachelor's Degree, Political Science	Administrator at a state university	First woman president of the board for a local non-profit serving the Hmong community

DAUGHTERS ACCESS PUBLIC LITERACY RESOURCES

Literacy facilitated these father-daughter relationships by offering them a site of connection that was new for Hmong daughters: access to education. As mentioned earlier, before daughters were expected (and required) to be educated in the US, they primarily occupied domestic spaces: doing chores, caring for younger siblings, cooking for the family. Daughters, by and large, did not have a public presence. After relocation, however, Hmong families had to readjust these practices to fit within a nation where the law would intervene if school-age daughters did not attend school. The place of daughters, and their relationships to other members of the family, were altered by their access to literacy. The women I interviewed told me their fathers responded by supporting their daughters' attendance and success in school, as long as she also contributed domestically as a traditional Hmong daughter might—and was at home when she was not in school.

By far, the most common literacy event between fathers and daughters—a narrative shared with me by twenty of my twenty-three participants—came in the form of "lectures" fathers gave to their daughters about the importance of an education, encouraging them to take full advantage of the opportunities presented to them. Fathers gave these lectures to both daughters and sons, which came up during interviews when participants commented that they weren't sure if they would have received the same encouragement to be educated if they'd grown up in Laos. Many participants told me that these lectures included a warning against taking work in manual labor. Five women voiced an experience that is common among children of migrant parents (Gonzalez et al.): that their fathers were supportive but "couldn't *really* help" them, meaning that these fathers were, like many immigrant parents no matter their previous home nation or languages, unfamiliar with school culture in the US. These interactions resulted in the building of father-daughter relationships where these women felt that their literacy, measured in their educational achievements, was a reason their fathers took notice of them and became involved in their lives. They felt valued because of these interactions. In these lectures, fathers directed positive attention and messages about literacy to their daughters, centering literacy as the site of the interaction. The women I interviewed honored this relationship and expectation: all have pursued higher education.

Crossing Borders, National and Local

In addition to receiving verbal encouragement to access literacy through schooling from their fathers, the women also mentioned more literal acts of border crossing within narratives of literacy events. As literacy informed the development of relationships between fathers and daughters, fathers took action to make access to literacy physically possible for their daughters. Some of the fathers who participants told me "couldn't *really* help" their daughters with education found ways to increase their literate access: taking daughters to the library, driving them to and from school, or taking them to college interviews. By increasing their mobility, these fathers did in fact help their daughters access literate resources.

Phoua and PaChoua are sisters who teach at the same elementary school, and I met with them together in Phoua's classroom at the end of a school day. They are the two oldest daughters in their family, just over a year apart in age, and are, according to PaChoua, "always two peas in a pod." As they told me their family's story of migration, they included a literacy event featuring their father's literate intentions for them. Part of their father's inspiration to move his young family, as he told them, was his two daughters: "so we could have a better life, not in just wealth or whatever. He knew that education was the key, and if he stayed in Laos his daughters would never have the education that he wanted for us." Phoua and PaChoua's father made clear to his daughters that the opportunity for them to acquire literacy inspired him to move his family across national borders: from the jungles in Laos to the refugee camps in Thailand, from where they would eventually cross the border into the US. In their retelling of this family story, their father told them that he knew that if he decided to stay in Laos, his daughters would not be able to be educated. They knew he had always valued them, since he left his home country in order to ensure their access to literacy. His decision is an origin of the literate relationship that they continued to build, and neither daughter took her access to education for granted. They both expressed gratitude for their father's forward-thinking decision.

Phoua also articulated the lasting effects in her life from her father's actions to provide her geographic access to literacy. Phoua prioritized her education, saying that she was partially inspired by her father's words and his own pursuit of literacy at the local technical college. She always wanted to be an educator, telling me she imagined herself as a child teaching English lessons to her elders at her home. Phoua now teaches second grade in a diverse elementary school, and PaChoua teaches fifth grade at the same school. They both mentioned that they are proud to be role models for all of their students, but especially for students who are learning English as a second language. Their father's decision to cross national borders not only mediated their access to literacy at school but continues that access for the students they teach, many of whom have also crossed geographic borders to attend school.

Mai shared a similar literacy event of geographic border crossing as an example of her father's support for her literacy. I first met Mai a few years ago, when she was the board president of a local non-profit that serves the local Hmong community and gave the keynote address at an annual Hmong fellowship dinner. She is the oldest daughter in her large family and told me that her father's support of her education was "extremely progressive"; she quickly added, "But what was he to do? He had seven girls!" In imagining her father's process of arriving at this progressive stance, Mai said that he had to "rewire that traditional brain of his and widen it a little bit" first to believe that his daughters could "be whatever we want to be here in the United States" and then to tell them that they could, and should, use their educations to find the way to live that life. Mai's father took action and decided to support her education in a strategic choice to move their family to live within a particular school's boundary, so she and her siblings would attend an elementary school with fewer Hmong students. In the mid-sized city where she grew up in the early 1980s, most Hmong families lived in the same neighborhoods and attended the same elementary schools. Mai told me that her father's decision to cross this border to relocate was bold at the time. As she told me, he wanted to create the conditions where she would "either sink or swim": he wanted her to be forced to rely on English as her primary language in school (saving Hmong for home, making sure she also remained fluent) so she wouldn't be behind and would have the "asset" of English fluency. Mai ultimately believes that her father's "design" was wise even as she admitted to feeling isolated at school. She credits her elementary school experience with her fluency in English and that she learned to be "very comfortable being the only minority student in class," both of which have served her well in professional settings. Mai told me that her father framed his choice to relocate as one that would help her "survive," and she agrees that it has.

Mai related the lasting effects of her access to the elementary school literacy resources her father ensured by moving to a new home: she told me that because she was enrolled in a school where she was one of the only Hmong students, she learned to take different types of opportunities, to take risks, and not to stay "stuck in a niche grouping." As an adult, Mai finds these lessons still serve her well: she is still not afraid to be uncomfortable, and she does not feel out of place when she is the only Hmong person, or the only woman, in a space. When she was elected board president of the non-profit organization, she was the first women ever to hold such a leadership position and faced resistance from many of those she worked to serve. Mai tells me her ability to endure as an outsider in majority-White or male-gendered spaces is shaped because "[my dad] has designed me to get to this place where, You want answers? I will figure that out for you. I can do that!" Her sense of her own capacity to increase the public visibility and leadership potential of Hmong women began to form during those elementary school experiences. She links this aspect of her personality to her father's intervention in her schooling.

These literacy events reveal the interconnections among fathers, daughters, access to literacy through education, and the lived consequences of crossing national and local political borders. These fathers encouraged their daughters to access public literacies through decisions that placed them in geographic locations that would make such access possible. These literacy events participate in the broader narrative of the Immigrant Bargain, which Alvarez notes migrant children often experience as a burden to succeed, since parents justify their sacrifices because of the potential opportunities for their children. Years after their schooling is complete and they have achieved work in professional settings, Phoua, PaChoua, and Mai all acknowledged the hardships these decisions brought to their fathers and to themselves, but they did not say that they felt burdened by their fathers' expectations. Instead, they ultimately expressed gratitude for their fathers' decision making and for the opportunities they had because of them. Crossing geographic borders not only mediated their access to school but affected their literacy throughout their lives.

CROSSING BORDERS BETWEEN HOME AND SCHOOL

Some literacy events the daughters remembered were their fathers sharing school-based literacies with them, relying on schooling they'd obtained before their relocation. These literacy lessons crossed borders as fathers relied on knowledge and instructional practices from their own schooling and lives abroad. The lessons also crossed from home to school, as daughters drew from them throughout their educations. Seventeen participants' fathers came to the US with some alphabetic literacy (most commonly in Lao, French, or Hmong) and numeracy they had acquired through formal education in Laos, military training, or adult education programs in the refugee camps. Of these seventeen, five created an instructional relationship with their daughters, often centered in nightly lessons, homework time, or trips to the local library or bookstores to find reading materials. These scenes of academic lessons were more rare in my interviews, even among the fathers who'd been educated, because most of the fathers worked long hours in manufacturing jobs that did not leave time for home lessons. Nhia and Nalee both shared extended stories about how their relationships with their fathers developed through these lessons in alphabetic literacy, numeracy, and languages. They remembered their fathers supporting their access to school-based literacy by assuming a teacher-like role in their lives.

Nhia and I met in her government office, where she works in public policy. When I asked her about her earliest memories of education, she shared this literacy event:

> My father and my uncle worked out a deal where, even as a teenager, my uncle would go to school, hold a part time job at a gas station, and then he would get home at around midnight. I always knew that my job was to stay up past midnight because then my father would go and pick up my uncle from the gas station where he worked at and my uncle would come in with all of the remaining donuts. We would eat donuts and we would learn our ABCs. It worked out well because I was waiting for the donuts and my father wouldn't let us go to sleep until my uncle Mickey was home and we had gone through our A is for Apple and B is for Banana kind of thing, And this is before I went to school.

In remembering her late-night lessons and donuts with her father and uncle, Nhia referred to it as a sort of Early Childhood Education. In addition to the lessons about the ABCs, her father drilled multiplication tables with her by papering her bedroom walls with large sheets of paper, writing multiplication tables all over them, and having her recite them nightly. She called these lessons her "bedtime reading," bringing together the cozy imagery of this often-maternal practice with the image of her joining her uncle and father around a table, eating donuts and trying to win dictionary competitions. Nhia pointed to these family literacy practices when she remembered her ease of access to school: they were the reason she excelled in math class until "at least ninth grade" and continues to be careful and aware of the words she chooses to use when speaking. She noted that her father's diligence in his lessons with her made her school experiences less burdensome. That he taught these lessons with no mind to her daily work in school—at times teaching her at levels far beyond what her teachers expected of her—also taught her to work hard to achieve the eventual ease of learning. She credited her father's lessons as part of how she developed her diligence and success throughout her schooling.

Nalee has worked in school-based settings her entire professional life and currently is the director of a Hmong language program. When Nalee and I met over coffee and began our conversation, it became immediately clear that her father is an important influence in her personal commitment to education. She proudly told me that her father was a language teacher in Ban Vinai refugee camp before his family relocated to the US and that her family was "different than the average Hmong refugee family" because her father created a homework station at the kitchen table and gathered his children there for nightly practice. She told me that he taught her all he could, until "eventually the education that we were part of became pretty much over his head." Nalee remembered learning to read and write in Hmong, multiplication tables, and how to count from one to eleven in French. She chuckled as she recalled the confused faces her teachers made when she repeated the lessons she learned from her father to them and they couldn't quite decipher what she was saying: "even before we went to school he was teaching us already, but he taught us in his accent." Nalee remembers feeling proud that she was ahead of her peers, even if her speech was marked as accented. For Nalee, education has always been and continues to be "a huge part of my life," and she connects her belief in the power of education to her father's influences that began with those lessons.

For both women, these nightly lessons facilitated their access to some literacies in school, but when fathers relied on the instructional methods they had experienced that did not align with classroom practices in American schools, there were some disconnects in expectations and consequences. Nhia remembers watching her sister play a multiplication game with her father that involved chopsticks and a ball, in which "if you recite any number that's off you would get hit with the chopsticks.... I had that luxury of watching, so I knew that I couldn't get any answers wrong." Nhia noted that her father's methods were less sympathetic than what she experienced in school. Nalee also said that her father's methods mirrored his own education experiences in Thailand where "once you learn the information you move on. It doesn't matter how old you are." When he introduced her to multiplication as a young child, she remembered, "I was just thinking what is this beast? I tried so hard . . . but I still didn't understand! I have to say though, when I got to third grade, we started doing actual multiplication and I was ahead. [I thought] is this all this is? Oh, this is easy!" Both Nhia and Nalee remarked that they believed their fathers emphasized numeracy because, as Nalee put it, "math is its own language" and their fathers were not hindered by a lack of English. They turned to numbers to mediate these interactions with their daughters. Both women found these family literacy practices beneficial in their ability to perform among public literacy work of school, especially in math class.

In addition to feeling prepared for success in school by her father's lessons, Nalee told me that she has always felt "blessed" that her father did not adhere to "that community assumption that there was this whole sons and daughters thing where daughters were expected to do more housework and things like that" but instead "as far as education goes and opportunities and all of that it was just about who was interested in what." Nalee said she knew that "whatever I wanted to be a part of, he would be right there." In addition to helping her land her first summer job as an adolescent, Nalee credits her father for her "knack for tutoring," which she drew from during her work as a translator in a charter high school for teen mothers. Her tutoring skills led her to develop support for Hmong-speaking students that was responsive to their language and culture, and she eventually assumed most of the instructional duties for these students: developing curriculum and planning and delivering lessons. Nalee highlighted this experience and her expertise in the Hmong language when she interviewed to be a Hmong language instructor at a university. She does not have all of the educational credentials the job asked for, but she accepted their job offer and has since received a promotion to direct the program. Nalee has spent her professional life in schools, and she traces her entry to working for these public institutions, and her desire to be the best teacher she can be, to her relationship with her father.

Nhia's professional path has led her to work in public policy, which she decided to pursue partway through her undergraduate degree, when she switched her major from pre-med to political science. Nhia's desire to be a leader stems both from her father's messages about education and from a message her grandfather recorded for her parents on a cassette he sent them from Laos: her grandfather said that "the future leaders of the world are sitting inside the classrooms of America." Nhia's father, himself a military leader, told her that education would help her find a seat at the table "where decisions, our very futures, are being made." The inspiration she found in her relationship with her father meant she made the bold move to pursue his dream that his children be leaders, while defying his desire that she become a doctor. Despite her prominence as a leader for the Hmong community in her state and particularly for women, she revealed that her father still believes she should have become a doctor. Even so, while her father's lessons may not have produced the specific result he wanted, they manifest in her work in public policy. Nhia's realization that she did in fact want to be a leader led her away from a more lucrative profession in medicine to a career where she uses literacy to advocate for justice for underrepresented groups. She is a visible, and at times controversial, leader in the Hmong community and in her state government. She chose to have this path because she grew up seated at her family's table where she learned her ABCs and her future possibilities.

The literacy events depicted in this section reveal the ways that these fathers enacted literacy instruction with their daughters, developing relationships centered on home literacies that also support their success in school-based literacies. Even with the indirect connection to school, these lessons are clearly primarily grounded in family literacy practices—as these fathers relied on their heritage language as they share their own literacies with their daughters. These lessons are not always immediately accessible to daughters in school, but they eventually became a resource they draw from as a knowledge base and as an orientation to education more broadly. The dual nature of these effects results in their continued ability to access the resources that schools offer them: first as students and later as professionals. These women credit the literacy events they had with their fathers as they locate the ways they developed and drew from these resources.

Family Literacies Revising Gender Roles

In the previous sections, I demonstrated how participants draw from their literate relationships with their fathers, crossing borders as they access public literacy resources in schools and workplaces. Many participants revealed that such access led them to question and revise the traditional gender roles they might have otherwise been expected to maintain when it came to marriage. Being married, becoming a daughter-in-law, and having children are central expectations for Hmong women. According to traditional practices, Hmong women marry young: in the US, if generation 1.5 and second generation daughters were not married during high school, then elders thought they should be shortly thereafter. Indeed, simply attending school during the day meant that these unmarried Hmong daughters had a public presence that resulted in great concern among many Hmong parents. They believed that their daughters' freedom outside the home would lead them to misbehave— making them less eligible for marriages into good families. Parents responded by restricting daughters' mobility outside of school hours, as participants told me during interviews and as Stacey

J. Lee finds in her study of Hmong youth in schools. Accessing school literacies and choosing to continue to pursue higher education—in response to their fathers' support—often resulted in the disruption of typical expectations for age of marriage for Hmong women. Among the women who shared their stories with me, three were married during or right after high school and pursued higher education while also filling the expected role of daughters-in-law in their husbands' families.[7] The rest of the women in my study delayed their marriages while they attended higher education and married after they had earned degrees. Three women were single at the time of our interview. Mai, who delayed her marriage not only until she had graduated but until her term as board president ended, told me that she was an "eyesore" among her extended family before she married, adding: "I mean, they've never had a Hmong female in their family beyond the age of sixteen, seventeen!" As in her experiences in school, she found support for this revision of her expected role in her relationship with her father, who, she reported, "was like, you do what you need to do [with school and work] and all that other stuff [getting married and having children] will happen." Her relationship with her father, and his support of her literate pursuits and public advocacy, offered her the resources she needed to withstand pressures to marry that came elsewhere in her community. Marriage, and the age at which Hmong women now get married, has shifted noticeably as Hmong women access public literacies. Delaying the age of marriage—and recognizing that a daughter has some agency in making the decision—is a clear revision of gender roles inspired by access to literacy.

The disruptions in expectations inspired by these relationships were not just in age of marriage, however. Literacy also became a resource that daughters could draw from as they measured their own value and attractiveness as future wives. Phoua shared one such literacy event that she said has informed one way she reconsidered her value as a Hmong woman. As a self-described "ugly duckling," Phoua told me that "in the Hmong culture, it's so natural for people to do this . . . they will compare everybody. They will say oh, you're not as pretty as this one." Phoua told me these comments were hurtful until "my dad sat me down one day . . . and he was like, Okay. You might not be pretty, but I don't want you think about just beauty. I want you to focus on education . . . one day you're going to be educated and then you will be beautiful to everybody." Laughing, Phoua ended this memory by saying "I cherish those words!" Her father intervened and interrupted the cultural practice of commenting on physical beauty of women to reframe Phoua's sense of what she could, and should, value about herself as a Hmong woman. His message taught Phoua that literacy could open a different path to achieve different goals, that she could focus on herself and achievement rather than worry about outside judgment. She learned that literacy could be her access to resources that would make her an attractive wife. In this reframing, the gender roles and values for Hmong women are revised.

Crossing Borders into Male-Coded Spaces

For some daughters, their relationships with their fathers resulted in gendered border crossings into male-coded spaces that mediated their access to traditional oral literacies typically shared between fathers and sons. Nhia received lessons in oral history, which she told me her father "meant to be for the sons but he didn't have any sons," during times they went fishing together. She said that her father told her about the history of the Hmong people and about her clan in particular: "stories of what could be, what has been, what's broken, what could be put together again...eventually [I could] begin to hear all of the other messages that were being told that he wasn't just really putting into words for me. I just walked away from those years of my life with the understanding that I have an opportunity [to become a leader]." She told me that she felt these oral family histories shared by her father positioned Nhia in the long lineage of the leaders in her family, that her own literacy could give her the opportunity to contribute to the historical memory of her family and clan.

Nhia's fishing trips and cultural literacy lessons demonstrate how such changed relationships between fathers and daughters opened space for fathers to include daughters in lessons previously reserved for sons, offering them access to privileged cultural literacies and the opportunity to imagine themselves part of them. Nhia's current leadership in government policy places her within the stories her father told her: she is working to put things together for the Hmong in the US. She continues this difficult work even as she faces backlash from those in her community who feel she is out of her place as a Hmong woman—that she's crossed the border too far in assuming her role as a public advocate for women. Nhia locates the resolve to stand firm in her advocacy in her knowledge of her family's leadership lineage.

Phoua and PaChoua's father also included his daughters in these male-only spaces. They told me that their father spent a lot of time with them and "literally imparted the knowledge and the wisdom that his dad passed onto him and his brother to us." In this account of inter-generational teaching, "us" means two daughters: Phoua and PaChoua interrupt the patriarchal chain. PaChoua elaborates:

> [My dad was able] to give us the knowledge and wisdom that they usually pass onto boys. Because boys sat in meetings, they took care of the family issues. And we did, we got to sit

> through those too. We got to listen to it. We brought the waters in for the males like girls do, but my dad would always allow us to stay in the room. We weren't shooed away like girls usually do. He would invite us to stay, you know: It's okay girls. You can stay. He made us feel like we were important in this decision making, even though it was a room full of males. He's like: Listen. Listen. How did this person talk? Listen, how did this person talk? And did you see how wise he was with his words? And don't be like the fool like this one. And he would coach us. But if we were girls, we would be in the kitchen. We wouldn't hear that. We wouldn't get that coaching.

Even though PaChoua's language implies that she sees some separation between "girls" and herself and her sister when she repeats "like girls" and says "*if* we were girls," at the time of this memory they *are* girls. PaChoua's language indicates that in this memory she recognizes that her father is not treating her like a girl. PaChoua's father not only encourages her and Phoua to witness the male elders in discussion but also debriefs those discussions with her later, encouraging her active listening and evaluation of what she heard. In her memories of this rhetorical training, her father is inviting her to imagine herself one day also participating in these discussions. She can stay. He asks her to try to emulate the good examples and tells her "don't be like the fool." PaChoua concluded the story of this memory by telling me that she felt able to be a leader, and to become a teacher, because her father not only encouraged her to speak her mind but taught her how to do it eloquently.

Entry into these male-coded spaces inspired further revision to traditional marriage expectations for these daughters beyond delaying the age at which it happened. In this particular case, Phoua and PaChoua were invited to stay in and learn from elders' discussions, and their father demonstrated that he appreciated them and valued their opinions. Perhaps because they had been treated as more than just "like girls" by their father, Phoua and PaChoua both expressed that when the time came for them to think about choosing their partners, they'd wanted to marry men who "appreciate us as equal partners" and who "value our opinions." They understood that while this might be uncommon among traditional Hmong men, it was possible to find husbands who might have similar beliefs about their wives. Phoua and PaChoua, laughing, both told me that their "independence" can at times result in conflict in their marriages, but that ultimately they have found husbands who do consider them as equals and they are grateful to have married them. Phoua and PaChoua revised the courtship script for Hmong daughters by expecting to be treated with equality.

These women's fathers invited their daughters to cross the gendered borders within their families and gave them access to Hmong cultural literacies typically shared with sons. These daughters look to these interactions as one place where they gained a sense of their own potential for leadership. They continue to assert themselves into these community spaces and rituals, crossing gendered borders and in so doing transforming their own gender roles as they also publicly represent revised images of Hmong women as leaders. This is an important enactment of their access to public literacies, as Mai and Nhia especially offer public enactment of these leadership roles and can be models for expanding notions of the realms Hmong women should occupy. In their personal and professional

lives, literacy has allowed these three women to cross multiple borders and to participate as Hmong women in their families and communities, but in these cases we see them being Hmong women on their own timelines and on their own terms.

FAMILY LITERACIES AS RESOURCES

Families, and their literacy practices, continue to move across borders. The current political unrest around the world is resulting in more displaced people seeking refugee status and protection. With the attention circulating around the migrations of groups of people, some of that focus has turned in particular to literacy access for young women and girls for whom education has been denied due to geopolitical interruptions and sexist forces.[8] It is clear that as families migrate, literacy will continue to mediate changes within families and as members of those families use literacy to access public resources. Literacy's role within these families is complicated: at times the source of conflict and strife, at times a source of relationship building and strengthening. Family literacy practices, regardless of whether or not they directly support or relate to the literacy practices of schools, workplaces, or governments, can have lifelong effects of the children of migrants as they continue to mediate borders and establish a public presence in their home nation.

In this article, I have shown how daughters rely on literate relationships with their fathers throughout their lives to access these public resources of literacy and to transform their gender roles within their families and communities. Literacy, and the relationships it mediated, supported their experiences of upward mobility as it also inspired them to revise their expected gender roles. While all migrant groups events will not necessarily follow the pattern of the Hmong relocation to the US and the introduction of widespread literacy for women in one generation, studies such as this should inspire transnational writing scholars to look to family literacy practices as capaciously as possible, in order to better understand these resources that individuals carry with them into classrooms, workplaces, and writing in public. Further, as we broaden notions of literacy's role in feminist agency, we better understand that transnational women's experiences mediating multiple gendered borders, and their revisions of gender roles, are also intricately connected to family literacy practices. These nuanced insights help us to recognize the complex interactions between individuals, family literacies, and access to the public resources of literacy—and should challenge us to rethink ways that migrant family literacies serve as assets, especially as they are carried from homes into public spaces.

Notes

1. I would like to express my deep gratitude to Catherine Prendergast for her feedback on this article from its earliest stages. Special thanks to Kate Vieira for on-point and insightful suggestions on multiple drafts. Thank you to Amy Wan and the anonymous reviewers for offering productive critique and providing suggestions for improvement. Most importantly, I owe all of this work to the generous women who shared their literacy histories with me.

2. The relocations of the Hmong after the end of the Vietnam War happened in waves, with one occurring between 1978-1982, one in 1987-8, and one in the mid 2000's at the closure of the last remaining refugee camp in Thailand. For more on this history, see Chan; Donnelly; Duffy; Tapp et al.; C. Vang.

3. In keeping with common definitions among transnational scholars (e.g., Danico; Louie; Suarez-Orozco et al.; Vertovec), I define generation 1.5 as those who migrate when they are younger than the age of twelve.

4. While these cultural specifics of gender bias are particular to the Hmong, these biased tendencies between fathers and their children are not, as sociologist Dalton Conley notes in *Pecking Order*. Conley's study of a wide

corpus of data as well as qualitative interviews reveals that these gender biases transcend culture and economic status and have real economic and emotional effects that last throughout adulthood. Sons tend to benefit in terms of their confidence, self-esteem, and economic stability while daughters tend to experience negative effects in these realms.

5. For another consideration of the "typical" roles and treatment of Hmong daughters, see Ka Vang.

6. Similar methodologies appear in the following: Brandt, *Literacy;* Duffy, *Writing;* Lagman; Mihut; Prendergast, *Buying;* Vieira, *American.*

7. When a Hmong woman marries, traditionally she becomes a member of her husband's family. Traditional kinship practices involve sons and daughters-in-law living with his parents, and the daughter-in-law (*nyab*, in Hmong) is expected to "serve" her in-laws through domestic labor: cooking, chores, caring for the family's children.

8. Malala Yousafzai (whose father plays a prominent role her education) won the Nobel Peace Prize in 2014 because of her work to bring education to girls. "Boko Haram," the common name in the West for a Nigerian terrorist organization, is most often translated as "Western education is a sin." This isn't a perfect translation, but the words link the concepts of "education" and "harm." The group notoriously kidnapped girls from their school in 2014, inspiring the #BringBackOurGirls movement. For more on the translation of the name, see Murphy.

Works Cited

Ahearn, Laura M. "Language and Agency." *Annual Review of Anthropology* 30.1 (2001): 109-37. Print. Al-Salmi, Laila Z., and Patrick H. Smith. "Arab Immigrant Mothers Parenting Their Way into Digital Biliteracy." *Literacy in Composition Studies* 3.3 (2015): 48-66. Web. 10 Nov. 2016.

Alvarez, Steven. "Brokering the Immigrant Bargain: Second-Generation Immigrant Youth Negotiating Orientations to Literacy." *Literacy in Composition Studies* 3.3 (2015): 25-47. Web. 10 Nov. 2016.

Auerbach, Elsa. "Deconstructing the Discourse of Strengths in Family Literacy." *Journal of Reading Behavior* 27.4 (1995): 643-61. Print.

Bascara, Victor. "'In the Middle': The Miseducation of a Refugee." *Strange Affinities: The Gender and Sexual Politics of Comparative Racialization.* Eds. Grace Kyungwon Hong and Roderick A. Ferguson. Durham: Duke UP, 2011. 195-214. Print.

Brandt, Deborah. "Accumulating Literacy: Writing and Learning to Write in the Twentieth Century."
College English 57.6 (1995): 649-68. Print.

—. *Literacy in American Lives.* Cambridge: Cambridge UP, 2001. Print.

Brandt, Deborah, and Kate Clinton. "Limits of the Local: Expanding Perspectives on Literacy as a Social Practice. *Journal of Literacy Research* 34.3 (2002): 337-356. Print.

Browne, Katherine. "Snowball Sampling: Using Social Networks to Research Non-Heterosexual Women." *International Journal of Social Research Methodology* 8.1 (2005): 47-60. Print.

Chang, Sucheng. *Hmong Means Free: Life in Laos and America.* Philadelphia: Temple UP, 1994. Print. Chao, Xia, and Miguel Mantero. "Church-Based ESL Adult Programs: Social Mediators for Empowering 'Family Literacy Ecology of Communities.'" *Journal of Literacy Research* 46.1 (2014): 90-114. Print.

Chua, Amy. *Battle Hymn of the Tiger Mother.* New York: Penguin, 2011. Print.

Cintron, Ralph. *Angel's Town: Chero Ways, Gang Life, and Rhetorics of the Everyday.* Boston: Beacon, 1998. Print.

Clark, Christina. *Why Fathers Matter to their Children's Literacy.* London: National Literacy Trust, 2009. Web. 15 April 2016.

Conley, Dalton. *Pecking Order: Which Siblings Succeed and Why.* New York: Pantheon Books, 2004. Print.

Danico, Mary Yu. *The 1.5 Generation: Becoming Korean American in Hawai'i.* Honolulu: U of Hawai'i P, 2004. Print.

Das, Veena. *Critical Events: An Anthropological Perspective on Contemporary India.* Delhi: Oxford UP, 1995. Print.

Da Silva Iddings, Ana Christina. "Bridging Home and School Literacy Practices: Empowering Families of Recent Immigrant Children." *Theory Into Practice* 48.4 (2009): 304-11. Print.

Donnelly, Nancy D. *Changing Lives of Refugee Hmong Women.* Seattle: U of Washington P, 1994. Print.

Duffy, John. "Recalling the Letter: The Uses of Oral Testimony in Historical Studies of Literacy." *Written Communication* 24.1 (2007): 84-107. Print.

---. *Writing From These Roots: Literacy in a Hmong American Community.* Honolulu: U of Hawai'i P, 2007. Print.

Figueroa, Ariana Mangual. "'I Have Papers So I Can Go Anywhere!': Everyday Talk About Citizenship in a Mixed-Status Mexican Family." *Journal of Language, Identity, and Education* 1.51 (2012): 291-311. Print.

Gilyard, Keith. *Voices of the Self: A Study of Language Competence.* Detroit: Wayne State UP, 1991. Print.

Gonzalez, Laura M., Jose A Villalba, and L. Dianne Borders. "Spanish-Speaking Immigrant Parents and Their Children: Reflections on the Path to College." *Journal of Humanistic Counseling* 54.2 (2015): 122-139. Print.

Guan, Shu-Sha A., Patricia M. Greenfield, and Marjorie F. Orellana. "Translating into Understanding: Language Brokering and Prosocial Development in Emerging Adults from Immigrant Families." *Journal of Adolescent Research* 29.3 (2014): 331-55. Print.

Heath, Shirley Brice. "Protean Shapes in Literacy Events: Ever-Shifting Oral and Literate Traditions." *Literacy: A Critical Sourcebook*. Eds. Ellen Cushman, et al. Boston: Bedford St. Martin's, 2001. 443-66. Print.

—. *Ways with Words: Language, Life, and Work in Communities and Classrooms*. Cambridge: Cambridge UP, 1983. Print.

Heath, Shirley Brice, and Brian V. Street. *On Ethnography: Approaches to Literacy and Language Research*. New York: Teachers College P, 2008. Print.

Ireson, Carol J. *Field, Forest, and Family: Women's Work and Power in Rural Laos*. New York: Westview P, 1996. Print.

Keown-Bomar, Julie, and Ka Vang. "Hmong Women, Family Assets, and Community Cultural Wealth." *Claiming Place: On the Agency of Hmong Women*. Eds. Chia Youyee Vang, Faith Nibbs, and Ma Vang. Minneapolis: U of Minnesota, 2016. 117-43. Print.

Kirkland, David E. *A Search Past Silence: The Literacy of Young Black Men*. New York: Teachers College P, 2013. Print.

Koshy, Susan. "Neoliberal Family Matters." *American Literary History* 25.2 (2013): 344-80. Print. Lagman, Eileen. "Moving Labor: Transnational Migrant Workers and Affective Literacies of Care." *Literacy in Composition Studies* 3.3 (2015): 1-24. Web. 10 Nov. 2016.

Lee, Richard M., et al. "The Family Life and Adjustment of Hmong American Sons and Daughters." *Sex Roles* 60.7 (2009): 549-58. Print.

Lee, Stacey J. *Up Against Whiteness: Race, School, and Immigrant Youth*. New York: Teachers College P, 2005. Print.

Louie, Vivian. *Keeping the Immigrant Bargain: The Costs and Rewards of Success in America*. New York: Russell Sage Foundation, 2012. Print.

Mahmood, Saba. *Politics of Piety: The Islamic Revival and the Feminist Subject*. Princeton: Princeton UP, 2005.

Mihut, Ligia Ana. "Literacy Brokers and the Emotional Work of Mediation." *Literacy in Composition Studies* 2.1 (2014): 57-79. Web. 10 Nov. 2016.

Mohanty, Chandra Talpade. *Feminism Without Borders: Decolonizing Theory, Practicing Solidarity*. Durham: Duke UP, 2003. Print.

Moll, Luis C., and Norma Gonzalez. "Lessons from Research with Language-Minority Children." *Literacy: A Critical Sourcebook*. Eds. Ellen Cushman, et al. Boston: Bedford/St. Martin's, 2001. 156-71. Print.

Murphy, Dan. "'Boko Haram' Doesn't Really Mean 'Western Education is a Sin.'" *The Christian Science Monitor*. The Christian Science Monitor, 6 May 2014. Web. 10 Nov. 2016.

Narayan, Uma. *Dislocating Cultures: Identities, Traditions, and Feminism*. New York: Routledge, 1997. Print.

Ngo, Bic, and Stacey J. Lee. "Complicating the Image of Model Minority Success: A Review of Southeast Asian American Education." *Review of Educational Research* 77.4 (2007): 415-53. Print.

Orellana, Marjorie Faulstich. *Translating Childhoods: Immigrant Youth, Language, and Culture.* Piscataway: Rutgers UP, 2009. Print.

Packer, Martin. "Qualitative Analysis Reconsidered." *The Science of Qualitative Research.* Cambridge: Cambridge UP, 2011. 99-120. Print.

Prendergast, Catherine. "Or You Don't: Talents, Tendencies, and the Pooka of Literacy." *Enculturation* 16 (2013). Web. 6 May 2016.

Rodriguez, Richard. *Hunger of Memory: The Education of Richard Rodriguez (An Autobiography).* Boston: D.R. Godline, 1982. Print.

Rose, Mike. *Lives on the Boundary: A Moving Account of the Struggles and Achievements of America's Educationally Underprepared.* New York: Free P, 1989. Print.

Sarroub, Loukia K. *All American Yemeni Girls: Being Muslim in a Public School.* Philadelphia: U of Pennsylvania P, 2005. Print.

Sato, Chizu. "A Self-Reflexive Analysis of Power and Positionality: Toward a Transnational Feminist Praxis." *Women, Literacy, and Development: Alternate Perspectives.* Ed. Anna Robinson-Pant. London: Routledge, 2004. 100-12. Print.

Suarez-Orozco, Carola, Marcelo M. Suarez-Orozco, and Irina Todorova. *Learning a New Land: Immigrant Students in American Society.* Cambridge: The Belknap P, 2008. Print.

Symonds, Patricia V. *Calling in the Soul in a Hmong Village: Gender and the Cycle of Life.* Seattle: U of Washington P, 2003. Print.

Tapp, Nicholas, et al., eds. *Hmong/Miao in Asia.* Bangkok: Silkworm, 2004. Print.

Vang, Chia Youyee. *Hmong America: Reconstructing Community in Diaspora.* Urbana: U of Illinois P, 2010. Print.

Vang, Ka. "The Good Hmong Girl Eats Raw *Laab.*" *Hmong and American: From Refugees to Citizens.* Eds. Vincent K. Her and Mary Louise Buley-Meissner. St. Paul: Minnesota Historical Society P, 2012. 101-12. Print.

Vertovec, Steven. "Migrant Transnationalism and Modes of Transformation." *The International Migration Review* 38.3 (2004): 970-1001. Print.

Vieira, Kate. *American By Paper: How Documents Matter in Immigrant Literacy.* Minneapolis: U of Minnesota P, 2016. Print.

—-. "Doing Transnational Writing Studies: A Case for the Literacy History Interview." *Composition Studies* 44.1 (2016): 138-40. Print.

Xiong, Yang Sao. "Hmong Americans' Educational Attainment: Recent Changes and Remaining Challenges." *Hmong Studies Journal* 13.2 (2012): 1-18. Print.

Young, Vershawn Ashanti. *Your Average Nigga: Performing Race, Literacy, and Masculinity.* Detroit: Wayne State UP, 2007. Print.

REFLECTIONS

Reflections is on the Web at https://reflectionsjournal.net/

Reflections, a peer reviewed journal, provides a forum for scholarship on public rhetoric, civic writing, service-learning, and community literacy. Originally founded as a venue for teachers, researchers, students and community partners to share research and discuss the theoretical, political and ethical implications of community-based writing and writing instruction, Reflections publishes a lively collection of scholarship on public rhetoric and civic writing, occasional essays and stories both from and about community writing and literacy projects, interviews with leading workers in the field, and reviews of current scholarship touching on these issues and topics.

Subalternity in Juvenile Justice: Gendered Oppression and the Rhetoric of Reform

Although a number of articles have focused on juvenile justice, few have addressed young women, especially the rhetoric surrounding them. Golden's article critically examines how oppressive rhetoric contributes to the silencing of these young women, especially given their subaltern status. Not only is Golden filling a critical gap in this research, but she also, as a creative writer, provides poignant poems from these women to counter their invisibility, as well as the misguided programs and "the system's isolated authoritarian environment" that serve to oppress them. From their empowering rhetoric as expressed in their writing, Golden provides insight on what will work for these women.

Subalternity in Juvenile Justice: Gendered Oppression and the Rhetoric of Reform

Tasha Golden

The proportion of young women in the juvenile justice system has increased substantially since the nineties, yet the rhetoric surrounding them remains under-studied and under-critiqued. The oppressive nature of this rhetoric thwarts the achievement of gender equity in juvenile justice, undermining the reforms that have been recommended over years of research. The following analysis examines this rhetoric for the ways in which it silences women and furthers gendered oppression in system; it also offers critical cautions regarding existing approaches to gender-responsive programming. By acknowledging the subalternity of young justice-involved women, further studies and community collaborations can be taken up to close the distance between the actual experiences and knowledges of young women and the rhetorical constructions of them that have long informed policy, programming, and daily interaction.

"*Who are you*
You now-grown teenager Who are you
Who is afraid to look in the mirror because of what she might see"

—N., an incarcerated teen woman
whose writing appears in *Call Me Strong*

"*[W]hatever point is made about such a low-status group gains credibility, validity, and reliability only as it can be redefined through the lives and contributions of others more credible, more legitimate, and more salient.*"

—Jacqueline Jones Royster, *Traces of a Stream*

I began working with young incarcerated women in 2012, when I was invited to be the Writer in Residence for the young women at a detention center in Ohio. While I knew the work would take me into new territory as a writer and scholar, I was unprepared for the consistency with which the participants in my workshops wrote about experiences such as sexual assault, domestic violence, sex work, imprisoned parents, mental illness diagnoses, and cutting. Brittany[1] demonstrates this in a poem to her father:

> *Dad, why do you hate us,*
> *your flesh and blood*
> *Don't tell us*
> *that you will dress us*
> *up like prostitutes and put us*
> *on the corner. Don't beat us*
> *like you would a man on the street"*
> *(Breaking Out of Silence).*

As I daily combed through their poems, I was alarmed at how tempting it became to allow my role with these writers to slip into that of mediator, mouthpiece, missionary.

So each evening of that first week-long writing workshop, I returned to my hotel reeling from my own emotional reactivity, anxious to replace it with concrete (if generalized) knowledge about the women with whom I was working. I spent hours hunched over my computer, beginning what would become years of research regarding young justice-involved women. I quickly discovered that a "history of physical or sexual victimization is one of the most common characteristics of girls in the justice system" (Sherman 21), and that young women are more likely than young men to suffer from mental illness and Post-Traumatic Stress Disorder (PTSD).[2] I also learned that, despite the

---

1. As in the books in which these poems originally appear, I use the authors' first names or initials only.

2. In a report for the Federal Office of Juvenile Justice and Delinquency Prevention (OJJDP), Francine Sherman writes, "Research from the Oregon Social Learning Center shows that while 3 percent of boys in their study had documented histories of physical abuse, 77.8 percent of the girls had histories of abuse" (Sherman 21). In addition, "[o]n every scale, delinquent girls studied by the Oregon Social Learning Center had more significant mental health problems than boys—over three-quarters of the girls in the study met

dozens of studies and reports since the nineties describing specific attributes and needs of young justice-involved women, little responsive action has been taken to address those needs (Watson and Edelman ii). More subtly, their lives are circumscribed discursively as well as physically: their experiences always depicted and "validated," as Royster describes above, by juvenile justice authorities, lawyers, and/or researchers whose rhetoric further silences the women they wish to help. For example, the words of young justice-involved women are almost wholly absent from scholarly literature about them; more troubling, their voices even in poetry and other creative arts are often stripped of power by the pity they engender in well-intended listeners, by patronizing interpretations of their statements as mere self-expression, and/or by the simple fact that their works are rarely seen or heard beyond the walls of detention centers or diversion program facilities.

While scholars in rhetoric and writing studies have addressed the rhetoric surrounding "at-risk" youth and adult women in prison,[3] young justice-involved women have remained under-acknowledged and under-studied in the field. This is a devastating gap in public rhetoric research, given that the juvenile justice system's failure to address women's needs is due at least in part to women's subaltern status in the system and to pervasive rhetorical constructions of them as other. I argue that young women in the justice system will not be given equitable and humane care until that system faces— and reforms—its long history of infantilizing, neglecting, and othering them. I thus offer the following critique, beginning with a delineation of the oppressive circumstances in which many young justice-involved women live, followed by an analysis of the extent to which their ways of know-

---

the criteria for three or more DSM IV Axis 1 diagnoses" (23). Sherman also cites a study of detained youth which "found that girls had higher rates of psychiatric disorders than boys—nearly three-quarters of girls met criteria for one or more psychiatric disorder and rates of depression and anxiety disorders were particularly high among girls. Notably, girls are more likely than boys to be diagnosed with more than one mental health disorder, often a mental health disorder with a substance use disorder" (23). This data is not meant to imply that reform for young detained men is unnecessary, or even that it is less urgent. It does, however, clarify that equitable treatment of young women requires that the system attend to gender disparities rather than simply maintaining a system designed for males.

3. See Tobi Jacobi, Meghan Sweeney, Ruby Tapia (see Solinger et al), Wendy Hinshaw, and Adela C. Licuna, among others.

ing are disqualified and dismissed by the rhetoric of those in positions of power. Finally, I offer critical cautions regarding gender-responsive programs: problematizing recidivism as a benchmark for success and critiquing the use of indoctrination and empowerment rhetoric as means of addressing oppression. By acknowledging the subalternity of young detained women, further studies and community collaborations can be taken up to close the distance between the actual experiences and knowledges of young women and the oppressive rhetorical constructions of them that have long informed policy, programming, and daily interaction.[4]

> *I would like to make people happy,*
> *help the world be better to live in.*
> *Try to talk to others to make sure that they're ok.*
> *And try to be a positive person*
> *to anyone in need of it.*
> *I would like to heal people*
> *from their pains and their suffering*
> *So that they won't have to be angry*
> *anymore.*
>
> —from *Shine Through*

I should first note that I approach this analysis with no small amount of wariness; as Gayatri Spivak has argued, Intellectuals who wish to "give silenced others a voice" often fail to recognize the opacity of their intercessional work and the heterogeneity of the "others" whom they seek to represent (Leitch 2193). Such failures result in a "benevolent effort" that "merely repeats the very silencing it aims to combat" (2193). I recognize the possibility that this endeavor could do the same, particularly as I am inevitably present as observer and intercessor. Furthermore, as William Banks has discussed in his work on embodied writing, I am unable to avoid bringing to this inquiry my own experiences of domestic dysfunction; indeed, the violence inscribed on my body may inform the significance I place on young women's abusive histories as determinative and powerful (25). I am also aware that my many personal, often emotional interactions with young in-

---

4. The present work is but a starting point for the continued analyses, collaborative and iterative program designs, and thorough evaluations that are ultimately necessary for reform.

carcerated women cannot but color my understanding(s) of them. Nevertheless, despite my misgivings, the absence of young women's voices in public conversations about justice, childhood adversity, and education demands the risk I take now in presuming to illuminate the unexamined rhetorics that perpetuate their oppression. In an effort to better expose this problematic and inevitable *speaking-for*, several poems by young women I've met in juvenile detention appear throughout the piece. My hope is that these highlight my observational standpoint: offering recurring reminders that the women of whom I speak are individuals with their own opinions, goals, knowledges, and beliefs regarding their circumstances.[5]

Landscape

I am a dark, lifeless forest
bare branches and rolling fog in every corner
I like being dark and cold sometimes
I keep to myself usually
I am a cloudy sky
and a wet, broken branch smushed into the mud s
ometimes I go unnoticed
but that's ok
I am a dark lifeless forest

—from Know Me

THE STATE OF OPPRESSION

The othering of young women who enter the juvenile justice system begins before they are arrested, and in fact, is often the cause of their arrests. For example, young females are more likely than males to be detained for minor offenses and technical violations (Sherman 11), in-

---

5. The use of published poems allows young women's voices to be present in this research despite confidentiality protections that typically limit descriptive research among young incarcerated women. While I support such protections, I do worry that they discourage researchers from conducting studies that rely heavily on firsthand interaction and information; one result is the near-absence of young women's voices in the literature about them. An increased demand for input and testimony could lead to collaborative research practices that protect the privacy of justice-involved youth while inviting and better utilizing their knowledge and feedback.

dicating that juvenile (mis)behavior is defined and punished in terms of gender. Similarly, parents are known to "have different expectations about their sons' and daughters' obedience to parental authority" (Zahn et al., "Violence by Teenage Girls" 7), and "[t]he use of the juvenile justice system by families in chaos in an effort to remove their daughters from their homes or to obtain services for them has been noted in the literature" (Sherman 35). In other words, young women are often punished not for criminal behavior per se but for a level of aggression or "unruliness" that fails to conform to traditional gender expectations (Sharpe and Gelsthorpe 195-196, 200). Indeed, "some professionals mistake expressions of gender-nonconformity (through choice of hairstyle, clothing, mannerisms, and name) as rebellious behavior to be corrected" (Majd, Marksamer, and Reyes 2).

Juvenile women are also disproportionately blamed and charged for occurrences of violence in their homes. Because of mandatory arrest laws for domestic violence, "law enforcement first responders may consider it more practical and efficient to identify the youth as the offender"—regardless of who (daughter, parent, or other) actually initiated a violent incident within the home (Zahn et al, "Violence by Teenage Girls" 7). This is deeply troubling, because such an expediency-driven approach is likely to punish victims rather than perpetrators. The literature has long shown that young women in the justice system have high rates of domestic victimization; in fact, this was reiterated in 2015 when an Annie E. Casey Foundation study reported that "girls' problem behavior, in contrast to that of boys, 'commonly relates to an abusive and traumatizing home life'" (Saar et al 12).

Studies have also "found that adjudicated girls had higher rates of clinical diagnoses of major depression, post-traumatic stress disorder, separation anxiety, and disruptive disorders than adjudicated boys. Furthermore, girls had significantly greater rates of physical, sexual, and emotional abuse and greater rates of physical neglect than boys" (Zahn et al, "Violence by Teenage Girls" 12; Baglivio et al) (see Figure 1). Any of these issues can be exacerbated by the experience of detention, which often reenacts abusive patterns and encourages further isolation from communities and families (Sherman 24, "Gender Responsiveness" 9).

Figure 1. Sexual abuse rates and ACE (Adverse Childhood Experiences) scores in juvenile justice, by gender (Saar et al 8).

Distressingly, the above issues disproportionately affect young women of color. For example, young Black women face disproportionate rates of disciplinary action in schools, which leads to justice involvement via the school-to-prison pipeline (Sherman and Balck 16). In addition, society's deeming of "middle-class, heterosexual, White femininity as normative" (Collins 193) often causes the behavior of young Black women to be perceived as deviant: "as disruptive to the order of a (supposedly race- and gender-neutral) social structure" (Morris 22); this often results in criminalization. Once they become involved with the justice system, young Black women face discriminatory treatment; they are "nearly three times as likely as their white peers to be referred to juvenile court for a delinquency offense," and "20 percent more likely to be detained" ("Girls and the Juvenile Justice System"). Young Native-American women experience similar inequities in the justice system. The Office of Juvenile Justice and Delinquency Prevention (OJJDP) reports that in 2013, "American Indian and Native Alaskan girls were 40 percent more likely [than their white peers] to be referred to juvenile court for delinquency, [and] 50 percent more likely to be detained" ("Girls and the Juvenile Justice System"). Additional racial disparities are difficult to analyze, because "many jurisdictions do not fully disaggregate data by race and ethnicity" (Saar et al 35). As a result, the extent to which Latina and Asian youth are represented in the juvenile justice system remains unclear. Indeed, the fact that they are often inaccurately identified, thus "inflat[ing] the numbers of white youth," is further evidence of the system's failure to recognize and address racial and ethnic disparities (35).

Young women also face discriminatory treatment based on sexual preference and gender identity. This often begins with lack of acceptance in family and school environments, which increases the risk of justice involvement "and negatively impacts their cases" (Majd, Marksamer, and Reyes 3). Non-heterosexual young women are "about twice as likely to be arrested and convicted as other girls who engaged in similar behavior" ("Girls and the Juvenile Justice System"); once convicted, detention facilities are "particularly dangerous and hostile places for LGBT youth," as biases and lack of training result in abuse, isolation, and/or misclassification in housing (Majd, Marksamer, and Reyes 5).[6] These data indicate that, despite an increase in studies of young justice-involved women, there is still too little understanding of how "layers of girls' identity bear on their social contexts and drive their behavior" (23).

In summary, young women often live in abusive and oppressive situations about which they cannot speak and *be heard*. Young LGBTQ+ women and women of color are often deemed deviant or disruptive due to white heteronormative expectations regarding female behavior, and young women in general may develop habits and behaviors designed to protect and defend themselves—behaviors that are later criminalized and used to further delegitimize their voices. Indeed, studies show that "[the most common crimes for which girls are arrested—including running away, substance abuse, and truancy—are also the most common symptoms of abuse" (Saar et al 9).

> *My heart is like a moon*
> *and it shines just like the evening blues.*
> *My heart is like a*
> *beat, because it beats*
> *and beats until you*
> *hear my sadness loud*
> *and clear.*
>
> —from *Shine Through*

---

6. "Once in the juvenile justice system, LBQ/GNCT girls report higher levels of self-harming behavior and are more likely to be discriminated against, become targets of violence and sexual victimization, and be placed in isolation" (Sherman and Balck 23).

Disqualified Knowledges

Given the distressing nature of the above information, and given the urgency with which advocates often wish to respond, we must take a critical view of how information about incarcerated teen women is rhetorically presented and to what extent this presentation may perpetuate the very issues it reveals. As I've mentioned, literature about young justice-involved women rarely employs those women's own words to describe their conditions, needs, or values.⁷⁷ The young women with whom I've worked are well aware of the absence of their voices in the discourse about them; they recognize when and how they are defined by those whose perceptions have been deemed legitimate. As Shana writes, "They say we're whores [...] / They say we're immoral [...] / They say I will be successful. / They say I am brave [...] / They say I'm a failure / They say I'm worthless" (*Know Me* 50). While many studies rely to some extent upon self-assessment among adjudicated young women, these assessments are later compiled, codified, and "translated" by experts who re-present the young women's observations within the context of "qualified" knowledge. As acknowledged in my introduction, the present work itself participates in a form of compilation and translation.

This absence of young women's voices in discourses about them is particularly striking in results published by the Girls Study Group: experts convened by the OJJDP to "assess current knowledge about the patterns and causes of female delinquency and to design appropriate intervention programs" (Zahn et al, "Causes and Correlates" 1;). The Girls Study Group published seven in-depth analyses from 2008-2013; not one includes a quote from a young woman served by the Ju-

---

7. This may be due in part to the difficulty of obtaining facility and IRB approval; in fact, inclusion of young women's narratives in the present work was precluded by these contraints. However, the field's seeming lack of interest in obtaining firsthand accounts is concerning. Two notable exceptions include Holsinger and Holsinger's 2005 study of African American and White girls in the system, which indicated "a willingness and capability on the part of incarcerated girls to help shape policies that adequately address their needs [...] There are lessons that can be learned from 'listening' to the girls" (236). In addition, Morris's *Pushout* "demonstrates through narratives the importance of... decreasing the institutional and individual risks that fuel mass incarceration and our collective overreliance on punishment" (14).

venile Justice System.[8] Similarly, a meta-analysis of studies regarding "Detention Reform and Girls" from the Annie B. Casey Foundation offers only one short quote from a young woman potentially impacted by such reform; ironically, the quote states that "they [the juvenile justice system] take your voice away" (Sherman 21). In fact, although the Casey Foundation document includes twenty-three pages of information about "promising gender-responsive programs," it offers no evaluations or perspectives from participants in these programs. In juvenile justice literature, even narratives of particular young women's experiences often appear to have been inferred based on juvenile records, rather than presented in their own words; this is a means of further homogenizing and codifying women's experiences.[9]

Winter Describes Me Best

the winter is pretty and bright
but it is also a really hard season
the wind, the hail, the snow

—from Breaking Out of Silence

The most troubling aspect of this silence may be the literature's apparent inability to recognize it as such. I have yet to see a report or study that mentions its own neglect of young women's voices or that attempts to explain or justify this neglect. Thus young women are not merely excluded from discourses about them; they are excluded to such an extent that no one recognizes the omission. It is therefore clear that young women's ways of knowing are, in Foucault's words, "disqualified as inadequate to their task or insufficiently elaborated: naïve knowledges, located low down on the hierarchy" (82). According to Foucault, we must resist this disqualification by bringing subjugated knowledges to the fore, combining them with "erudite knowledges" to create a genealogy of conflict—"a painstaking rediscovery of struggles" (83). In gender-reform efforts within juvenile justice, this means elevating and relying on the direct voices of young justice-involved women in any studies and publications that purport to represent them.

---

8. See Zahn et al "The Girls Study Group;" Zahn et al, "Causes and Correlates;" Zahn et al, "Violence by Teenage Girls;" Hawkins et al; Huizinga et al; etcetera.

9. For examples, see the "Sarah" narrative in "Better Solutions for Youth" (1) and the "Tamika" narrative in Sherman (45-47).

When we do not, we risk further silencing the very women we seek to assist.

THE OTHER-ING OF JUVENILE WOMEN

In addition to disqualifying their knowledges, delineations of "problems" among young women in the justice system, including my earlier discussion, risk forcefully ejecting them from a normative discourse in which they already lack power. For example, studies and reports about young justice-involved women often render them non-normative (1) as daughters and siblings, given high rates of family abuse; (2) as people, given high rates of mental illness, PTSD, and learning disabilities; (3) as young people, given their involvement in the juvenile justice system; (4) as women, given aggressive behaviors that transgress gender norms; and even (5) as juvenile offenders, in that they are women. This raises a critical issue in gender-reform rhetoric: that consistent calls for equal treatment and gender-responsive programming have resulted less in an equitable system than in additional public depictions of young incarcerated women as "unique," "different," and/or "special" participants in the juvenile justice system.

For example, the OJJDP has published "Why Are Girls' Needs Different?" along with many girl-specific reports (Zahn et al); the National Council on Crime and Delinquency released "Girls *Do* Matter;" and the Physicians for Human Rights created a list of "Unique Needs of Girls in the Juvenile Justice System." Such careful gender differentiations result in part from the fact that the U.S. Juvenile Justice System was originally designed to meet the needs of male offenders (Watson and Edelman 3). This original design continues to be perceived as the "normal" system against which accommodations for females require special arrangements. In fact, The Berkeley Center for Criminal Justice has stated that funding for gender-responsive programming in juvenile justice is difficult to find due to "the tyranny of numbers. There are more boys than girls in the juvenile system and where the numbers are, that's where the money goes" ("Gender Responsiveness" 8). The implication is that because women are in the minority, the meeting of their needs can be deferred; it is elective or conditional.

Young detained women are often aware of this deferral; in one facility in which I conducted a writing workshop, participants thanked me many times every day, telling me this was their first experience of a program or activity being offered "to girls." For months, they said, they had watched "the boys" walk down the hall to various activities while they "were stuck in [their] pod."[10] When I asked facility staff about this, they confirmed that even programs that were designed for both males and females, such as learning how to train shelter dogs, had been relegated to male participants due to lack of funding and staff.

Years of insisting upon young women's "unique needs and experiences" has perpetuated the notion that men are the norm against which women are judged to have "special needs." Of course, as detailed above, young women's experiences and needs *are* often quite different from those of young men. However, acknowledgements of gender disparities must result in a reassessment of "norms" within the juvenile justice system, *not* in reassertions of young women as anomalous others whose presence in the justice system is notable primarily because it requires accommodations from a male-defined system. The latter approach only decreases the possibility that young women will receive equitable treatment in arrest, sentencing, and juvenile justice programming.

In addition, highlighting the "unusual" properties of young justice-involved women as a gender group too often obscures the significant impact of women's intersectional experiences of oppression. Despite evidence that race, sexuality, and gender identity influence justice decisions and confinement (Holsinger 235), the juvenile justice system has not consistently been held accountable for gathering and disaggregating data that enables truly intersectional understandings of young women's circumstances.[11] Meanwhile, researchers and justice system employees should be aware of the extent to which our calls for this accountability may rely on or contribute to the delegitimization of young women's knowledges and experiences. For example, as a hetero white woman in academia without a criminal record, I have at times sensed that my advocacy for descriptive intersectional juvenile justice

---

10. Many detention facilities are constructed with multiple "pods" that include several individual cells opening to a shared/common room. While such facilities generally require several pods to house males, the relatively small number of female inmates can often be housed in a single pod.

11. Following community-based participatory research (CBPR) and critical pedagogy methods, this "understanding" must also be discussed with and confirmed by the young women under study, to help ensure that any published "interpretions" of their stories and data are accurate in their view (Israel et al 180, 190; "Education for Critical Consciousness" 37).

research is heard and considered precisely because I myself am read as normative. Those of us with privilege should indeed use it to dismantle oppressive structures; however, if our perceived legitimacy is achieved primarily via contrast with those for whom we advocate, we unwittingly rely on the ongoing delegitimization of those whose experiences deserve respect, study, and action. As bell hooks has written, "[often] this speech about the 'other' is also a mask, an oppressive talk hiding gaps...Often this speech about the 'other' annihilates, erases" (208).

When I Wear a Mask

*I give in to peer pressure
and sometimes I have to fight
in order to have people trust me
Sometimes I am not a leader
I am a follower. I be mean
to people so that I can look tough
So no one will think that I'm scared*

*I have to show them I'll do anything
for my family and friends. I walk around
mad sometimes. Sometimes I don't
like acting tough
But I have to be, for my siblings
cause if I don't who will?*

*I feel I have to wear a mask
for random people
but if I took it off t
hey'd see a very smart
and nice girl*

—from *Know Me*

Gendered Dismissal

Unfortunately, even when young women in the justice system *do* speak about their ideas and experiences, their voices are regularly dismissed—due in large part to popular rhetoric within the justice system that defines young women as "difficult." This is evident in an article by the Director of Projects for the National Center for Juvenile Justice, which opens with a simple lament: "No one wants to work with girls"

(Griffin 1). The article is an attempt to counter the common view that "girls" are "the monsters of the juvenile justice system" by explaining the effects of PTSD on their behavior (1). But adolescent women on both sides of a jail's walls are regularly accused of being overemotional, dramatic, and manipulative, based on "conventional beliefs that girls and women are untrustworthy" (Chesney-Lind and Irwin 45).[12] This widespread negative discourse is at least partly responsible for many arrests of young women (28); once they are in the justice system, the bias has far-reaching implications for sentencing, treatment by staff, and the denial of rehabilitative opportunities (Schaffner 9).

In fact, the negative discourse about teenaged women is so powerful that, in daily practice within juvenile detention centers, it effectively overrides the justice system's accumulated knowledge about mental illness, PTSD, and abuse histories. For example, a study of probation officers' views of girls revealed that even when officers know that young women's paths to detention are affected (if not determined) by experiences of abuse, poverty, and/or pregnancy, they fail to respond in practice by addressing these issues. Instead, many admit to believing that young women are making up stories. One probation officer told researchers,

> They feel like they're the victim. They try from, "Mom kicked me out" to "Mom's boyfriend molested me" to "My brother was sexually assaulting me." They'll find all kinds of excuses to justify their actions. Because they feel if I say I was victimized at home that justifies me being out on the streets. (Gaarder, Rodriguez, Zatz 557)

Many officers "recognize that girls have problems due to their histories of victimization but do not respond in sympathetic ways, instead writing the girls off through gendered stereotypes and treating the victimization and manipulative behaviors as independent realities" (Gaarder, Rodriguez, and Zatz 560). A participant in one of my workshops articulated this dismissive response, writing, "What if I told you my mind wasn't right, / would you tell me it's a phase until it's too late?" (*Shine Through* 35).

---

12. Chesney-Lind and Irwin further note that "[b]eing mean, nasty, petty, and entirely incapable of meaningful friendship is just one more mainstream message announcing how 'bad' girls and women are" (45).

I have also encountered this gender bias in conversations with detention and probation officers, who regularly tell me they "don't like working with girls," or that "there's just so much drama in the girls' unit." In these disclosures, the use of the word "drama" suggests that young women's situations, behaviors, and complaints are not taken seriously; the young women of which they speak are "merely" teenaged girls being (dramatic, emotional, manipulative) teenaged girls.

i am a road

in the middle of nowhere
i have cracks but can still get you
where you needa go.

i am also a meadow
calm & beautiful
and I just keep on going.
i have a lot of room for you.

—from *Know Me*

The refusal to take young women seriously has also been apparent in detention staff's responses to young women's poetry. For example, after seeing a poem in which a writer described having raised herself without help, a detention officer (DO) noted to me that this individual "makes a lot of things up."[13] Later, upon reading a poem in which the same writer expressed determination to be a better mother to her baby boy, another staff member replied, "Yeah, we'll see."[14]

Thus even when young women in the justice system are given a place and time in which to voice their experiences, they are not heard.

---

13. In the workshops I conduct, at least one DO is always present in the room. Because workshop participants see DOs daily and develop relationships with them, they often invite the officers to read their poems. The DO(s) may also walk around the room, asking to read writers' work.

14. I do not wish to suggest that detention staff are always careless or cold toward the young women with whom they work; on the contrary, I've had the privilege to work alongside staff and detention officers who exhibit an openness to and understanding of young women (and their complex situations) that have deepened over years of work in the field. Nevertheless, the impact of (what are often implicit) gender biases within the juvenile justice system—even among those who mean well and who work hard to help youth—cannot be denied.

Their knowledge is always already dismissed by accusations that they are merely emotional, deflecting blame, or manipulating staff; such dismissals are especially common among young women of color and LGBTQ+ women.[15] Yet because staff members occupy positions of power, their interpretations of young women's words almost always determine the official and/or institutional response(s) to them.

My Heart
That broken lamp that got fixed
That bottle of memories
That teddy bear you kept but hate
That vase that is thinner than paper

—from *Call Me Strong*

Design, Evaluation, and Critical Awareness

In response to the juvenile justice system's failure to adequately address the needs of young women, many facilities and external organizations have established programs and initiatives to fill gaps in gender-responsive offerings. Given the extent to which young women have been oppressed and silenced, critical analysis of programming approaches is necessary to prevent further oppression under the rhetorical guise of philanthropy and/or empowerment. Thus in this final section, I consider four ways in which programming efforts within juvenile justice may unintentionally perpetuate the oppression of young women. This is meant not to dissuade agencies or volunteers from supporting, creating, and/or facilitating juvenile justice programming, but rather to spur innovative, culturally-sustaining pedagogies by cautioning against uncritical interventions.

The Reign of Recidivism

The OJJDP's "Model Programs Guide" lists the prevention and reduction of crime, violent behavior, and detention as its first mark of "program efficacy." While such a gauge is apt for an agency whose purpose is to prevent juvenile delinquency, it risks "impoverish[ing] the idea of education" and of the arts by subordinating them to a single

---

15. See "The State of Oppression," above.

institutional goal (Sweeney 255). More broadly, it rhetorically undercuts the many other benefits young women could receive from quality interventions. With recidivism as their primary focus, juvenile justice programs are likely to meet young women's needs only when (or insofar as) doing so serves larger institutional concerns such as regulating behavior, preventing rebellion, and increasing participation in the economy. Of course, young women generally do not wish to be incarcerated, and to this extent, attempts to reduce recidivism do advance participants' own goals. In addition, programs that are *not* set up specifically to serve institutional concerns are unlikely to receive court or facility access and support. Therefore, best practices for gender-responsive programming in juvenile justice must accommodate the material and institutional constraints (such as a focus on recidivism) under which interventions are designed. But they should also include approaches based on critical and culturally sustaining pedagogies,[16] social justice youth development, and radical healing[17]—particularly when working with young women of color. The creative pursuit of such practices will allow programs and their designers/administrators to accommodate institutional interests while avoiding the strict equation of program success with the perpetuation and enforcement of conforming behaviors and speech acts.

---

16. According to Django Paris, "[t]he term *culturally* sustaining requires that our pedagogies be more than responsive of or relevant to the cultural experiences and practices of young people—it requires that they support young people in sustaining the cultural and linguistic competence of their communities while simultaneously offering access to dominant cultural competence" (95).

17. Youth development expert Shawn Ginwright defines radical healing as a pedagogical and developmental approach "which builds the capacity of young people to act upon their environment in ways that contribute to well-being for the common good. This process contributes to individual well-being, community health and broader social justice where young people can act on behalf of others with hope, joy and a sense of possibility [...] When black youth are conscious of the root causes of the problems they face, they act in profound ways to resist and transform issues they view as unjust" (85).

> ***Sometimes I'm Afraid***
>
> *That you will turn your back*
> *I'm afraid I will give up completely I*
> *'m afraid you won't understand*
> *I'm afraid I will break*
> *Something I'm not ready for.*
> *I'm afraid I will be nothing*
> *I'm afraid no one will ever really*
> *know me.*
>
> —from Breaking Out of Silence

A Failure of Confidence

In *Pedagogy of the Oppressed*, Paulo Freire offers a critique of well-meaning individuals in positions of power who, in their attempt to "move to the side of the exploited," fail to leave behind "their prejudices and their deformations, which include a lack of confidence in the [exploited] people's ability to think, to want, and to know" (60). As noted above, most studies and reports regarding justice-involved young women fail to incorporate their voices, opting instead to speak for them. This choice betrays a lingering belief that young women are incapable of speaking (to) their own oppression(s), and it risks reducing young women to "objects which must be saved from a burning building" (65). Those who work with justice-involved young women can show confidence and solidarity by inviting young women's participation in program development, arranging for in-depth program evaluations, and seeking personal narratives and firsthand descriptions of individual needs.[18] As Freire argues, an educational or political program that fails to respect the perspectives of the oppressed will not have positive results; in fact, "such a program constitutes cultural invasion, good intentions notwithstanding" (95).

---

18. Despite the acknowledged lack of these elements in the present work, my hope is that this discussion increases demand for first-person accounts, and argues convincingly for the improved representation of young women in juvenile justice programs and publications. By recognizing that these changes are critical to the equitable treatment of young justice-involved women, those of us who work in the field can creatively and collaboratively endeavor to improve programs and practices.

The lighthouse

I am the strong wind
I'm the high waves coming
to take over my family
I am the storm
protecting my family
I'm the moving waves
trying to motivate my family
I'm the high water
taking care of my family
I'm the wind
pulling all of us together
I'm also the lighthouse
bringing light to my family's eyes!
—from Call Me Strong

Indoctrination as Oppression

Unfortunately, reliance upon young women's input is often hindered by the perception that their involvement with the justice system is evidence of a *lack* of knowledge—or at least of an inability to adopt normalized views and behaviors. While this perception is not always (technically) false, it takes condescension and lack as its starting points for interaction with young women. When combined with institutional equations of reduced recidivism with program success, such starting points may lead to programs centered on training young women in normalized views and behaviors, rather than on developing critical consciousness. Ultimately, such training moves young women not from disempowerment to agency, but from one oppressive situation (such as abuse, unaddressed mental illness, poverty) to another (corrections system) to another (psychological, educational, and/or social indoctrination). Indoctrination-oriented programs, often based on a perception of "middle-class, heterosexual, White femininity as normative" (Collins 193), are particularly oppressive for young women of color and LGBTQ+ women. In addition, any young woman's success in such environments may come at the cost of suppressing her sexual, cultural, and/or ethnic identities. Yet women are incentivized to pay these costs, because those who assimilate are labeled by institutional and societal structures as "successful": reformed, transformed, convalesced. They therefore find both literal and metaphorical doors opening for them based on their achievements in acquiescence, which may condition future self-subjugation.

I have regularly witnessed subtle (and likely unconscious) methods of indoctrination during my writing sessions, despite my active promotion of safe expressive writing spaces. For example, detention officers regularly celebrate young writers for poetry that expresses belief in God, dedication to school, praise for parents, and/or remorse for poor choices. By contrast, poetry that describes abuse, drug use, romantic love, self-destructive habits, or disappointment in parents is regularly second-guessed by staff. In one workshop, a writer was applauded by several officers after reading a poem in which she states, "I am learning about God because he is my all and my savior" (*Shine Through* 56). A few minutes later, a writer in the same workshop was asked by an officer to change a poem about her hurting heart (22), first by taking out an "offensive word" it contained, and then by "adding something hopeful."[19]

Further examples of an indoctrinating approach can be seen in the criteria used to evaluate effective juvenile justice programs. In addition to decreased recidivism, criteria include pro-social behavior, lack of pregnancy, "school engagement, school satisfaction, and grades" ("Determining What Works" 281). In other words, programs are "effective" if they successfully teach women how to achieve a hegemonic definition of female adolescent success. Such teaching by the youth "corrections" system is another way in which, as feminist theorist Susan Bordo has described, "female bodies become docile bodies—bodies whose forces and energies are habituated to external regulation, subjection, transformation, 'improvement'" (Bordo 2362). Moreover, because young women are rarely consulted to develop program goals and parameters, and because their vulnerable positions compel their compliance, it is far from clear that achieving hegemonic female adolescent success is actually desired by young women. Even when it is, researchers cannot

---

19. To be clear, interactions between DOs and writers are often beneficial; as mentioned in note 10, participants often know the officers and invite them to read their work. When they do, the writing can provide staff with insights about the young women in their care. However, while this officer likely meant well, her response contributes to indoctrination and assimilation by suggesting that certain thoughts, feelings, or experiences should be censored. This impedes young women's expression, and may hinder open and trusting participation.

know to what extent this desire is itself driven by emotional dependence or habitual deferral, versus by critical consciousness followed by deliberate, personal choice. The indoctrinating approach can be counteracted by collaborating with young women in the development of programs, evaluation measures, and culturally sustaining practices.

Empowerment Rhetoric.

Empowerment rhetoric in juvenile justice programming, particularly among creative writing and arts initiatives, is immensely popular with many programs claiming to "give youth a voice" in their lives and communities.[20] This rhetoric is problematic in that, as Jamila Lyiscott has noted, youth "woke up" with a voice; they do not need "some salvific external force" to "gift them with the privilege to speak." While the *dissemination* and/or *amplification* of their voices could indeed provide a legitimate benefit to young justice-involved women, these actions are often absent in creative arts programming. The art and written work produced by justice-involved youths is rarely studied for what it reveals about its writers, their oppression, and/or systemic issues, nor is it strategically disseminated to community leaders, local educators, policy makers, or the public.[21] The ethical risk here is that, if "giving youth

---

20. For example, see the emphasis on girls' "authentic voices" in "Containment and Resistance: Girls' Writing in the Juvenile Justice System" (Briggs); rhetoric throughout "InsideOUT Writers (IOW) Fact Sheet;" and a workshop at the MacArthur Foundation conference devoted to "[g]iving youths a bigger voice in juvenile justice reform" (Gately). Also, note the following quotes: "[A] rarely-heard voice in juvenile justice: the girls themselves" (Corbally); "57 texts that give voice to the reflections of young people in detention" ("Juvenile In Justice"); "Youth offenders will also have more of a voice in the new system" (Highfield); "The Media Awareness Project exists solely for the purpose of empowering youth by giving them a voice!" ("The Home of Youth Voice"); "a sustainable program that will give dozens of youth the chance to find their voice" (Brouwer); "youth should have a voice in the decisions that affect them" (Willison et al); "Voices UnBroken nurtures the inherent need in all people to tell their stories and be heard"; "WritersCorps has given young people a voice since 1994" (Simonton); "It is my hope that these pieces celebrate the urgent voices of incarcerated youth" ("Free Me Fast"); "Empowerment teaches girls to use their voice, to speak for themselves" ("Chapter 2"); "we help young people connect with their creativity, strengthen their voices, and confidently express their ideas" ("Words Within the Walls"); etc.

21. Notable exceptions include a 2003 effort by PACE Center for Girls,

a voice" is a program's stated goal, young women may believe their concerns and stories will be heard and considered—while the justice system (and the public) continue to effectively disregard their needs. Regrettably, when juvenile justice programs *do* publicize the work of their participants via documentaries, performances, or books, audiences and readers often respond to it with pity or benevolent condescension. By doing so, they assume a position of power relative to the writers and artists, thus invalidating the notion that "having a voice" is axiomatically empowering or even desirable.

Given these realities, the "voice-giving" of gender-responsive programs may be rhetorically disingenuous. Creative courses and workshops are accurately represented as efforts to teach communication skills, provide opportunities for therapeutic self-expression, create safe spaces for difficult conversations, and/or improve group dynamics among participants. But these significant and worthy goals should not be confused with "giving youth a voice," which suggests a dialogic exchange rarely offered to juvenile offenders.

> ***To Prisoners***
>
> *I hope you realize that you are worth way more*
> *Than people controlling your life. The truth is*
> *in your hands, and you are the only one*
> *who can set it free.*
>
> —from *Know Me*

Empowerment rhetoric without follow-through again reveals a lack of confidence in young women to insightfully inform the policies, practices, and programs that impact their lives. Quality research, programming, and juvenile justice reform require that the voices of young women be actively, consistently sought—not merely for personal expression or audience sympathy but for serious dialogue, mu-

---

Inc that led "roughly 500 girls under the supervision of the state juvenile justice system" to protest at the Florida state capital "against funding cuts to community-based programs for girls in the juvenile justice system" ("Pace Center for Girls; Watson and Edelman). Also, The Beat Within, based in San Francisco, widely publishes writing and art from youth in the juvenile justice system; however, I was unable to determine its circulation or its rates of female involvement. Some JJS programs strive to get participant work disseminated via publications, radio, video, and/or live performances; these too present possible exceptions to this critique.

tual learning, critical analysis, policy input, and the transformation of oppressive structures. In arts programming, this work can begin with culminating performances for external audiences—during which facility staff, city government leaders, and/or local educators witness young women sharing their experiences. Publication and active circulation of young women's written work could also ensure that it makes its way to those who can effect change.[22] Increased investments in social justice youth development and in the cultivation of civic agency in juvenile justice programming would help young women develop a voice in their communities. Finally, those who study gender inequities in the system could invite young justice-involved women to be fellow researchers in assessment, program design, implementation, analysis, and/or evaluation.

Conclusion

The continued increase in studies about juvenile women indicates a genuine, increasing concern among researchers, government agencies, activists, and the public about young women's visibility in the justice system. It also marks society's rising level of disturbance regarding inequitable treatment and its growing motivation to pressure policymakers and funding bodies to improve conditions for young women. However, precisely because this level of oppression can engender urgent and emotional responses from relatively privileged individuals, its rhetorical representations often elicit missionary impulses and/or the confirmation of unexamined biases. In addition, the urgent need for equity in the justice system can give rise to well-intended programs and measures that ultimately perpetuate oppression. Ongoing critical awareness is therefore necessary to identify and alter discourses that inadvertently support the very conditions by which many of us are rightly appalled.

---

22. The performance and/or publication of personal material should always be optional. When young women have preferred not to read their work during programs in juvenile facilities, we have found other poems or quotes for them to read, or involved them in other roles (such as the emcee). When publishing young women's work in print or online, always obtain their permission first. Be sure to use pseudonyms (that they choose), initials, or first names only when circulating their work.

I have shown that the subjectivity of young justice-involved women is always already obscured by their sociocultural positions. Young women come into the system particularly vulnerable; once "justice-involved," they can be further victimized by the system's isolating, authoritarian environment. Even if they are not, they too rarely find help for the issues that influenced their involvement. Rather, when young women voice their needs or experiences, their words are regularly dismissed due to powerful rhetorical constructions of teenaged women as manipulative, cruel, or over-emotional (Gaarder, Rodriguez, and Zatz 560); this has been particularly true for women of color and LGBTQ+ women. On the rare occasions young women find sympathetic ears, their words are valued only to the extent that they represent self-expression or a therapeutic benefit; they typically are not perceived as capable (or worthy) of influencing policy, programming, or society. In such subaltern conditions, there is no possibility of speech. Young women's interests are acknowledged ("heard") only when they are codified and translated by authorities whose knowledges are qualified by the hegemony. Moreover, the language used by these authorities further subjugates young women by repeatedly marking them as "other."

In his foreword to Paulo Freire's *Pedagogy of the Oppressed*, Richard Shaull describes Freire as being driven by the conviction that "every human being, no matter how 'ignorant' or submerged in the 'culture of silence' he or she may be, is capable of looking critically at the world in a dialogical encounter with others" (32). This same conviction regarding young justice-involved women must be assiduously cultivated and enacted so that we consistently open ourselves to learning from them: acknowledging their deserved roles as "students-teachers," (80), as women to whom we are accountable, as our partners in a "courageous dialogue" (128). By noting the extent to which young justice-involved women have been muted, it is my hope that this analysis initiates an energetic effort within and beyond the juvenile justice system to seek, study, and disseminate young women's voices. Doing so is necessary not only to improve their wellbeing, but also to inform and transform our own conceptions of justice, and to help create a better and more equitable system for all of us.

You Don't Know Me

You know why?
Because you don't know what I go through.
You don't know what I'm capable of.
You don't know how I think.
You don't know what I'm facing. Y
ou don't know how much I hold in

—from *Shine Through*

WORKS CITED

"Addressing the Intersection of Gender and Racial Disparities: A Snapshot from the Juvenile Justice Resource Hub." *National Juvenile Justice Network*. April 2016, www.njjn.org/our-work/ addressing-the-intersection-of-gender-and-racial-disparities-a-snapshot-from-the-juvenile-justice-resource-hub.

Baglivio, Michael T., Kimberly Swartz, Mona Sayedul Huq, Amy Sheer, Nancy S. Hardt, and Nathan Epps. "The Prevalence of Adverse Childhood Experiences (ACE) in the Lives of Juvenile Offenders." *OJJDP Journal of Juvenile Justice* vol. 3, no. 2, 2014, pp.1-23. www.journalofjuvjustice.org/JOJJ0302/article01.htm.

Banks, William P. "Written Through the Body: Disruptions and 'Personal' Writing." *The Personal in Academic Writing*, special issues of *College English*, vol. 66, no. 1, 2003, pp. 21-40. www. jstor.org/stable/3594232.

"Better Solutions for Youth with Mental Health Needs in the Juvenile Justice System." *Models for Change*. Mental Health and Juvenile Justice Collaborative for Change. Jan. 2014.

Bordo, Susan. "The Body and the Reproduction of Femininity." *The Norton Anthology of Theory and Criticism*, edited by Vincent B. Leitch, 1st edition, W.W. Norton & Company, 2001, 2360-2362.

Breaking Out of Silence: A Collection of Poetry Written by Young Women at the Clark County Juvenile Detention Center. Project Jericho, 2014.

Briggs, Katherine C. "Containment and Resistance: Girls' Writing in the Juvenile Justice System." *Intersections*, no. 9, 2011, pp. 48-66. journals.tdl.org/intersections/index.php/intersections/ article/view/14/4.

Brouwer, Matthew. "Whatcom Juvenile Justice Creative Writing Project." *Kickstarter*. Whatcom Juvenile Justice Creative Writing Project, July 2013. www.kickstarter.com/projects/1363369594/ whatcom-juvenile-justice-creative-writing-project.

Call Me Strong: A Compilation of Poetry by the Young Women at the St.

Joseph Juvenile Justice Center. Project Uncaged, 2014. "Chapter 1: Why Are Girls' Needs Different?" *Guiding Principles for Promising Female Programming*. Office of Juvenile Justice and Delinquency Prevention, October 1998. www.ojjdp.gov/pubs/ principles/ch1_4.html.

"Chapter 2: What Does Gender-Specific Programming Look Like In Practice?" *Guiding Principles for Promising Female Programming*. Office of Juvenile Justice and Delinquency Prevention, October 1998. www.ojjdp.gov/pubs/principles/ch2_6.html.

Chesney-Lind, Meda, and Katherine Irwin. *Beyond Bad Girls: Gender, Violence and Hype*. Routledge, 2008.

Collins, Patricia Hill. *Black Sexual Politics: African Americans, Gender, and the New Racism*. Routledge, 2004.

Corbally, Sarah F, Donald C. Bross, and Victor E. Flango. "Filing of Amicus Curiae Briefs in State Courts of Last Resort: 1960-2000." *The Justice System Journal* vol. 25, no. 1, 2004, pp. 39-56. www.tandfonline.com/doi/pdf/10.1080/0098261X.2004.10767 707?needAccess=true.

Foucault, Michel. *Power/knowledge: Selected Interviews and Other Writings, 1972-1977*. Edited by and Colin Gordon. Pantheon, 1980.

"Free Me Fast: Voices From Inside SF's Juvenile Justice Center." *WritersCorps RSS*. WritersCorps, 30 May 2014. www. sfartscommission.org/WC/free-me-fast-voices-from-inside-sfs-juvenile-justice-center.

Freire, Paulo. *Education for Critical Consciousness*. Seabury Press, 1 Jan. 1990.

Freire, Paulo. *Pedagogy of the Oppressed*. Continuum, 2000. Gately, Gary. "Confronting Bias in the Juvenile Justice System."

Juvenile Justice Information Exchange. 19 Dec. 2013. jjie. org/2013/12/19/confronting-bias-in-the-juvenile-justice-system.

"Gender Responsiveness and Equity in California's Juvenile Justice System." *www.law.berkeley.edu*. Berkeley Law University of California, 2010. www.law.berkeley.edu/img/Gender_ Responsiveness_and_Equity.pdf.

Ginwright, S. A. "Peace out to Revolution! Activism Among African American Youth: An Argument for Radical Healing." *Young*, vol. 18, no. 1, 1 Feb. 2010, pp. 77–96, doi: 10.1177/110330880901800106.

"Girls and the Juvenile Justice System." *Office of Juvenile Justice and Delinquency Prevention*. n.d. www.ojjdp.gov/policyguidance/ girls-juvenile-justice-system/#nav.

Griffin, Patrick. "Painful Secrets: Helping Traumatized Girls in Pennsylvania's Juvenile Justice System." *Pennsylvania Progress* vol. 7, no. 4, 2001,, pp. 1-7. *National Center for Juvenile Justice*. www.ncjj.org/Publication/Painful-Secrets-Helping-Traumatized-Girls-in-Pennsylvanias-Juvenile-Justice-System. aspx.

Hawkins, Stephanie R., Phillip W. Graham, Jason Williams, and Margaret A. Zahn. "Resilient Girls—Factors That Protect Against Delinquency."

Girls Study Group. Office of Juvenile Justice and Delinquency Prevention. Jan. 2009. www.ncjrs.gov/ pdffiles1/ojjdp/220124.pdf.
Highfield, Travis. "Juvenile Justice Reform Could Save Taxpayers Money." *The Augusta Chronicle.* The Augusta Chronicle, 14 Oct. 2013. chronicle.augusta.com/news-metro-latest-news/2013-10-14/juvenile-justice-reform-could-save-taxpayers-money.
Hinshaw, Wendy Wolters and Tobi Jacobi. "What Words Might Do: The Challenge of Representing Women in Prison and Their Writing." *Feminist Formations* vol. 27, no. 1, 2015, pp. 67-90. Project Muse. muse.jhu.edu/article/582252.
Holsinger, K. "Differential Pathways to Violence and Self-Injurious Behavior: African American and White Girls in the Juvenile Justice System." *Journal of Research in Crime and Delinquency*, vol. 42, no. 2, 1 May 2005, pp. 211–242, doi: 10.1177/0022427804271938.
"The Home of Youth Voice." *Media Awareness Project.* www. mediaawarenessproject.org/.
hooks, bell. "Choosing the Margin as a Space of Radical Openness." *Gender, Space, Architecture: An Interdisciplinary Introduction.* Edited by Jane Rendell, Barbara Penner, and Iain Borden. Routledge, 2000. pp. 203-09.
Huizinga, David, and Shari Miller. "Developmental Sequences of Girls' Delinquent Behavior." *Girls Study Group.* Office of Juvenile Justice and Delinquency Prevention. December 2013. www. ojjdp.gov/pubs/238276.pdf.
InsideOUT Writers Fact Sheet. InsideOUT Writers, 2014.
Israel, Barbara A., et al. "Review of Community-Based Research: Assessing Partnership Approaches to Improve Public Health." *Annual Review of Public Health*, vol. 19, no. 1, May 1998, pp. 173–202. doi: 10.1146/annurev.publhealth.19.1.173.
Jacobi, Tobi, and Ann Folwell Stanford. *Women, Writing, and Prison: Activists, Scholars, and Writers Speak out.* Rowman & Littlefield Publishers, 2014.
"Juvenile in Justice." *CRANE ARTS A Community of Art Culture in Philadelphia.* CRANE Arts, 8 July 2013. www.cranearts.com/ juvenile-in-justice.
Leitch, Vincent B. "Gayatri Chakravorty Spivak." *The Norton Anthology of Theory and Criticism.* 1st ed. W.W. Norton and Company, 2001, 2193-2197.
Know Me: A Compilation of Poetry and Art by the Young Women at the Miami Valley Juvenile Rehabilitation Center. Project Jericho, 2014.
Lyiscott, Jamila. "If You Think You're Giving Students of Color a Voice, Get Over Yourself." *Blackness in Bold Black Professors Black Experiences and Black Magic. wordpress.com.* 25 Mar. 2016. blackprofessorblog.wordpress.com/2016/03/25/if-you-think-youre-giving-students-of-color-a-voice-get-over-yourself.

Majd, Katayoon, Jody Marksamer, and Carolyn Reyes. *Hidden Injustice: Lesbian, Gay, Bisexual, and Transgender Youth in Juvenile Courts*. Legal Services for Children and National Center for Lesbian Rights, 2009.

Morris, Monique W. *Pushout: The Criminalization of Black Girls in Schools*. The New Press, 2016.

National Council on Crime and Delinquency. *Girls Do Matter*.

National Council on Crime and Delinquency, 11 May 2009. http:// www. nccdglobal.org/sites/default/files/publication_pdf/ girlsdomatter.pdf.

"OJJDP Model Programs Guide –." *OJJDP Model Programs Guide –. Office of Juvenile Justice and Detention Prevention*. www.ojjdp. gov/mpg/.

Paris, D. "Culturally Sustaining Pedagogy: A Needed Change in Stance, Terminology, and Practice." *Educational Researcher*, vol. 41, no. 3, 29 Mar. 2012, pp. 93–97, doi: 10.3102/0013189x12441244.

Royster, Jacqueline Jones. "A View from a Bridge." *Traces of a Stream: Literacy and Social Change among African American Women*. U of Pittsburgh, 2000.

Saar, Malika, Rebecca Epstein, Lindsay Rosenthal, and Yasmin Vafa. "Sexual Abuse to Prison Pipeline: The Girls' Story." Rights4girls.org, Human Rights Project for Girls, 1 June 2015. rights4girls.org/wp-content/ uploads/r4g/2015/02/2015_ COP_sexual-abuse_layout_web-1.pdf.

Saar, Malika, Rebecca Epstein, Lindsay Rosenthal, and Yasmin Vafa. "Figure 1." Rights4girls.org, Human Rights Project for Girls, 1 June 2015. Author's Screenshot. rights4girls.org/wp-content/ uploads/r4g/2015/02/2015_COP_sexual-abuse_layout_web-1. pdf.

Schaffner, Laurie. "Female Juvenile Delinquency: Sexual Solutions, Gender Bias, and Juvenile Justice." *Hastings Women's Law Journal* vol. 9, 1998. pp.1-25.

Sharpe, G., and L. Gelsthorpe. "Engendering the Agenda: Girls, Young Women and Youth Justice." *Girls, Young Women and Youth Justice*. Special issue of *Youth Justice*. vol. 9, no. 3, 2009, pp.195-208. DOI: 10.1177/1473225409345098

Sherman, Francine T. "Detention Reform and Girls: Challenges and Solutions." *The Annie E. Casey Foundation*. Pathways to Juvenile Detention Reform Series, 01 Jan. 2005. www.aecf.org/m/ resourcedoc/AECF-DetentionReformAndGirls-2005.pdf.

Sherman, Francine T. and Annie Balck. "Gender Injustice: System-Level Juvenile Justice Reforms for Girls." *National Crittenton Foundation*. 2015. nationalcrittenton.org/wp-content/ uploads/2015/09/Gender_Injustice_Report.pdf.

Shine Through: A Compilation of Poetry by the Young Women at the Hamilton County Youth Center. Project Uncaged, 2014.

Simonton, Stell. "Young Voices Become Strong Through WritersCorps." *Juvenile Justice Information Exchange.* 25 Feb. 2014. jjie.org/2014/02/25/young-voices-become-strong-through-writerscorps/.

Solinger, Rickie, Ruby Tapia, Paula C. Johnson, Martha L. Raimon, and Tina Reynolds. *Interrupted Life: Experiences of Incarcerated Women in the United States.* U of California, 2010.

Spivak, Gayatri Chakravorty. "Can the Subaltern Speak?" *Marxism and the Interpretation of Culture,* edited by Cary Nelson and Lawrence Grossberg, U of Illinois, 1988, 271-313.

Sweeney, Megan. *Reading Is My Window: Books and the Art of Reading in Women's Prisons.* U of North Carolina, 2010.

"Unique Needs of Girls in the Juvenile Justice System." n.d. *Health and Justice for Youth Campaign.* Physicians for Human Rights. createoutcomesmodel.com/wp-content/uploads/2012/08/ PHR-Factsheet.pdf.

"Voices UnBroken | Bronx Poetry, Bronx Creative Writing, Voices UnBroken." *Voices UnBroken| Bronx Poetry, Bronx Creative Writing, Voices UnBroken.*

Watson, Liz, and Peter Edelman. "Improving the Juvenile Justice System for Girls: Lessons from the States." Georgetown Center on Poverty, Inequality and Public Policy, Oct. 2012. www. law.georgetown.edu/academics/centers-institutes/poverty-inequality/upload/jds_v1r4_web_singles.pdf.

Willison, Janeen B., Lisa Brooks, Meghan Salas, Meredith Dank, Elissa Gitlow, John K. Roman, and Jeffrey A. Butts. "Reforming Juvenile Justice Systems: Beyond Treatment." *Robert Wood Johnson Foundation.* Reclaiming Futures, 2010. reclaimingfutures.org/members/sites/default/files/main_ documents/reforming_juvenilejustice2010.pdf.

"Words Within the Walls -A Journal for Youth in Jail." *Indiegogo.* WritersCorps, May 2014. www.indiegogo.com/projects/words-within-the-walls-a-journal-for-youth-in-jail#/.

Zahn, Margaret A., J. C. Day, S. F. Mihalic, and L. Tichavsky. "Determining What Works for Girls in the Juvenile Justice System: A Summary of Evaluation Evidence." *Crime & Delinquency* vol. 55, no. 2, 2009, pp.266-93. doi:10.1177/0011128708330649.

Zahn, Margaret A., Stephanie R. Hawkins, Janet Chiancone, and Ariel Whitworth. "The Girls Study Group—Charting the Way to Delinquency Prevention for Girls." *Girls Study Group.* Office of Juvenile Justice and Delinquency Prevention. October 2008. www.ncjrs.gov/pdffiles1/ojjdp/223434.pdf.

Zahn, Margaret A., Robert Agnew, Diana Fishbein, Shari Miller, Donna-Marie Winn, Gayle Dakoff, Candace Kruttschnitt, Peggy Giordano, Denise C. Gottfredson, Allison A. Payne, Barry C. Feld, and Meda Chesney-Lind. "Causes and Correlates of Girls' Delinquency." *Girls Study Group.*

Office of Juvenile Justice and Delinquency Prevention. April 2010. www. ncjrs. gov/pdffiles1/ojjdp/226358.pdf.

Zahn, Margaret A., Susan Brumbaugh, Darrell Steffensmeier, Barry C. Feld, Merry Morash, Meda Chesney-Lind, Jody Miller, Allison A. Payne, Denise C. Gottfredson, and Candace Kruttschnitt. "Violence by Teenage Girls: Trends and Context." *Girls Study Group.* Office of Juvenile Justice and Delinquency Prevention. May 2008. www.ncjrs.gov/pdffiles1/ojjdp/218905. pdf.

Tasha Golden is a doctoral student at the University of Louisville's School of Public Health and Information Sciences, where she researches the impact of writing and the arts on stigma, discourse, and public health. Her research and prose have been published in *Ploughshares, Pleaides,* and *Ethos Journal,* among others, and her first book of poems, *Once You Had Hands* (Humanist Press), was a finalist for the 2016 Ohioana Book Award. Golden is also the frontwoman and songwriter for the critically acclaimed band Ellery; her songs have been heard in major motion pictures, TV dramas, and more. She regularly leads writing workshops for incarcerated teen women. www.tashagolden.com

COLLEGE COMPOSITION AND COMMUNICATION

CCC is on the Web at http://cccc.ncte.org/cccc/ccc

College Composition and Communication publishes research and scholarship in rhetoric and composition studies that supports college teachers in reflecting on and improving their practices in teaching writing and that reflects the most current scholarship and theory in the field. The field of composition studies draws on research and theories from a broad range of humanistic disciplines—English studies, rhetoric, cultural studies, LGBT studies, gender studies, critical theory, education, technology studies, race studies, communication, philosophy of language, anthropology, sociology, and others—and from within composition and rhetoric studies, where a number of subfields have also developed, such as technical communication, computers and composition, writing across the curriculum, research practices, and the history of these fields.

Veterans in the Writing Classroom: Three Programmatic Approaches to Facilitate the Transition from the Military to Higher Education

Based on an extensive, multi-campus research project which received funding support from CCCC, Hart and Thompson offer a wide-ranging glimpse at how colleges are responding to expanding military student enrollments. Beyond any particular pedagogical or administrative recommendations, Hart and Thompson are most interested in encouraging proactive discussions about how best to support student veterans. Hart and Thompson's article provides an excellent starting place for these conversations and for readers wanting to learn more about this burgeoning area of teaching and research.

Veterans in the Writing Classroom: Three Programmatic Approaches to Facilitate the Transition from the Military to Higher Education

D. Alexis Hart and Roger Thompson

Drawing upon a two-year study of student-veterans in college writing classrooms, this article analyzes three types of courses developed in an effort to respond to increased military-affiliated student enrollments: veterans-only, veteran-focused, and veteran-friendly. The article concludes with recommendations for an asset-based approach to professional development for writing faculty.

The purpose of this article is to report on institutional approaches to veteran enrollments in writing classes and to recommend a reorientation of those approaches toward asset-based professional orientation and course development. These recommendations derive from the findings of a 2010 Conference on College Composition and Communication (CCCC) Research Initiative Grant that funded a two-year study of student veterans in the writing classroom.

Since at least 2003, the CCCC has made public comment on US military engagements in Iraq and Afghanistan.[1] Subsequently, veteran populations—particularly those from Operation Iraqi Freedom (OIF) and Operation Enduring Freedom (OEF) who are taking advantage of the generous benefits of the Post-9/11 GI Bill—have surged on college campuses, with over one million veterans and eligible family members using these benefits since 2009 ("One Million"). A spike of veteran enrollments in core courses such as first-year writing (FYW) has followed.[2] Because FYW courses are typically small enough for students to interact one-on-one with their instructors and to collaborate with their classmates,[3] and because expressive and reflective writing theories shape many first-year students' writing experiences,[4] writing classes often function as a transitional space between veterans' military experiences and their college experiences.

Current Landscape

Sue Doe and William Doe have termed this transitional time for service members *residence time*, which they describe as the amount of time it takes for a person to become fully acclimated to a new environment, and they call on the concept of *induction* as the process by which veterans transition into residence time ("Residence"). For Doe and Doe, veterans, in moving from military life to civilian life, may experience a more extended period of induction than during their original transition into the military, and so the goal of educators should be, at least in part, to reduce the length of residence time through close attention to the varied literacies of military service members.

Residence time provides a useful framework for engaging with veterans on college campuses in that it emphasizes the sometimes dramatic transitions veterans undergo. While we would emphasize that not every institution or writing program will be affected by a veteran surge, we nonetheless urge writing program administrators (WPAs) to investigate veteran enrollments on their campuses to determine the degree to which these transitions may be taking place in their classrooms. Such a task is not easy. Very few colleges, if any, disclose veteran status to faculty,[5] so instructors often only become aware through veterans' self-disclosure as a result of classroom discussion, one-to-one conferences, informal or formal writing assignments, or, in some cases, discussion of accommodation for disability.[6] Absent such self-disclosure, many student-veterans remain invisible, especially in classes populated by other adult learners.

Nonetheless, the number of veterans entering our classrooms continues to climb. The Department of Veterans Affairs (VA) reports that the US veteran population is nearing twenty-two million people, with one million from the current wars now enrolled in colleges and universities (*2015 Veteran* 18–19). That constitutes nearly 4 percent of students nationwide, though in some geographical locations that percentage is much higher. Further, estimated enrollments reflect only those students receiving GI Bill benefits, and no study has produced reliable data on the number of veterans seeking college degrees after their benefits have lapsed, have been transferred to a family member, or have otherwise remained unused.[7] Reflecting the rapid growth of veterans on college campuses, the national Student Veterans Association (SVA) has seen the number of its campus chapters multiply exponentially, from fewer than 50 before 2010 to 950 in fall 2014, with membership doubling from 2013 to 2014 alone (Romney). In 2014, SVA reported that just over half of all veterans who enroll in degree programs receive degrees, a number close to the traditional college population and significantly above the more-comparable "nontraditional" student body, whose graduation rates linger around 40 percent. The overwhelming majority—nearly 80 percent—of student-veterans enroll in public institutions (Cate), and the largest number of graduates in the SVA study sought degrees in the liberal arts and sciences. Both the SVA and the VA estimate that growth in student-veteran enrollments will continue in the short term.

The fact that the current GI Bill affords educational opportunities to family members of veterans will also ensure ongoing military-affiliated student enrollment growth ("Transfer"). The implications of shared benefits are far-reaching. First, it reminds us that our classrooms contain not only veterans but also spouses and children of veterans. In communities with high numbers of National Guard members or reservists, this may be especially true, as those veteran populations tend to be older and often already have families and grown children. Additionally, the extension of educational benefits to family members means those who have been deeply connected to OIF and OEF will continue to fill in our classrooms for generations.[8] Military dependents—many of whom will have been significantly impacted by the length and severity of two concurrent wars[9]—will enroll in college up to two decades from now, and as ample research testifies, they will be bringing with them the generational costs of war.[10]

The impact of military service on both veterans and their family members suggests that WPAs have a special need to identify and understand the student-veteran populations on their campuses. Several strategies may help determine whether special outreach for veterans or military family members is necessary. Discussing veteran enrollments with the staff of a campus veterans resource center or with a school's certifying official[11] will provide an initial sense of how many veterans or military family members are on campus. Further, making contact with a veterans' student group can offer insight into the student-veteran identity on a particular campus. Finally, reviewing and discussing institutional recruitment initiatives with senior administrators can be especially helpful in anticipating potential future enrollment trends. Many schools have very active recruitment initiatives to encourage veteran enrollments,[12] and while the motivations for such recruitment have been the subject of significant speculation (and even congressional testimony), reviewing and understanding campus initiatives can aid WPAs in determining the likelihood that the effects of military service may find their way into writing classrooms.

For many schools, that likelihood is slim. Private, four-year institutions as a group enroll far fewer veterans than state institutions despite a provision of the Post-9/11 GI Bill that encourages broad enrollments.[13] The Yellow Ribbon Program "allows approved institutions of higher learning and the VA to partially or fully fund tuition and fee expenses that exceed the established thresholds under the Post-9/11 GI Bill" ("Post-9/11") for those student-veterans who have earned 100 percent benefits eligibility by funding the difference between the maximum benefit allowed to veterans under the GI Bill and the private school tuition.[14]

Public four-year institutions enroll veterans in greater numbers than do private institutions, but their numbers are still lower than those of community colleges. As Kelly Field reports, "Many veterans prefer community colleges and for-profit institutions because they are more convenient and cater to their needs. . . . The majority of veterans today use their GI benefits to attend institutions that offer two-year degrees or emphasize vocational training." The SVA Million Records Project indicates that roughly 35 percent of veterans initially earn an associate's degree—the largest percentage of degrees earned by veterans (Cate), likely because the student-veteran demographic parallels other adult populations. The American Council on Education (ACE) indicates that the average student-veteran is thirty-three years old, more than ten years older than the nonveteran-student average of twenty-two ("Veteran Students"), and as a result, they often seek community colleges with programs designed to balance academics, work, and family.[15] Unlike traditional students, who, as Caroline Bird suggested during the post-Vietnam surge, frequently attend college "because it has become the thing to do or because college is a pleasant place to be; because it's the only way they can get parents or taxpayers to support them without getting a job they don't like," student-veterans expect institutions of higher education to be more than "a social center or aging vat." Instead, many seek accelerated entry into a productive and sustainable economic life, and community colleges and vocational and technical schools are often viewed as the most efficient way to get there. In addition, for student-veterans who are initially uncertain about how successful they may be academically, earning an associate's degree can give them the confidence to continue to a bachelor's degree.[16] Well-established articulation agreements between many state two-year and four-year colleges make such transfers particularly viable options.[17]

The varied reasons for and paths by which veterans seek college degrees, however, should not obscure the larger story that many institutions with diverse student bodies are experiencing substantial veteran enrollments. In fact, military undergraduates represent "a significant minority population on college and university campuses" (Bonar and Domenici 205). In addition, these students are often undertaking a fundamental shift in identify—from military to civilian, from professional soldier/airman/sailor/ marine to student. Those points of transition provide rich opportunities for writing and writing instruction and as such were at the heart of many of the inquiries we made while conducting our research.[18]

A Brief Statement on Methodology

We have discussed our methodology for the CCCC Research Grant in detail elsewhere (see Hart and Thompson, "Ethical"), but before exploring our key findings, we highlight some of our methodological approaches. As an initial step for our work, we conducted a national survey of writing instructors. We collected more than four hundred survey responses, processed some results at the inaugural Dartmouth Summer Seminar for Composition Research, and, using grant funding, conducted follow-up site visits at forty university and college campuses. Our site visits were determined by two factors: density of veteran populations (the top four states for veteran populations are California, Texas, Florida, and Virginia) and institutions whose work with veterans emerged from the survey as especially noteworthy. While we did not in our data collection and do not here aim to be exhaustive in describing trends across the country, we identified one major development across many institutions: the expansion of classes explicitly for veterans.

Across the country generally three types of courses have been created to account for increases in military student populations: *veterans-only courses*, *veteran-focused courses*, and *veteran-friendly courses*. We provide below a taxonomy of these classes. While we focused our research on writing classrooms, these classifications also appear regularly in other disciplines and college orientation courses. Here, we trace the constituentparts of each category, but we also discuss governing assumptions behind each model and some of the theoretical architecture that supports those assumptions. We draw special attention to the fact that implementation of classes oriented to military audiences requires significant intellectual engagement with "the veteran" as a cultural trope or stereotype (see Vacchi). Our culture has been saturated with the rhetoric of war for over a decade, forcing us to formulate our own positions not only about the wars but also about those who fight them. Confronting those positions, which are often forged in moments of intense emotion, is necessary to move ourselves and our classrooms beyond the essentializing language of the "hero," the "wounded warrior," the "war criminal," or other convenientcategorizations.[19] Our hope is that, much as we observed on campuses where new courses for veterans were being offered, the categories of classes we describe will foster more nuanced exploration of the connections between military service and academic inquiry.

Veterans-Only Courses

A sense of alienation among student-veterans is well-documented (see, e.g., DiRamio, Ackerman, and Mitchell; Elliot, Gonzalez, and Larsen; Glasser, Powers, and Zywiak; Livingston et al.), and the first category of classes we describe—veterans-only classes—aim to remedy this estrangement by restricting course enrollment to veterans or members of the military. Such classes recognize the challenges thatservice-members have in transitioning from military to civilian life, and they attempt to ease that transition by ensuring that student-veterans are surrounded by peers who understand military culture and the wartime experience (see also Valentino, "Serving"). For veterans, a sense of "difference" can be heightened when they encounter student lives that seem fundamentally disconnected from their own lived experiences. In many of our interviews with students and faculty, the image of privileged undergraduate students who talk incessantly about their social lives emerged as a kind of trope, a stereotype against which many veterans positioned themselves. The stereotype served, in the veterans' minds, as evidence of the fundamental differences between the student-veteran, who matured and was professionalized in a military (and often international) setting, and the "typical undergraduate," whose concerns focus on dating, alcohol, and parties.

Because (as Janet Lucas reminds us) the writing classroom is a space where disclosures of life's personal details often emerge, this sense of difference can be exacerbated. Even in instances when instructors may try to avoid prompting such disclosures, the use of experience as a type of evidence or as an organizing principle of a piece of writing may still lead to disclosure of a veteran's status. We note that even an assignment as seemingly innocuous as a "how-to" assignment may unexpectedly reveal military experience. Writing professors who explicitly assign personal narratives increase such opportunities. In fact, our research suggests that, regardless of course goals, some form of personal narrative remains a mainstay of many composition classes.[20] Thus, the possibility that any particular student will disclose personal information that either his or her classmates, the instructor, or even the student himself or herself finds difficult to negotiate increases. For veterans, who already report a higher sense of alienation, personal writing may exacerbate those feelings, especially if their professors, like Melanie Burdick so openly discusses, find themselves unready for war stories and "afraid to respond" (354). Therefore, "the question becomes how to respond thoughtfully, intelligently, and professionally to these disclosures" (Lucas 368).

Veterans-only classes partially mitigate this issue because, on the one hand, faculty leading the class have typically received special preparation and, on the other hand, students share, at least broadly, a military context that can provide common touchstones for discussion and support. The model mirrors similar courses that have developed to aid other populations in higher education. Just as ESL or developmental writing sections of FYW seek to adapt shared learning objectives by acknowledging a need within the student population, so too do veterans-only writing courses. First popularized through the Supportive Education for Returning Veterans (SERV) program at Cleveland State

University, initiated by chemistry professor John Schupp, the typical veterans-only course aims to provide a safe learning environment for veterans who may feel distracted or anxious in classes containing students without military backgrounds. Schupp believes that veterans-only classes allow students to focus on their educational goals while finding support among peers, and his program received significant media attention for its innovative approach to helping veterans in postsecondary education. These classes help students establish a sense of "unit cohesion" that allows them to focus more directly on the "mission" of class (Stripling). Such courses become "like the VFW hall without the alcohol," spaces where veterans "can talk about problems they may have, whether it's educational or personal" (Hall 8).

Several institutions have piloted veterans-only writing courses. An instructor at a community college in a large state with a significant military population created a veterans-only class that received national exposure in part because it recognized that the strong sense of camaraderie that service members feel while in the military could be harnessed as part of a writing class. As such, the initial class included trips to ropes courses and whitewater rafting to help create a strong learning cohort. The second semester the course was offered built on the lessons from the first and provided a shared reading experience on the subject of war. The course enjoyed significant success, but by the third semester it was offered, the instructor began to shift the focus away from the students' military experience because they found ongoing discussion about aspects of service and war at times frustrating and tedious. As a result, the instructor modified the course to focus on education and the college experience.

One professor at a regional comprehensive university in close proximity to a military base launched a veterans learning community as part of her institution's introductory composition sequence. While debate about the desirability of the course emerged from discussions with student-veterans, they nonetheless supported the pilot, which included service members from all the different branches. The approach was to provide "a space where if you want to write about service, it's a safe space," and while students reported some resistance to the writing process and to the "book learning" nature of the college setting, the instructor noted their ongoing strong sense of motivation and initiative.

Despite the many benefits reported from courses like the ones described above, they nonetheless present significant challenges, some pragmatic and some ethical. While the first institution discussed above continues to offer the veterans learning community FYW course in conjunction with a personal development course, the veterans-only course sequence at the latter institution was canceled in subsequent semesters, despite its relative success in achieving its goals. At Cleveland State, the Veterans Student Success Program website shows that 2010 was the last year "SERV-only" English courses were offered, and an *Inside Higher Ed* article in 2012 reported that Cleveland State had discontinued the SERV program entirely; a similar program at Ohio State was also discontinued (Grasgreen).

The relatively short history of veterans-only classes demonstrates that their viability often rests on issues of "logistics and demand": on the one hand, a class that is consistently under-enrolled becomes unsustainable and a drain on limited resources, while on the other hand, "a model based on one-on-one interactions and exceptionally small class sizes (which have to fit into everyone's schedules) can only reach so many people" (Grasgreen), so staffing veterans-only courses that are experiencing exceptionally high demand is often not feasible either. Further, in some cases, student-veterans are not interested in taking courses that deliberately separate them from their civilian counterparts because they are seeking opportunities to reintegrate into a nonmilitary community. As one veterans' coordinator explained, "isolating veterans from the rest of the population is not necessarily positive. . . . [T]he worst thing we [can] do is continue to isolate them from that immersion and that process" or reinforce "reclusive-veteran stereotypes" (Grasgreen). In other cases, some student-veterans choose not to sign up for the veterans-only designated sections because they feel their need or desire to be around other veterans is less acute than some of their "battle buddies," so they don't sign up in order to allow others with a perceived greater need to do so. A concern that veterans-only classes might be stigmatized as "remedial" is another apprehension some veterans voice.

Institutions offering veterans-only courses have recognized that providing professional development opportunities to faculty to ensure clarity of purpose is crucial. While the impulse of an instructor to teach a veterans-only course may be well meaning, doing so without a keen sense of the varied motives for military service and the complexity of the many different kinds of professional work service in which members have engaged can lead to profound assumptions and misconceptions about the students in the class. For instance, notorious cultural divides exist between different branches of the military, and those divides may find their way into the classroom. Army veterans may, for reasons that have nothing to do with collegiate life, dismiss contributions to the course by navy veterans. Even deeper schisms often exist between ranks or, perhaps most poignantly, between combat veterans and noncombat veterans (though those lines are increasingly blurry). It is worth noting that the 2010 Department of Veterans Affairs National Survey of Veterans found that of veterans from all eras "34 percent . . . reported that they had served in combat or a war zone"("National"); the number is notably higher for post-9/11 veterans, with "60% [being] deployed to a combat zone" (Taylor). Yet our vision of the student-veteran experience likely includes combat. Such visions, however, are contrary to the actualities: many service members will never have been deployed to a foreign country, and among those who have, many will not have served in an active war zone, let alone engaged in direct combat. Certainly, service members working in a military at war will and do feel the effects of those wars—even those working in an office in the Pentagon or a missile silo in Wyoming are immersed in a culture of war—but the figure of the combat-hardened (male) soldier or marine that occupies a central place in our imaginations has displaced the realities of a very large, complex, and diverse military force.[21] Instructors without knowledge of this complexity, or at least sensitivity to it, not only undermine their own credibility but also jeopardize the possibility of fashioning a safe zone for student-veterans that, as noted earlier, is the very purpose of most veterans-only classes.

Further, we would point out that the governing assumption of most of veterans-only classes is that veterans are in need of some sort of buffer from the rest of the student body. Indeed, such classes are predicated on students' deficits, most often characterized by diagnostic medical and psychological language. When courses' starting points are the presumption of need for rehabilitation or, more simply, protection, broader educational goals can be sacrificed. Later in our argument, we recommend an asset-based approach that reorients class creation away from an underlying vision of veterans as deficient and toward a vision of veterans as students with notable assets.

Veteran-Focused Courses

Some institutions have responded to (or even anticipated) the enrollment challenges and pedagogical hurdles that veterans-only classes pose, and one resulting strategy has been to form courses that take the veteran or the military as their subject without limiting enrollment to veterans. These classes target service members, their families, or others affected by war, and while enrollment is not limited to those particular students, their presumed interests and anticipated engagement are central motivations for such courses.

Publication of a wide range of teaching materials that engage with issues of war has facilitated the development of these courses. For example, OIF army infantryman Alex Horton's essay "On Getting By: Advice for College-Bound Vets" has been anthologized in one of Norton's FYW readers, and Jena McGregor's essay "Military Women in Combat: Why Making It Official Matters" appears in Bedford's best-selling FYW anthology *Current Issues and Enduring Questions*, which also includes a complete chaptertitled "Service: A Duty? A Benefit? Or Both, or Perhaps Neither?" Accordingly, faculty have created syllabi with sequences focused on the wars or some aspect of them. For example, torture became a common topic for student writing after Abu-Ghraib, as did the issue of the draft, military recruitment on college campuses, the idea of a "just war," and similar topics.

Course sequences and lessons on these topics, however, are not precisely what we mean by veteran-focused courses. By *veteran-focused*, we mean those courses whose genesis or revision stem from the attempt to address within a curriculum the needs of veterans, military family members, or others affected by military action. They are courses in which faculty members arrange course materials and activities by focusing on the needs of the veteran population in order to recruit veterans to the course.

Veteran-focused courses envision veterans as the primary audience for the course, and engagement with materials about war functions, in part, to attract students with a particular experience or interest in the military, combat, or the effects of war. The faculty teaching veteran-focused classes may also attempt to address the needs of student-veterans by crafting what they regard as especially relevant writing assignments for these students.[22]

The veteran-focused classroom provides a meaningful learning environment for veterans because it rests on a deliberate attempt to understand the values of the student-veteran population and, often, their family members. Those needs may be quite straightforward. They may include providing students with options on writing assignments so that they can choose whether or not to disclose their veteran status, providing students with options on seating within a classroom, providing accommodations for out-of-classroom responsibilities (such as work, reserve or National Guard duty, medical appointments, or family obligations), or providing options on readings or film viewings for veterans who find particular texts or images difficult to endure.[23] Further, faculty development on how to handle the complexities of the wartime experience helps ensure the classroom remains a safe place for intellectual curiosity. For example, helping faculty negotiate the issue of combat casualties may require extensive support or, more subtly, helping faculty understand that even seemingly supportive statements such as "I could never imagine what you've been through" may result, as Phil Klay notes, in the veteran feeling "in a corner by himself [sic], able to proclaim about war but not discuss it," while simultaneously shutting out the civilian "from a conversation about one of the most morally fraught activities our nation engages in—war."

For those considering a veteran-focused course, then, we suggest that it be developed in coordination with other stakeholders in veterans' issues on campus. The image we have of the "veteran" may bear very little resemblance to the actual veterans on a particular campus, so identifying local campus trends in veteran demographics is crucial. Some campuses, for example, may have primarily air force veterans, others primarily marines. Some campuses may have a veteran population concentrated in an MBA program, whereas others may be concentrated in undergraduate offerings in international studies, engineering, or social work. Some campuses may have a high concentration of combat veterans, whereas others may have a high concentration of support personnel. Some campuses may have a rich tradition of veterans of foreign militaries on the campus, or they may have an unusually high concentration of female veterans, or a large number of military dependents. Understanding these distinctions and others provides a foundation for crafting intentional courses.[24]

Often, veteran services offices have demographic information that can be useful, but simply opening discussions within a writing department or program is important to ensure a clear understanding of the student-veteran population on campus. In other words, forming a veteran-focused class requires nuanced understanding of the veterans on a campus and in a community. Without such an understanding, the goal of recruiting veterans and their dependents for a class will likely result in some of the same issues that veterans-only courses seem to face: inconsistent enrollments, lack of ability to staff under-enrolled classes, and inability to create courses that engage veterans in meaningful ways.

Veteran-Friendly Courses

Darren Keast at the City College of San Francisco has recently written about developing a veteran-friendly writing course, and we would suggest that his model provides an avenue for creating the "safe space" that the veterans-only course attempts to provide while also mitigating the pragmatic problems, such as staff resource allocation and student enrollment, that recur in both veterans-only and veteran-focused courses. By the designation *veteran-friendly*, Keast means simply a course that, in its preparation and execution, is mindful of the veteran presence on a campus and in a classroom. It does not limit enrollments, nor does it imply a special focus of the coursework or audience for the class. Instead, the course instructor recognizes the particular strengths and challenges veteran and active duty service members may bring to a classroom and campus, and those strengths and challenges become a measure by which the instructor organizes class material, activities, and assignments.

Keast's syllabus and accompanying reflection on his process for creating and running the course provide a useful roadmap for instructors. We would draw attention to two particular aspects of his work. First, Keast envisions his course as mitigating the sense of alienation veterans experience in a university setting while simultaneously providing civilians with "public forums to discuss moral issues related to these wars." Keast emphasizes that a veteran-friendly class provides veterans, as one student reported, "street cred" in the academic exchange of the class, but that the goals of research and careful argumentation require students to engage with topics beyond personal experience alone. Secondly, while Keast indicates that his course is "themed," he maintains a focus on his institutional and departmental composition outcomes. The result is that he ultimately sees veterans in much the same way as other students. As he says in the closing of his article: "Veterans and civilian students, from what I can tell from my anecdotal experience with their work, have essentially the same needs as writers." Instead of a veteran-focused class, then, a veteran-friendly class is one whose "primary goal . . . is to create a space broad enough for students with a wide range of experiences and predilections to write essays that engage and challenge them and are informed by careful research." The class, Keast hopes, will "bridge the civilian-military gap that many critics have observed."

Keast's classroom, therefore, is a conscious attempt to bridge a cultural divide within the context of a writing classroom, and it does so by mitigating one of the central concerns of veterans-only classes. That concern is perhaps best articulated by Matt Gallagher, the author of the critically acclaimed Iraq memoir *Kaboom*. Gallagher argues that veterans-only writing workshops, for all their promise and good intentions, might fail to accomplish one of their primary (often unstated) goals, which is to help veterans more easily join new communities and to ease their transition from the military to civilian life. Gallagher observes that for all the benefits of veterans-only writing workshops, the exclusive nature of them "reinforce[s] an ugly undercurrent of thought in military writing—that one shouldn't write about war unless one participated in it as a combatant or otherwise survived its destruction." Gallagher argues that for veteran writing workshops to work, "they [need] to stress the writing part over the veteran part," and while his position focuses on creative writing, his final words point to what much of our research identifies as well, which is that "inclusion" should start with a broadminded approach of how "to involve talented, driven people" in giving voice to complex issues.

From our perspective, then, the veteran-friendly class model offers the most viable opportunity for many schools to address veteran enrollments in writing classes. On the one hand, such courses recognize veterans as a group with particular strengths and challenges that recur with some regularity across institutions, and, on the other hand, these courses provide a means of, to invoke military language, remobilization that allows student-veterans more transparency in making their educational decisions. Whereas even a veteran-focused class relies on the notion of the "veteran" to animate the course material (effectively asking veterans to participate in the class *as veterans*), the veteran-friendly class acknowledges without demand the role that the veteran identity may have played in shaping a sense of self while the student negotiates new roles as civilian and student. The classroom becomes a space where both the veteran identity and the student identity can be honored and performed.

An Asset-Based Approach to the Question of Faculty Development

Throughout our research, we repeatedly encountered anxiety among WPAs or veteran services staff over the need for professional development about veterans on campus. The sense was that forcing (or even inviting) faculty to be prepared for "yet another special interest group" would create more work for those conducting the professional development as well as resentment among those receiving it. Such concerns are not groundless, as overburdened faculty and staff may question the need for more training: "Why add more professional development workshops?"

We submit three answers to this question. The first is that for many programs, specialized professional development on veterans' issues is unnecessary. WPAs and writing faculty should base their decisions on relevant data collected on their local campuses. Thoughtful questions provide avenues for gathering that data:

- How many veterans are on campus (not just how many are receiving educational benefits)?
- How many are undergraduate students? Transfer students? Graduate students?
- How many are veterans of the US military? Other countries' militaries?
- Is the campus near a military site or in a community with a historical military presence?
- How many dependents of service members and veterans are likely to be on campus?
- What professional development is already being conducted by a veterans coordinator or service office?
- Is there a Student Veterans Association? Is there an ROTC presence?

These kinds of questions can help WPAs shape a local response to the national student-veteran surge, and while we do not believe every campus will need to formulate a response, we maintain that program administrators in core fields such as writing have, in Marilyn Valentino's words, an "ethical obligation" to investigate and determine the level of need ("CCCC Chair's Address").

Secondly, when professional development is appropriate, we recommend an asset-based model. According to a report prepared by Drew Lieberman and Kathryn Stewart for Greenberg Quinlan Rosner Research, presenting post-9/11 veterans in an "asset" frame "produces an even better [perception] than portraying veterans as heroic. It also begins to reorient the way people think about how best to 'thank' veterans returning from service by shifting the focus from charity [or accommodation] to opportunity" (Lieberman and Stewart).[25] However, virtually every professional development module or program we encountered focused on veteran "deficits": PTSD, TBI, trauma, lack of preparedness for college, absenteeism, disability, substance abuse, gender discrimination, sexual assault, transition issues. Such a deficit-based approach, we suggest, creates "a priori expectations about a student," which, as Eugenia L. Weiss explains, "can lead an educator to treat the student differently and in accord with those expectations." As a result, "students are likely to respond accordingly, regardless of their intellectual ability" (Weiss 120). While the effects of military service during a time of active warfare are real and may require significant interventions,[26] they do not exclusively or even primarily constitute the student-veteran experience. As Pamela Woll makes clear, "the subject of war and its effects can easily tip over into a dramatic focus on the negative or a stereotypical portrait of service members and veterans as dangerous, unstable, or objects of sympathy. The best focus will emphasize respect for these individuals . . . and belief in their strength and potential" (24). Indeed, our research affirms what other studies demonstrate: veterans tend to be an asset to the classroom. Many bring broad worldviews to complex issues, and all members of the military receive extensive training in leadership and team building. Further, promotion within the military is often linked to education and professional development, so that veterans' capacity for learning per se is less of a hurdle than is the need for them to learn to apply already well-developed learning processes to the relatively unfamiliar learning environment of the college classroom. Therefore, when faculty approach veterans as experts in their own fields—as highly trained professionals seeking to become proficient in new ways of knowing and learning—the significant assets of military students can strengthen classroom dynamics. In his 2014 op-ed, Mark Street points out that "in an academic community we are all there to question our own assumptions, to be surprised, and to be willing to let another's viewpoint or reaction challenge our own," which is why he appreciates how student-veterans "enliven [his] classes . . . day to day." Erin Hadlock and Sue Doe also call attention to student veterans' "aptitude, agency, and critical thinking, all of which situate them to thrive in higher-education settings" (74). Among our interviewees, one of the most repeated sentiments was that faculty highly valued student-veterans because of their professionalism, motivation, varied experiences, and maturity.

Emphasizing assets is at the heart of our third and final recommendation: WPAs should consider asset-based pedagogical research for any professional development. Such research traditionally centers on issues of educational justice in K–12 schools. As Django Paris and H. Samy Alim explain, "the vast majority of asset pedagogy research and practice has focused on the racialized and culturally situated heritage practices of [Indigenous American and African American] communities" (90). While we do not mean to suggest that the culturally situated practices of (former) military members are equivalent to the culturally situated heritage practices of marginalized student populations such as Indigenous Americans and African Americans, we concur with Lew Zipin that teaching and learning become more difficult when "learners' culturally inherited ways of knowing do not match those privileged in school curriculum" (317). For studentveterans, this may mean a shift from actionand mission-oriented training to less immediately concrete educational objectives. As Angie Mallory and Doug Downs note in their chapter in the collection *Generation Vet*, studentveterans typically "do not cast [their military habits] aside. For example, every veteran [they] interviewed reported following the military script of showing up to a scheduled event (class) fifteen minutes early—to find no one else there" (61). Other student-veterans shared with Mallory and Downs their initial dismay at what they perceived to be slovenliness in the dressing habits or physical postures of their professors and fellow classmates,[27] or the apparent lack of respect students demonstrated by calling a professor by his first name. These elements of academic culture can be unsettling to student-veterans. By making an effort to "design curriculum that makes meaningful connections with ways of knowing in learners' lives beyond school, . . . that is, to become open to learning about and from the lives of others, with conviction that these lives embody both intelligence and knowledge assets," writing instructors can potentially create a "more egalitarian, democratic and intellectually rich curriculum that puts diverse lifeworld learning assets to use" (Zipin 317–19). In asset-based frameworks, like that proposed by John Saltmarsh, "student's assets are embraced because the experience and knowledge they contribute to the learning process, and the authority of the knowledge they possess, contribute necessarily to the construction of new knowledge" (342). As former marine and current college writing instructor Galen Leonhardy reminds us, "we have much to learn" from student veterans (342).

Corrine Hinton's research on US Marine Corps student-veterans shows that those "who [are] able to identify and then translate previous learning and rhetorical experiences from the military into academic writing contexts [are more likely to report] positive perceptions about that writing," and Cathleen Morreale similarly argues that "the educational quality of military students can be improved through the development of socio-educational relationships . . . such as recognizing a student's knowledge by having them provide spontaneous accounts, presenting alternative versions of arguments, engaging various participants holding contradictory opinions, [and] building arguments collectively through work in small groups" (138). By setting aside preconceptions and guiding student-veterans to recognize similarities between academic writing and military writing, we help them "identify and unpack the kinds of action agency that were valued in the military and compare these to the kinds of learning and writing agency that will be needed in college classrooms" (Hadlock and Doe 90).

This is all to say that veterans' lived experiences promise to help shape classroom discussions, and their professional writing experiences stand to enrich students' considerations of various academic and nonacademic literacies. Prompting dialogue about what helps veterans on a particular campus learn better will, we believe, prompt greater engagement with different ways of knowing and seeing the world, and such epistemological discussions may consequently help transform our ways of approaching our writing classrooms. Acknowledging student-veterans' needs while also recognizing their assets not only helps us enact good pedagogy, but it is at the very heart of the veteran ethos: service. In this case, to our students.

Acknowledgments

We extend our sincere thanks to the CCCC Research Initiative; Tiane Donahue and the inaugural Dartmouth Summer Seminar for Composition Research program leaders and participants; supportive colleagues at VMI, Allegheny College, and Stony Brook University; survey respondents; the generous faculty, staff, administrators, and students who took the time to speak with us on our visits to campuses; and Jonathan Alexander and the anonymous reviewers who provided valuable suggestions for revision.

Notes

1. See Resolution 3 of the Executive Committee of the Conference on College Composition and Communication, Annual Business Meeting, 22 Mar. 2003, New York.

2. In our 2010 survey of WPAs and writing instructors, 44.2 percent of respondents (some of whom represent the same institutions) stated that they had noticed an increase of student-veterans in their writing classes.

3. In the same survey, 62.3 percent of respondents stated that their FYW classes are capped at between 20 and 25 students, while 23.8 percent had caps between 15 and 20 students. Only 10.8 percent of respondents had caps of more than 25. We also want to note here that we deliberately used the term *classmates* rather than *peers*, as many student-veterans would not identify their classmates as their peers due to differences in age and experience.

4. In the same survey, 71 percent of respondents indicated that FYW classes at their institutions "typically include assignments of personal narrative essays." Similarly, 69.5 percent of respondents concurred that some form of "journals" are assigned in FYW.

5. During our research, we learned that during the Vietnam era, faculty members at some institutions were provided with class rosters that *did* indicate which, if any, of their students were receiving educational benefits from the military. According to our sources, this practice was instituted in order to "catch" veterans who were cashing in on their benefits without actually attending classes or working toward degree completion. A 1978 article in the *Atlantic* points out that "by 1977, only 30 percent of the Vietnam-era veterans without a high school education had used any part of their GI Bill benefits. And, of course, there [was] no way of telling how many Vietnam veterans [used] the Bill [which was distributed in monthly lump sum payments to cover tuition only], not primarily to go to school and learn a trade, but to get cash and keep themselves and their families in food" (Kidder).

6. While we don't want to downplay the significant impact of posttraumatic stress disorder (PTSD) and traumatic brain injury (TBI)—the "signa-

ture wounds" of the most recent wars—we also want to make it clear that according to the Pew Research Center's 2011 report *War and Sacrifice in the Post-9/11 Era*, the Veterans Administration (VA) has stated that only 11–20 percent of OIF/ OEF veterans have been diagnosed with PTSD, although 37 percent believe they have suffered from it, whether diagnosed or not (Taylor 1). According to a report by the RAND Corporation, 20 percent of OIF/ OEF veterans have PTSD, while 19 percent have TBI (Tanielian).

7. Not all student-veterans draw from the GI Bill or other military educational benefit programs; as a result, some may not be "counted" in an institution's demographic data.

8. Dependents may use the benefits while the service member is on active duty or after he or she has separated or retired from the service. Spouses must use transferred benefits within fifteen years from the service member's separation date; children must use transferred benefits prior to reaching the age of twenty-six ("Transfer").

9. "More than eight-in-ten post-9/11 veterans (84%) say they were deployed at least once while serving—and nearly four-in-ten (38%) say they have been deployed three times or more. Among veterans who were married while they were on active duty, nearly half say deployment had a negative impact on their relationship with their spouse (48%) and nearly as many parents reported that their relationship with their children suffered when they were away (44%)"(Taylor 15–16). Additionally, "[a]lthough historically, the suicide death rates in the U.S. Army have been below the civilian rate, the suicide rate in the U.S. Army began climbing in the early 2000s, and by 2008, it exceeded the demographicallymatched civilian rate (20.2 suicide deaths per 100,000 vs. 19.2)" ("Suicide").

10. The evidence that the legacy of war is passed from veterans to children is overwhelming, and while here we use *cost* in the broadest possible way, the monetary costs for war are no less real. For examples of studies on the emotional costs, see Motta et al.; Dahl, McCubbin, and Ross; Scharf; Dekel and Goldblatt. For an accessible and personal account of the generational effects of war, see Levinson. Levinson has coordinated writing groups for veterans and their families in the Austin area, and she has taught war literature and writing at several colleges.

11. The Department of Veterans Affairs defines a *school certifying official (SCO)* as "the individual assigned the authority of completing all paperwork necessary to certify the enrollment and changes in enrollment for students eligible for VA educational benefits at their college or university" (Hobbes).

12. See, for example, the "*Top Military-Friendly Colleges and Universities*" guide published by *Military Advanced Education* (*MAE*), which promises to encapsulate "in 75 words or less why [each school is] appealing to the prospective military student" and is funded by advertisements purchased by the colleges featured in the publication. See also Brooks, Morse, and Tolis

on *US News & World Report*'s methodology for ranking the "best colleges for veterans."

13. "About 16 percent of veterans use the GI Bill to attend private institutions, roughly the same proportion as students generally" (Sander). See also Fairbanks; Sloane, "Annual"; Sloan, "Veterans."

14. "To qualify for the full benefit a veteran must have served at least 3 years of active duty after September 10, 2001" ("Post-9/11"). A veteran with 100 percent benefits eligibility can receive up to thirty-six months of education benefits, a monthly housing allowance, and an annual books and supplies stipend.

15. In the state of California in 2009, fewer than 800 veterans were enrolled in the University of California system's four-year colleges, while 15,000 veterans were enrolled in California community colleges. This may partially be due to the thirty-six-month limit on benefits in addition to the reasons Field outlines.

16. As Michelle Navarre Cleary's research on adult students demonstrates, "Anxiety about how school works is intensified in writing classes for those adult students who discover that what they remember about academic writing has lost currency. . . . Writing process methods, kinds of assignments, citations methods and the nature of sources have all changed since many adults were in school. As a result, writing classes can be sites of extreme, potentially paralyzing anxiety for them" (116).

17. For-profit institutions and online institutions provide significant benefits to veterans, such as twelvemonth programs, no breaks in benefits, and flexibility in scheduling. Indeed, many servicemembers take courses while deployed, even in combat zones. Nonetheless, our research was limited to two-year and four-year traditional institutions.

18. Former marine Micah Wright proposes the term *remobilization* rather than *transition* as a key term: "The term *transition* reflects the civilian culture's idea that the service member needs to change to reflect the civilian ideals; however, the term *remobilization* rhetorically motivates the service member to move from one mission to the other. This term includes the military identity in the civilian discourse" (22–23).

19. As retired army Captain Shannon Meehan argues, "The stories we tell consistently portray veterans in extremes—either emphasizing vets' heroism beyond comprehension or their propensity for erratic violence. . . . Because of the unreal, formulaic depictions of vets in our culture, [veterans] remain distanced from society, leaving little chance that anyone will actually see [vets] as real people with both strengths and struggles."

20. In response to the question, "Do first-year writing classes at your institution typically include assignments of personal narrative essays?," 71.3 percent of respondents to our survey answered "Yes," with 5.4 percent answering "Don't know."

21. See Hart and Thompson ("War") for discussion of women as outsiders in the military (42–45).

22. Former marine and current two-year college writing professor Galen Leonhardy, for example, suggests that we should be open to offering veterans opportunities to explore their military experiences (and, indeed, research shows that many student veterans appreciate the opportunity to write about VA benefits—whether educational or medical; about veteran homelessness, etc.). We should not, however, require or expect them to do so.

23. We concur with Sarah Roff with regard to "trigger warnings": "Since triggers are a contagious phenomenon, there will never be enough trigger warnings to keep up with them. It should not be the job of college educators to foster this process. It would be *much more useful for faculty members and students to be trained how to respond* if they are concerned that a student or peer has suffered trauma" (emphasis added). See also Valentino ("Serving") on considerations to take into account when deciding whether to assign readings, films, and essays on war.

24. In addition, instructors might need to recognize that most students participating in the Reserve Officers Training Corps (ROTC) do not have veteran status and have not been deployed.

25. Similarly, Eileen E. Schell and Ivy Kleinbart encourage veteran writers outside of a classroom context "to think about how their military training is an asset" when it comes to "the act of writing" (137).

26. For example, in her *Generation Vet* chapter "Faculty as First Responders: Willing but Unprepared," Linda De La Ysla, whose student Charles Whittington published his essay "War Is a Drug" in the college newspaper and who never completed his degree after being told by school officials that he would not be allowed on campus until he had a psychological evaluation, acknowledges her lack of preparation for "what to do or what to say" and points out that "many teachers of writing" also lack clarity about how to provide "supportive and pedagogically sound responses" when confronted with veterans' narratives of trauma (97). Reflecting on the situation, De La Ysla concludes that "faculty [need] to recognize the existence of student-veterans as a distinct yet heterogeneous group . . . and realize that within that diversity [are] individuals [who are] suffering," and that writing teachers need "to be aware of whatever resources [exist] on campus as well as off " (110).

27. Indeed, one of the many concerns expressed on our survey was how to productively engage student-veterans with their civilian classmates. According to Eugenia Weiss, faculty members who strive to promote "safety and community in the classroom . . . should do all they can to foster student-to-student connections in a nonthreatening and culturally responsive manner." She references "Allport's Intergroup Contact Theory as a starting point" (116).

Works Cited

Bird, Caroline. "College Is a Waste of Time and Money." 1975. PDF.
Bonar, Ted C., and Paula L. Domenici. "Counseling and Connecting with the Military Undergraduate: The Intersection of Military Service and University Life." *Journal of College Student Psychotherapy* 25.3 (2011): 204–19. Print.
Brooks, Eric, Robert Morse, and Diane Tolis. "Best Colleges for Veterans Methodology." *US News & World Report*. 8 Sept. 2014. Web.
Burdick, Melanie. "Grading the War Story." *Teaching English in the TwoYear College* 36.4 (2009): 353–54. Print.
Cate, C. A. *A Review of Veteran Achievement in Higher Education. Million Records Project: Research from Student Veterans of America*. Washington: Student Veterans of America, 2014. PDF.
Dahl, Barbara, H. I. McCubbin, and K. L. Ross. "Second Generational Effects of War-Induced Separations: Comparing the Adjustment of Children in Reunited and Non-Reunited Families." Paper presented at the National Council for Family Relations. Aug. 1975. Print.
Dekel, Rachel, and Hadass Goldblatt. "Is There Intergenerational Transmission of Trauma? The Case of Combat Veterans' Children." *American Journal of Orthopsychiatry* 78.3 (2008): 281–89. Print.
De La Ysla, Linda S. "Faculty as First Responders: Willing but Unprepared." Doe and Langstraat 95–116.
DiRamio, David, Robert Ackerman, and Regina L. Garza Mitchell. "From Combat to Campus: Voices of StudentVeterans." *NASPA Journal* 45.1 (2008): 73–102. Print.
Doe, Sue, and William W. Doe. "Residence Time and Military Workplace Literacies." *Composition Forum* 28 (Fall 2013). Web.
Doe, Sue, and Lisa Langstraat, eds. *Generation Vet: Composition, StudentVeterans, and the Post-9/11 University*. Logan: Utah State UP, 2014. Print.
Elliott, M., C. Gonzalez, and B. Larsen. "U.S. Military Veterans Transition to College: Combat, PTSD, and Alienation on Campus." *Journal of Student Affairs Research and Practice* 48.3 (2011): 279–96. Print.
Fairbanks, Amanda. "Military Veterans at Private Universities Fear Being Robbed of G.I. Bill Dollars." *Huffington Post* 19 Apr. 2011. Web.
Field, Kelly. "Cost, Convenience Drive Veterans' College Choices." *Chronicle of Higher Education* 25 July 2008. Web.
Gallagher, Matt. "How to Run a Successful Writing Workshop for Veterans." *New York Times* 9 Sept. 2013. Web.
Glasser, Irene, John T. Powers, and William H. Zywiak. "Military Veterans at Universities: A Case of Culture Clash." *Anthropology News* 50.5 (2009): 33. Print.

Grasgreen, Allie. "Veterans-Only Classes Both Expanding and Closing." *Inside Higher Ed* 4 Jan. 2012. Web.

Hadlock, Erin, and Sue Doe. "Not Just 'Yes Sir, No Sir': How Genre and Agency Interact in Student-Veteran Writing." Doe and Langstraat 73–94.

Hall, Kristin. "Colleges Focus on Veterans as GI Bill Ups Numbers." *Community College Week* 27 July 2009: 8–9. Print.

Hart, D. Alexis, and Roger Thompson. "'An Ethical Obligation': Promising Practices for Student Veterans in College Writing Classrooms." Conference on College Composition and Communication White Paper. June 2013. Web.

— "War, Trauma, and the Writing Classroom: A Response to Travis Martin's 'Combat in the Classroom.'" *Writing on the Edge* 23.2 (2014): 37–47. Print.

Hinton, Corrine. "'The Military Taught Me Something about Writing': How Student Veterans Complicate the Novice-to-Expert Continuum in First-Year Composition." *Composition Forum* 28 (Fall 2013). Web.

Hobbes, Laural. "The Role of the School Certifying Official." *Military Advanced Education and Transition.* 22 Jul 2013. Web.

Horton, Alex. "On Getting By: Advice for College-Bound Vets." *Back to the Lake: A Reader for Writers*. Ed. Thomas Cooley. 3rd ed. New York: Norton, 2015. 311–16. Print.

Keast, Darren. "A Class for Vets, Not by a Vet: Developing a Veteran-Friendly Composition Course at City College of San Francisco." *Composition Forum* 28 (Fall 2013). Web.

Kidder, Tracy. "Soldiers of Misfortune: A Report on the Veterans of Vietnam—And on the Often Disgraceful Treatment They Have Received from Their Countrymen." *Atlantic* Mar. 1978. Web.

Klay, Phil. "After War, a Failure of the Imagination." *New York Times*. 8 Feb. 2014. Web.

Leonhardy, Galen. "Transformations: Working with Veterans in the Composition Classroom." *Teaching English in the Two-Year College* 36.4 (2009): 339–52. Print.

Levinson, Leila. *Gated Grief: The Daughter of a GI Concentration Camp Liberator Discovers a Legacy of Trauma*. Brule: Cable Books, 2011. Print.

Lieberman, Drew, and Kathryn Stewart. "Strengthening Perceptions of America's Post-9/11 Veterans: Survey Analysis Report." Greenberg Quinlan Rosner Research. 17 June 2014. Web.

Livingston, Wade G., Pamela A. Havice, Tony W. Cawthon, and David S. Fleming. "Coming Home: Student Veterans' Articulation of College Reenrollment." *Journal of Student Affairs Research and Practice* 48.3 (2011): 315–31. Print.

Lucas, Janet. "Getting Personal: Responding to Student Self-Disclosure." *Teaching English in the Two-Year College* 34.4 (2007): 367–79. Print.

Mallory, Angie, and Doug Downs. "Uniform Meets Rhetoric: Excellence through Interaction." Doe and Langstraat 51–72.

McGregor, Jena. "Military Women in Combat: Why Making It Official Matters." *Current Issues and Enduring Questions.* Ed. Sylvan Barnet and Hugo Bedau. 10th ed. Boston: Macmillan Education, 2014. 28–31. Print.

Meehan, Shannon. "Why We Don't Need a Parade: One Vet's Dissent." *New York Daily News* 15 Mar. 2012. Web.

Morreale, Cathleen. "Academic Motivation and Academic Self-Concept: Military Veteran Students in Higher Education." Diss. State U of New York at Buffalo, 2011. Print.

Motta, Robert W., Jamie M. Joseph, Raphael D. Rose, John M. Suozzi, and Laura J. Leiderman. "Secondary Trauma: Assessing Intergenerational Transmission of War Experiences with a Modified Stroop Procedure." *Journal of Clinical Psychology* 53.8 (1997): 895–903. Print.

"National Survey of Veterans, Active Duty Service Members, Demobilized National Guard and Reserve Members, Family Members, and Surviving Spouses." Washington, D.C.: Department of Veterans Affairs, 18 Oct. 2010. PDF.

Navarre Cleary, Michelle. "What WPAs Need to Know to Prepare New Teachers to Work with Adult Students." *WPA* 32.1 (2008): 113–28. Print.

"One Million Now Benefit from Post-9/11 GI Bill." *Department of Veterans Affairs.* Office of Public and Intergovernmental Affairs. News release. 8 Nov. 2013. Web.

Paris, Django, and H. Samy Alim. "What Are We Seeking to Sustain through Culturally Sustaining Pedagogy? A Loving Critique Forward." *Harvard Educational Review* 84.1 (2014): 85–100. Print.

"Post-9/11 GI Bill: Yellow Ribbon FAQs." *Department of Veterans Affairs.* Education and Training. 2012. Web.

Roff, Sarah. "Treatment, Not Trigger Warnings." *Chronicle of Higher Education* 23 May 2014. Web.

Romney, Andy. "SVA Nearing Release of GI Bill Graduation Rates." *American Legion Online Newsletter* 8 Jan. 2014. Web.

Saltmarsh, John. "Changing Pedagogies." *Handbook of Engaged Scholarship: Contemporary Landscapes, Future Directions.* Vol. 1: *Institutional Change.* Ed. H. E. Fitzgerald, C. Burack, and S. Seifer. East Lansing: Michigan State UP, 2010. 331–52. Print.

Sander, Libby. "Veterans Tell Elite Colleges: 'We Belong.'" *Chronicle of Higher Education* 7 Jan. 2013. Web.

Scharf, Miri. "Long-Term Effects of Trauma: Psychosocial Functioning of the Second and Third Generation of Holocaust Survivors." *Development and Psychopathology* 19.2 (2007): 603–22. Print.

Schell, Eileen E., and Ivy Kleinbart. "'I Have to Speak Out': Writing with Veterans in a Community Writing Group." Doe and Langstraat 119–39.

Sloane, Wick. "Annual Veterans Count, 2013." *Inside Higher Ed* 11 Nov. 2013. Web.

—. "Veterans Day 2012." *Inside Higher Ed* 12 Nov. 2012. Web.

Street, Mark. "Military Veterans Bring Value to the Classroom." *Chronicle of Higher Education* 21 Apr. 2014. Web.

Stripling, Jack. "Tillman's Legacy." *Inside Higher Ed* 12 Mar. 2010. Web.

"Suicide in the Military: Army-NIH Funded Study Points to Risk and Protective Factors." *National Institute of Mental Health*. Press release. 3 Mar. 2014. Web.

Tanielian, Terri, et al. "Invisible Wounds: Mental Health and Cognitive Care Needs of America's Returning Veterans." *RAND Corp*. Center for Military Health Policy Research, 2008. Web.

Taylor, Paul, ed. *War and Sacrifice in the Post-9/11 Era: The Military-Civilian Gap*. Washington: Pew Research Center, 2011. Print.

"Top Military-Friendly Colleges and Universities: 4th Annual Guide, 2010–2011." *Military Advanced Education* May 2010. PDF.

"Transfer Post-9/11 GI Bill to Spouse and Dependents." *U.S. Department of Veterans Affairs*. Education and Training, 2 Mar. 2016. Web.

2015 Veteran Economic Opportunity Report. U.S. Department of Veterans Affairs, 2015. PDF.

Vacchi, David T. "Considering Student Veterans on the Twenty-First-Century College Campus." *About Campus* 17.2 (2012): 15–21. Print.

Valentino, Marilyn. "CCCC Chair's Address: Rethinking the Fourth C: Call to Action." *College Composition and Communication* 62.2 (2010): 364–78. Print.

—. "Serving Those Who Have Served: Preparing for Student Veterans in Our Writing Programs, Classes, and Writing Centers." *WPA* 36.1 (2012): 164–78. Print.

"Veteran Students Study Harder, But Are Less Engaged in Campus Life, Says New ACE Report." American Council on Education. 3 Dec. 2013. Web.

Weiss, Eugenia L. "Building Community in a Diverse College Classroom." *Supporting Veterans in Higher Education: A Primer for Administrators, Faculty, and Advisors*. Ed. Jose E. Coll and Eugenia L. Weiss. Chicago: Lyceum, 2015. 104–29. Print.

Woll, Pamela. "Teaching America's Best: Preparing Your Classrooms to Welcome Returning Veterans and Service Members." New York: National Organization on Disability, 2010. PDF.

Wright, Micah. "Improvise, Adapt, and Overcome: The Student Veteran and Considerations of Identity, Space, and Pedagogy." Master's thesis, Texas State U, 2013. Print.

Zipin, Lew. "Dark Funds of Knowledge, Deep Funds of Pedagogy: Exploring Boundaries between Lifeworlds and Schools." *Discourse: Studies in the Cultural Politics of Education* 30.3 (2009): 317–31. Print.

D. Alexis Hart is associate professor of English and director of writing at Allegheny College in Meadville, Pennsylvania. A US Navy veteran, she has published and edited scholarly work on veterans' issues and was the corecipient, with Roger Thompson, of a 2010 Conference on College Composition and Communication Research Initiative Grantto study veterans returning to college writing classrooms. She is co-chair of the CCCC Task Force on Veterans and an NCTE Policy Analyst for Higher Education in Pennsylvania.

Roger Thompson is associate professor in the Program in Writing and Rhetoric at Stony Brook University and serves as senior fellow at Syracuse University's Institute for Veterans and Military Families. He is coauthor of *Beyond Duty: Life on the Frontline of Iraq*, and his work has appeared in *College English, Philosophy and Rhetoric*, and other journals.

RHETORIC SOCIETY QUARTERLY

> *RSQ* is on the Web at https://associationdatabase.com/aws/RSA/pt/sp/rsq

Rhetoric Society Quarterly is published in the months of January, April, July, October and December by Taylor & Francis Group for the Rhetoric Society of America. RSQ invites article-length manuscripts on all areas of rhetorical studies, including theory, history, criticism, and pedagogy. Readers of RSQ are rhetoricians working in communication, composition, English, history, philosophy, politics, classics, and other allied fields. Consequently, RSQ publishes work that advances a shared understanding of a multi-disciplinary field.

Children Speaking: Agency and Public Memory in the Children's Peace Statue Project

Risa Applegarth's rhetorical analysis of the Children's Peace Statue Project, designed and funded by children and dedicated in Albuquerque, New Mexico, in 1995. The rhetorical contest was between the statue's supporters (children)—specifically, children who were seen as threatening sanctioned public memories of Los Alamos's role in World War II—and those who wanted to protect and preserve the honor and integrity of those who worked for the Manhattan Project. Applegarth concludes that children who petitioned the Los Alamos County Councle exercised agency in ways that challenge rhetorical scholars to revise our tendency to position children primarily as figures or objects of discourse.

Children Speaking: Agency and Public Memory in the Children's Peace Statue Project

Risa Applegarth

Scholars in rhetoric have been slow to recognize children as capable of exercising rhetorical agency. This oversight inadvertently recapitulates the divestment of agency experienced by children who speak publicly about civic concerns. This essay examines the argumentative and organizational strategies of a group of children from New Mexico who worked in the early 1990s to publicize, design, and fund the Children's Peace Statue and who repeatedly petitioned the Los Alamos County Council to accept the statue as a gift to the city of Los Alamos. Analyzing the children's rhetorical strategies alongside responses of adult opponents, I show how opponents rejected the statue in part by resisting engaging with children as rhetorical agents. This research underscores the stakes of recognizing children's agency as complexly meaningful.

Keywords: *children, Los Alamos, public memory, rhetorical agency, World War II*

The Children's Peace Statue generated numerous headlines in 1995, the year that marked the 50th anniversary of the bombing of Hiroshima and Nagasaki by the United States. The first national memorial in the United States to be designed and funded by children, the Children's Peace Statue materialized the hopes of children around the world: some 50,000 individuals from sixty-five countries who mailed donations to an Albuquerque post office box to express their desire for peace. Reporting on the statue's origins in an Albuquerque elementary school, the national competition to select a design, and the statue's dedication in August of 1995, periodicals across the country found noteworthy not only the novelty of a monument created by children but also the resonant significance of the location these children had identified for the statue: Los Alamos, "the birthplace of the bomb," as the *Washington Times* and many other newspapers reported.[1]

Because the statue had been promoted so widely as a gift to the city of Los Alamos, the decision of the Los Alamos County Council (LACC) in early 1995 *against* permitting the statue to be installed on county land prompted surprised headlines in newspapers across the country. Although the Council initially voted in 1992 to provide land for the project, two subsequent meetings—in November 1994 and February 1995—had been attended by vocal opposition, resulting in the failure of a motion to find land for the statue. News coverage of these contentious meetings emphasized their unusual—if not sensational—scene of intergenerational confrontation. Dana Kaplan, a fourteen-year-old member of the Kids' Committee for the Children's Peace Statue, "couldn't finish her presentation in support of the statue because of heckling from the audience" (Armijo C3). One Los Alamos resident displayed his opposition by holding up World War II–era posters showing Neville Chamberlain cooperating with Adolf Hitler and charged that the peace statue represented a similarly dangerous gesture of placation (Schaller, "What Was Said" A3). Another opponent expressed her resentment at "the fact that people generations away from the times, people who seem never to have heard of Pearl Harbor ... should take it upon themselves to try to shame Los Alamos into saying—yes, we were wrong to try to win the war to do what our country asked, and you're right to come here and tell us to give land, time and money to expiate our guilt" (LACC, *Council Work Session* 9–10). Some members of the Kids' Committee were fighting back tears as they talked with the press after these tense public meetings; in one widely quoted interview, fourteen-year-old David Rosoff said to reporters, "I am very, very frustrated, because they can't seem to get past the past" (Cortwright 6).

Rosoff's diagnosis that adult opponents and local officials refused to "get past the past" points to the complex nexus of children's agen-

---

1. See "Students Plan." In 1994, a story about the children's plan to dedicate the statue in Los Alamos ran in *Parade Magazine*, a Sunday supplement with a circulation of 30 million, generating enormous visibility for the project.

cy and public memory that I explore through rhetorical analysis of this case. Although supporters insisted that the statue spoke of the desire of children worldwide for future peace, residents of Los Alamos voiced fears that the statue would "dishonor the memory of the men and women of the Manhattan Project" (LACC, *Council Work Session* 9). Opponents of the statue repeatedly voiced dominant U.S. public memories that maintain the war as just, the bomb as necessary and life-saving, and the people of Los Alamos as working sacrificially in service of a peace-initiating scientific achievement.[2] Residents asserted that Los Alamos National Laboratories is itself "a living peace monument" (LACC, *Council Regular Session Meeting* [1992] 5) and that the "the last fifty years of peace have come [about] because of Los Alamos" (LACC, *Council Regular Session Meeting* [1994] 10). As one resident explained, she "would like Los Alamos to be remembered as having played a large part in ending the very tragic war and not as the place that built the weapon that killed many hundreds of children" (*On Wings of Peace* 3).

Because materiality and design play such a significant role in the capacity of memorials to solidify or revise dominant public memories, scholars in rhetoric might imagine that the statue's innocuous design would allay such fears. Selected by a panel of adult and child judges from six thousand entries in a national competition, the statue's design (Figure 1) and final form (Figure 2) avoid reference to World War II, Hiroshima, or nuclear weapons.

---

2. For historical accounts that counter this dominant justification for the bombing of Hiroshima and Nagasaki, see Tsuyoshi Hasegawa; Robert J. Lifton and Greg Mitchell; Howard Zinn

Figure 1 Design of Children's Peace Statue in one proposed location in Los Alamos. Reprinted with permission from Bill Perkins, formerly of Campbell Okuma Perkins Associates.

Figure 2 Children's Peace Statue, adorned with strands of paper cranes, in its current location at the Anderson-Abruzzo Albuquerque International Balloon Museum. Photo courtesy of Richard Loyd.

The original design, by eighteen-year old Noe Martinez, depicts an open globe surrounded by a garden, and originally included garden space where visitors could plant flowers to participate in creating the memorial collectively. Martinez's design was modified for a desert environment by New Mexico landscape architect Bill Perkins, and further modified by Colorado sculptor Tim Joseph, who incorporated the design's collaborative dimension by sending cubes of wax to schools in the United States and around the world, which children molded into plants and animals and sent back to the sculptor's foundry. Joseph then cast some three thousand wax figures into bronze, which he assembled to form continents over the steel frame of the globe (Figure 3). The open steel frame, reminiscent of a molecule, subtly evokes the atomic age, while the small bronze figures, forming filigreed continents and bearing the fingerprints of the children who molded them, simultaneously suggest the fragility of the earth, the delicacy of children's care, and the durability of children's collective efforts on behalf of peace.[3]

Although sustained analysis of the statue's materiality would be typical in rhetorical scholarship on public memory, in what follows I instead focus on children's (unsuccessful) efforts to place the statue in Los Alamos. Although the design avoids the message of blame residents feared, it did not alleviate opponents' resistance. Minutes from County Council meetings show that concern over design diminished as the controversy proceeded, replaced by more diffuse anxieties. Consequently, I prioritize the rhetorical strategies of supporters and opponents because I argue that one highly salient factor in this unfolding rhetorical situation was the identity of the statue's supporters as *children*—specifically, children who were seen as threatening sanctioned public memories of Los Alamos's role in World War II.

---

3. See Dingmann, "Statue Unites" and "Peace and Perseverance."

Figure 3 Detail from Children's Peace Statue. Photo courtesy of Richard Loyd.

The children who raised funds and mobilized supporters make this case an instance—rarely studied in rhetorical scholarship—of children exercising rhetorical agency. Even as our field has embraced theories of agency that include objects, environments, and nonhuman animals, we still have difficulty perceiving children as rhetorical agents.[4] As posthumanist conceptions of agency as dispersed, partial, and contingent have gained ground, children have persisted as figures that elude even our capacious theories. When I speak about this case with other scholars in rhetoric, I am often met with skepticism about the extent to which the children who supported the statue—children as young as eight and as old as eighteen— acted "on their own," or without adult or teacher guidance. Certainly, the children who wrote letters, called press conferences, spoke in churches and bookstores, and gave radio and television interviews did not act alone. Two teachers at Arroyo del Oso Elementary School, Christine Luke and Caroline Gassner, provided space for the project's creation when they led a discussion with their third and fourth grade class about what kids could do to prevent war. Luke and Gassner also invited an Albuquerque-based international educator, Camy Condon, to talk with students about the book *Sadako and the Thousand Paper Cranes*, by Eleanor Coerr, which

---

4. My thanks to Paul Lynch for this insight. Among recent scholarship on agency, see Jane Bennett; Marilyn M. Cooper; Thomas Rickert.

helped students link their plan to build a peace statue with the statue dedicated to Sadako Sasaki in Hiroshima. Condon's experience with international peacebuilding efforts made her an important advisor as the children outlined and pursued a five-year plan for promoting, fundraising, designing, and dedicating a "sister statue" to the peace statue in Hiroshima. As the roster of children involved in the project shifted over the years, teachers and librarians who incorporated the project into their classrooms provided important continuity; and certain strategies for garnering support, such as inviting Sig Hecker, director of Los Alamos National Laboratory, to become an honorary advisor to the project, would not likely have occurred to children lacking prior experience in municipal governance.

Yet even as I acknowledge this support, I could also recount the project's development in terms that emphasize the children's independence and rhetorical savvy. It was children who decided at the first press conference in 1990 to locate the statue in Los Alamos; who composed press releases for newspapers around the country; who decided what to say at public meetings to persuade the Council to respond to their requests. Students who participated in the project recall it as student-directed, and major decisions—about timelines, strategies for fundraising and publicizing, design and location for the statue, and so on—lay with the children who spoke, not with parents and teachers who drove them to meetings. Children sent information about the statue to newspapers, magazines, and religious publications across the country; they spoke at unscripted events at bookstores, churches, convention centers, and in radio and television interviews; they advertised in area newspapers to invite other students to monthly meetings at an Albuquerque pizza place; they created a newsletter, *The Crane*, distributing thousands of copies of each issue; and they created an early computer database to log donations and keep track of the names of donors—all 50,000 of which were read aloud during the statue's 31-day dedication ceremony in August 1995. I am reluctant to discount these collective activities by reciting a narrative that prioritizes adult guidance, rather than permits that children could in fact be the instigators and organizers of such rhetorical activity.

More significantly, posing the question of agency in relation to this case—to what extent were these children *really* agents?—highlights the recalcitrance of our collective ideas about what constitutes agency. This reluctance echoes that of the peace statue's opponents and motivates my investigation into children's collective rhetorical activity. Through this essay I document children's efforts in the early 1990s to constitute an international constituency capable of revising the inherited global politics of the Cold War era. Through rhetorical tactics of amplification and through strategic spatial and temporal linkages that asserted their existence as a powerful speaking body, supporters of the Children's Peace Statue asserted their agency and the legitimacy of their political collective. These tactics were subverted by adult dissent, which not only reasserted dominant public memories—of the bomb as necessary and peace-initiating—but also resisted recognizing the agency of children speakers.

In what follows, I first discuss contemporary scholarship from the emerging field of childhood studies not only to highlight *childhood* as a constructed, historically shifting category, but also to argue that children are yoked to temporality in ways that undermine their rhetorical agency. I then analyze competing claims surrounding public memories of Los Alamos and World War II voiced by statue supporters and opponents as members of the Kids' Committee petitioned the Los Alamos County Council in 1992, 1994, and 1995 to request a site for the statue. As I show, despite efforts of children rhetors to garner support for the future-oriented meanings they hoped the statue would generate, opponents of the statue disputed these meanings to reassert dominant public memories of the bombings of Hiroshima and Nagasaki as peace-initiating. Adult opponents reaffirmed the legitimacy of these dominant public memories by resisting engaging with children as speaking agents, figuring the children instead as (at best) innocent idealists and (at worst) puppets being maneuvered by adults into arguments and agendas they were incapable of understanding. Drawing upon a range of materials, including minutes from Los Alamos County Council meetings, news coverage of these meetings, and archival materials retained by participants in the project, I highlight the strategies children adopted, then trace the tactics by which adult opponents divested these speakers of agency.

Children, Agency, and Public Memory

The interdisciplinary field of childhood studies has drawn new and sustained attention to the ways in which *childhood* is a historically contingent category, imbued with meanings and contained by boundaries that vary across time and place.[5] Such scholarship underscores the myriad ways in which childhood is "not only a biological fact but a cultural construct that encodes the complex, ever-shifting logic of a given group" (Levander and Singley 4). By tracing this shifting logic, scholars have highlighted the distinction between children as figures exchanged within an adult discourse that excludes them (Rose) and children as actual political subjects—or, in Karen Sánchez-Eppler's phrase, the "disjunction between the rhetorical power of childhood and its lived precariousness" (xv). For instance, scholars have contrasted how crucial children are as *figures*—of innocence, of technological savvy, of heteronormative futurity, and so on—with how frequently they are vacated of agency in the media. Advertisements, news features, and pleas for international aid often employ representations of children to motivate adult action (Moeller 39), while displacing actual children's complex experiences of agency and vulnerability.

The pervasive power of children as figures depends on their association with future and past temporalities. Queer theorist Lee Edelman, in particular, has argued that children serve as "obligatory token[s] of futurity" (12), figures that constrain political possibilities by serving as "the repository of variously sentimentalized cultural identifications" and by embodying "the telos of the social order," which must be maintained for the sake of the sentimentalized future child (11). Terming this figurative regime "reproductive futurism" (4), Edelman critiques the unquestioned way in which "the image of the Child, not to be confused with the lived experiences of any historical children, serves to regulate political discourse" (11). Other theorists have found children's temporal associations backward-turned, linking the past to the present through appeals to nostalgia. Erica Burman, for instance, argues that children serve as an "appeal to the past" (296) that mobilizes "nostalgias that ... are far from innocent" (297). Children serve both as idealized, hazy reminders of adults' own (scarcely or un-remembered) past, as well as equally idealized portents of the (unseeable, unreachable) future. These temporal linkages divest children of meaningful relationships with their own present, a present in which children do not only signify adult investments in past and future but also act with agentive capacity to influence the world around them. In other words, figurations of children as *the past of adults*, as *future adults*, and as *the future of adults* all rely on a fundamental binary that maintains children as

---

5. See Philippe Ariès; Jacqueline Rose; Sánchez-Eppler.

not adults, and, in particular, not *coeval* with adults, but inhabiting a different time; their agency is deferred to a later date, when they attain the status of adulthood. Scholarship in childhood studies has sought to challenge this practice by refusing to depict "children as locked into a process of becoming" and instead portraying children "as beings in the present, as creating their own cultures and ... as competent social actors" (Raby 79).

These pervasive representations reinforce the diminished agency of actual children. As Marah Gubar has argued, "the mere act of describing young people as voiceless can itself help *render* them voiceless" (452, emphasis in the original). For instance, persistently figuring children as "priceless, lovable, vulnerable innocents" (Best 4) creates a contingent relation of protection, in which adult protectiveness demands innocence and a corresponding lack of agency. Entrenched Romantic notions link children with "'innocence,' 'incapacity,' 'dependence,' 'wonder,'" and aphasia, or the inability to speak (Davis 20), making the child emblematic of a person who lacks the ability to speak for herself. As figures, children must bear uncomplicated meanings to motivate adult action; children who act with complex intentions lose their claim on adult protection and relinquish their hold on the status of *child*. Young children in particular are deployed as symbols of straightforward innocence, in contrast to "older children, especially teenagers," whose assertions of agency and capacity for independent meaning-making destabilize portrayals of them as "innocent" (Moeller 44). Because of the persistent connection between innocence and aphasia, children who *speak*—who assert, insist, and disagree, as in the case below—are rendered as anomalous, either not children or not innocent. As Gabrielle Owen has argued, "when we grant the child this kind of personhood, we no longer see a child" (256).

Recognizing children as agents asks scholars to revisit the ideals of competency and self-sufficiency that still infuse notions of adult agency as well. Wendy Hesford has argued this in relation to representations of children within transnational human rights discourses, where recognizing children as agents unsettles clear distinctions between dependency and self-sufficiency. Instead, Hesford suggests, "if we are to recognize children as political and moral subjects," we must acknowledge that "tensions between individual capacity and vulnerability, and between protection and empowerment, are not easily resolved" (*Spectacular* 186, 187). Similarly, Gubar has called for scholars to reckon with the shared quality of the forms of agency adults and children exercise. Gubar, echoing Bakhtin, argues that "from the moment we are born (and even before then) we are immersed in multiple discourses not of our own making that influence who we are, how we think, what we do and say—and we never grow out of this compromised state" (454). Viewing children as agents, that is, does not merely entail bestowing (adult) agency on children, but also foregrounds experiences of dependency, insufficiency, and limitation as characteristics of the agency adults exercise as well.

Scholarship in rhetoric has largely engaged with children as *objects* of discourse rather than as actors who produce discourse, who introduce complex meanings into their social worlds.[6] For instance, some scholars have examined how children are solicited or recruited into certain ideologies. Amy Lynn Heyse has analyzed how the United Daughters of the Confederacy (UDC) catechize children into distorted, mythical memories of the South; likewise, Michael S. Waltman has examined the pernicious tactics used by the Ku Klux Klan (KKK) to encourage children to consume hate speech uncritically. Yet both of these studies treat children as objects rather than agents of rhetorical practice. For instance, Waltman argues that "only by understanding the nature of these [unscrupulous rhetorical techniques] may we optimally inoculate our children against their vile messages" (23); to posit *inoculation* as a metaphor for children's engagement with the world of persuasion is to limit children's capacity for critical action and reflection quite significantly. Heyse similarly critiques the UDC for "target[ing] the South's most impressionable—its children—to carry on the Confederate cause into the future" (429). Such a focus aims to exonerate children from blame for their upbringing into racist ideologies, as well as to amplify the wrongness of the racist rhetorical practices these studies examine. Yet by focusing on how adults solicit children into problematic identifications, such scholarship resists understanding children as people whose meaning-making practices contribute to rather than merely receive cultural formations.

On the whole, rhetorical scholarship has treated children as "what fieldworkers would call a 'muted group,' rarely present in their own voices or testimonies and mediated for the most part in the officially sanctioned canons of adult reportage" (Davis 19). Because rhetorical

---

6. Two exceptions to this tendency can be found in recent work by Phyllis Mentzell Ryder and Hesford on Malala Yousafzai, which I discuss below.

agency is a measure of power, portraying children as recipients rather than agents of culture serves "only to disguise the gradient of power under which children [have been] comprehensively subjugated" (Davis 20). Scholars in rhetoric could contribute in important ways to the project of disrupting that subjugation by examining children's rhetorical activity as a mechanism for engaging with and intervening in unequal systems of power.

As the supporters of the peace statue quickly discovered, public memory is inescapably involved in such systems of power. Greg Dickinson, Brian L. Ott, and Eric Aoki have shown that "public museums, memorials, and other historical sites play a crucial role in the construction and maintenance of national mythologies, histories, and identities" (29). Memorial sites concretize certain public memories at the expense of others through processes of negotiation that are often highly contested. As Stephen H. Browne has suggested, "public memory does not just entail conflict but is in some way defined by it" (243); similarly, Carole Blair and Neil Michel have characterized public memory as "the very battleground upon which are fought issues of contemporary concern" (596). Rhetorical scholars have collectively demonstrated that public memory "speaks primarily about the structure of power in society" (Bodnar 15). Seeking to articulate their experiences of Cold War–era conflict, children supporters of the peace statue troubled official public memories in ways that prompted vociferous disagreement.

Public acts of remembering link past events to a community's present and future collective identity. Historian W. Fitzhugh Brundage has argued that "the identity of any group goes hand in hand with the continuous creation of its sense of the past" (9), making struggles over memory inevitably struggles about present and future configurations of a community. Memory formation is never static, but an ongoing production that employs narratives about the past in relation to shifting contemporary concerns. Voting against the statue, Councilor Denise Smith explained, "As a community, we have a right to define ourselves. This would define us as the people who bear the sole responsibility for the destruction of Hiroshima, and that's not appropriate" (Easthouse). Such assertions underscore the threat that unsanctioned public memories pose to a community's identity. The collective identity of Los Alamos, a town created for the Manhattan Project and still significantly dependent on federal contracts, depends on maintaining public memories that celebrate the bomb as a scientific accomplishment rather than a source of blame, trauma, or tragedy.

The interventions into public memory posed by supporters of the peace statue were doubly threatening to residents of Los Alamos because of the identity of these rhetors as children. Temporal associations of children with futurity extend their figurative power forward in time; consequently, the promotion of a peace statue by children portended a generational loss of control over public memory. The ideological anxieties the project raised for opponents were heightened by these temporal linkages, prompting opponents to see the project as signifying a usurpation of cherished community identities, as "the greatest generation" would be supplanted by children—future adults—who, lacking first-hand recollections of wartime sacrifice, promulgated unacceptable counter-memories.

Perhaps in retrospect it seems inevitable that such a project would fail. One of my goals in approaching these materials, however, is *not* to assume that failure was inevitable. As I show below, one tactic of opponents was to characterize the children as out of their depth, unaware of the broader context that made their arguments threatening to cherished public memories. Approaching these children as rhetorical agents means holding open the prospect of their success rather than recapitulating to the assertions of opponents who drew substantial rhetorical power from characterizing the children who addressed them as naïvely unaware of the complexities of adult conflicts. Consequently, I show how these children acted to shape public memory through the creation of a material object meant to concretize children *as* a collectivity capable of engaging in public acts of meaning-making. Turning later to adult responses, I show how the association of children with innocence provides adult opponents with argumentative resources for subverting children's efforts to act as meaning-making agents in public life.

Children's Rhetorical Tactics

From the project's beginnings in 1990 through the dedication of the statue in 1995, children worked persistently to intervene in public life. Members of the Kids' Committee drafted flyers, mimeographed donation forms, organized scores of events to promote the project and raise funds, worked to identify a sculptor and foundry to craft the statue, and debated with elected officials and adult citizens over the meanings of peace, war, and memorialization.

Despite this wide-reaching rhetorical activity, children clearly constitute a "muted group" in the minutes of the LACC meetings at which they spoke. In contrast to detailed quotations recorded from councilors and adult members of the public who attended the meetings, arguments made by children on behalf of the statue are summarized in two sentences: "Approximately fifteen young children and teenagers from as far away as Albuquerque addressed the Council concerning the peace monument. The Council was encouraged to provide a place in the County for the placement of the monument" (LACC, *Council Regular Session Meeting* [1992] 4). In the analysis that follows, I read promotional material and correspondence alongside news coverage and meeting minutes to locate evidence of the rhetorical strategies children employed. These materials suggest that children speaking in support of the statue employed three major rhetorical tactics: *amplification, spatial linkages*, and *temporal identifications*.

Amplification

Children used amplification as a rhetorical strategy to increase the force of their voices by positioning themselves as speaking for thousands of other children. At the 1992 meeting when the group first petitioned the Council for land, numerous students asserted that they were speaking for others—for a group of youth at Los Alamos High School, for students who collected signatures from other supporters, for other kids who learned about the project and sent letters, and so on. One said: "I got several letters from kids in Silver City and I am sending these to you but I decided that I'd read one ... 'Dear City Council People, My name is Crystal Ness. Please give the land for the Peace Statue because I would like to see a statue for peace'" (*On Wings of Peace* 6–7). Many of the promotional materials circulated by the Kids' Committee recount the support the project had received from others—both adult and child, individual and collective—in ways that frame the statue as a project pursued by a broad national and international collective. For instance, the first issue of *The Crane*, the kid-produced newsletter for supporters of the project, features a large two-page spread containing all the names of supporters collected through May 1991 (Figures 4 and 5).

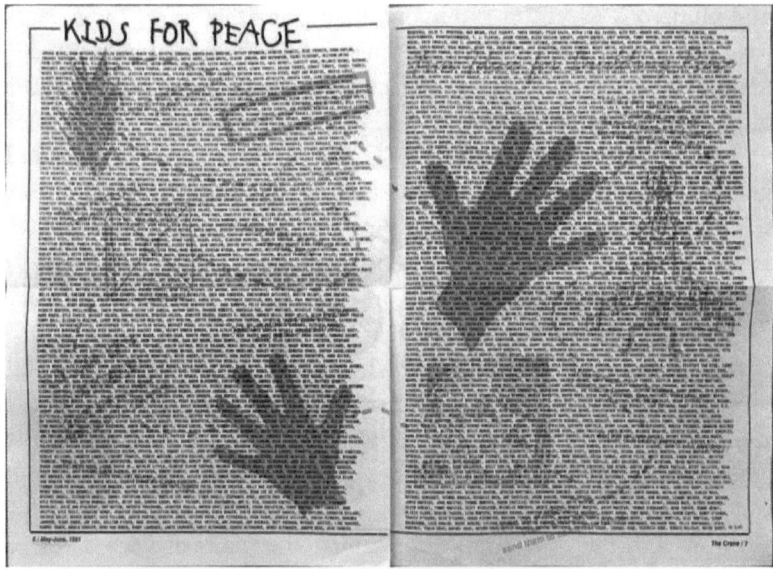

Figure 4 "Kids for Peace." Names of supporters, printed in The Crane 1.1 (1991). Courtesy of Camy Condon.

SALAZAR, BENJI GUILLEN, BETH ESQUIVEL, MAGGY ROMERO, GENE WILLIAMS, ANTONIO
ACSHANE, NINO ANGELINO, ASHLEY WEITZEL, REBECCA COHEN, SHAYNA LAZAR,LUCAS
IN HARVEY, KARA HARVEY, MARGARET HARVEY, AMANDA KUEHNTOPZ, ANNA KUISUR,
KARISSA MCCALL, PAULA ROSA PODEHL, ANNA JENNIFER PODEHL, SHOHREH BIAJAR,
, CORY GUINEE, ELISE GUINEE, ZACHARIE JACOBS, CASSIE JACOBS, ALEXANDRA JACOBS
ISEN, KATY MOSES, JEFFRY MOSES, GRETCHEN MOSES, HEIDI MOSES, LETTA NIGGLI,
AN DEWALD, SARA SCHMOE, MIWA ITO, CHIE HIROSE, YOKO AKANA, SASHA SCHENK,
KEMORE, CHRISTINE MURRAY, ANDREA GOULD, STEPHEN WEIL, MATTHEW GENNETT,
, NICOLE BOWDICH, JEREMY ROTUNNO, JASON ROTUNNO, MATTHEW ROTUNNO, KIAH ROTUNN
AH JOHNSON, KYLE JOHNSON, KENNETH JOHNSON, NATHAN JOHNSON, MARTIN LOPEZ,
TE, JUAN MONTES, GRANT DRUMMOND, REBECCA CLARK, JOELLE STEINBECK, HERMETTA
JENNY RILL, REBECCA SYNDERGUARD, ANGIE RUIZ, CHRIS CHAVEZ, CHRISTY STRAIGHT,
I, BRADLEY SCHRAMM, MINDY SCHRAMM, TREVOR SCHRAMM, MELISA JONES, TYLER JONES,
AN, ERIK BROADUS, JASON BROADUS, SKHYE GARCIA-WIX, BRIANA GARCIA-WIX, ERTUGRUL
HERTEL, CHRISTIANNE HERTEL, MICHELLE TRUJILLO, SHAWN VON DREELE, ROSA HAGAR,
IN, SHOSHANNA, DAVID CHAVEZ, HEATHER GATT, NATHANIEL GOTTLIEB, BLAISE TREESON,
TOMMY TECHENTIEN, NATHAN GARCIA, SARA TWEIST, ABRA ANCLIFFE, DAVID MAESTES,
ARRASCO, ANNAROSE SCHWARTZ, KATIE KELLY, JESSICA FRELUND, JUDD FRELUND,
LY ROSE VOGLER, JESSIE VOGLER, PHOENIX YOUNG-TANTUM, SARAH YOUNG, KAYLA LYALL,
ON, LINDI LANCON, CAMILLE LANCON, KYLE POIRIER, SHAWN POIRIER, JONATHAN POIRIE
STINE PAPPIAN, BRANDDON PAPILLION, RAQUEL CHARLES, MARKEYNA DICKS,
WITHERWAX, SHARHONDA OTIS, RACHELLE LANDRY, VINDETTA JOHNSON, NICOLE CHRÉTIEN
JIMMY GUILLORY, BRANDON RELEFORD, JASMINE OLIVIER, ADAM THIBODEAUX, RICHARD
UNT, TIFFANIE HARMON, KIMBERLY THIBODEAUX, JOHN BILLIOT, DURRELL WASHINGTON,
THON, MAJORIE ELIZABETH BREDA, ADRIENNE BELLOW JOLIVETTE, MICHAEL GAVAZZA,
ICERO, JEREMY MONTOYA, JEANETTE R. LONGO, VERONICA SANCHEZ, JESSICA CARRILLO,
ALBAS, AMBER YOUNG, MONICA MENDOZA, CAROLINA MARIE CALDERON, JESSICA ELLEN
AMES MATHEW SCHWECHERL, SARAH SIMPSON, KATIE GUIFFRE, TRACY O'BRIEN,
OLTS, CORINE CHESTER, MOLLY MAE CHESTER, ERIKA GUISTI, ERIN SUE MOCHRIE,
ATHER LYNN DE VILLIERS, RYAN LEE DE VILLIERS, BRADLEY JAMES DE VILLIERS,
NDA ANGELL, STEPHANIE HYDE, JUSTIN PAUL HYDE, ERIN CHRISTINE REEVE,
ERICA SOUTHWORTH, AMY C. PIA, CHARLES CORTEZ, MELISSA GRIFFIN, STEPHANIE
DREW GRAY, JULIE CONNER, CHAVA EDELSTEIN, TORRE HUNTER, TREY LANGLEY, ANNE
SON, ROBIN BANKER, CHRIS REEVES, QUINCY HARRIS, TODD GAYLORD, CHAQUITA WILLARD,
HODGE, AMY FITZGERALD, CHAD FLOYD, JENELLE WILLIAMS, JANIKA FLOWERS, DURENDA
GRIFFIN, AMY PARHAM, AMY ROEBUCK, MATT SHERMAN, MICHAEL JUSTICE, LINC HANCOCK,
LY ALTHAUSER, CASSIE ALTHAUSER, DEREK ALTHAUSER, JOSEPH BECK, JESS CHARLES

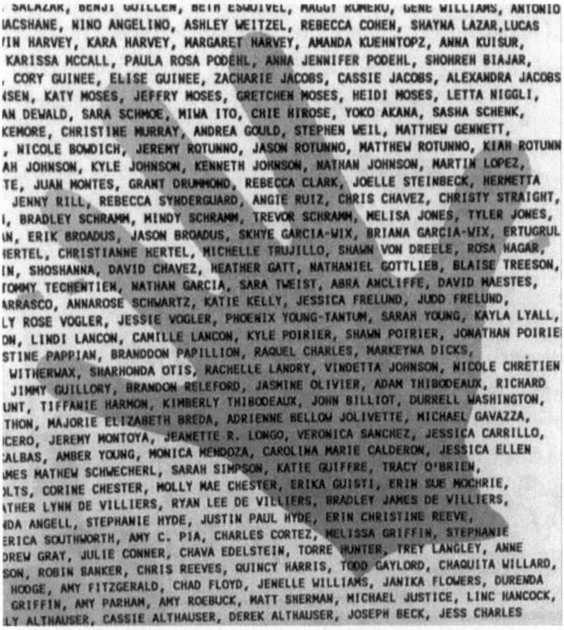

Figure 5 Detail from "Kids for Peace," printed in The Crane 1.1 (1991). Courtesy of Camy Condon.

The numerous names in extremely small print that cover these pages have an augmentative effect, becoming not merely a list but accumulating into a visual representation of mass support. Blue text behind the printed names invites readers to join this collective by suggesting "Fun Ideas for Building Peace," such as "Take photos of peace events and send them to us" or "Have an art show or auction." Blue handprints stand out against the names, signaling the members of this collective as *children*, even as the names themselves evoke the (typically adult) political project of petitioning—a time-honored amplification strategy employed by the disenfranchised that I discuss more fully below.

Children's amplification strategies took embodied and material forms as well. Although approximately twenty children spoke at the 1992 LACC meeting, those twenty were augmented by a large, visible group of supporters in the audience— roughly one hundred children and two dozen parents and teachers who attended to show their support. In addition, one speaker presented the Council with a list of names of thousands of other children—more than 10,000—who had contributed money in support of the project. A document of this size is obviously not meant to be read; its purpose is to amplify the force of the children's petition by portraying— and helping the Council to visualize—thousands of absent others who likewise support the project. As she presented this list to the Council, Bonnie Malcolm said, "in these names, of 10,000 children, we ask for land" (*On Wings of Peace* 2).

Presenting the list of names to the Council as a request on behalf of 10,000 individuals connects this amplification strategy to the long-standing practice of public petition. Rhetorical scholars Alisse Theodore Portnoy and Susan Zaeske have articulated the importance of public petition among nineteenth-century U.S. women, for whom the act of petitioning signaled not only specific political desires but also their right to speak to a governing body that granted them no voting rights. Through anti-removal campaigns, women "intruded into an exclusive discourse community" and laid claim to national, political space (Portnoy 603); likewise, women who participated in abolitionist petition campaigns "bypassed the requirement of suffrage to participate publicly in the political debate over the heated national issue of slavery" (Zaeske 148). The strategy of amplification employed by children supporters of the peace statue functioned similarly by simultaneously strengthening the speakers' request and *constituting* the speakers themselves within a civic space that grants children no legal right of address. As Zaeske argues, understanding public petitions in this way focuses our attention on petitioning as a political act that "reformulate[s] ... the political subjectivity of the rhetors themselves" (148). In the antebellum United States, exclusions from voting were based on an ideal political subject "who was to be a rational actor capable of independent thought and action" (149). Many disenfranchised residents "fell outside" categorization as political subjects because of "their status as dependents ... believed to lack capacity for rational thought" (149). The amplification tactics of peace statue supporters likewise draw attention to political exclusion; supporters amplified their claims and claimed political subjectivity not only at Council meetings but also—perhaps most insistently—at the dedication itself, when names of all 50,000 supporters were read aloud dur ing a month of events held throughout August 1995. Reading supporters' names aloud extends the act of petition into public space, claiming status as members of a collective who speak their desires through the statue.

The strands of folded paper cranes that frequently figured in the public discourse of children supporters constituted a further form of material amplification. The children often located their project's origins in the narrative of Sadako Sasaki, a Japanese girl who died of leukemia at age twelve in 1955; Sasaki, following a Japanese folk belief, hoped to be granted her wish for health if she folded one thousand origami cranes. After her death, her classmates organized a youth movement to dedicate a peace memorial in her honor; strands of one thousand paper cranes are still left daily at this statue in Hiroshima. While single origami cranes symbolize peace, the chains of one thousand cranes folded by student supporters of the statue make visible and material both the care of individual children and the collective power of their work together. That is, each delicate origami crane is folded by a particular individual, an act that takes only a slight amount of skill, time, and resources, but these individual contributions become substantial when linked into chains of one thousand. Strands of folded cranes consequently emblematize the collective, the pooling of energies toward a project that would be, similarly, the linked, larger result of small individual efforts joined together.

In 1992, in addition to a massive list of names, the children employed the visible, material abundance of nine thousand folded paper cranes to augment the presence of speakers in the room by recalling the presence of thousands of other supporters elsewhere. This connection was reinforced by the student who presented the cranes, saying, "In addition to the 10,000 children [who contributed their money and names], we represent many other thousands of children who have sent their support in the form of paper cranes. ... I guess what this means to you is that those of us here tonight represent the 10,000 people and others who have helped us make all these cranes. We all ask for your support" (*On Wings of Peace* 4–5). Students' amplification strategies attempt to make manifest to the Council their collective of thousands, and suggest that the children anticipated the difficulty they faced in addressing an elected body where their collective had no formal standing.

Spatial Linkages

Forming spatial linkages with children around the world offered supporters a further avenue for amplification by constituting their discourse as originating from a national and international rather than merely local community. Presenting their original petition to the Council, children highlighted the geographic scope of the letters and donations they had received. One speaker emphasized that the children in the room "have come from all over New Mexico tonight; from Albuquerque, from Los Alamos, from Espanola" (*On Wings of Peace* 2); another explained that the 10,000 names presented to the Council come from "49 states in the US" as well as kids in "53 countries who support our dream" (*On Wings of Peace* 2). A flyer created by the Kids' Committee in 1994 likewise emphasized that the project had "received support from all over the world with names of over 41,000 children from all 50 states and 63 different countries." Highlighting origins of donations helped the Albuquerque-based group invoke a global collective of children supporting the statue's message of peace.

In addition, the Kids' Committee created more specific spatial linkages with Japan. They identified their proposed statue as a "sister statue" to Japan's Children's Peace Monument, *Genbaku no ko no zo*, dedicated in 1958 in the Hiroshima Peace Memorial Park that occupies central Hiroshima. Through the "sister statue" designation, the Kids' Committee highlighted the precedent-setting nature of that earlier statue as one proposed and funded by children. For instance, a photograph and drawing of the Japanese statue were featured in the initial issue of *The Crane*, with a narrative explaining that the current project

> was inspired by the Japanese statue called "Genbaku No Ko No Zo," (Atomic Bombed Children), constructed in the Hiroshima Peace Park after the Second World War. Following the war, Japanese children raised funds and urged the building of a peace statue. They were led by the classmates of Sadako Sasaki, a young girl who was a victim of radiation sickness and who died ten years after the war. The dream of U.S. children today is to design and build a "sister" statue, to be created by student design and student raised funds, in New Mexico, the state in which the first nuclear bombs were built and where the first nuclear test bomb was dropped on July 16, 1945. (Condon 1)

The Japanese statue is likewise depicted on a 1990 flyer that was reprinted in numerous periodicals, and a prayer attributed to Sasaki, "I will write peace on your wings and you will fly all over the world," was printed on promotional materials and donation forms. During the initial presentation to the Council in 1992, Ben Nathanson, a student supporter, recounted Sasaki's story in detail, beginning with the bombing of Hiroshima during her childhood and concluding with the unveiling of the Japanese statue in 1958, a story that, Nathanson argues, "shows even little children have big dreams and I think this story inspires young minds" (*On Wings of Peace* 3–4).

Although the Japanese statue provided a precedent for the children's public action, symbolically linking Los Alamos with Hiroshima through a parallel statue was important as well. In a 1990 flyer distributed to periodicals across the country, members of the Kids' Committee explain:

> Maybe you don't know it, but Los Alamos, New Mexico was the place where the first nuclear bombs were made during World War II. From Los Alamos, two atomic bombs named "Little Boy" and "Fat Man" were carried by plane to Japan and dropped on the cities of Hiroshima and Nagasaki at the end of the war in 1945. ... Now we want to create a Children's Peace Statue in the United States in the city of Los Alamos. By this action we are saying NO to war.

When addressing the LACC, supporters did not invoke the trajectory of the bombs so directly but instead emphasized the message of peace the statue in Hiroshima bears. The children deployed the project's links to Japan in a polysemic fashion, finding this spatial connection useful for different arguments and audiences— although their opponents likewise used these spatial connections to assert that the statue was tied "too much to World War II" (LACC, *Council Work Session* 12) to be acceptable, as I discuss more fully below.

Temporal Identifications

In addition to creating international linkages, children used temporal tactics to constitute their collective. Supporters emphasized age, rather than language or nationality, as the primary identification organizing the dispersed global community they sought to construct. For instance, they reprinted in *The Crane*, in their original languages, letters from Russian and Japanese supporters; poetry, drawings, and photographs printed in the newsletter usually included the age of the children who submitted them. The title of their governing organization, the Kids' Committee for Peace, itself reinforces this age-based identification, attaching "kid" as a possessive modifier to the bureaucratic, adult structure of a "committee." In their ambition to "reach one million kids who want peace," the Kids' Committee reinforced their agency by reminding readers that *kids* were in charge of the project, generating its energy and scope.

They also oriented their project toward the future rather than the past. In public statements and printed documents, supporters reiterated the statue's message: that kids want peace for the future. In their widely reprinted 1990 flyer, members of the Kids' Committee introduce themselves as "36 kids in New Mexico who have a dream of making a peaceful future for our world" and ask for support because "the future of the earth needs us to be united." A flyer from 1994 places this message in bold and all caps: "The Albuquerque children decided that their statue would represent their **HOPE FOR A PEACEFUL FUTURE**." Students worked to create a collective that could overcome geographical, national, and linguistic differences, unified around its members' identities as children who shared this desire for the future.

By emphasizing the statue's future orientation, supporters sought to eschew the perception that the statue would *memorialize* past events. For instance, responding to residents' concerns over "rewriting history" (*On Wings of Peace* 3), one member of the Kids' Committee, Jack Thornton, tried to redirect discussion toward the statue's future orientation, explaining

> If we didn't make it sufficiently clear earlier, this monument is not intended as a reminder that Hiroshima happened. Rather, this monument is intended as a sister statue to one that happens to be in Hiroshima, for peace. Our purpose here is not to remember wars that have happened, not to forget them or the people who died serving our country, or other countries. Rather, our purpose here is to look forward into time and do at least, in our way, some small project or something that will hopefully lead to a peaceful future where we won't have to be remembering wars and people who have died protecting others. (*On Wings of Peace* 7)

Another student invited the audience to "all look forward towards peace and not back on pain and suffering" (*On Wings of Peace* 5). At the 1994 meeting, asked to comment on why Los Alamos was chosen, Bonnie Malcolm explained that the members of the Kids' Committee "want a peaceful future, nothing more, nothing less ... [and] to work together to get over the past" (LACC *Council Regular Session Meeting* [1994] 10). Similarly, David Rosoff reiterated that "the statue's message would be that adults of today would use their power to create a peaceful future for those of tomorrow" (*Council Regular Session Meeting* [1994] 10). At the final meeting in 1995, Dana Kaplan insisted "that the project evolved beyond World War II. It is a hope for a peaceful future, and has nothing to do with Hiroshima or the atomic bomb" (LACC, *Council Work Session* 11). Adult supporters likewise reinforced this future orientation; Councilor Ginger Welch, the member of the Council who most strongly supported the statue, said at the final meeting, "the children ... want peace for the future of the world and ... that is what [the statue] stands for" (LACC, *Council Work Session* 9). A nun representing the Sisters of Loretto argued that the statue was "not a statement about the past, it is not about whether or not to have a defense program, Los Alamos bashing, or about making anyone feel guilty .. it is a children's prayer that the future of the world be without war" (LACC, *Council Work Session* 11). Such repeated assertions highlight the importance supporters accorded to the statue's future orientation; yet the necessity of insisting upon that orientation reflects the extent to which future meanings, present desires, and past narratives are deeply enmeshed. The vehement response the statue prompted from adult opponents underscores the fact that this project unavoidably offered an intervention into public memory, not merely a statement about the future.

Adult Re-Articulations

Recognizing agency as something children exercise in complex ways requires that we register the diverse effects of their public activism, even when their efforts appear to fail. Although opponents prevailed in preventing the statue from being located in Los Alamos, in what follows I argue that the intensity and variety of opponents' responses provide evidence of children's rhetorical agency. If children were incapable of public action, rejecting their project would not have demanded so much urgent rhetorical effort.

Even as supporters' status as children heightened the opposition their project provoked, the proposed intervention into public memory was itself provocative for residents of Los Alamos. Almost certainly, if a group of children had proposed a statue with symbolic valences more aligned with dominant memories of World War II—a memorial to commemorate the scientists of the Manhattan Project, for instance—the response from Los Alamos residents would have taken a different form. The nature of the children's project—its opposition to Cold War–era political formations, its posing of alternative forms of collectivities, and its supporters' status as unauthorized speakers—prompted the range and vigor of the oppositional tactics I chart below. This analysis invites rhetorical scholars to attend to how ideological opposition can be masked by strategies of re-articulation that draw on pervasive figurations of children as innocent, naïve, and lacking in agency. In this way, I argue, widespread representations of children as politically ineffectual served as an argumentative resource for opponents who employed such representations to resist the public action these children pursued and, thus, to reinforce the impossibility of children acting publicly.

Adults who opposed the statue resisted children's agency in myriad ways. For instance, some adults' tactics of heckling and shouting to prevent teenagers from speaking during Council meetings serve as an effective, if uncivil, way to foreclose the possibility of rhetorical exchange. Such behavior bespeaks not only the intensity of local investment in dominant public memories of Los Alamos's wartime role, but also a deep reluctance to address and be addressed by children. Other tactics of resistance operate more subtly—and more civilly—than simply shouting to prevent a child from speaking. These tactics enable adult opponents to refuse not only the children's petition, but more fundamentally the claim to agency and political subjectivity they staged through the project.

Adult opponents subjected the students who addressed the LACC to a range of kinds of dismissal. Some raised concerns about the "process" the students had adopted in petitioning the Council for land. Councilor Morris Pongratz, for instance, who was fiercely opposed to the statue—he spoke against it at length as a member of the public in 1992, before he was elected to the Council—argued in the final public meeting that "the United States has a ratified way for addressing ways to change government policies and he is concerned that the process that is being advocated is not one of electing people and changing something if you don't like it" (LACC, *Council Work Session* 7–8). Other Los Alamos residents likewise proposed that the issue "should be referred to the voters" (LACC, *Council Work Session* 9). Yet children do not have access to the electoral citizenship Pongratz privileges, and resistance to the *form* of children's advocacy ignores the extent to which these citizens lack access to electoral channels.

Frequently, children were subjected to lessons about the futility of their project. Pongratz, for instance, argued in the 1992 meeting that "the real place where we need peace is within our hearts and he is not sure how much a monument does for that" (LACC, *Council Regular Session Meeting* [1992] 5). Praising "actions" over "monuments," Pongratz "would rather see $1 million spent trying to feed the hungry people in Somalia rather than spend $1 million on a statue" (LACC, *Council Regular Session Meeting* [1992] 6). Many others repeated the idea that more good could be accomplished in some other way—by providing food or housing for the poor, assistance for children whose parents are unemployed, medications for children in Russia, and so on. Opponents characterized the project as "dewy-eyed sentiment" (Schaller, "What Was Said" A3) or "wishful thinking" (LACC, *Council Work Session* 9) that could never accomplish the children's ambitious goals. These dismissive characterizations deny children's agency by denying that the project could have the effects children claimed for it.

Adult opponents (as well as many supporters) repeatedly asserted the children's innocence. Many who voiced concern about the potential message of the statue tempered their critiques by affirming that they trusted the children's "pure" motives. One critical resident, for instance, granted that "the project has been promulgated with excellent intentions, but is misdirected" (LACC, *Council Regular Session Meeting* [1992] 4), and Councilor Bob Fisher noted that, although he opposed the statue, "no one in the room doubts the intentions of the children here tonight" (LACC, *Council Regular Session Meeting* [1992] 6). Adult supporters of the project voiced similar affirmations; JoAnn Dowler, a Los Alamos teacher, introduced the children by stating that their "motives are pure and uncomplicated" (LACC, *Council Regular Session Meeting* [1992] 3), and Councilor Welch affirmed numerous times that "the children have a sincere and honest motive" (LACC, *Council Work Session* 9). Such repetition, although intended as support, represents the children as incapable of voicing any serious challenge to preferred public memories of Los Alamos. The strong association of children with innocence has the effect of blunting and subverting the power they claimed—both in the act of petitioning the Council and in the possibilities they ascribed to the statue in their own letters and promotional flyers.

The insistence on viewing children as innocent also reveals the contingent nature of adult protection, which children can expect only so long as they refrain from asserting their agency. Many opponents' civility diminished as their certainty of the children's innocence weakened. One city official wrote to the Council that she was "forced to question the motives of the Kids['] Committee and their adult advisors" because the children's stubborn resolve to hold an August dedication caused her to suspect that they were planning disruptive anti-war demonstrations (LACC, *Council Regular Session Meeting* [1994] 11). Pongratz likewise expressed skepticism regarding the children's innocence, complaining that the Council was "told that they are innocent children, pure of heart and untainted by the adult world and that the Council should not question that" (LACC, *Council Work Session* 8). Pongratz was particularly willing to engage with children confrontationally. In the 1994 meeting, after teenager Bonnie Malcolm explained that "the point is that [Sadako's] statue was built and funded by children," and that an August dedication is important "because this symbolizes the beginning of a new era to come, since the nuclear age is coming to its end" (LACC, *Council Regular Session Meeting* [1994] 10), Pongratz responded that he "did not 'buy' her comments. If it is to be a sister image to the one in Hiroshima, Japan, one might think that it would be dedicated in the month in which she died" (LACC, *Council Regular Session Meeting* [1994] 10). Through strong associations between innocence and incapacity, the tolerant attitude adopted by some opponents eroded as the children's requests threatened to become reality.

One consequence of opponents' resistance to children's agency is that statements about the children as *innocent* could be converted into assertions about the children as *dupes*. As Kathleene Parker, writer for the Santa Fe *New Mexican*, reported in 1995, "opponents have claimed the idea in fact originated with adult peace activists who are exploiting children as a way to get the statue built in Los Alamos" ("Councilor" B1). Councilor Pongratz circulated an agenda packet before the 1995 meeting that asserted that the entire project, in Pongratz's words, was "all part of an adult put-up plan," specifically by Camy Condon, the adult advisor who Pongratz said "went shopping for kids gullible enough to think [the idea] was their own" (Parker, "Councilor" B1). Letters to the *Los Alamos Monitor* likewise asserted that adult activists were exploiting the children "to further their questionable cause" (Vigil 4). Under the guise of concern over "exploitation," these portrayals reveal a reluctance to engage with children as speaking agents. If children are innocent, they are not agents but puppets, which allows opponents to argue more comfortably against the adult activists who are seen as ultimately generating their discourse. This tactic suggests analytically what childhood studies scholars have argued more theoretically: that our ideas about, and language about, children as powerless innocents help to constitute that powerlessness.

Opponents also adopted tactics of rearticulation by which they revised the children's lines of argument. Specifically, adult opponents reframed the project's spatial and temporal linkages in ways that recast supporters as outsiders, irrelevantly distant from the meaningful community of Los Alamos residents, and that generated anxiety about future uses of the statue—especially future demonstrations by antinuclear activists.

Children's efforts to forge spatial links with Japan in particular and with an international community of children more generally were rearticulated by adult opponents in ways that turned supporters of the statue into community outsiders. Despite the presence of many Los Alamos students and teachers among the supporters, councilors and members of the public who spoke against the statue effectively reframed the project as one originating *outside* Los Alamos, and consequently without jurisdiction. For instance, in the final meeting in 1995, when Councilor Greenwood "stated that he was elected to represent Los Alamos, not Northern New Mexico, Albuquerque, etc." (LACC, *Council Work Session* 8), this statement was greeted with applause (Schaller, "What Was Said" A3). Even though two hundred Los Alamos residents submitted their signatures in support of the statue (Parker, "Los Alamos," A1), opponents who attended the meeting referred to the statue's supporters as "external people" (LACC, *Council Work Session* 10) and asserted that Los Alamos "should not accept anything from outside the community" (LACC, *Council Work Session* 10). After voting again to reject the statue, Councilor Greenwood closed discussion of the matter by reminding the audience that the Council would not "prohibit doing something like this if there is an interest within the community. His opposition is primarily the external nature of it" (LACC, *Council Work Session* 13). Framing the children as outsiders permits opponents to reject the statue while insisting that their community supports children and peace, casting their opposition as a problem of jurisdiction rather than of message.

The project's specific spatial linkages with Japan provided opponents with further resources for positioning it as inappropriate for Los Alamos. These included racist and xenophobic responses from opponents who figured Japan as an enemy. One woman asserted that if not for the atomic bomb, "everyone in the room" would be "speaking Japanese and bowing to the Japanese" if not "being kicked by them" (Schaller, "What Was Said" A3). Another opponent, Al Charmatz, proposed a design for the statue that would feature "a panel showing Battleship Row at Pearl Harbor listing the names of the thousands of seamen who are still inside the Arizona ... another panel showing the New Mexico National Guard and the Bataan Death March with soldiers being decapitated and shot ... right across the top should be the immortal words of Harold Agnew, former Director [of Los Alamos National Labs], 'They bloody well deserved it'" (LACC, *Council*

Regular Session Meeting [1992] 5). The hostility of these responses underscores how deeply the project threatened local identities and public memories. The designation of the project as a "sister statue" to the peace statue in Hiroshima prompted many opponents to propose alternate locations, especially Pearl Harbor and Washington, D.C., as more "parallel" to Hiroshima. Councilor Denise Smith, for instance, suggested Washington, D.C., as "a place where decisions are really made as to whether we enter into conflicts" (LACC, *Council Regular Session Meeting* [1994] 10), and Councilor Pongratz argued that "symmetry" with the peace statue in Hiroshima "would suggest a Pearl Harbor memorial—perhaps in Japan" (Pongratz 4). Although the children tried to assert that the project "evolved beyond WWII" (LACC, *Council Work Session* 11), opponents drew upon the project's links to Hiroshima to rearticulate the project as unsuitable.

Likewise, although the children used age to constitute an international community of supporters, opponents used this to position them as outsiders in a temporal sense, arguing that children could not legitimately participate in public memory formation about events they had not witnessed. This argument is implicit in opponents' characterization of children as "people generations away from the times, people who seem never to have heard of Pearl Harbor" (LACC, *Council Work Session* 10). Not only the specific children who represented the statue at meetings, but children and teenagers in general were depicted as disqualified from participating in public memories of World War II. For instance, a long editorial by Evelyn Vigil, publisher of the *Los Alamos Monitor*, recounted a visit to the *USS Arizona* Memorial during which "a couple of teen-agers in front of me ... giggled and pointed and acted up enough to draw a sharp retort from the tour guide" and, eventually, to be prevented from entering the memorial (4). Vigil's diagnosis was that "these kids didn't know history. They had no sense of what had happened at this site, no sense of what it means to go to war, and so they had no sense of what is proper respect at a place like this" (4). These unruly teenagers were excluded, Vigil suggested, not only because they misbehaved, but more fundamentally because of their inability to access the wartime experience of earlier generations. Vigil linked the teenagers in this anecdote with those supporting the peace statue, writing that "while it's right to seek peace at every opportunity ... the teen-agers who acted up ... probably never knew anyone who went to war. They probably never really thought about the sacrifice a war demands. And, I wonder, would they be tough enough to answer the call, if they were needed?" (4). This perennial complaint about disrespectful teenagers serves, in the context of the peace statue controversy, to substitute disruptive teenagers, ignorant of history, for the collective of thousands of children working together to create a monument to peace. In place of the specific children who had attended County Council meetings and endeavored to speak while opponents shouted them down, Vigil substitutes generic teenagers at a memorial site where the only way to behave respectfully is to be silent. Furthermore, she shows these teenagers receiving a lesson in which their unruly behavior secures their exclusion. The anecdote depicts children simultaneously as disruptive—for failing to sustain imperiled public memories—and incapable of action, as figures who cannot be trusted with the future, because they will fail to act.

Finally, opponents shifted the temporal orientation of the statue into a source of fear about its durability—its capacity to enable unsanctioned uses and disruptive public memories in the future. Councilor Greenwood, for instance, called the statue a "soap box for people to come to Los Alamos to speak general opposition to what the community has believed over the years" (LACC, *Council Work Session* 12). Councilors were "worried that peace activists would employ the park for rallies" (Editorial A4), on the 50th anniversary and beyond. One editor of the *Los Alamos Monitor* conceded these fears in an editorial supporting the statue, explaining residents' "genuine concern about just what will happen in Los Alamos ... on the 50th anniversary of Hiroshima Day, when demonstrators who feel the bombing was wrong might interact with veterans ... and the presence of hundreds of children wouldn't help" (Schaller, "Peace Statue" 4). This fear over who might control the statue's future meanings underscores the way in which children's associations with futurity undermine their agency in the present.

Conclusion

Children who petitioned the LACC exercised agency in ways that challenge rhetorical scholars to revise our tendency to position children primarily as figures or objects of discourse. Using a range of strategies to address a forum where they lacked standing, children constituted an international collective of tens of thousands and employed the weight of that collective to stage an intervention into public memory. The vehemence of adult efforts to refuse the children's petition registers the viability of the children's strategies, even as opponents resisted acknowledging children as capable of such a meaningful public act. Children's complex rhetorical agency can be seen in the constellated effects their project generated, including not only materializing a statue but also provoking outrage, anxiety, and fevered attempts to reassert dominant public memories of World War II and the bombing of Hiroshima. Disrupting public space through their acts of speaking, organizing, and petitioning, these children in turn resisted the continuity of dominant public memories that adults in Los Alamos demanded. Treating children as "tokens of futurity," as Edelman and Gubar have argued, thus not only discounts the potential efficacy of their words and actions, but also, as this case shows, enables rhetorical practices that weaken their political possibilities in the present. Scholarship in rhetoric might better support such collective efforts not only by attending to children's argumentative tactics, but also by grappling with the way their presence shapes unfolding rhetorical situations, enabling and constraining patterns of response among the publics they address.

Further scholarship on the public activism of children might illuminate whether and to what extent children's possibilities for collective action have altered over the past two decades. Certainly, global and technological transformations since 1995 have shaped public life and collective possibility significantly. Yet recent rhetorical scholarship on the young activist Malala Yousafzai, for instance, draws attention to the ongoing challenge of acknowledging and grappling with the complexity of children's agency. Phyllis Mentzell Ryder and Wendy S. Hesford have both highlighted the tendency among international media to treat Yousafzai as a symbol—of liberal values of freedom and individual fulfillment, or of the cooptation of Muslim girlhood by the West—in ways that "lessen Malala's political agency by transforming her into a diminutive humanitarian subject" (Hesford, "Malala Effect" 145). Resisting such a tendency, Ryder argues, requires scholars to attend to Yousafzai's lived agency and actual words and tactics as a speaker. Hesford, likewise, asks rhetorical scholars to recognize "the intelligibility of Malala as an agent navigating the complex political machinery of rights, cultural norms, and the protocols of global engagement" ("Malala Effect" 143). As Hesford and Ryder's work shows, not only must scholars resist the tendency to discount or overlook children as rhetorical agents, but we must also identify how the scripts by which children are divested of agency intersect with other circulating narratives—narratives animated by gendered, geographic, racialized, and myriad other axes of difference. Scholars in rhetoric might, by undertaking further investigations into children's public activism, help to reveal the unfinished work of agency across a wide range of contemporary public sites.

Children speaking—collectively, publicly, insistently about past and future— undermine more comfortable practices that figure children as symbols of hope and goodness. Instead, children who speak designate themselves as agents who will bring about the world they desire. For instance, when children organize protests for immigration reform, advocate for particular local or national policies, form collectives to speak out against anti-Muslim or transphobic public discourse, scholars in rhetoric must work to register these activities as rhetorical efforts to articulate and bring about particular futures. Figuring children as "hope" signals their futurity, but children speaking about their hopes demand a stake in, and promise a struggle over, specific possible futures. Children speaking threaten to revise their own symbolic associations; they promise that past and present narratives will mean and do unsanctioned things in the future. They threaten, as this case in particular demonstrates, a loss of control over how a community is configured, who it includes, and what it values; in these ways children speaking demand our collective attention.

Acknowledgments

For generously sharing primary materials and discussing this project with me numerous times, I thank Camy Condon, Marilee Nason of the Anderson-Abruzzo Albuquerque International Balloon Museum, and my husband Matthew Loyd, who was one of the original participants in the Children's Peace Statue Project. Thanks as well to my writing group, Heather Branstetter, Sarah Hallenbeck, Chelsea Redeker Milbourne, Lindsay Rose Russell, and Erin Branch, and to two anonymous reviewers who provided generous feedback on this essay.

Works Cited

Ariès, Philippe. *Centuries of Childhood: A Social History of Family Life*. Trans. Robert Baldick. New York: Vintage, 1965. Print.

Armijo, Patrick. "Peace Statue Loses New Battle." *Albuquerque Journal* 15 Feb. 1995: C3. Print. Bennett, Jane. *Vibrant Matter: A Political Ecology of Things*. Durham: Duke UP, 2010. Print.

Best, Joel. *Threatened Children: Rhetoric and Concern about Child-Victims*. Chicago: U of Chicago P, 1990. Print.

Blair, Carole, and Neil Michel. "The AIDS Memorial Quilt and the Contemporary Culture of Public Commemoration." *Rhetoric and Public Affairs* 10.4 (2007): 595–626. Print.

Bodnar, John. *Remaking America: Public Memory, Commemoration, and Patriotism in the Twentieth Century*. Princeton: Princeton UP, 1991. Print.

Browne, Stephen H. "Reading, Rhetoric, and the Texture of Public Memory." *Quarterly Journal of Speech* 81 (1995): 237–65. Print.

Brundage, W. Fitzhugh. "No Deed But Memory." *Where These Memories Grow: History, Memory, and Southern Identity*. Ed. W. Fitzhugh Brundage. Chapel Hill: U of North Carolina P, 2000. 1–28. Print.

Burman, Erica. "Between Identification and Subjectification: Affective Technologies of Expertise and Temporality in the Contemporary Cultural Representation of Gendered Childhoods." *Pedagogy, Culture, and Society* 20.2 (2012): 295–315. Print.

Condon, Camy. "Kids Invited to Build a Dream." *The Crane* 1.1 (1991): 1. Print.

Cooper, Marilyn M. "Rhetorical Agency as Emergent and Enacted." *College Composition and Communication* 62.3 (2011): 420–49. Print.

Cortwright, David. "Los Alamos's Little War with Peace." *The Bulletin of the Atomic Scientists* 51.2 (1995): 5–6. Print.

Davis, Robert A. "Religion, Education, and the Post-Secular Child." *Critical Studies in Education* 55.1 (2014): 18–31. Print.

Dickinson, Greg, Brian L. Ott, and Eric Aoki. "Spaces of Remembering and Forgetting: The Reverent Eye/I at the Plains Indian Museum." *Communication and Critical/Cultural Studies* 3.1 (2006): 27–47. Print.

Dingmann, Tracy. "Peace and Perseverance." *Albuquerque Journal* 6 Aug. 1995: D1 D4. Print.

—. "Statue Unites World's Kids." *Albuquerque Journal* 1 Aug. 1995. n.p. Print. Easthouse, Keith. "Why Los Alamos Said No." *Santa Fe New Mexican* 4 Dec. 1994: A1. Print.

Edelman, Lee. *No Future: Queer Theory and the Death Drive*. Durham: Duke UP, 2004. Print. "Editorial." *Los Alamos Monitor* 27 Nov. 1994: A4. Print.

Gubar, Marah. "Risky Business: Talking about Children in Children's Literature Criticism." *Children's Literature Association Quarterly* 38.4 (2013): 450–57. Print.

Hasegawa, Tsuyoshi. "The Atomic Bombs and the Soviet Invasion: Which Was More Important in Japan's Decision to Surrender?" *The End of the Pacific War: Reappraisals*. Ed. Tsuyoshi Hasegawa. Stanford: Stanford UP, 2007. 113–44. Print.

Hesford, Wendy S. "The Malala Effect." *JAC: A Journal of Composition Theory* 34.1–2 (2014): 139–64. Print.

—. *Spectacular Rhetorics: Human Rights Visions, Recognitions, Feminisms*. Durham: Duke UP, 2011. Print.

Heyse, Amy Lynn. "The Rhetoric of Memory-Making: Lessons from the UDC's Catechisms for Children." *Rhetoric Society Quarterly* 38.4 (2008): 408–32. Print.

Levander, Caroline F., and Carol J. Singley, eds. *The American Child: A Cultural Studies Reader*. New Brunswick: Rutgers UP, 2003. Print.

Lifton, Robert J., and Greg Mitchell. *Hiroshima in America: A Half Century of Denial*. New York: Putnam, 1995. Print.

Los Alamos County Council. *Council Regular Session Meeting*. 16 Nov. 1992. Minutes. Print.

—. *Council Regular Session Meeting*. 21 Nov. 1994. Minutes. Print.

—. *Council Work Session Meeting*. 13 Feb. 1995. Minutes. Print.

Moeller, Susan D. "A Hierarchy of Innocence: The Media's Use of Children in the Telling of International News." *Press/Politics* 7.1 (2002): 36–56. Print.

On Wings of Peace. Video of Children's Peace Statue Presentation at the Los Alamos County Council Meeting. 16 Nov. 1992. Print Transcript.

Owen, Gabrielle. "Queer Theory Wrestles the 'Real' Child: Impossibility, Identity, and Language in Jacqueline Rose's *The Case of Peter Pan*." *Children's Literature Association Quarterly* 35.3 (2010): 255–73. Print.

Parker, Kathleene. "Councilor: Peace Park Adults' Idea." *Santa Fe New Mexican* 13 Feb. 1995: B1. Print.

—. "Los Alamos Gives Kids' Peace Park Another Chance." *Santa Fe New Mexican* 2 Feb. 1995: A1. Print.

Pongratz, Morris B. "This and That." *Los Alamos Monitor* 6 Dec. 1994: 4. Print.

Portnoy, Alisse Theodore. "'A Right to Speak on the Subject': The U.S. Women's Antiremoval Petition Campaign, 1829–1831." *Rhetoric and Public Affairs* 5.4 (2002): 601–24. Print.

Raby, Rebecca. "Children's Participation as Neo-Liberal Governance?" *Discourse: Studies in the Cultural Politics of Education* 35.1 (2014): 77–89. Print.

Rickert, Thomas. *Ambient Rhetoric: The Attunements of Rhetorical Being.* Pittsburgh: U of Pittsburgh P, 2013. Print.
Rose, Jacqueline. *The Case of Peter Pan, or the Impossibility of Children's Fiction.* London: Macmillan, 1984. Print.
Ryder, Phyllis Mentzell. "Beyond Critique: Global Activism and the Case of Malala Yousafzai." *Literacy in Composition Studies* 3.1 (2015): 175–87. Print.
Sánchez-Eppler, Karen. *Dependent States: The Child's Part in Nineteenth-Century American Culture.* Chicago: U of Chicago P, 2005. Print.
Schaller, Charmian. "Peace Statue Should Live in LA." *Los Alamos Monitor* 6 Dec. 1994: 4. Print.
—. "What Was Said About the Statue." *Los Alamos Monitor* 15 Feb. 1995: A3. Print. "Students Plan Peace Monument." *Washington Times* 26 Aug. 1991: B10. Print.
Vigil, Evelyn. "Remembering Pearl Harbor." *Los Alamos Monitor* 7 Dec. 1994: 4. Print.
Waltman, Michael S. "Stratagems and Heuristics in the Recruitment of Children into Communities of Hate: The Fabric of our Future Nightmares." *The Southern Communication Journal* 69.1 (2003): 22–36. Print.
Zaeske, Susan. "Signatures of Citizenship: The Rhetoric of Women's Antislavery Petitions." *Quarterly Journal of Speech* 88.2 (2002): 147–68. Print.
Zinn, Howard. *The Bomb.* San Francisco: City Lights Books, 2010. Print.

Risa Applegarth is Associate Professor in the Department of English, University of North Carolina at Greensboro, 3143 MHRA Building, 1111 Spring Garden St., Greensboro, NC 27412, USA. E-mail: Risa_Applegarth@uncg.edu

www.ingramcontent.com/pod-product-compliance
Lightning Source LLC
Chambersburg PA
CBHW031417230426
43668CB00007B/336